THE MASTERS AMONG US

AN EXPLORATION OF SUPERNAL ENCOUNTERS
AND MIRACULOUS PHENOMENA

THOMAS CURLEY

Wilder Street Press

Copyright ©2000, 2004 by Thomas Curley. Revised Edition ©2019, 2020. All rights reserved. No part of this publication may be reproduced, stored in a retrieval system, or transmitted in any form or by any means, electronic, mechanical, recording or otherwise, without the prior written permission of the author.

© 2020 Thomas Curley
All Rights Reserved

Third Edition. Published by Wilder Street Press, Kirklyn, PA

ISBN: 978-0-578-62742-7

Library of Congress Control Number: 2019920979 (Paperback)

Cover and Book Design by

Wilder Street Press LLC
wspressllc@gmail.com

Dedicated to the memory of my father.

Dad, I'd like to think I've written a book that you would have liked to have read yourself.

CONTENTS

FORWARD	3
PREFACE	5
1: SIGNS, WONDERS, AND WARNINGS	13
2: PREPARING THE WAY	41
3: THE REAPPEARANCE OF THE CHRIST	61
4: THE PLAN OF THE MASTERS	81
5: SCIENCE, SAINTS, AND SIDDHAS	130
6: JESUS ON THE MAIN LINE	140
7: THE DIPLOMAT	175
8: THE MASTER AND MR. CREME	191
9: SENSING THE PRESENCE	215
10: FAITH AND RATIONALISM	239
11: A MASTER EMERGES IN INDIA	249
12: AWAKENING	292
13: CONCLUSION	312
ACKNOLWEDGEMENTS	344
BIBLIOGRAPHY	346

FORWARD

One evening while scrolling my phone for a routine daily news fix, I noted with interest one particular headline which read: "Crowds Flock to Virgin "miracle tree" in New Jersey."[1] Adjoining it was a photograph of a knot in a tree that looked remarkably identical to images of "Our Lady of Guadalupe," a photo of which was tacked above for obvious comparison.

The story went on to describe the scene where throngs of the faithful had flocked to pray and offer gifts to the arboreal visage after being discovered by a woman who claimed to have seen a light that spoke to her, identifying itself as being "the Virgin." Skeptics, the author noted, had walked past, shaking their heads and scoffing at the assembled devout, remarking on the impossibility of their claims. One of those skeptics who was interviewed had remarked "I'm a Catholic and I believe very much in the Virgin, but the picture in this knot is just a coincidence." Immediately following, this same person had perhaps offered the best, most accurate summary, by adding: "However, I believe that whether or not it's real, the important thing is that it motivates people's faith. It gets them to go back to church and remember that God exists."

Twenty years ago, I sat down with a pile of similar stories I had compiled over the course of the twenty years prior. Many I had heard since childhood, had never failed to intrigue me, and the new ones continued to peak my fascination to no end. These stories manifest in the first version of this book published in 2000. After 9-11-2001, the world had changed dramatically. This inspired a revision released in 2004, and yet, by 2006, I had put the manuscript away. Though the book had achieved moderate success with relatively favorable reviews from readers on several continents, it seemed to me that the majority of people had become more self-interested in personal ideology to ever want to heed stories of a quasi-spiritual or miraculous nature. Few, I perceived, really wanted to discuss the contents of the book, hesitant to

---

[1] Posted July 25, 2012, accredited to Sebastian Smith, reporter for AFP (Agence France-Presse, a global news agency). The yahoo link: http://news.yahoo.com/crowds-flock-virgin-miracle-tree-jersey-072636975.html

shake the status quo with regard to issues of belief, and seemed to be fearful of venturing beyond a learned spiritual comfort zone. I arrived at the conclusion that few really cared about this sort of information. How wrong I was. More people than I realized were actually starving for these stories.

Until then, I had spent the better part of my life searching for some sort of quantifiable measure that could shed deeper insight about the nature and existence of this God of whom I had been taught since childhood. When I read this particular story about the miraculous tree, my heart lifted. It seemed there were many who still chose to believe, who still yearned for hopeful signs that we are not alone, that we are loved, that we are cared for and being watched over, and that there are skeptics who, though they may or may not want to believe, can still glean even a modicum of inspiration. This made me think: maybe it is still true that we ourselves are, collectively and individually, the very quantifiable proof of the existence of a God. That it can't be measured or sanitized or cloned in a laboratory, that it only exists within ourselves, within our own perception, our own experience, and with our own choosing. Maybe, I thought, people really would like to hear more of these stories, and just maybe they could provide some of the medicine we need in what at times seems to be a hostile, unforgiving and disparate existence in the world today. It is in this spirit that I offer the following collection of stories and experiences.

Thomas Curley, June 9, 2019

PREFACE

The great religions and philosophical systems that have endured through the ages have, at their core, a very simple root message: that the realm of God can be found nestled right within the human heart. Whether Christian, Muslim or Jew, Hindu or Buddhist, Jain or Sikh, the essential teaching remains the same.

Yet, while these systems would direct human focus to a realm not necessarily perceived by the naked eye, all have in common a tradition of legend and lore of apparent otherworldly instances and super-human and supernatural phenomena. The Old Testament teaches us of great prophets like Moses, who parted the Red Sea, turned his staff into a serpent, and the River Nile into blood. The Hindu traditions speak of saints who have fried bread on their backs, manifested fruit and other objects out of thin air, and levitate, or appear and disappear at will.

The Christian traditions offer legends of statues and icons that weep blood or pure, precious oils; of *stigmatists* who spontaneously bleed from wounds corresponding to those of the crucified Jesus, or saints who have a natural capacity to heal sickness and cure afflictions, beginning with Jesus Himself.

In all of the world's many diverse religious traditions one will find similar tales. A common note found within such sources is the alleged, science and rationally defying allure of the respective prophets, teachers, saints, and those defined as *Masters* of these traditions. Such exalted and venerated persons of legend have been described to not only have possessed a compelling measure of faith and devotion, but in addition, a veiled, obscure natural capacity to manipulate physical forces, to, as it were, command nature. But more importantly, they possessed a peculiarly effective charisma that enabled them to uplift the limited, compromised level of perception and understanding of everyday people to the very precipice of virtual enlightenment, of personal and/or collective religious epiphany.

Countless charlatans and fakirs through the ages have endeavored to demonstrate such an alleged veiled ability to simply entertain or to purposefully take advantage of the feeble minded and less fortunate. Yet, for many kind-hearted, well-intentioned, and spiritually aspiring sages of historical legend, these abilities have been used, it would seem, as a specific means of inspiring the spiritually hungry, the devotionally aspiring. Their acts are referenced frequently in the context of events geared to draw focus on a particular lesson of a religious teaching. Regardless, they do seem to be used to inspire belief in something greater and unseen.

This is a book about miracles and related supernatural phenomena, about a broad prevalence of mystic experience, and about the sort of alleged persons or iconic figures that have been or are at present purportedly vested with extraordinary, super-human powers and capabilities. While the focus of much of the dialog in this book refers to recognized historical figures renown for having possessed such powers, it should be made clear that in no manner do these qualities summarize the sum purpose or life-focus of the aggrandizement of such persons, nor any assertion of superiority of the traditions which they represent. In short, the author is not endorsing one point of view or another, one tradition or another, but rather attempting to shed some light on phenomena that is more commonly experienced or believed in than one might wish to believe.

Other issues addressed are a potential fallibility of rational thought, and exclusion from the viewpoint that creation can only be substantiated scientifically. While not in denial of these perspectives, miracles and related phenomena do seem to defy orthodox reason. On the whole, the phenomenon of the miraculous is consistent with one of the primary tenets central to all ancient religious and philosophical traditions, that one should not maintain an absolute faith in the reliability of the transient, material world.

Why is this repeatedly addressed? What lies beyond that to with which we are most familiar, to what we have so endeared and attached ourselves? What else beside that which we can see, touch, hold, taste? Is there something more? Is there a transcendent aspect beyond that which can be proven within the confines of a laboratory?

Certain aspects of religious teachings often seem to conflict. On one hand, it is suggested that living a moral life is our assurance for an exalted afterlife. However, another will say the goal of life is to exercise a balanced, ethical life in this world, in the here and now while living, that the notion of an afterlife is just another illusion.

Some traditions address this philosophical continuum by declaring, consistent with the teachings of Jesus and other great prophets, that the Kingdom of God "is at hand," that it is right here and now, that if only one "had eyes that could see" the truth of a transcendent level of reality would be apparent. Following this vein of thought, it is further declared that the saints, prophets, and emissaries of God are, likewise, among us even now. Great beings of lore are claimed by some to be living in spirit form, not as 'ghosts' as we would understand it, but as eternal souls who have transcended human death, dwelling in an ageless realm beyond the limits of known material physics. And most peculiar of all is a consistently expressed conviction that these unseen spiritual ancestors of ours visit us often, purposely leaving behind a trail of mystifying clues - such as the appearance of Our Lady of Guadalupe in the knot of a tree in New Jersey - that would have us stand and wonder. These concepts, originating from many traditions, are explored in the pages that follow.

Some clarifications should be made in advance to enable the reader to understand distinctions in usage of terminology, however similar, from one tradition to another.

It should be noted that a distinction is made between the capitalized terms Theosophy, Theosophic, and Theosophical, and the same terms minus the capitalization. The capitalized terms are used as specific references to anything affiliated with *The Theosophical Society*, and that organization's philosophical perspectives and canon, etc. The non-capitalized terms are used more generally, with theosophical denoting a universally inclusive philosophical perspective that includes all religions, spiritual or philosophical paths, their teachers and icons, etc., regardless or not whether any of these maintain any formal affiliation (as they likely do not) with the Theosophical Society per se. It is the author's opinion that 'theosophy', used generally, includes all philosophical, spiritual, and theological paths and perspectives.

In the same way, the author wishes to distinguish between the use of the term Master(s) as opposed to master(s). The capitalized form of the word refers specifically to those accorded an advanced status of human spiritual achievement and evolution by members and authors of various schools of arcane thought that are referenced herein, none of which necessarily have a direct affiliation with each other.

With lower-case designation, 'masters' is a more liberally applied term with reference made to individuals who have achieved or have been accorded advanced status in the area of their respective religious or philosophical tradition.

To the best of the author's ability, it is hoped that all the religious and philosophical traditions referred to herein are regarded with an equally due measure of respect and consideration, and without any intent to promulgate one or another specific path.

Thomas Curley, June, 2004

"Are you looking for me?
I am in the next seat. My shoulder is against yours.
When you really look for me,
you will see me instantly."

        Kabir Granthvali,
        15th Century Poet

THE MASTERS AMONG US

Chapter One

SIGNS, WONDERS, AND WARNINGS

> "About 6,000 worshippers at Muslim Village, Kawangware, Nairobi, believe they saw Jesus Christ, in broad daylight last week. "Jesus! Jesus! Jesus of Nazareth!" went the loud whispers from the crowd as they raised up their hands in divine welcome. The tall figure of a barefooted white-robed and bearded man appeared from nowhere and stood in the middle of the crowd."
>
> Kenya Times, June 11, 1988[2]

Prior to the advent of television, radio, or film, the spiritual upliftment of the masses was the business of organized religious institutions. Where a ritual dance or spell binding oration may have been common in older traditions, we find evidence of the need for convincing special effects that enabled the priests, shamans and spin doctors to sufficiently 'wow' the curious into subscription. Such examples are found in unearthed temples from the remote past; the imposing structures of Stonehenge, Easter Island, or Egypt, right up through the arrival of the stirring, prodigious architecture and stained-glass cathedral windows of the European middle ages. Yet, consistently used throughout history on all such structures, whether adorning walls or ceilings, entrance or arch, is reliance upon perhaps the true cornerstone of all the varied theological marketing plans. That is, the legends and exploits of the prophets and those deemed gods or saints - the fabled, ancestral men and woman of God.

Through the ages, many a tale have arisen of visions, appearances and visitations from angels, deceased saints, deities, and heavenly beings in all world cultures and traditions. Though primarily relegated to the lore of mystics, saintly persons, and other devotees of God, many tales of divine visitation

---

[2] Source: Share International Magazine, September, 1988 issue.

involve secular individuals as well.

There is a legend, for example, that no less a person than the American founding father George Washington had such an occasion while encamped at *Valley Forge* in the Winter of 1777, during the American Revolutionary War. The account was first published in 1859 in *The National Tribune*, a popular news journal at the time. The story, as written by reporter Wesley Bradshaw, features an interview with then 99-year-old Anthony Sherman, a former American Revolutionary War officer who had served under Washington at Valley Forge, and who claimed to have been present when Washington revealed a disquieting experience to a close companion officer. As Sherman recounted:

"One day, [Washington] remained in his quarters nearly all the afternoon alone. When he came out, I noticed that his face was a shade paler than usual, and there seemed to be something on his mind of more than ordinary importance...After a preliminary conversation of about half an hour, Washington, gazing upon his companion with that strange look of dignity which he alone could command, said to the latter:

'This afternoon, as I was sitting...engaged in preparing a dispatch, looking up I saw standing opposite a singularly beautiful female. So astonished was I, for I had given strict orders not to be disturbed, that it was some moments before I found language to inquire into the cause of her presence. A second, a third, and even a fourth time did I repeat my question, but received no answer from my mysterious visitor except a slight raising of her eyes. By this time, I felt strange sentiments spreading through me. I would have risen, but the riveted gaze of the being before me rendered volition impossible. I assayed once more to address her, but my tongue had become useless, even thought itself had become paralyzed. A new influence, mysterious, potent, irresistible, took possession of me. All I could do was to gaze steadily, vacantly at my unknown visitor. Gradually, the surrounding atmosphere seemed as though becoming filled with sensations and luminous. Everything about me seemed to rarify, the mysterious visitor herself becoming more airy, and yet more distinct to my sight than before. I now began to feel as one dying, or rather to experience the sensations which I have sometimes imagined accompany dissolution. I did not think, I did not reason, I did not move; all were alike impossible. I was only conscious of gazing fixedly, vacantly at my companion. Presently, I heard a voice say: 'Son of the Republic, look and learn!'[3]

Washington continued to explain how the visitor proceeded to reveal a vision of the future of the United States, showing him the growing cities, images of the American Civil War, the dark specter of slavery and its consequences, and a third, ominous fate that only caught my attention as I was revising this work in 2018. In the overview for the 1950 publication, while listing the three primary visions, the editor had written:

> "These were the Revolutionary War, the Civil War, and the greatest threat, a war fought on the soil of the United States near the time of Jesus' return to reign on the earth. It is this third battle, that holds our interest as the day draws near."[4]

For that third vision, Washington explained:

> "I at last saw nothing but the rising, curling vapor I at first beheld. This also disappearing, I found myself once more gazing upon the mysterious visitor, who, in the same voice I had heard before, said,
>
> 'Son of the Republic, what you have seen is thus interpreted: Three great perils will come upon the Republic. The most fearful is the third, passing which the whole world united shall not prevail against her. Let every child of the Republic learn to live for his God, his land, and the Union.'

Washington had concluded, simply, "With these words the woman vanished from my sight."

Was this account[i] merely the fabrication of latter political adherents seeking to prey on the religious sentiments of the growing American population? Or had it been it a genuine mystical experience for Washington - a known practitioner of Freemasonry? There is a sense of authenticity for an 1859 article, because the added description of Washington's personal experience, i.e. paralyzed thought, a 'new influence' possessing him, etc., are all classic symptoms cited in both traditional Eastern mysticism, as well as contemporary research in Western Psychology. These are key points to consider.

Although Washington doesn't identify his visitor, the semblance and accompanying message are consistent with the varied and numerous accounts of visits from Mary, the mother of Jesus.

---

[3] Source: The National Tribune archives. The Nat'l Tribune Corp. was eventually acquired by another company that filed for Chapter 7 Bankruptcy in August of 2002. The entire text of Bradshaw's article may be found in the endnote section in the back of this book.

[4] Ibid

For those who were raised and schooled in the Catholic tradition, the legends of the 'Marian Apparitions' were an integral part of their spiritual development. A young Catholic child was taught to assume that those apparition occasions that were sanctioned by the Church were real events that happened to real people. Such documented apparition events are numerous, with those of the latter 19th and early 20-century being most influential to modern Catholicism.

To name just a few of the better-known incidents:
- Spain - 1206;
- Cambridge, England - 1251;
- Guadeloupe, Mexico - 1531, to Juan Diego;[5]
- Paris, France - 1830, to Saint Catherine Laboure, a Parisian nun, and in 1840 to Sister Justine Bisqueyburu
- LaSalette, France - 1846, to Melanie Calvat and Maximin Giraud, two shepherd children;
- Lourdes, France - 1858, to Bernadette Soubirous;
- Pontmain, France - 1871, to Eugene and Joseph Barbadette, along with some children
- Knock, Ireland - 1879, to fifteen eyewitnesses;
- and, Fatima, Portugal, in 1917, to three shepherd children.

Most instances of recorded Marian apparition occurred to one or more secular individuals, religious novitiates of a lesser ecclesiastical status such as priests and nuns, and, primarily, to children of no elevated social or class distinction.

Take, for instance, the account of the Madonna's first appearance in 1858 to Bernadette Soubirous, the young native of Lourdes, France. Initially no one believed her: not her friends, her parents, nor her parish priest, who, like most Catholic clergy at the time, held significant political and social influence in such small, European communities. On numerous occasions throughout the course of that year, Bernadette claimed she had been visited repeatedly by 'the beautiful Lady' on the fringes of what had been a village dumping ground. Since no one else could see the Lady, people thought her mad, while civic leaders attempted to have her institutionalized.

Frustrated by her inability to convince anyone of the reality of her experiences, Bernadette asked "the Lady" for a sign, and the Lady, in turn,

---

[5] The Feast Day of Our Lady of Guadeloupe is still annually celebrated today on December 12, recalling an apparition in 1531 to Juan Diego, a Native American. Our Lady of Guadeloupe is the patron saint of Mexico, Latin America, and the Philippines.

promised to Bernadette that one would be given on the occasion of her final visit. As word spread from village to village, an increasing crowd of curious faithful travelled to the Lourdes dumping ground to see for themselves if the tales were true. By the time of the anticipated final appearance of 'the beautiful Lady' had come, thousands had assembled near Bernadette to bear witness. When the moment of the visit arrived, those close to Bernadette saw her demeanor become suddenly enraptured. Though they saw nothing themselves, many fervently began to pray, some in wonder, some in fear, some with faith.

Then, Bernadette, who had been kneeling prayerfully, began to suddenly dig in the earth with her hands. Many grew concerned and doubtful, wondering if they'd been deceived by a deranged psychotic, and started to leave and return to their villages. Finally, from the very spot where Bernadette had been digging, a previously nonexistent spring of water emerged to the amazement of all, who concurred they had indeed witnessed a miracle. That same spring at Lourdes continues to flow today. The countless tales of miraculous healing since attributed to those waters are well documented, and Lourdes still flourishes as one of the primary points of Christian pilgrimage in the world.

The Fatima Controversy

The Catholic Church is known for its cautious, methodical approach to openly acknowledging claims or rumors of apparitions or anything of a similarly spectacular, supernal nature. Perhaps the most evocative and widely known incident, even by non-Catholics and agnostics the world over, has been that of Fatima, Portugal, in 1917, where a message so profound was issued that the Vatican guarded it in secrecy for nearly a century afterwards.

At the request of the otherworldly lady who appeared at Lourdes, according to the witnesses to whom she spoke, that message was to have been disclosed to the world in 1960, an event subsequently anticipated by millions of Catholics for the next 43 years. In 1944, Lucia dos Santos - one of the three shepherd children and the primary recipient of the Madonna's messages -was urged by a local bishop to record the secret message in writing. Once this was done, it was sealed in an envelope and promptly delivered to the Papal office in Rome, where it would remain untouched until 1960.

It is said that when the fateful year finally arrived, Pope John XXIII opened the envelope, read its contents, and consequently ordered it resealed immediately. In 1967, with still no disclosure and mounting public pressure, an official Vatican Statement announced it had been concluded by Pope Paul VI, the recently elected successor to John XXIII, that the time "had not yet come" to reveal its contents. While many were no doubt disappointed, it's also likely that such a move exonerated skeptics and critics, with speculation about the secret message prevailing in the years that followed.

In 1997, after decades of an explosive increase in claims of Marian encounters, the Fatima topic was again in the news. In an interview on Italian television, Father Rene Laurentin - a Catholic theologian and historian who had gained special prominence and recognition for his work on Marian apparitions - remarked that Pope John XXIII had chosen to keep the secret from the public in 1960 due to fear of causing *further* intramural division within the Catholic Church. Had the message contributed to division previously?

Responding to Laurentin's comments in an interview with the Italian publication *Gazettino di Venezia*, Cardinal Joseph Ratzinger - prefect of the Vatican's Congregation for the Doctrine of the Faith - dismissed speculations that Our Lady of Fatima's third secret had been a prediction about a future period of dissent from Catholic doctrine, and would lead to grave divisions within the Church.

Ratzinger urged the faithful not to be preoccupied with such "fantasies and fictions," pointedly adding that only a few people had been informed about the third secret of Fatima, and Father Laurentin had not been among those so privileged.

"Three popes have become acquainted [with the secret]," Ratzinger explained, "and none of them has judged it opportune to make it public. They had good reasons for their decision."

In a separate interview with a Portuguese radio station, Cardinal Ratzinger added: "For those who are curious, I can offer assurance: the Virgin is not engaged in sensationalism, nor in feeding fears, or offering apocalyptic visions…The key to the understanding of the message of Fatima, he said, lies in Mary's emphasis on prayer and penance. That is what is essential."[6]

Undoubtedly due to unceasing pressure originating from the Laurentin incident, in May of 2000, the Vatican publicly announced that the apocalyptic message of Fatima would be finally be revealed. Pope John Paul II declared that, in light of the Catholic Church's *Millennial Jubilee* - the official celebration of two millennia of Christianity - the time had come to reveal the message. It was explained that the reasoning behind his predecessor's choice to withhold prior disclosure was that the message primarily concerned "the popes of the 20th century."

In an interview with the Italian daily *Corriere della Sera*, Vatican Secretary of State Cardinal Angelo Sodano said that with the 20th century now

[6] Source: Catholic World News. Reprinted with permission.

concluded, the Holy Father saw no reason to further delay public announcement of the message, adding, that, in light of historical developments, "the symbolic visions contain nothing mysterious."

Vatican spokesman Joaquin Navarro-Valls said that Pope John Paul had chosen not to release the secret himself, but to allow Cardinal Sodano to make the dramatic announcement for two reasons: First, that the Pope felt a measure of personal reserve about publicizing the message since he himself is clearly a principal figure in the prophetic vision due to his view that the 1981 assassination attempt on his life was related to the message. Such a reference to Papal assassination in the message may also explain the similar reservation of the previous Pontiffs. Secondly, according to Navarro-Valls, the Pope wished to indicate the official character of the announcement while still clearly preserving the distinction between the "private revelation" of Lucia dos Santos' vision, and the body of Revelation that had been transmitted through the Christian scriptures and Church tradition itself.

Finally, on June 26th, 2000, the Vatican formally released the contents of the message to the public, read in its entirety, as follows:

> "I write in obedience to you, my God, who commands me to do so through his Excellency the Bishop of Leiria and through your Most Holy Mother and mine. After the two parts which I have already explained, at the left of Our Lady and a little above, we saw an Angel with a flaming sword. It gave out flames that looked as though they would set the world on fire; but they died out in contact with the splendor that Our Lady radiated towards him from her right hand. Pointing to the earth with his right hand, the Angel cried out in a loud voice: "Penance, Penance, Penance!" And we saw "something similar to how people appear in a mirror when they pass in front of it" a Bishop dressed in White ("we had the impression that it was the Holy Father."); Other Bishops, Priests, men and women Religious going up a steep mountain, at the top of which there was a big Cross of rough-hewn trunks. Before reaching there the Holy Father passed through a big city half in ruins and half trembling with halting step, afflicted with pain and sorrow, he prayed for the souls of the corpses he met on his way. Having reached the top of the mountain, on his knees at the foot of the big Cross he was killed by a group of soldiers who fired bullets and arrows at him, and in the same way there died one after another the other Bishops, Priests, men and women Religious, and various lay people of different ranks and positions. Beneath the two arms of the Cross there were two Angels each with a crystal

aspergillum[7] in his hand, in which they gathered up the blood of the Martyrs and with it sprinkled the souls that were making their way to God."[8]

What most surprised many is that the contents of the message seemed to somewhat contradict the remarks made by Cardinal Ratzinger in his 1997 interview. Foremost is that the message *was* evidently apocalyptic in nature, and, secondly, is the suggested reference of possible assassination of a Pope. In 1981, shortly after the assassination attempt, John Paul II remarked at the time that the Fatima prophecy had been fulfilled, and that he believed his survival had been due to the Madonna's divine intervention. As a result, many maintain that *the whole* message was not released in 2000. The mystery of the message continues to intrigue many.

Since the Church had been given instructions to reveal the message in 1960, one ponders the notion of the bureaucratic bungling of a divine request. Was Father Laurentin, a known authority on Marian issues, correct, then, that Vatican insiders had quibbled over the point for decades, fearing internal dissent and corruption? Further, why does controversy continue to circulate about the message despite the fact that its public disclosure should have ended further speculation? To fully comprehend the legacy of interest and impact of the events of Fatima so many years ago, a review of its profound details would be in order. For the significant difference between the relatively Catholic, religious overtones inherent in apparitions such as Lourdes and that of Mary's 1917 appearance in Fatima, is an emphasis specifically addressing points critical to world affairs, and humanity in whole.

Wars and Rumors of Wars

The story begins in the spring of 1916, when Lucia dos Santos, eight-year-old Francisco Marto, and six-year-old Jacinta Marto, were routinely tending their flock of sheep in a field on the outskirts of their village. To their astonishment, a massive orb of radiant white light seemingly appeared out of thin air and suddenly approached them. From the said orb emerged an extraordinarily beautiful young man with a body as brilliant as the light itself. "Do not fear," he said, "I am the angel of Peace. Pray with me." The angel then prostrated himself, touching his forehead to the ground in a fashion reminiscent of the 'pranam' of Hindu and Buddhist tradition, or the 'sajdah' of Islamic prayer.

The children complied by mimicking this alien gesture while three

---

[7] A ceremonial vessel, normally used to hold holy water.
[8] Source: Catholic World News, with permission.

times the angel repeated: "My God, I believe, I adore, I hope, and I love you. I implore your pardon for those who do not believe, do not adore, do not hope and do not love you." The angel then stood and said "The hearts of Jesus and Mary are attentive to the voice of your supplications." and then vanished. He would again appear twice more in that year, repeating the same ritual each time.

In the following Spring, at precisely 12 noon on the 13th day of May, 1917, a woman of extraordinary beauty - "more brilliant than the sun" - adorned in an ankle length gown and tenderly draped veil on her head - then appeared in the same manner as the angelic young man to these most humble of emissaries. Though uncertain, the children assumed it could be none other than the Blessed Virgin Mary herself. On that first visit, Mary asked if the children would be willing to assist her, to endure any consequential 'suffering' and ridicule that undoubtedly would accompany their involvement, and to live their lives dedicated to the conversion of humanity to spirituality. The children agreed. She then asked them to "Say the beads..." - the Rosary, referring to the Catholic prayer beads similar to those used in the Eastern traditions - "each day to obtain peace for the world and the end of war."

In the months that followed, the "Lady more brilliant than the sun" as the children had initially described her, would offer the most provocative, apocalyptic, and fearful message of any previously relayed by her to humanity. Mary's appearances and messages of Fatima hold an even greater significance when now viewed in light of recorded historical world events.

For example, in March 1917, the first revolt of the Russian Revolution occurred, culminating with the armed insurrection of the Bolsheviks that November.[9] The following month, the United States officially entered World War One, inaugurating its final phase. And on May 13th, the very day of the Madonna's first Fatima visit, it has since been learned that a group of armed Bolshevik horsemen, under orders from Nikolai Lenin, charged into a Moscow church filled with children, killing many of them while destroying the altar and statues.[10]

Bearing these facts in mind, it is most intriguing to review the warning and message given by Mary on the third Fatima visit of July, 1917, when she addressed the potential danger facing humanity;

'I come to ask the consecration of Russia...If people heed my request, Russia will be converted and there will be peace. If not, she shall spread her errors throughout the world, promoting wars and persecution of the church. The good will be martyred; the Holy Father

---

[9] Widely referred to as the 'October Revolution', it was designated as such due to Russia's use of the old Julian Calendar until January of 1918.
[10] Source material for this accusation remains subject to speculation.

will suffer much; different nations will be destroyed, but in the end my 'Immaculate Heart' will triumph. The Holy Father will consecrate Russia to me, which will be converted and some time of peace will be given to the world.'[11]

It is fascinating to wonder why such a profound issue would be addressed with three shepherd children in rural Portugal, why an announcement of such critical import and magnitude wasn't directed instead to some key envoy in the global political and diplomatic arena. At the very least, if it was decided that the message would spread further if channeled through the Catholic Church, why not through a Vatican ambassador? Why not appear directly to the Pope?

Regardless, for argument sake, we can assume that the right people for the job were found in these three children, as the word did spread adequately.

As if that warning weren't alarming enough, it was also on the third visit that Mary prophetically warned of the potential imminence of what became World War II, when she said:

'If men do what I tell you, many souls will be saved and there will be peace. This war (WWI) is going to end soon, but if men do not stop offending God, not much time will elapse before another and more terrible war will begin in the reign of Pius XI.'[12]

The warning was much more substantial than realized. Mary continued:

'When a night illumined by an unknown light is seen, know that this is the signal that God gives that the chastisement of the world for its many transgressions is at hand.'

Another twenty years would pass before any 'night illumined' would arrive. But when it did, it was a night so unusual, extraordinary, and of such magnitude that the world, and its press, stopped and took notice.

On January 26th, 1938, the *New York Times* printed the following account:

'LONDON - JANUARY 25TH, 1938 - The Aurora Borealis, rarely seen in Southern or Western Europe, spread fear in parts of Portugal and lower tonight while thousands of Britons were brought running into the streets in wonderment. The ruddy glow led many to think half the city was ablaze. The Windsor Fire Department was called out thinking that Windsor castle was afire. The lights were

---

[11] According to Lucia, who was asked about this in 2000, the consecration was performed in 1984.
[12] Pius XI reigned as Pope from 1922 to 1939.

clearly seen in Italy, Spain, and even Gibraltar. The glow bathing snow-clad mountaintops in Austria and Switzerland was a beautiful sight but firemen turned out to chase non-existent fires. *Portuguese villagers* rushed in fright from their homes fearing the end of the world.'

Was the reporter knowledgeable of the forecast made in Fatima twenty years earlier? A report from Grenoble, France of the same day, also reprinted in the Times, described it thus:

'A huge blood-red beam of light which scientists said was an Aurora Borealis of exceptional amplitude tied up telephone systems in parts of France tonight and spread anxiety in numerous Swiss Alpine villages. Emblazoned in the Northern sky the light brought thousands of telephone calls to Swiss and French authorities asking whether it was a Fire? War? or the End of the World?'

In February of 1938, *'The Literary Digest'*, one of the most popular journalistic reviews of the day, also published a summary compiled from various worldwide press coverage of the event. Reciting the references as published in the Times, the Digest added, that, in Holland, the sight was 'regarded as a good omen', while the Scottish press remarked "Northern lights always spell misfortune for Scotland." The lights were said to have been seen as far south as Bermuda, and the Canadian press reported that "wire services throughout northern Ontario were disrupted, while radio transmission went dead."

The lights of January 25th could have certainly been the prophetic sign referenced at Fatima, for less than two months later, on March 11, 1938, Hitler's troops annexed Austria. In October of that year - with anti-Semitism having become government policy - over 15,000 Jewish citizens were expelled from Germany without warning, then forcibly transported by train in boxcars and dumped at the Polish border. On November 9, a massive, coordinated attack on Jews throughout the German Reich came to be known as *Kristallnacht* - The Night of Broken Glass. Mob violence broke out as the German police stood by and crowds of spectators watched as Nazi storm troopers along with members of the SS and Hitler Youth beat and murdered Jews, broke into and wrecked Jewish homes, and brutalized Jewish women and children. All over Germany, Austria and other Nazi controlled areas, Jewish shops and department stores had their windows smashed and contents destroyed. Synagogues were especially targeted for vandalism, including the desecration of sacred Torah scrolls. Hundreds of synagogues were systematically burned while local fire departments stood by or simply prevented the fire from spreading to surrounding buildings. About 25,000 Jewish men were rounded up and later sent to concentration camps where they were often brutalized by SS guards and in some cases randomly chosen to be beaten to death.

On September 1, 1939, Poland was subject to a full-on Nazi invasion, and by October 6 - with the aid of Soviet forces - was taken over, occupied and divided, with jurisdiction split between the Nazis and Soviets. Jews again became primary targets of brutality, deportation, and systematic extermination, with native Poles declared as slaves of the German Empire. The Second "and more terrible" World War predicted by Mary had begun. In the five years to follow, humanity would witness and endure a measure of abject savagery like nothing before. No recorded period of human civilization or history of conquest could compare to or augur the horror of the Nazi death camps, the diabolical human torture and experimentation of captive European Jews and other 'undesirable' minorities, and the blood of millions flowing from the four corners of the globe.

After numerous Herculean efforts on behalf of the combined Allied forces, it finally took no less than the harnessing of the atom - the core essence of creation itself - to produce the ultimate weapon of mass destruction that would end the global reign of terror and threat of world domination. How ominous, in light of the Fatima messages, is the now infamous response made by Robert Oppenheimer upon having witnessed the first test detonation of an Atomic Bomb, the creation of which he spearheaded. Oppenheimer watched in simultaneous awe and horror, uttering to himself a quote from a Hindu scripture:

"I am Shiva, destroyer of Worlds."

History has shown that Mary indeed meant business on the occasions of her Fatima visits. Between the threats of global, Stalinist communism and its subsequent squelching of Christianity and religion in general; Hitler's 'final solution' to obliterate Judaism and *non-Aryan*, Semitic peoples by means of genocide, the deviate tyranny of Mussolini, and Japan's equally threatening, monomaniacal quest for world domination, we can begin to surmise the full weight of Mary's warning. In addition to detestable holocaust was an evident objective for the systematic elimination of the world's largest and most influential religions from the face of the Earth.

Beginning with Christianity and Judaism, it would have been just a matter of time until the remaining 'big three' - Hinduism, Buddhism, and Islam - along with the numerous minor religions and sects - were gone as well. To support this argument, one only need to look at the extent to which communism would eventually spread, from Eastern Europe to China, through

Southeast Asia and elsewhere. Furthermore, we today are quite aware of Communist China's cruel attempt to annihilate Tibet's theocratic culture and the ethnic cleansing of its people. The chilling thought of an enforced, Godless civilization was more a potentiality than realized.

In 1917, the visions and messages of the shepherd children had been officially denounced as lunacy. Word of the Fatima apparitions aroused the concern and suspicion of public officials throughout Portugal, many of whom, including the district administrator of Fatima, were members of an anticlerical movement known as the *Freethinkers*. So powerful was their political influence at the time that they already had effectively brought about a suppression of Catholicism in that country. Ironically, their attempts to squelch the events at Fatima backfired.

Jacinto Marto, Francisco Marto, and Lucia dos Santos at the time of the Fatima apparitions. Source: www.fatima.org with permission.

On the day of what was to have been the 4th visitation from Mary, an estimated 18,000 people converged on the small village. So outraged were the government officials that arrangements were made for the children to be purposely kidnapped and detained for the duration of the appointed apparition time. While the children were being brutally interrogated and threatened, many among the gathered multitude grew disappointed, then skeptical, then angry, and began to leave.

As had Bernadette at Lourdes 60 years earlier, Lucia, previous to her kidnap, petitioned the Madonna for a sign so that she and her cousins might be believed. Her plea would be acknowledged that day. At noon, an explosive sound like thunder was heard and a brilliant flash of light was witnessed. The sun grew dim, and around the small oak tree where the visitations regularly occurred, a small white cloud formed, which shortly afterwards rose and dissolved in the air. The whole area was then bathed in a kaleidoscopic spectrum of brilliant Technicolor, permeating the crowd and entire landscape. Faith and belief returned instantly to the throngs, and those who had decided to leave returned en masse, initiating a prayerful vigil. Two days afterwards, the children were released due to growing concern of an uprising.

On August 19th, as if to make up for the lost appointment, Mary appeared to the children, and explained, that, due to their kidnapping, the previously promised grand miracle, which was to have been given on Her final visit in October, would be considerably less than anticipated.

What would *not* occur, as a result of the detainment, had been a planned visit from Saint Joseph, father to the child Jesus, followed by an appearance of Jesus himself!

One wonders why, in light of Mary's critical warnings with regard to the menacing and ultimately worsening state of world affairs, such a significant world event would be withdrawn. Is humanity so inextricably linked that the sins of the few could sufficiently outweigh the virtues of many, lending credence to the old maxim; "one bad apple spoils the whole bunch"?

On September 13th, an estimated 30,000 people gathered to witness a similar visual spectacle as before. The noon sun dimmed so much that stars were visible in the sky as the great orb of light descended to the oak tree. The enthralled witnesses gazed in awe as clusters of flower petals drifted from the sky and dissolved like snow before touching the ground. On this day, simple prayer instructions were given with emphasis on the rosary. Mary then repeated her promise of a greater and more fantastic miracle on October 13th.

When that final day arrived, it is estimated that 80 to 100 thousand people thronged to the fields surrounding the small oak tree. Torrents of rain had fallen all morning, hindering travel on the rural roads, yet none were deterred. Skeptics, atheists, and Freethinkers, with intentions of disrupting and denouncing the event once more, scoffed and laughed at the faithful, who, pathetically drenched, sloshed relentlessly to assemble in the muddy pasture.

Then, at noon, eyewitnesses report first seeing a column of blue smoke that appeared and disappeared three times near the children, an indication that Mary had arrived. Her message was brief:

'People must cease offending my divine son, whom they have already much offended. Therefore, let the rosary be recited daily. Sincerely ask pardon for sins. The war will end soon, and the soldiers will return to their homes.'

With that, Mary then spread her hands from which incredible beams of extraordinary light reached into the sky to reveal a brilliant disc of light. "Behold, the sun!" cried Lucia, as instantaneously the rain ceased, and the dark, foreboding clouds were quickly torn apart.

Eyewitnesses described 'the sun' as "a disc of smoky silver, with a sharp rim and clear edge" which had "the luster of a pearl," clear, rich and opaque in color. The awestruck crowd remained silent and motionless as the disc began to quiver in the sky, and increased their fright as it began to spin at a terrific and continually increasing speed. A fantastic montage of changing, pure, translucent hues was cast simultaneously across the landscape, and was reportedly visible for up to twelve miles away.

After four minutes, the spinning stopped, only to resume, repeating the spectacle for another four minutes. As the disc began to spin yet a third time, it appeared to suddenly dislodge from its place in the sky and hurtle towards the Earth at a fantastic speed while emitting an intense and increasing

The assembled faithful at Fatima in 1917.
Source: www.fatima.org, with permission.

heat. All who were gathered shrieked in terror, assuming the world was about to end, and threw themselves on the ground in prayer and contrition. Finally, just at the point when the falling 'sun' was about to consume them, the disc retreated into the now clear blue sky, and disappeared.

Remarkably, those present, who had been soaked to the skin and enveloped in mud only minutes before, discovered that their clothes and the ground were now completely dry. Thousands shouted spontaneous, joyous prayers of thanks and praise, and the three children were carried off triumphantly on the shoulders of the faithful.

But while the tens of thousands who gathered witnessed this spectacle, Lucia, Jacinta, and Francisco had alone experienced the promised miracle that was withdrawn due to the children's kidnapping and detainment. All three saw the Lady, now dressed in white and blue, trimmed in gold, accompanied by Saint Joseph and the infant Jesus, dressed in red, their hands raised as they blessed those who were unable to see them.

Lucia alone then saw the Lady transform into the sorrowful mother of the crucified adult Jesus, who then appeared before Lucia alone, while blessing the crowd, and the world unseen.

In 1927, having entered the convent and taken the vows of a Catholic nun, Lucia claimed to have received a message from Jesus while in prayer, instructing her to reveal part of the 'secret' Fatima message that was to remain concealed until 1960. She was to reveal five 'scourges' that were to transpire. The first of these referred to what would be the 'aurora borealis' incident of January 25th, 1938. The second referred to the threat of complete, global, communistic, and hence, enforced godless domination. The third and fourth were specifically pertinent to the Catholic Church, involving references to many who would be martyred, and the first mention of the possible assassination of a pope, as detailed in the Vatican release of June 26, 2000.

We are well aware of the many Christian clergy who were tortured, violently molested and/or slain in the Second World War, the Korean conflict and other great wars and more political insurrections in South America, the Middle East, and elsewhere. We know that Pope John Paul I died mysteriously, shortly after assuming the Papal seat. His successor, Pope John Paul II has, as mentioned, asserted with conviction that the assassination attempt made on him in 1981 was the fulfillment of the prophetic reference made at Fatima, and credits his survival to Mary's divine intervention. Even more compelling is the fact that the assassination attempt occurred on May 13, the very day of the first Fatima visit sixty-four years earlier.

The fifth scourge, according to Fatima scholars, has yet to be seen, and warns of "the annihilation of entire nations." To what is Mary referring? Are claims true that the Vatican's June 26th public disclosure of the Fatima message was only partially disclosed?

The message comes alarmingly too close for comfort as we witness the more recent, countless bloody insurgencies and revolutions that have played out around the globe in recent years. Yugoslavia, Bosnia-Herzegovina, Indonesia, Kashmir - are these just the rumbling of a far worse cataclysm yet to come? Have we arrived at the precipice of the foretold 'annihilation of entire nations'?

Many agree with the assertions of biblical fundamentalists that we are living in the 'end times', the 'last days' as prophesied by biblical prophets, as well as contemporary seers, shamans, visionaries and holy men from all cultural and theistic traditions. Aztec, Native American, Aboriginal and other such traditions all possess oral legends, calendars, ancient scriptures and hieroglyphics that some say conspicuously point to this time in history as a critical juncture.

Around the year 2000 when I was working on the first draft of this book, a headline blared from one of the tabloids proclaiming that "startling new evidence" had been found that the "Day of Judgment is at hand," and was attributed to the late Billy Graham, chief among Christian biblical proponents. Taking into account the 5th scourge of Fatima, seasoned with a few foreboding quotes from the Koran, the Old Testament Book of Isaiah, or St. John's Revelations, one ponders the plausibility of such doomsayers. Perhaps the tabloids aren't as preposterous as we tend to believe.

On the other hand, what if humanity *has* adequately heeded Mary's innumerable warnings and petitions for prayer, thus averting an impending horror from which we may have been spared, or of which we may never know? Adding to the confusion and coinciding with the 'wars and rumors of wars' and other, similar gloomy messages of 'end time' prognosticators, there have consistently been an equally considerable number of positive, hopeful 'signs' of an extraordinary nature.

Signs and Wonders

While the Fatima apparitions remain the most renowned, they were by no means the last. In 1932 and 33, Mary appeared no less than thirty-three times in Beauraing, Belgium; in 1946, as previously mentioned, in Marionfried, Germany, and 15 years later in 1961, to two women in Garabandal, Spain. From 1968 through 1971, particularly astounding apparitions occurred above a Coptic church in Zeitoun, Egypt. Initially witnessed by thousands, it was perhaps the first such event filmed live and broadcast on international television. Interestingly, it was Zeitoun, tradition holds, to which Joseph, Mary, and the infant Jesus fled for safety during King Herod's 'slaughter of the innocents' after the nativity. Accordingly, all three members of the holy family were seen in the visions, along with their donkey! On one occasion, an exceptionally brilliant appearance remained wholly in view for seven and a half hours!

But unique to the Zeitoun apparitions, apart from all previous, was the noticeable circumstance of a multi-denominational acceptance. There, Christians of all sects, Catholic, Protestant, and Coptic, gathered and tearfully prayed side by side with an equal number of Muslims. In fact, over those four years, an estimated one million people from all walks of life, the largest number up to that time, had witnessed the fantastic spectacle firsthand. So convincing were these appearances that the Egyptian Government, in clear support and acknowledgement of what was happening, tore buildings down to create more open space around the church to accommodate the steadily increasing number of pilgrims.

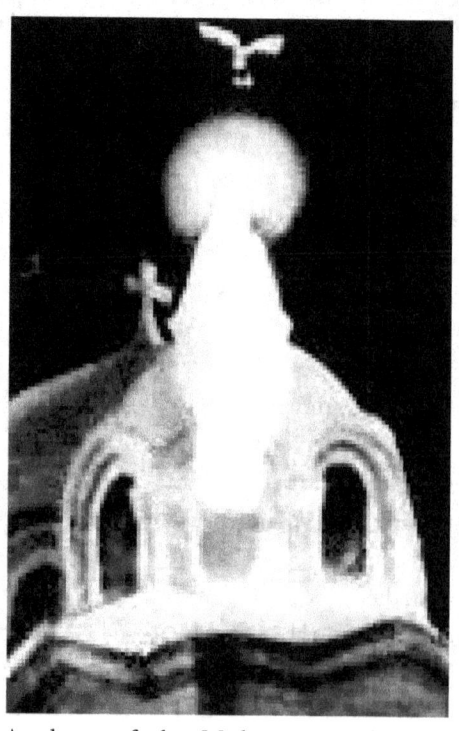

A photo of the Madonna apparition at Zeitoun, 1968. Note the dove over the figure's head. At times as many as 12 dove apparitions were seen flying about the image. Source: www.zeitun-eg.org

Some claimed that, due to the deep impression made after witnessing the apparition firsthand, Egypt's president Anwar Sadat was able to open his mind and heart to begin unprecedented peace negotiations with Israel. Further, the number of photographs taken at Zeitoun, tested, scrutinized, thoroughly examined and consequently given credence by experts, offer some of the strongest evidence to date of Marian phenomena.

Medjugorje

On June 25th, 1981, Mary appeared in Medjugorje, Yugoslavia, again to peasant children, six in all. Like Fatima and Lourdes, these six children alone have been able to see and converse with Her. Yet unlike any known, previous account, visits have continued ever since - thirty-eight years at this writing. For three decades, Mary has appeared first daily, then weekly, and now monthly - to one of the original six, who are now mature adults. More than ten million pilgrims - and, perhaps as indication of present-day indifference - tourists - have visited and witnessed the same, profound, pulsation and dancing, dimming and brightening of the sun, events now conclusively documented on film with greater frequency since the advent of video cameras. In addition, like Fatima, the visitations in Medjugorje have been accented with a significant number of weighty warnings and profound secrets that remain unrevealed.[13]

As recently as October of 2018, Mary appeared to the visionary Mirjana, who relayed this message:

"Dear children, I am calling you to be courageous and to not grow weary, because even the smallest good—the smallest sign of love—conquers evil which is all the more visible. My children, listen to me so that good may overcome, so that you may come to know the love of my Son. This is the greatest happiness—the hands of my Son that embrace, of Him who loves the soul, of Him who has given Himself for you and is always giving Himself anew in the Eucharist, of Him who has the words of eternal life. To come to know His love, to follow in His footsteps, means to have a wealth of spirituality. This is the wealth which gives good feelings and sees love and goodness everywhere. Apostles of my love, my children, be like the rays of the sun which with the warmth of my Son's love warm everyone around them. My children, the world needs apostles of love; the world needs much prayer, but prayer spoken with the heart and the soul and not only pronounced with the lips. My children, long for holiness but in humility, in the humility which permits my Son to do that which He desires through you. My children, your prayers, your words, thoughts and actions—all of this either opens or closes the doors to the Kingdom of Heaven for you. My Son showed you the way and gave you hope, and I am consoling and encouraging you because, my children, I had come to know pain, but I had faith and hope. Now I have the reward of life in the Kingdom of my Son. Therefore, listen

---

[13] In Chapter 4, an in depth look at some of the more significant messages from Medjugorje are further discussed.

to me, have courage and do not grow weary. Thank you."[14]

Between 1981 and 2001, the number of Marian apparitions - often flavored with an uncharacteristic manner of manifestation - have been staggering. At least thirty-eight-plus documented occasions of Marian apparition - not including *all* the repeated appearances of Medjugorje - or related miracles have been noted since 1980. There have been references made to dozens more from all corners of the globe, incredible reports that have engendered worldwide attention.

In addition to the historically familiar manner of Mary's visits, reports of unique and humorous twists of her presence have become commonplace. For example, in Elsa, Texas in 1993, an image of Mary is said to have appeared on the rear fender of a car. Members of the car-owner's family were moved enough to camp beside the vehicle, maintaining an overnight vigil. After some time, the skeptical owner decided the activity was just deranged foolishness, and attempted to remove the image by giving the car a good washing. Instead, the image only enhanced and enlarged, with hundreds more then flocking to the car on a daily basis, making it a veritable drive-in shrine.[15]

In Oregon in 1994, an image of Mary appeared in a landscape painting.[16] In a Barberton, Ohio church in 1992, tears began flowing from the eyes of a painting of Mary which hung there.[17] In fact, reports of photographs, paintings, and statues of Mary 'crying' tears of water, oil, even blood are too numerable to mention. The ABC television news magazine *20/20* reported on such an occurrence and broadcast astounding, videotaped footage of oil weeping so prolifically that buckets, bowls and cooking pots were needed to contain it.[18]

On one occasion in Boston a Catholic procession statue of Mary is alleged to have winked at those in attendance.[19] Her image has been seen organically manifested on rose petals,[20] in natural formations on the bark of trees, and in rainbows.[21]

For three weeks in December, 1996, 450,000 people flocked to Clearwater, Florida, to view an image of Mary 50 feet wide and 35 feet tall that

---

[14] https://www.medjugorje.com/medjugorje-today/headlines/our-lady-of-medjugorje-s-october-2-2018-message-given-through-mirjana.html. Accessed December 10, 2018.
[15] Source: Share International Magazine, December 1993, from *The Wall Street Journal*.
[16] Source: Share International Magazine, June 1994, from *The News Review*, Roseburg, Oregon.
[17] Source: Share International Magazine, May, 1992, from Knight Ridder Newspapers.
[18] See footnote #49.
[19] Source: Share International Magazine, October, 1991, from *The Boston Herald*
[20] Source: Share International Magazine, October, 1993
[21] Source: Share International Magazine, various issues; Video: *"Miracles and Visions: Fact or Fiction,"* ©MCMXCVI, Kiviat Productions, Vidmark Entertainment.

lingered on the glass wall of a two-story office building![22] That image became a shrine until 2004, when the upper section of windows were broken by a teenager with a slingshot.

In 1997, almost 2000 visitors per hour flocked to see an image of Mary formed in a puddle of water in a Mexico City subway station! Now a dried stain resembling Mexico's 'Virgin of Guadeloupe' (as an artist depicted her appearance in the year 1531!), the image continues to attract the faithful.[23]

Such incidents seem to impart a message - that we are not alone. Even the most ardent of skeptics must acknowledge some measure of curiosity or interest. There is almost a palpable, reassuring effect when left with the impression of Mary, assuming her representation of the legendary, unseen overseers, that *someone* is watching, looking out for us, caring for us. For consistent throughout all the known, recorded messages are repeated expressions of concern. The general, consistent tone of the messages seems to be one of admonishment, of warning that relay some manner of dire consequence if humanity did not mend its unconscious, irresponsible ways. Have we learned to listen to this omnipresent, doting divine mom? One need only to look at the news on any given day to see just how enmeshed we've become in loveless ignorance, psychosis, delusion, and agnosticism.

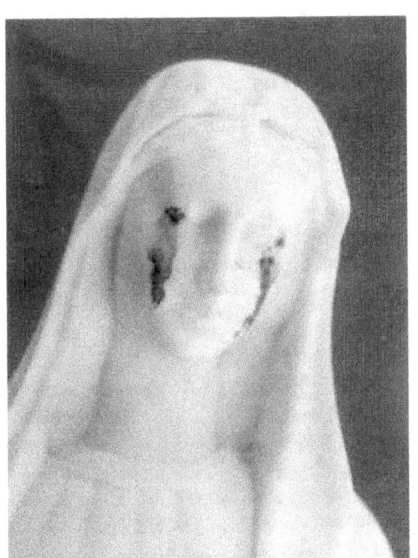 

Statues of Mary shown 'bleeding' tears.
Source: Share International Foundation

[22] Source: Share International Magazine, January 1997.
[23] Source: Catholic World News / Share International, July 1997.

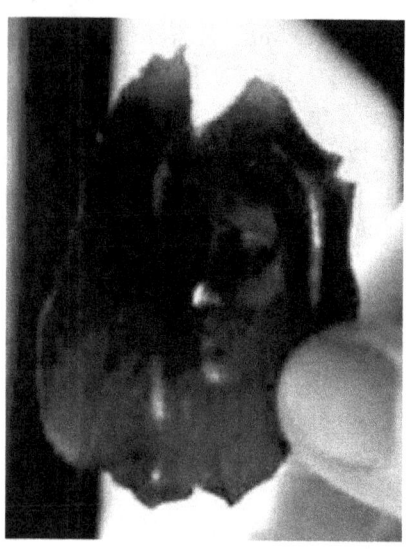 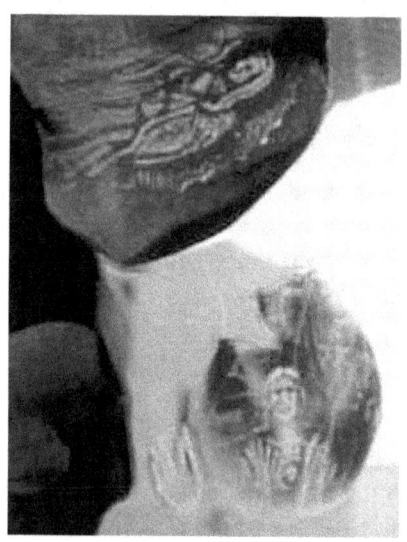

Above: Images of Mary (left) and Jesus (right) have appeared naturally etched into Rose petals. Note the petal on top of the photo on right with a depiction consistent with 'Virgin of Guadalupe' images. Source: Share International Foundation. Below, Left: The office building in Clearwater, Florida. The outline of the Madonna was visible from 1996 until a vandal shattered the top 3 panes in 2004. Below, right: A photo capturing an apparition of Mary in Medjugorje. Source: Share International Foundation

 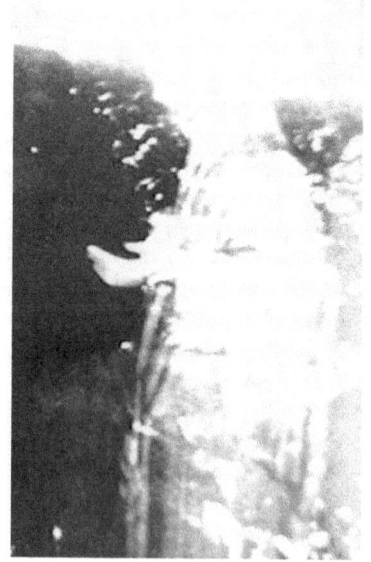

Despite the foreboding overtures associated with the Marian apparitions, there is indication that some of the more recent incidents, such as those listed above, are notably light-hearted in tone. Have we respected her wishes adequately since the foreboding, weighty messages of Fatima? Is her message getting through to us?

On December 20, 2001, Vatican City issued a press release stating that a high-ranking Church official met with 94-year-old Lucia, the sole surviving Fatima visionary on November 17th of that year. She was asked to put to rest the controversy of any unreleased secrets, and the status of the requests made of the Madonna in 1917. "Everything has been published; there are no more secrets. If I had received new revelations, I would not have communicated them to anyone, but I would have told them directly to the Holy Father." With regard to the Russian issue, she remarked, "I have already said that the consecration requested by Our Lady was done in 1984, and it has been accepted in heaven." Referring to the persistent public demand for clarification, she said,

> "How many things they attribute to me! How many things they make me do! They should read my book ["The Appeals of the Fátima Message"]; the advice and appeals that correspond to Our Lady's wishes are there. Prayer and penance, with great faith in God's power, will save the world."

It is increasingly apparent that humanity, despite its extensive dark side and capabilities, and potential course of blind self-annihilation, has made great strides. From the ashes of World War II, we have seen the advent of our modern world.

Through an unprecedented level of international cooperation, no matter how strained at times, it was universally avowed to 'never again' allow such a horrific catastrophe like the world war again mar or threaten our civilization. This is why it is doubly painful for the human family to witness virtual reenactments on the evening news of, for example, ethnic slaughter of a people solely based on their ancestral and religious difference, of the continued plight of starvation and poverty. Yet, despite what seems to be politically sanctioned, calculated barbarism through the protection of selfish and nationalistic interests at the expense of others, we also need to acknowledge our progress and achievements.

Peace negotiations between nations and factions continue despite lengthy stalemates, such as the unilateral disarmament and nuclear test ban agreements; the abolishment of Apartheid in South Africa; the advancement of civil and humanitarian rights in general; and the development of such increasingly persuasive philanthropic and humanely oriented organizations as UNICEF; Amnesty International, Oxfam, and more. We forget that such organizations did not exist in great numbers before WWII, and certainly didn't hold the degree of global influence enjoyed today.

With the demise of Soviet communism and the subsequent end of the Cold War and destruction of the Berlin Wall, witnessed was an event unexpected and universally unanticipated - the ending of the most dangerous, self-created threat to civilization in human history, and to life on Earth in general. Remarkable achievements, when viewed in history's light. On the whole, it could be said that we really aren't a completely bad lot, but still have far to go.

In 1946, on what would be her parting visit for a while, the Madonna allegedly again appeared in Germany, just as it was beginning to dig itself out from its own devastating chastisement. After explanation of the reasons for the war ("Because the nations rejected His Son, the Father poured out His cup of wrath upon them."), she once again forewarned of what to expect. But it was then, for the first time in exactly 100 years of repeated visits, that her message was considerably toned down, and the focus of content seemed to shift gears. She explained how, from that point on, she would be with us behind the scenes, looking after us, and that a personal 'peace of heart', as she called it, is easily available, if humanity continued to comply with her requests.

Though the similar strain of warning, admonition and request for prayer and faith was present, the messages delivered near Marionfried, seemed to specifically address the role of Man's own choice in the matter, i.e., our free will.

"Because," Mary exhorted,

'...the devil knows how to deceive men so that *they permit themselves to be completely blinded* to the higher things... I cannot manifest my power to the world in general. In secret I shall work marvels in souls ...Upon *you* it depends to shorten the days of darkness.'

She also indicated, that, despite what we might experience as an escalation of our darker nature in the coming years, it is a necessary process that must work itself out. Mary puts it thus:

'[The 'devil'] will rage more violently than ever and will cause frightful destruction...[and] will kill many, because he knows that his time is short.' 'The world will have to drain the cup of wrath to the dregs...' 'But, I want to tell you, my children, not to forget that the very cross of those bloody days is a grace.' 'Pray. Pray not so much for external things - weightier things are at stake in these times.'

One Hundred years earlier, in 1846, prior to Lourdes, prior to Fatima, Mary's first extensive message of warning was a forecast that also pointed to our own time. As in biblical passages, she warned of "terrible earthquakes, bloody wars, famines, pestilence, and contagious diseases [that] will develop...men will desert religion and become worse and worse."

But also, during this appearance to Melanie Calvat and Maximin Giraud in LaSalette, France, she twice made a profound statement:

'Many will allow themselves to be seduced, because they have not believed *the true Christ living among them.*'

And again, as if to reinforce and specifically clarify that remark, she said:

'Men will let themselves be deceived because they refused to adore *the real Christ who lives bodily among them.*'

Could the 'tall, white robed figure', that appeared, as reported and photographed in Nairobi in 1988, and proclaimed by witnesses to have been "Jesus of Nazareth," possibly have been the "Christ living among us" of which Mary foretold? Has Christ returned, unnoticed and unannounced, congruous with the New Testament prophecy "Like a thief in the night"?

News of the Nairobi incident flashed across the globe. Yet, few today recall anything about it, many never heard about it, or it seems to have been ignored altogether. However, like the countless, unconfirmed or validated incidents of Marian apparition in recent years, a virtually equal number of reports of alleged visits and personal encounters with Christ have proliferated, a broad topic discussed in ensuing chapters of this book.

Because, despite the overwhelmingly Christian angle relative to discussion of apparitions or encounters with Mary and/or Jesus, an equally substantial and growing number of incredible, miraculous incidents exclusive of the realm of Christianity altogether have had just as much impact in their respective traditions as that of Lourdes, Fatima, or Medjugorje.

Native Americans have reported appearances of 'deities', spurring their own spiritual revival.[24] The birth of 'Miracle', an aptly named, rare, white buffalo calf has prompted tribal councils to recognize in unison the fulfillment of their ancestral prophecies.

For Buddhists, images and statues of Buddha, like the blood and oil phenomenon of Christian icons, have also manifest supernatural attributes and

[24] Source: Share International Magazine, September 1996, from *The Dallas Morning News*

appendages. In one such report, a Japanese couple claimed that an image of the *Bodhisattva*, emanating a rainbow of light, had manifested on their bathroom window,[25] and a second emerged from a stain in the wall immediately below, prompting the home's owners to renovate the room into a shrine.

For Muslims, where worship of deities or idols of any sort is prohibited, it was reported and received with great astonishment when, on numerous occasions, the name of *'Allah'*, the phrase *'Allah exists'*, or *'Ya-Allah'*,[26] in Arabic script, was found imprinted on kilos of beans and scales of fish, or composed by the arrangement of seeds in melons[27] and other fruits and vegetables. In one instance, even the shape of some eggs appeared to spell out the name of 'Allah.'[28]

In 1995, in an event that eagerly received extensive international press and television coverage, millions of Hindus around the globe watched in euphoric amazement as statues of beloved deities such as *Ganesh*, *Shiva*, *Nandi*, and *Shash Naag* drank milk offerings from spoons, cups and saucepans. The entire nation of India came to virtual standstill, with Government offices shutting down and stock markets in Bombay and New Delhi grinding to a halt, as millions rushed to their homes and temples to make offerings of their own and witness the miracle firsthand. Reports of similar activity came in from Nepal, Singapore, Hong Kong, England, America, and elsewhere.[29]

The *Times of India* reported: "This was clearly a message from the Gods saying: 'We are here, here's the proof.'" A temple spokesperson was quoted as saying, "All I know is that our Holy Book says that whenever evil prevails on earth then some great Soul will descend to remove the bondage of evil so that right shall reign. We believe this miracle...may be a sign that a great Soul has descended, like Lord Krishna or Jesus Christ."[30]

While many of these and other stories have been frequently used as incidental filler in back sections of newspapers, the overwhelming increase of spiritually oriented phenomena worldwide has aroused interest to such an extent that many key publications now think them worthy of a coveted headline or cover story - a risky venture for a legitimate news organ in a realm hitherto reserved for the tabloids.

---

[25] Source: Share International Magazine, April 1993.
[26] Lit.: 'Oh God!', or, 'Dear God!.' Also, possibly – "Allah is here."
[27] Source: Share International Magazine, July, 1996, from *L'Actualite Religieuse*, France
[28] Source: Share International Magazine, November 1997.
[29] Source: Video: "*Miracles and Visions: Fact or Fiction*," ©MCMXCVI, Kiviat Productions, Vidmark Entertainment. Also reported in Share International magazine, November 1995, from *The Guardian*, UK.
[30] Source: Share International magazine, November 1995, from *The Guardian*, UK.

But it wouldn't be the first time such claims have been made. In fact, the very history of the modern press is demonstrative of how an attempted fulfillment of the spiritual yearning of the masses was big business. Nouveau spiritual movements have routinely sprung up in all parts of the globe, most markedly in the past 150 years, and many of these movements have embedded themselves into popular culture and lore to the extent that the source is now relatively unrecognized.

Coinciding with the frequent accounts of the appearance of Mary in the latter half of the 19th and the early 20th centuries were a number of movements that endeavored to yoke religious fervor with academic and scientific credibility. By simultaneously synthesizing the eastern and western, the oriental and occidental, the rational with the irrational, and blended with the essences of assorted cultural elements from the four corners of the globe, new perspectives on the 'old time religion' hit the mark for many who sought an alternative to the fire and brimstone stance of the dominant Christian faiths. For those who dreamed of building a modern utopia as the industrial age was just beginning to gain steam, a new religious perspective was needed. One that drew from antiquity and one that did not wholly denounce the varied traditions, but, like their material counterpart in the physical world, could form the foundation upon which a new church could be built. Religion could be manufactured, marketed, and promoted, just like the many new wonder items being produced in the ever-increasing number of factories and sweatshops.

Yet, while countless charlatans swindled naive believers, there were those who sincerely wished to really bring about a religious revolution. One that could realistically and intellectually uplift the masses out of the industrial mire, one that could truly offer a scientifically based redemption and understanding, an epiphany within which all could participate.

Who would guide such a new revelation? Who would teach this new philosophy? Some promoted themselves in ways that would have been formerly considered heretical, and just 100 or so years prior would have had them imprisoned, exiled, or burned as heretics. Some came up with remarkable packages, and to fully implement the agenda, it was evident that what would really help and be most effective would be the interpretation of obscure scripture of the past accompanied with signs of the fulfillment of ancient prophecies. But the real icing on the cake would be to find and announce the arrival of a modern messiah. One that would understand the needs of the modern age, a peer who could guide us into the new century, the new time, the new age.

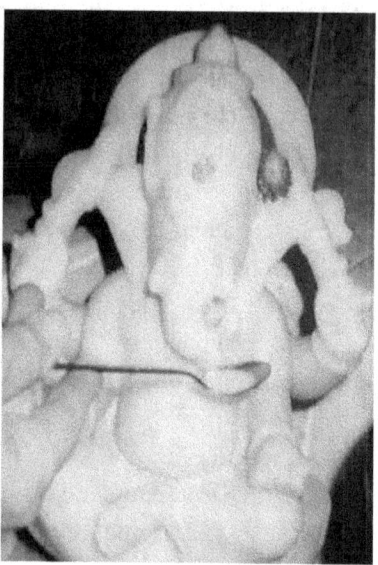

Above: Photos taken while the respective statues of Ganesh (right) and Krishna (left) were witnessed to have miraculously "drink" milk from a spoon. Below: A Muslim miracle: Eggplant seeds spell sacred words or phrases in Classic Arabic script. Source: Share International Foundation

Chapter Two

PREPARING THE WAY

"God has a few of us whom He whispers in the ear."

Robert Browning

Born on the heels of the spread of occult spiritualism in the West, the *Theosophical Society* has been subject to scorn, scrutiny, criticism - as well as praise by some noteworthy intellectuals - from the beginning. The very name of the organization denotes an ongoing attempt that occurred throughout the 19th century to establish academic credibility within the realm of spiritual phenomenon. The term *Theosophical* implies 'the science of religion'; practically a misnomer up to then in the West but which had been the status quo in the Orient for countless ages.

Prior to the Society's founding, many organizations and cults claimed ever-new angles as to why they held authority in their representation of the 'spirit world.' As early as 1841 there were extreme claims proclaiming that the returned Christ was among us. It was then found in the person of an Anglican minister - Reverend H. J. Prince - who initiated a charismatic revival within that church that was so potent that Prince eventually left the Church of England altogether to found his own religious community called 'The Abode of Love.' Prince declared himself an *avatar*,[31] and the modern successor to Jesus, whom Prince claimed had been just one of a long lineage of avatar-redeemers, of which he himself was the current chosen scion. One could say it was then, in 1841, that began what we today know as 'the New Age.'

Meanwhile, in America, the interest in spirit mediumship and seances had gained enormous popularity, eventually attracting the naive, curious, and spiritually deficient of the upper middle and elite social classes. Wealthy people poured their fortunes into backing many of the so-called mystics, attracting the

---

[31] A divinely born, appointed intermediary or medium of divine grace.

attention of the era's entrepreneurs, such as P. T. Barnum, which only further entrenched a broader public interest.

One individual so smitten by spiritualism was Henry Olcott, a former American Union Army Colonel who sat on the official investigation panel of President Abraham Lincoln's assassination, and later dabbled in a variety of careers as a farmer and agricultural expert, lawyer, and writer. Having grown disillusioned by the failure of his many career attempts as well as a marriage that ended in divorce, Olcott sought distraction and solace through investigations into the spiritualist climate, publications, and activities, as well as Freemasonry. It was after writing a series of articles in a popular spiritualist circular on the activities at Mary Baker Eddy's[32] Chittenden Farm in Vermont - which was known in its day for putting on a spectacular show of spirit world activities - that Olcott met an expatriate Russian aristocrat, Madame Helena Blavatsky. Blavatsky was not only a fan of Olcott's written articles, but found in him a kindred spirit.

Born in a prominent family of noble ancestry, Blavatsky abandoned the required social conditions consistent with her family background, as well as her aged husband whom she later claimed had been interested only in sexual relations. She lived an incredible life of world travel and adventure, primarily on her own. Accentuated by love affairs with elite members of international society, Blavatsky was infamous for her tales of: journeys through the American West in a covered wagon; her stint as a circus performer; touring as a concert pianist; running businesses in Odessa and Paris; extended stays in exotic lands, and her conversations and tenures of study with Tibetan Lamas, Indian Yogis, Middle Eastern Kabbalists, Asian secret agents, and Voodoo magicians in the American South. She claimed to have fought in battles and to have been once shipwrecked off the coast of Greece. But of all such adventures, the most enduring and significant moment, as later recounted in her biography, was her initial meeting with a most phenomenal being by the name of El Morya Khan, a Rajput Prince living in the Himalayas at the time. Known then as Master Morya, Blavatsky claimed he was one of an extended group of Masters of Wisdom whose work is concerned with the unseen governing of humanity. It was after meeting Morya, she said, that the course of her life's direction was thereafter altered.

Her scholarly influences were many and diverse, and anything reeking of the occult attracted the interest and insatiable hunger for wisdom that possessed Blavatsky. Among these were contemporary works written by

---

[32] The 19th century founder of the *Church of Christian Science*, a sect which proclaimed the then revolutionary notion that a personal relationship with the divine was available to us while here on earth, as opposed to the prevailing notion that living a good life earned its reward in a heavenly afterlife.

members of the Freemasons and the Rosicrucians, whose roots are said to have originated with the Knights Templar, the order of secular, Catholic warrior-monks who spearheaded the Crusades, gained control of Jerusalem for the benefit of securing safety for medieval Christian pilgrims for nearly 80 years, and who were eventually persecuted and slain as heretics by the Vatican's office of Inquisition.

It was rumored that during their tenure in the Holy Land, the Templars had allegedly unearthed ancient written documents which had been buried in secret, hidden vaults beneath the Temple of Jerusalem, and which shook the very foundations of Papal power and Christianity itself. The possession of this secret, radical occult knowledge had secured for the Templar Knights a unique position of unquestionable power and authority in 10th Century Christendom, as well as an extraordinary measure of financial wealth due to their funding by Europe's wealthiest families, and allegedly due to having simultaneously unearthed the Treasury vaults of ancient Israel.[33]

Helena Blavatsky

Whatever written material the Templars had discovered required a sworn oath of secrecy from each member until death. New recruits arriving from Europe were required to endure a rigorous series of initiation rituals, with only the most tenured members privileged to full disclosures. Legend holds that each high-ranking Templar had been revealed a segment of an alleged secret doctrine, which would be passed to another select, advanced initiate just prior to the former's death. As guardians of these portions of the doctrine, they collectively contained an ancient secret that was said to enable one to gain insight into the mysteries of the ages and the life of the immortals - ageless beings who defy time, space, and all properties inherent in the material world. Further, by possession of this ancient, esoteric secret, the bearers believed they themselves could attain a degree of immortality equal to that of Jesus himself. Naturally, such a perspective instilled a queasy feeling in the Papal house, and thus the ultimate demise of the Templars.

---

[33] Ref: The Hiram Key © Christopher Knight and Robert Lomas

In her book of the same title, Blavatsky claimed that *The Secret Doctrine* was the essence of a singular theism from which all historical theological systems had sprung, and which, in her case, had been revealed to her by several of these same alleged immortals with whom she claimed to have made contact. Most notably was the aforementioned El Morya Khan, along with another adept and fraternal brother of his - Master Koot Hoomi.

Left: An alleged photograph of Koot Hoomi. Right: El Morya, the Rajput Prince, circa 1890. Well known in his time, El Morya passed in 1898. Photo source unknown.

The general public and specifically the educated upper classes of Blavatsky's day were obsessed with fantastic legends such as that of the Templars. Academics competed in a race to offer scientific and intellectual evidence of such phenomena at the same rate at which many tried to debunk it. In fact, new scientific fields of study were being created regularly, and it was Galileo vs. the Vatican all over again, as science began to openly challenge religious hierarchy. The debate over Darwinism - culminating decades later in the Scopes trial - was just beginning to get warm.

Having witnessed a number of nouveau, quasi spiritual/scientific expositions both in person and via articles written by various celebrities of the spiritualist movement, Blavatsky and Olcott, now inseparable companions, saw an opportunity in the void created by the growing well-publicized disillusionment in spiritualism. To fill that void, the two 'chums' as Olcott referred to themselves, organized their views, research, and experience, and scheduled a public meeting in New York in 1875. Invited were a number of socially prominent - and wealthy - individuals who had supported or believed in the principals behind spiritualism for some time. After Blavatsky and Olcott presented, discussed, and demonstrated their credentials - which allegedly included the public demonstration of alleged miracles - the group of supporters would form what became known as The Theosophical Society.

The measure of public spectacle that surrounded Spiritualism at the time needs to be taken into consideration, for, as in the example of Chittenden Farm, an almost persuasive, vaudevillian presentation was often sufficient enough to convince those eager enough to investigate. Despite the public's general suspicion aroused by the number of previously exposed, spiritualist frauds, one needs to view, in perspective, the more than likely stimulating presentation made by Blavatsky and Olcott, along with the specific nature of the sort of claims which were asserted and demonstrated by Madame Blavatsky herself. Blavatsky stood firmly on the assertion that she was in constant telepathic contact with two, then physically living Masters - Morya and Koot Hoomi. The technique is a skill routinely taught in traditional Buddhism and Raja Yoga, and her teachers, she claimed, were Masters of both. Hence, the credentials offered to those first potential inductees of the Theosophical Society were the alleged display of miracles, which Blavatsky contended was due to the intervention by these unseen Masters.

As the Society grew, its influence spread far and wide, attracting and impressing a significant number of the world's influential thinkers and personalities both during Blavatsky's life and afterward. Among those who praised Blavatsky's works and included themselves as members of the organization at one time or another were William Butler Yeats, Oscar Wilde, Mohandas K. "Mahatma" Gandhi, Rudolf Steiner, Albert Einstein, and Thomas Edison. As the new century dawned and the influence of the Society under Olcott's initial direction as President continued, The Theosophical Society would do innumerable philanthropic and humanitarian works which included the printing of school books and the establishment of schools in many developing nations.

After a period of unresolved interpersonal conflict, Blavatsky and Olcott parted company, with Blavatsky settling in London. It was there, having succumbed to a number of serious health conditions, that Blavatsky completed *The Secret Doctrine*.

Offered by Blavatsky as a commentary on an arcane, ancient book entitled *The Book of Dyzan*, it was believed that Blavatsky had her hands on the very information so guarded by the Templars, and so feared by the Vatican.

In one, brilliant academic swing, Blavatsky had simultaneously earned international academic and social respect while boldly standing in defiance of all religious establishment of the day. She was the conquering hero of the spiritualists, a New Age David against the Papal Goliath, and her connections amongst the international social registry made her virtually untouchable.

Though broken into four sections, only the first two sections of The Secret Doctrine were initially published. The first section, entitled *Cosmogenesis*, details the origin of the universe and the corresponding symbolic references found throughout the glyphs, legends, and writings of ancient civilizations. In the second part - *Anthropogenesis* - the origin, history, and both the natural and metaphysical evolution of the human species is explained. It is said that Blavatsky so abhorred and disagreed with the finite theories of Charles Darwin, which were widely accepted by the scientific community at the time, that Anthropogenesis was written in direct response to Darwin's *The Origin of Species*. In contrast to Darwin's work, Blavatsky's Anthropogenesis offered a convincing, combined scientific and philosophically based argument for the divine, spiritual origin of man.

Since its publication in 1883, The Secret Doctrine had become a virtual, academic Rosetta Stone of human endeavor, evolution, and civilization, and more importantly, it purported to offer a sound explanation for the historical origin and basis of the lore, myths, and legends of all the world's cultural heritages. Simultaneously hailed and scorned, it is a mystifying book. Many of the assertions made in the two-volume set continue to be given broader credibility and substantiation in contemporary thesis such as those posed in works like researcher Graham Hancock's 1995 publication *Fingerprints of the Gods*. Such works cite claim to offer modern scientific data that would lend a large measure of plausibility to Blavatsky's assertions. If some of her archeological suggestions have since passed the acid test through more recent findings in the 20th century, could the theological and philosophical purports of Blavatsky be true as well?

Theosophy and Christ

Theosophy holds that 'Christ' - in its proper interpretation of the term - as a persona, had rarely incarnated, and has historically worked *through* his best and brightest disciples by *overshadowing them*. According to succeeding arbiters of the arcane in the 20th century, as well as Blavatsky herself, it was The Secret Doctrine that specifically opened the door and began to pave the way for the unfolding of a divine 'master plan' that would result in the ushering in of the return of the Christ in the modern era. In fact, it was Blavatsky's contention that one objective of the Theosophical Society in those early years was to locate and assist in the grooming of a suitable candidate through whom the Christ would 'descend', overshadow, and work once more among humanity. In the late 1880's, Madame Blavatsky informed her students of this plan, and that a primary purpose behind the establishment of the Theosophical Society was to specifically help humanity prepare to receive the coming messiah of our time, a World Teacher by the name of *Maitreya*, the same name historically assigned in Buddhism to the expected 5th and final incarnation of Buddha.

According to that theory, the Christ - not confined to the Christian use of the term - has historically worked in this manner of overshadowing through some of the most popular names in the combined canons of the world's theosophies. Among them - the Vedic Rishi *Vyasa*; *Sri Krishna* of Hinduism's *Bhagavad-Gita*; Jesus the Nazarene; and more recently, the great eighth century Indian exponent of *Vedanta*, *Sri Shankara of Kerala*, among others.[34] These great disciples, it was claimed, are fully and constantly overshadowed by the higher, soul-infused principle of *Christ Consciousness*. Having perfected and mastered the goal of discipleship, such candidates have consciously surrendered and merged their limited, egoic personalities with the infinite, which is consistent with the true theopathic goal of the world's older religious traditions, such as Buddhism, Vedanta, Sufism, etc. In the New Testament Gospel of John, Chapter 7, vs.28 -29, Jesus indicates his full awareness of this form of personal surrender:

> "You both know me, and know where I am from. Yet I have not come of myself, but he who is true has sent me, whom you do not know. I know him because I am from him, and he has sent me."

Based on the contention of a tradition of divine overshadowing, and in a manner similar to the Tibetan Buddhist search process for the reincarnated heir apparent of Dalai Lamaship, the Theosophical society sought and did locate several select individuals whom they saw fit to be perfect candidates and who could be properly groomed to fill those largest of sandals. The intention was that if one of the candidates held all the essential qualifications and could complete the rigorous preparatory process to a sufficient degree, that they, for all intents and purposes, would be ordained with the mantle of Christ, and become the next messiah, the *Mahavatar* of *The New Age*.

Two of Madame Blavatsky's students - Annie Besant, who would succeed Olcott as president of the Theosophical Society (and who would eventually take her place in history as a co-founding member of the *All India Home Rule League* with Mahatma Gandhi and Ali Jinnah), and her controversial

---

[34] As based on the writings of Benjamin Creme in *Maitreya's Mission*, volumes one through three.

companion Charles W. Leadbeater - had found such a candidate in the person of the young Jiddu Krishnamurti, who would later come to be regarded as one of the preeminent philosophical thinkers of the 20th century. After other candidates had failed to make the grade, allegedly due to Leadbeater's preference and intervention, Krishnamurti alone was left in the running, and, to the Theosophists, was certain to be the first high caliber Christ-avatar since Jesus.

The First Second Coming

Born on May 12, 1895 in Andhra Pradesh, India, Jiddu Krishnamurti[35] was the eighth of nine children in a middle-class Brahmin family. His mother, a profoundly devout Hindu, had an intuitive sense during pregnancy that this child had a sacred destiny, and arranged to give birth in the family's *puja* room - the Hindu equivalent of a home chapel. As the boy grew, he was, oddly enough, denounced as being mentally retarded by schoolteachers and other adults, due to a lackluster academic performance.

At the age of fourteen, while playing with his brother Nityananda[36] on a beach which was adjacent to the headquarters of the Theosophical Society in India, the boy then caught the attention of C.W. Leadbeater, who sensed the same "sacredness" foreseen by Krishnamurti's mother. Believing that they'd found the awaited vehicle for the returned, incarnating World Teacher, Annie Besant adopted Krishnamurti as a ward of the Theosophical Society, and brought him to England to be educated at Oxford.

Meanwhile, Leadbeater took on the role of personal tutor, coaching Krishnamurti in an advanced curriculum of austere yogic practices as part of the rigorous preparatory program he'd co-developed with Besant. Included and emphasized, for example, were esoteric methods of conscious astral travel which were practiced during periods of deep sleep, techniques long employed by the adepts and masters of Yoga and Tibetan Buddhism.

In Krishnamurti's biography, *The Years of Awakening*, author and lifelong friend Mary Lutyens recounts in amazing detail the intricate process of Krishnamurti's preparation to become the World Teacher. She describes some of the 'astrally escorted' journeys with Leadbeater, when Krishnamurti was said to have met the Master Koot Hoomi and others who further 'prepared' and trained the boy by giving assorted tests. Such tests required, for example, that Krishnamurti recall a series of sentences that were given during the course of his discarnate journeys, which he was then required to write down upon his

---

[35] 'Jiddu' is the family surname.
[36] Not to be confused with the Indian Saint, Bhagavan Nityananda.

return/waking in the morning. Many of these early 'training' notes are recorded in a small book entitled *At the Feet of the Master*, which is still in print today.

But most extraordinary is Krishnamurti's own documented description of his experience, in which he lucidly describes his otherworldly, dream-state encounters with the Masters - those same Masters first introduced - if only in theory - by Blavatsky.

"It was very beautiful," wrote Krishnamurti,

> "When we went to our Master's house, we found [Master Koot Hoomi] and Master Morya and the Master Djwal Khul all standing, talking, and they spoke very kindly. We all prostrated ourselves, and the Master drew me to His knee, and asked me whether I would forget myself entirely and never have a selfish thought, but think only how to help the world; and I said indeed I would, and I wanted only to be like Him some day. Then He kissed me and passed his hand over me, and I seemed to be somehow part of Him, and I felt quite different and very happy, and I have had that feeling ever since. Then all three blessed me and we came away."[37]

After this encounter, Leadbeater wrote to Annie Besant, informing her that Krishnamurti had passed his 'probation period' and was to be initiated in a ceremony which was to presided by Maitreya, the World Teacher - *the Christ* - and that the boy would require a period of thirty-six hours in seclusion. After this event, the young Krishnamurti awoke the following morning shouting "I remember! I remember!" recording the account of his initiation as follows:

> 'When I left my body the first night, I went at once to [Master Koot Hoomi's] house and found Him there with [Masters Morya and Djwhal Khul]. The Master talked to me very kindly for a long time, and told me about the Initiation, and what I should have to do. Then we all went together to the house of the Lord Maitreya, where I had been once before, and there we found many of the Masters - The Venetian Master, the Master Jesus, the Master the Count [St. Germain], the Master Serapis, the Master Hilarion,[38] and the two Masters Morya and [Koot Hoomi]. The Lord Maitreya sat in the middle, and the others stood round Him in a semicircle...Then the Master [Koot Hoomi] took my right hand, and the Master Djwhal Khul my left, and they led me in front of the Lord Maitreya, you [Besant] and

---

[37] Courtesy of the Krishnamurti Foundation of America, Ojai, California.
[38] Believed, in the Theosophical canon, to have been Saint Paul in a previous incarnation.

[Leadbeater] standing close behind me. The Lord smiled at me, but He said to the Master [Koot Hoomi]:

"Who is this that you thus bring before me?'

And the Master answered: 'This is the candidate who seeks admission...'

Then the Lord asked: - 'Do you vouch for him as worthy of admission?'

The Master replied: - 'I do.'

The Lord continued: 'Will you undertake to guide his steps along the path which he desires to enter?'

And the Master answered: - 'I will.'"[39]

Krishnamurti's whole account of the event is very reminiscent of several known initiatory rites of established organizations. For one, it is very close to that of the Freemasons. Without added detail, it's virtually interchangeable. Secondly, it's curiously similar to the Catholic ritual of the sacrament of Confirmation, the third sacrament bestowed upon a Catholic once having been baptized and received Holy Communion for the first time. In that ceremony, the baptized candidate, after going through a period of catechism study and 'spiritual cleansing' through prayer and confession of sins to a priest, is presented to a regional Bishop for the anointing. Pre-selected, and vowing to guide the child in his spiritual life in the event that his or her parents are unable to, are two Godparents, who are usually two, devout, pious adherents of the faith. In Freemasonry, two sponsoring, previously initiated and ranking members vouch for the new candidate.

Confirmation is much like the Jewish Bar-and Bat-Mitzvah ceremony in that it marks, if only in theory, the independent adult life of the confirmed, and undoubtedly both of those religion's practices were closely linked if not synonymous in the remote past, as asserted by Blavatsky. In fact, while reading Krishnamurti's account one gets the impression that perhaps his own described initiation ceremony was an ancient practice which preceded all subsequent, historical rituals of a similar nature, as suggested by the Theosophists. This would lend some measure of credence to the potential likelihood that both the Jewish Mitzvah and Catholic Confirmation ceremonies are based on the same ritual practice, or the memory of such, reaching far into antiquity. Was this also the basis of the secret initiation ceremony of the Freemasons, who openly acknowledge that the actual origin of their rites is today only speculated? Was it the same ritual employed by the Templars?

---

[39] Courtesy of the Krishnamurti Foundation of America, Ojai, California.

Just as in Confirmation, a second 'God-parent' or sponsor was asked to support Krishnamurti. The Master Djwal Khul volunteered, saying: "I am prepared to do so." Thereafter, both Leadbeater and Besant accepted the responsibility to act as guides for the young Krishnamurti in his developing years.

According to Krishnamurti's account, Maitreya then addressed him again, by saying:

"[Will you] gladly submit yourself to their [Leadbeater and Besant] guidance?"

K: "Indeed, I do love them with all my heart."

Maitreya: "You desire then to join the Brotherhood which exists from eternity unto eternity?"

K: "I wish to join when I am fit to do so."

Maitreya: "Do you know the object of this Brotherhood?"

K: "To do the work of the Logos[40] by helping the world."

Maitreya: "Will you pledge yourself to devote all your life and all your strength henceforth to this work, forgetting yourself absolutely for the good of the world, making your life all love, even as He is all love?"

K: "I will."[41]

Krishnamurti explains that he was then shown a variety of things that he promised to keep secret which are not revealed in the book. He was further asked a number of compelling questions and requests, such as distinguishing between the subtle bodies of a living and a dead man, between a spirit and a ghost. Then he was asked if he could distinguish between a real person and a *'familiar'* - a thought-created facsimile of a living person - a feat accomplished by Eastern adepts in complete defiance of the currently known laws of physics.

The full account of Krishnamuti's testimony is quite lengthy and detailed, and interested readers might like to further investigate Mary Lutyen's book. Included therein are similar experiences of the Masters that occurred in just the first half of Krishnamurti's life,[42] as well as the accounts of others with whom he was associated.

The Public Life of Krishnamurti

The initial years of Krishnamurti's public life were wrought with controversy, as few ultimately accepted the messianic claims of his sponsors. He endured much mudslinging, humiliation, and rejection from the press and

---

[40] Relatively speaking, God in a triune aspect, a.k.a. 'The Holy Trinity.'
[41] Courtesy of the Krishnamurti Foundation of America, Ojai, California.
[42] Lutyen's 'Awakening...' is part one of a three-volume set.

public, and went through numerous periods of strong doubt and consternation. After a particularly difficult period, which was further strained by what were thought to be at the time a variety of unusual and unknown physical maladies, at the age of 27, Krishnamurti felt relief only after yet another powerful encounter with the Masters.

After he retreated one evening by sitting quietly beneath a pepper tree to meditate, the close associates who had gathered around Krishnamurti were quite concerned for his well-being and maintained a constant watchful eye on him. In an eyewitness account of what was described as an unexpected radical transformation, Krishnamurti's brother, Nitya, wrote the following details in a written correspondence to Annie Besant:

"Krishna seemed much worse, he seemed to be suffering a great deal... toward six o'clock [p.m.] he quietened down... Then suddenly the whole house seemed full of a terrific force and Krishna was as if possessed. He would have none of us near and began to complain bitterly... and in a voice full of pain said he longed to go to the woods. Now he was sobbing aloud... he expressed a desire for solitude. [He was urged] to go out under [a fragrant, blossoming pepper tree].

We sat with eyes fixed, wondering if all was well, for now there was a perfect silence, and as we looked I saw suddenly a great Star shining above the tree, and I knew that Krishna... was being prepared for the Great One. The place seemed to be filled with a Great Presence...and I knew that the Great Lord...had come Himself; and though we saw Him not, yet all felt the splendour of His presence."

Another woman had accompanied Nitya that evening. She also witnessed the scene with concern, until, at one point, Nitya described:

"Her face was transfigured, as she said to us, 'Do you see Him?'...we who could not see saw [the experience] mirrored in her face... I who could not see but who gloried in the presence of [Maitreya] felt He turned towards us and spoke some words to [her; for] her face shone...as she answered, 'I will, I will,' ... as if [her words] were a promise given with splendid joy.

The radiance and the glory of the many Beings present lasted nearly an half hour....[the woman] saw it all; 'Look, do you see?' she would often repeat, or 'Do you hear the music?' Then presently we heard Krishna's footsteps...and all was over.

All [the next] day [Krishnamurti] lay under the tree in samadhi and in the evening, as he sat in meditation as on the night before, [the woman] again saw three figures round him who quickly went away... Since then and every evening he sits in meditation under the tree."

In the annals of many a disciple of great beings are recorded accounts similar to Nitya's. Yet rarely are found the intimate sharings of the inner experience of those great beings themselves. In our time there are a number of them that have been made available for the benefit of both student and seeker wishing to gain insight into the hidden lives of Saints. Examples of such work can be found in *The Confessions of Saint Augustine*; the autobiographical works of *Saint Therese of Lisieux*; Paramahansa Yogananda's *Autobiography of a Yogi*; and Swami Muktananda's *Play of Consciousness*.

Mary Lutyens biography of Krishnamurti is unique in that it offers the view as written by a dear friend and confidant of the book's subject, and also includes a wealth of passages personally written by the subject himself. With regard to the events described above by Krishnamurti's brother, Nitya, it is fortunate that Krishnamurti sheds further profound insight by describing his own view of what occurred. Thus, Krishnamurti explains:

"When I had sat thus for some time, I felt myself going out of my body, I saw myself sitting down with the delicate tender leaves of the tree over me. I was facing the east. In front of me was my body and over my head I saw the Star, bright and clear. Then I could feel the vibrations of the Lord Buddha; I beheld Lord Maitreya and Master [Koot Hoomi]. I was so happy, calm and at peace. I could still see my body and I was hovering near it. There was such profound calmness both in the air and within myself, the calmness of the bottom of a deep unfathomable lake. Like the lake, I felt my physical body, with its mind and emotions, could be ruffled on the surface but nothing, nay nothing, could disturb the calmness of my soul. The Presence of the mighty Beings was with me for some time and then They were gone. I was supremely happy, for I had seen. Nothing could ever be the same. I have drunk at the clear and pure waters at the source of the fountain of life and my thirst was appeased. Never more could I be thirsty, never more could I be in utter darkness. I have seen the Light. I have touched compassion which heals all sorrow and suffering; it is not for myself, but for the world. I have stood on the mountaintop and gazed at the mighty Beings. Never can I be in utter darkness; I have seen the glorious and healing Light. The fountain of Truth has been revealed to me and the darkness has been dispersed. Love in all its glory has intoxicated my heart; my heart can never be closed. I have drunk at the fountain of Joy and eternal Beauty. I am God-intoxicated."

Thus, is laid the foundation for Krishnamurti's life's work. In the time that followed, he entered, according to he, a phase when he was thereafter in constant telepathic rapport with Maitreya, or, perhaps more accurately, permanently *overshadowed*, a state of consciousness in which he was completely aware of his own soul's melding with the universal spirit of the Christ. Krishnamurti termed his experience of this "the Process."

Around Krishnamurti the ceremonial "Order of the Star" was created by Annie Besant, but would ultimately be dissolved by Krishnamurti himself. It was his observation that too much emphasis was being placed on hierarchical status within the Theosophical Society and its many sub-branches. Splinter organization members, such as those of the Star Order itself, the 'Esoteric Division' - the original sect formed by Madame Blavatsky, and (in the footsteps of the Templars) the *Liberal Catholic Church* (in which C.W. Leadbeater had ordained himself a bishop), were all bickering about initiatory status: 'Whom was 'higher' than or equal to whom?'

Those who bristled over Krishnamurti's message of criticism and opposition had decided, since they had obtained the ability to astrally travel and visit and work with their own respective Masters, that they didn't need to heed Krishnamurti. In their view, he spoke to 'the little ones', the masses that had greater need for a Messiah than they. In contrast, the snobbish clerics decided that as - in their minds - senior initiates and disciples, they needed only to tend to themselves, and their own kind. This sort of rhetoric infuriated Krishnamurti, who, having indeed merged in consciousness with Maitreya, preached equality and personal independence, but not indifference and separatism.

In 1925, while speaking at a convention of members of the Order of the Star, all in attendance witnessed the transforming moment when Krishnamurti became fully immersed and overshadowed by Maitreya, who was believed to be the Christ. Prior to this moment, Krishnamurti typically spoke of Maitreya in second person, with Maitreya's teachings essentially being relayed through him. In this 1925 lecture, all present detected a shift from the normal second person manner of speaking to a noticeable, unexpected first-person format. As Mary Lutyens recalls:

> "It came at the end of his talk. He had been speaking about the World Teacher: "He comes" [said Krishnamurti] "only to those who want, who desire, who long..." and then his voice changed completely and rang out, "and I come for those who want sympathy, who want happiness, who are longing to be released, who are longing

to find happiness in all things. I come to reform and not to tear down, I come not to destroy but to build.'

Annie Besant, who awaited and helped pave the way for this moment since her days with Madame Blavatsky, knowingly noticed the change at once, recognizing the familiar voice and manner of speaking of the Theosophical Master of Masters. In a series of speeches and written articles, she hastily made the announcement to the world.

"That event," Besant wrote, "...marked the definite consecration of the chosen vehicle...The coming has begun...That there should be opposition is natural; did the Hebrews acknowledge Him or the Romans welcome Him? History repeats itself'; 'A new life, a new storm has swept the world... the morning star has risen above the horizon."

Annie Besant, circa 1920.

Besant herself had noticed the unbecoming pettiness within the Theosophical Society's personal infrastructure, and she too began to grow disillusioned with the Order of the Star, becoming sympathetic to Krishnamurti's view. She observed in horror how, shortly after hearing the news of Maitreya's overshadowing of K., the other officers of the Theosophical Society seemed more concerned with how the event would affect their ecclesiastical status, instead of finding cause for celebration. They went as far as opening a dialog, for example, on whom among them should be the appointed apostles, an issue that was never initiated and instantly detested by Krishnamurti. He made his sentiments truthfully clear in a correspondence to Leadbeater, saying:

"I have woken up so often with feelings of revolt and distrust that my impressions and intuitions are growing stronger and stronger and I feel that the events...aren't wholesome...Of course, none of them are very important, but this apostle business is the limit. I don't believe in it all...I think it's wrong... It's a trivial thing but other people are making a mountain of it... [so and so] is distributing initiations around...and sacred things will be a joke presently... it makes me weep to see these sacred things dragged in the dirt."

The strength of conviction in Krishnamurti's words became immovably entrenched. All those who had known him from day one and who remained supportive were taken aback by this unprecedented resoluteness. One close associate offered the following:

"Krishna spoke as never before and one feels now that his consciousness and that of [Maitreya] are so completely blended that there is no distinction any more.... The face of the Lord shone through the face of Krishna and His glorious aura encompassed us in an almost blinding light."

The world press, of course, had a field day with the controversy surrounding the rumors of bickering, which was having the effect of drastically undermining all the groundwork laid by Olcott, Blavatsky, Leadbeater, Besant, and Krishnamurti himself, along with the believed unseen but involved hands of Maitreya and the Masters. Despite this, Krishnamurti and Besant held their heads high, confronting the opposition head on and staying the course. Both K. and Besant scheduled conferences and lecture tours, with Besant issuing press releases in advance of their arrival, such as the following sent to the Associated Press:

Krishnamurti, circa 1925.

"The Divine Spirit has descended once more on a man, Krishnamurti, one who in his life is literally perfect, as those who know him can testify...The World Teacher is here."

Arriving by ocean liner in America in 1926 for one such lecture tour, news reporters and photographers were eagerly on hand to greet 'the World Teacher', the news of which had rapidly spread from Europe. Disappointed with Krishnamurti's appearance in Western style, contemporary clothing, skeptical reporters "tried to trip him up with shrewdly worded questions," the *New York Times* reported. "He skillfully avoided all these pitfalls and earned their admiration by coming out triumphant."[43]

In those days before the advent of television, the word of the press was bible. Krishnamurti toured America to mixed, though primarily positive reviews. False accusations, rumors of scandal and love affairs, as well as a general denouncement of his acclaimed status stained a possible greater reception than it was believed he'd initially receive. Yet this did not deter the sincerely devout, who hoped and yearned that the rumor of the returned 'World Teacher' was true. Scandalous rumors or not, by 1928, at meetings around the globe in all the major cities - New York, Bombay, Genoa, Paris, London, and many more - hundreds of people had to be turned away from sold out venues.

Upon his arrival in America, 16,000 or so people attended his first American lecture at the Hollywood Bowl. He was adored by the socialites in young Hollywood, and was even offered a five thousand-dollar per week salary - a considerably substantial sum in those days - by a Hollywood film mogul who wanted Krishnamurti to play the lead role in a film on the life of Buddha.

Returning to Europe, thousands now attended his lectures in capacity filled venues. In June of 1928, Krishnamurti spoke in fluent French during a radio broadcast from the Eiffel Tower to his largest audience to date - an estimated two million listeners. His penetrating lectures mesmerized audiences, and his breadth of insight, knowledge, and the ability to engage in intelligent discourse with the world's greatest thinkers and innovators captured their allegiance and respect. Einstein, Gandhi, the conductor Leopold Stokowski, author and 'transcendental researcher' Aldous Huxley (who remained a lifelong friend and supporter of K) - many who were making the news - requested private counsel and discourse with Krishnamurti, all of whom came away deeply inspired. A great spirit was indeed with the man.

Early in 1929, Krishnamurti was shocked to learn the full measure of dissent engendered by the Theosophical Society elders. In August of that year he publicly dissolved the Order of the Star, of which he had been appointed head, and by December had resigned from the Theosophical Society altogether. At a conference of card-carrying Theosophical and Order members, Krishnamurti expressed his disappointment in the attitudes of the Society leaders, offering a covert warning to those who allowed themselves to be shepherded by his jealous, egocentric colleagues.

"The time has come when you must no longer subject yourself to anything," he said. "I hope you will not listen to anyone, but will listen only to

---

[43] New York Times, August 25, 1926: "Krishnamurti due with Besant Today: Theosophists to Greet Young Hindu at Pier on His Arrival on the Majestic. NO FORMAL RECEPTION. Arrangements Canceled Because of "Flippant" Treatment of "Vehicle for World Teacher."

your own intuition, your own understanding, and give a public refusal to those who would be your interpreters" with implication directed to the leaders of the Theosophical Society.

It was during this period that the strong rhetoric for which Krishnamurti became best known began to flower. His talks were, by then, consistently discomforting in that they had the effect of shattering all preconceived notions of what a person with such an attributed stature would have to say. "I have no disciples," Krishnamurti explained,

> "Every one of you is a disciple of the Truth if you understand the Truth... Truth does not give hope, it gives understanding... There is no understanding in the worship of personalities... I still maintain that all ceremonies are unnecessary for spiritual growth. Truth is within yourself. Life itself [is] the guide, the Master, and the God. I say that liberation can be attained at any stage of evolution by [those who understand], and that to worship stages [of initiation] as you do, is not essential....
>
> Do not quote me ...as an authority, I refuse to be your crutch. I am not going to be brought into a cage for your worship.... I am not concerned with societies, with religions, with dogmas, but I am concerned with Life... Friend, do not concern yourself with who I am; you will never know...If I say I am the Christ, you will create another authority. If I say I am not, you will also create another authority. Do you think Truth has anything to do with what you think I am? You are not concerned with the Truth but you are concerned with the vessel that contains the Truth. There have been many thousands of people at [gatherings such as where this speech occurred] and what could they not do in the world if they all understood. They could change the face of the world tomorrow."

Spoken with pragmatic wisdom, Krishnamurti admonished those in attendance to recognize that each individual needed to walk the path themselves to do the work. According to his view, grace is a resource of unseen support always open for the taking, and that our own meritorious actions and mode of thought and being was the key to 'downloading' that grace into our lives. Hence, the old adage of 'God helps those who help themselves' is offered as an essential truth. It is we who need to pick ourselves up from the bootstraps, examine and alter our thoughts and actions. This was not too far removed from similar remarks delivered by the Madonna visionaries throughout history.

Despite the controversy that surrounded him, the story of Jiddu Krishnamurti serves as a demonstration of the evolutionary potential in each of us. Krishnamurti rejected all labels, such as Guru, apostle, prophet, or Christ, announcing and living by the credo that he was just a man, a man living the potential that is a birthright of all.

"I do not desire popularity; I do not want your flattery, your following. I do not want anything....'

'I am concerning myself with only one essential thing: to set man free. I desire to free him from all cages, all fears, and not to found religions, new sects, nor to establish new theories and new philosophies...'

'Truth is a pathless land"

Jiddu Krishnamurti circa 1983

According to historians at the Krishnamurti Foundation, no one human being spoke personally to so many people in the history of human civilization as had Jiddu Krishnamurti. He was passionate in his concern about the modern global crisis, and for 60 years addressed the issue with millions the world over, imploring them to discover that all the ills which beleaguer humanity at this time have their roots in our personal, collective, and social psychological conditioning. This is the core teaching of most spiritual teachers, life coaches, and counselors. Krishnamurti expressed with conviction that the hope of salvaging our troubled world wasn't to be found by adhering to a dogmatic creed or depend on following someone with a perceived advanced wisdom, but could be found right in our own hands. All that was required was a simple, conscious, and responsible shift in attitude, a change in heart and mind, a re-cognition of our true inherent dignity as children of the one source of creation, of the one Life, which could be found within ourselves.

Directly or indirectly, his tireless efforts, which engaged him until his death in 1986 at the age of 90, influenced and molded the minds of some of the greatest thinkers, educators, politicos, scientists, philosophers, theologians, social reformers, theorists, and artists of the 20th century. Namely, in addition to those already mentioned: Mahatma Gandhi, who met frequently with K in the late 1930's, more than likely as a result of their mutual friendship with Annie Besant; Huston Smith - widely hailed as one of the foremost authorities on world religions of our era; religious scholar Christopher Isherwood; the physicist David Bohm; Silent film legend Charlie Chaplin; medical pioneer Jonas Salk; the writer Henry Miller; the singer Van Morrison; and acclaimed health author and advocate Dr. Deepak Chopra, to name but a few.

Krishnamurti was undoubtedly one of the most engaging teacher/guides of the 20th century. It could be said that it was his influence that indirectly seemed to help hold the world together at a time when it was tearing apart at the seams. Living the promise made in that original journey to the Master's home as a young boy, he dedicated every ounce of his life and being for the upliftment of mankind. Like an attentive gardener, K steadily planted seeds that would mold positive and progressive human thought and conditioning, evolution, and civilization as it approached the threshold of the new millennium.

The true impact of his influence continues to become visible, as a generation of minds unconsciously affected by his influence by proxy now step to the helm, navigating the ark of collective human endeavor into an unparalleled era of human achievement.

Chapter Three

THE REAPPEARANCE OF THE CHRIST

> "Now in those days, brethren, there shall arise in the world an exalted one by name 'Maitreya', an Arhat, a Fully Enlightened One, endowed with wisdom and righteousness, a Happy One, a World-knower, the Peerless Charioteer of men to be tamed, a teacher of the devas and mankind, an exalted one, a Buddha like myself."
>
> Gautama Buddha in *Digha Nikaya*[44]

As the twentieth century progressed, the influence of Blavatsky and, subsequently, Krishnamurti opened countless doors which resulted in a virtual renaissance of thought, inquisitiveness, and investigation in realms scientific, philosophical, psychological, political, and beyond. After WWII, earnest, unbiased study in the realm of metaphysics became an accepted curriculum in leading universities. A literal quantum shift in global awareness and interconnectedness, brought closer to home during the war by way of the medium of radio, was altering the way people lived, learned, and looked at things. A formerly tight-knit social fabric had begun to unweave, and more and more individuals began to stake their claim in their personal freedom and God-given right to worship God as they saw fit, and to freely search for a mode of worship that might perhaps bring on a more direct experience of God. Yoga, Buddhism, and eastern philosophical traditions were approached with a more scientific and academic view, thus gaining acceptance and furthering social influence in the west.

Seemingly overnight, the art of the era also grew more philosophically sophisticated. Prior to the war, gangster films, cowboy serials, society farces, screw-ball comedies and children's fantasies were the mainstays of the

---

[44] Ref: Share International magazine - Special information issue

burgeoning entertainment industry. During the war, tales addressing sophisticated, humanitarian issues were introduced, but in the waning years of the war and those that immediately followed, films dealing with issues of a more spiritual nature began to emerge. Consequently, books offering alternatives to personal spiritual guidance also began to appear in bookstores with greater frequency. Having survived the tribulations of war, people now sought in earnest for answers to the most ancient yet common questions. Thus begins the age of information. The remainder of the 20th century would mark the most revolutionary era of achievement in all arenas of human thought and endeavor in the history of the world. To top it all off by century's end is the explosion of the information super highway. Again, with virtual suddenness, a globe that had become fragmented and divided over political difference was abruptly linked to an extent never before imagined, altering political, social, and economic limits on a scale heretofore unprecedented. It has been said that the pen is mightier than the sword, but I'm convinced that the stroke of a computer keyboard or the click of a mouse may be the mightiest and swiftest yet.

The late 20th Century also saw a cultural explosion of interest in the topic of Ascended Masters, demonstrating just how influential Theosophy and its many spin-offs had become in western culture. Nouveau spiritual organizations were founded by assorted individuals who claimed that the Masters Morya or Djwal Khul had contacted and spoke to or through them. Such were the IAM movement, the Summit Lighthouse, which eventually became the Church Universal and Triumphant, and countless other sects, churches and movements. In my youth I found many such organizations confusing and I tended to avoid the whole topic of Masters in general because of it. As far as those who had claimed to be channels, I recalled having read Paramahansa Yogananda's suggestion that one not give too much credence to self-proclaimed channels as they were simply voicing a naturally ordained capacity for personal awakening, and building a religion around it. I'd developed a trust in Yogananda based on perceived credibility, and I could live with his assessments.

The 1970s in America seemed to provide a ripe climate for many more such movements like Elizabeth Claire Prophet's Church Universal and Triumphant, which regularly packed sport stadiums. The Reverend Sun Yung Moon and his Unification Church virtually mimicked the Krishnamurti saga, with Moon all but declaring himself as the awaited Messiah. Such mass fanaticism had always been an instant turnoff for me. As for issues pertaining to 'the Masters', I had no idea just how many such "Ascended Master

Activities" had sprouted in the last 50 years until I plunged into research for this particular book. How to weed through so many? Was there any credence whatsoever to any of this?

In 1982, I had written a brief, investigative report on the then circulating news topic of the imminent, physical world return of Maitreya. I questioned the credibility of the claim and related assertions for a plausible connection between what seemed to be an emerging Maitreya movement and the radical changes then occurring in world affairs. I thought the subject would just wither away as another contrived, spiritual business pitch endorsed by wishful thinking. Yet, in the fifteen or so years that followed, the topic would keep coming up in magazine articles, in conversations with friends or coworkers, and in televised or printed newspaper features.

One night in the late 90s after the topic came up in conversation, I found it fascinating that people were still talking about it. It was then when I decided to do some internet investigating of my own on the subject of Maitreya. A driving curiosity had preoccupied the background of my thoughts for almost 20 years simply because the name kept coming up. I grew curious to know why this still engaged people. Was there any substance to all of the stories of alleged ascended Masters and such? What captivated so many people to believe and have hope in these things? Could the stories told by Krishnamurti actually be true? Was there a connection to the tales and prophetic hints associated with Marian apparitions as asserted by some? As I scoured the internet, I found links to countless books, magazines, and individuals claiming to have their own personal link with one or more such alleged Masters, with angels, and some even made claims of being in contact aliens. There were even a few websites of people claiming to be Maitreya. With such information so readily available, I wondered if weeding through all of this might turn up any modicum of definitive authenticity out there. Whenever I watched the nightly news or CNN during times of critical or threatening world events, I would often wonder if there was any truth to the messianic hullabaloo. What inspired certain individuals to take bold stands or initiate a revolutionary action that seemed to instill hope in a world weary of the shadow of nuclear exchange, terrorism, and other inhumane acts and policies? Whose words or deeds had offered a brief respite from basic human suffering even for a day? That offered a brief sliver of light piercing an overcast gloominess?

Such were my thoughts, for example, while watching news footage of the Berlin Wall being torn down; during the compassionate, global outreach that was the worldwide telecast of Live Aid; the heightening influence of human rights organizations such as Amnesty International; while watching the crushing defeat of South African apartheid and subsequent release of Nelson Mandela; and without a doubt - especially in light of my understanding of the Fatima messages - the demise of Soviet Communism and the former USSR.

It was amazing to witness the end of the cold war. The paralyzing chill of the greatest potential threat to the annihilation of the planet in its history - which was a decision away from actually occurring during the Cuban missile crisis in 1963 - had been reduced to a proverbial sputter. After nearly 40 years, humanity had been liberated from the ominous grip of nuclear captivity. It was difficult to not consider, as I sat in awe upon hearing the news, that such events may have possessed a hallmark and signature I felt I had seen repeatedly throughout the 80s and 90s, the postwar equivalent of 'Kilroy was here.' Could this deference to sound, sane reason been due to the influence of unseen, divine beings as described by the Madonna in her many apparitions since WWII? Was there any truth to J.D Krishnamurti's early claims of having met Maitreya and other reclusive spiritual Masters who allegedly governed the affairs of humanity as protectors?

Humanity's search for answers and guidance in the decades following WWII unveiled the need to look beyond its self-imposed cultural box for new or previously unexplored avenues of edification, and one such cultural influence was a wide spread interest in all things eastern and oriental. Martin Luther King cited Mahatma Gandhi as "the guiding light of our technique of nonviolent social change."[45] Sirhan Sirhan, the assassin of former US Attorney General and Presidential Candidate Robert Kennedy, was a known fan of *The Secret Doctrine* by Madame Blavatsky. A virtual second wave of interest in spirituality was evident everywhere, the likes of which had not been popular since Blavatsky's era in the century prior. Krishnamurti, still very much alive and active at the time, had gained a substantially larger following than anything witnessed at the height of his initial, global popularity some 50 years prior. Riding this wave were a significant number of advanced adepts from the Hindu yoga tradition.

In my own youth during this era, my interests had begun to shift dramatically towards a more introspective vein. Where I had once focused on issues typically important to an American teenager - football, Star Trek, Rock n Roll, and working part time jobs to ensure my ability to purchase of the latest popular record - I was also growing addicted to the written works of the likes of Ralph Waldo Emerson, Henry Thoreau, Thomas Merton, and other authors offering non-orthodox social views and a more liberal, if not directly, Eastern

---

[45] The Martin Luther King, Jr. Research and Education Institute, Stanford University. https://kinginstitute.stanford.edu/encyclopedia/india-trip. Accessed 12/11/2018

perspective on Christianity, the religious background of my family and community.

By the time I'd entered my first year of art college in 1979, I'd begun a formal study of yoga and meditation with Swami Muktananda, a remarkable, internationally respected, charismatic master of yoga who, by that time, had secured enormous popularity among younger, counter culture seekers as well as acknowledged scholars and professionals of every field. The Indian Government once declared Muktananda as "one of our greatest natural resources." Prime Minister Indira Gandhi, a known student of his, regularly sought his council on any number of government affairs and personal matters.

It was while I was with Muktananda on a one-month retreat at his Ashram in South Fallsburg, New York, that I first heard about the name and concept of Maitreya from a young woman I had met named Sophia. Like myself, Sophia had also been a student of mystic Christianity, yoga and meditation, eastern philosophy and Asian studies throughout her teens. This common ground founded a great friendship that continues to this day. In the years since, we shared countless hours conversing about relatively unknown esoteric writings and conjectures by innumerable authors of varying degrees of popularity or obscurity.

We would pick over, analyze, discuss, contemplate, and ultimately relate and compare the various dockets and precepts to our own unfolding lives, both internal and external. We would talk endlessly for hours and without exhaustion, reading aloud to each other excerpts from such authors as Blavatsky, Patanjali, Muktananda, Venkateshananda, Jaideva Singh, and others. Any new source of revelation offered great enjoyment for us.

During one of these sessions, Sophia gave me a copy of an obscure, theosophically themed publication entitled *The Reappearance of the Christ* by British author Alice A. Bailey, who had written numerous volumes dealing with arcane, esoteric philosophy in a vein quite similar to that of Madame Blavatsky.

Once a member of the Theosophical Society herself, Bailey became disillusioned with many of the Society's views, and, following the footsteps of Krishnamurti, severed her own affiliation as well. But, based on her own transcendental experiences while practicing the meditation techniques and disciplines as taught by the society, Bailey, too, claimed to have developed a telepathic interchange with one of the alleged, aforementioned, ascended Masters, whom, she asserted, had been responsible for dictating a considerable volume of book material over the majority of her life.

In *The Reappearance of the Christ*, originally published in 1948, Bailey, under the said guidance of the ascended Tibetan Buddhist Lama *Djwhal Khul* (pr. Jwa-koo) - the same Master Djwhal Khul mentioned by Krishnamurti - elaborates on the evolution and progressively ripening metaphysical, worldly and humanitarian conditions that have, essentially, opened the door for the prophetic fulfillment and imminent return of Christ to the physical world. This, mind you, published some 20 years after the Krishnamurti saga. It was in this book that I first found the ascended and soon-to-return Christ referred to by the name 'Maitreya.' Naturally, as Djwhal Khul was purportedly a Tibetan, then the name Maitreya as the returning one would be consistent with his tradition. How that meshes with traditional Christianity is another story. In fact, it doesn't mesh at all, and is, quite frankly, considered outright heresy.

Alice A. Bailey

While referring to him as 'The World Teacher' as did Krishnamurti, Bailey further asserted that Maitreya was the expected savior/messiah of *all* cultural traditions.

On the opening page, co-authors Bailey and Khul state:

'Right down the ages...great points of tension have occurred which have been characterized by a hopeful sense of expectancy. Someone is expected and His coming is anticipated. Always in the past, it has been the religious teachers of the period who have fostered and proclaimed this expectancy and the time has always been one of chaos and difficulty, of a climaxing point at the close of a civilization or culture and when the resources of the old religions have seemed inadequate to meet men's difficulties or to solve their problems. The coming of the Avatar, the advent of a Coming One and, in terms of today, the reappearance of the Christ are the keynotes of the prevalent expectancy. When the times are ripe, the invocation of the masses is strident enough and the faith of those who know is keen enough, then always He has come and today will be no exception to this ancient rule or to this universal law. For decades, the reappearance of the Christ, the Avatar, has been anticipated by the faithful in both hemispheres - not only by the Christian faithful, but by those who look for Maitreya and for the Bodhisattva as well as those who expect the Imam Mahdi.'

From there, Bailey's disclosure of the Tibetan's pronouncements is beyond provocative. While directly addressing some of the most fundamental and ageless philosophical questions posed by man, the book comes across as a compelling work inciting great hope and anticipation in the plausible reality of Christ returning, right now, in our time, *in our lifetime*. The last segment of the above excerpt is key, for Bailey's Christ refers not only to the anticipated return of a teacher of and for Christianity, but a great, advanced soul who comes as a guide for people of *all* faiths.

As one who was raised Catholic, this is bit hard to digest. Yet, like many Christians, we are taught to anticipate the return of Jesus Christ. In the Oriental traditions, Jesus is revered as just one of a number of divine avatars who have descended to our world in times of crisis and need. It was their culture from which Christianity arose. So, maybe they know something we in the west don't? Or is this just plain, delusional, heretical thinking? What if, just what if, the Eastern view is right? Are we blinding ourselves from fear of being wrong? In the East, Jesus is known by other names: Saint Issa, Issu, Sananda, Emmanuel, Yeshua, Yesu. Names of God are assigned depending on what characteristic is being addressed, such as God of Mercy or God of Love. If Bailey's words are being guided by a Tibetan adept, then, naturally, in his tradition, he would regard the prophesized Maitreya Buddha and returning Christ as the same. Is it possible, then, that they are?

In Jesus' time, there were many who didn't recognize who he was, or who he was claimed to be. In the first chapter of John's Gospel, the Apostle wrote:

> "[19] And this is the record of John, when the Jews sent priests and Levites from Jerusalem to ask him, Who art thou? [20] And he confessed, and denied not; but confessed, I am not the Christ. [21] And they asked him, What then? Art thou Elias? And he saith, I am not. Art thou that prophet? And he answered, No. [22] Then said they unto him, Who art thou? that we may give an answer to them that sent us. What sayest thou of thyself? [23] He said, I am the voice of one crying in the wilderness. Make straight the way of the Lord, as said the prophet Esaias. [24] And they which were sent were of the Pharisees. [25] And they asked him, and said unto him, Why baptizest thou then, if thou be not that Christ, nor Elias, neither that prophet? [26] John answered them, saying, I baptize with water: but there standeth one among you, whom ye know not"[46]

---

[46] Wikisource contributors, "Bible (King James)/John," *Wikisource*, https://en.wikisource.org/w/index.php?title=Bible_(King_James)/John&oldid=8889408 (accessed December 12, 2018).

"In such an hour as ye think not, He will come."

It is true that assertions similar to Bailey's have been made throughout history, as illustrated earlier herein. As a result, culturally we've become somewhat desensitized. In fact, we've generally adopted a prevalent condescension towards use of messianic parlance. Although many adherents of the various branches of Christendom are taught to believe in and expect the return of Christ, the plausibility of such an event actually occurring in our time is often trivially dismissed as an irrationally conceived, fanatical concept by the larger general population, primarily because they haven't been relayed by those in authoritative positions.

Despite an expanding acceptance for metaphysical thought, I'm sure Bailey herself found little academic acknowledgment in her day, save for a relatively small, select group of students of the arcane. Even today, similar pronouncements found online or in supermarket tabloids incite amusement. In the past few years alone, dramatic headlines have been so kind as to inform us that God has spoken through a radio signal from space, that Satan's face was seen in cloud formations, that the face of Jesus was seen through telescopes in Nebula formations in space, and so on.

Although I've been able to take an objective and humorous posture towards such publications and pronouncements with the assumption that most of them are a fabricated hoax, interestingly enough, I must admit I *have* occasionally glanced at those headlines that periodically offer "new biblical signs" of the second coming or declaring Christ's return, with the curiosity that such stories might be a haphazard reference to the Maitreya mentioned in the context of the works of Bailey, Blavatsky, and Krishnamurti.

The primary stimulus behind my curiosity for keeping abreast of current events in this manner was due to my friend's introduction of the name and work of one Benjamin Creme - a more current author, lecturer, arbiter of the esoteric and arcane, and whose writings - expressed with a non-denominational yet theocentric and humanitarian standpoint - make the remarkable assertion that all of the miraculous and astounding accounts that are and have been occurring worldwide can be primarily attributed to the presence of one extraordinary, theanthropic individual who *now* lives sequestered among us.

Submitted for Your Approval, Meet Benjamin Creme...

Benjamin Creme, for lack of a more fitting description, has been referred to as today's equivalent of John the Baptist, paving the way for this current day, as-yet-to-be publicly known Christ. A self-described student of the works of both Blavatsky and Bailey, since the mid 1970s Mr. Creme has claimed to be the key message-bearer with regard to the return of the World Teacher as based on the precepts of Theosophy. In addition to authoring several, best-selling books, one of Mr. Creme's primary vehicles has been *Share International Magazine* - a publication of the Share International Foundation, a non-profit, public information service associated with the United Nations Department of Public Information. It simultaneously serves as a forum focusing specifically on the global proliferation of miraculous events, as a journal of the activity of grass roots and well-respected humanitarian organizations and individuals, and as an outlet for the first-hand testimonies of the beneficiaries of miracles, related healings, and alleged encounters with angelic or peculiar beings believed to be, curiously, some of the same ascended Masters Krishnamurti once claimed to have met. But, above all, the magazine makes the unique claim of being the main organ in the world dedicated to spreading the awareness, in our time, of the reappearance of the Christ.

From an early age, Benjamin Creme displayed an apparent predilection for metaphysics. In his quest to understand an inherent talent for heightened sensory perception, at age fourteen Creme was encouraged by a book[47] that detailed the personal chronicle of a Polish woman who'd penetrated the clandestine realm of Tibetan Buddhism and secured tutorship under an advanced Lama. It was by reading the woman's description of the Lama's extraordinary code of mental discipline that Creme was introduced to the world of esotericism.

In the early 1950's, Benjamin Creme read *The Power of the Mind*, by Rolf Alexander - also a student of a Tibetan Master of Yoga - which served as both introduction and impetus to his practice of meditation. Subsequently, Creme studied in-depth the works of Patanjali, Alice Bailey, H. P. Blavatsky, Swami Vivekananda, Paramahansa Yogananda, and others focused on the topics of theosophy, metaphysics, yoga, and similar.

As an ardent practitioner of *Raja* yoga, Creme gradually achieved a greater measure of awareness of an inner sensitivity to spiritual energies and the natural development of heightened psychic faculties. By January of 1959, he'd developed - as previously claimed by Blavatsky, Bailey, and others - the capacity for telepathic communication, and began to receive inner communications that offered spiritual instruction, advice, or guidance, which he was requested to record.

Having established that his telepathic rapport was with one of the theosophically described *Masters of Wisdom*, Mr. Creme was telepathically instructed one night to switch off his tape recorder during such a transmission, with which he respectfully complied. It was then, says Creme, that Maitreya himself telepathically informed him of his own imminent reappearance in the world, and of Creme's requested role in its manifestation.

---

[47] The book which Mr. Creme read was *With Mystics and Magicians in Tibet*, by Alexandra David Neel.

Many years passed as Benjamin continued to grow more adept in his yogic practice. Little was further said of Maitreya's remarks until 1972, when Creme was again contacted for the purpose of preparing for the future work of which he is now known. For up to twenty hours a day over the course of many months, says Creme, he endured "the most intensive period of de-glamorization, disillusioning, [and] training" under his Master's guidance.

"For months we worked together," Creme explains,

"deepening and strengthening the telepathic link until it was two-way with equal ease... He forged in this period an instrument through whom He could work, and which would be responsive to His slightest impression (of course, with my complete co-operation and without the slightest infringement of my free will). Everything I see and hear, He sees and hears. When He wishes, a look from me can be a look from Him; my touch, His. So, with the minimum expenditure of energy, He has a window on the world, an outpost of His consciousness; He can heal and teach. He himself remains, in a fully physical body, thousands of miles away. I am not suggesting I am His only "window on the world." I do not know how rare this is, but I am sure it is not unique. He asked me not to reveal His identity for the time being - not even to [those] with which I work, and through whom He works. I know of two reasons for His request, and respect them, but I may say that He is one of the Senior Members of the Hierarchy, a Master of the Wisdom, whose name is well known to esotericists in the West."[48]

By 1974, Creme formed the first Transmission Meditation group with instructions from his Master, and later that same year, he claims to have begun receiving telepathically transmitted messages from Maitreya, who informed Creme about the progress of his return based on initial remarks made fourteen years prior.

In 1975, while delivering his first public lecture, Creme claimed to have been suddenly overshadowed by Maitreya, who imparted the following words to those in attendance:

"When the Christ returns, He will not at first reveal His presence, nor will the Masters Who precede Him; but gradually steps will be taken which will reveal to men that there lives among them now a man of outstanding, extraordinary, potency, a capacity for love and service, and with a breadth of view, far beyond the ordinary. Men and

[48] Extracted from *The Reappearance of the Christ and The Masters of Wisdom*, by Benjamin Creme. ©1980, Tara Press, London. Pg. 11 - 22.

women, all over the world, will find themselves drawn into the awareness of the point in the modern world wherein this man will live; and from that centre of force will flow the True Spirit of the Christ, which will gradually reveal to men that He is with us. Those who can respond to His Presence and His Teaching will find themselves somewhat reflecting this love, this potency, this breadth of vision, and will go into the world and spread abroad the fact that the Christ is in the world, and that men should look to that country from which a certain Teaching is emanating. This will take place in a very, relatively, short period of time, and will lead to conclusive evidence that the Christ is in our midst.

From that time onwards, the changes which will take place in the world will proceed with a speed unprecedented in the whole history of the planet. The next twenty-five years will show such changes, changes so radical, so fundamental, that the world will be entirely changed for the better."[49]

Between 1976 and 1977, Creme explained that such messages were transmitted with increased frequency. Then, on July 7th, 1977, Creme said he was informed by Maitreya, that he had completely manifested in the physical world by having donned a *Mayavirupa* - a fully mature, physical form of *his own* creation. On July 8th, Maitreya began his descent from his Himalayan retreat by way of Pakistan, from where he then boarded a flight with the assumed credentials of 'teacher.' On July 19th, Creme was informed by his own Yoga Master that Maitreya had arrived in his "point of focus" in the modern world.

On May 14, 1982, Benjamin Creme held a major press conference in Los Angeles. There, he formally announced to an audience of over ninety international journalists from all media outlets that Maitreya - the World Teacher - returned to the world in flesh and blood, and had specifically taken up residence in the Asian community of London. Creme challenged the media by extending to them an invitation on behalf of Maitreya to go to London and look for him in that community. It was stressed that a sufficiently high level of media involvement was required if they wished to meet him. Otherwise, they would not find him. By using the world's media only after having been so invited, Creme informed them, the proclaimed Christ would then publicly step forward. Only in this way would humanity's free will not be infringed upon - an

---

[49] Extracted from *The Reappearance of the Christ and The Masters of Wisdom*, by Benjamin Creme. ©1980, Tara Press, London, pg. 20.

issue, stressed repeatedly by Mr. Creme, as one of vital importance to these Masters.

The excited reaction to Creme's announcement in America and Britain was unprecedented, ultimately spreading like wildfire around the globe. Reports were broadcast on all major television networks, with the British media covering the story for days. In the United States, Benjamin Creme was invited to appear on nationally broadcast television programs such as the then popular *Merv Griffin Show*. Yet, strangely, due to distractions and reassignments related to other, world events at the time - most notably the Falkland Island crisis - the press did not take up Creme's invitation to make a purely token search in the London Asian community. Therefore, according to Mr. Creme, the Christ could not come forward and make himself known.

In the years following, a great measure of skepticism for Creme's words arose with the sustained absence of Maitreya. Meanwhile, a corresponding wave of remarkable, unprecedented world events unfolded that would dramatically alter the course of world affairs. Simultaneously, the increasing incidence of eyewitness reports of miracles and spiritually uplifting paranormal phenomena as referenced in chapter one made their way into news journals and television programs with engaging regularity. All the while, Mr. Creme stood his ground, never wavering in his view that Maitreya, the World Teacher, whose coming was claimed to fulfil the prophecies of all traditions, was now in the world, and was directly responsible for many internationally significant newsworthy events.

In November, 1997, Creme held another significant press conference, in which a second, formal announcement was made that Christ had returned to the world. Serving as a sort of public reminder of sorts, Creme offered the added news that it was very likely Maitreya would be seen on television in the very near future due to an invitation extended by a major American television network, whom he purposely declined to name for the time-being.

Despite the fact that Maitreya has not publicly stepped forward as hoped after the passing of many years, thousands of individuals and organized groups around the world continue to release new and updated testimonies in response to Mr. Creme's announcements, claiming to have encountered a remarkable individual who would suddenly appear, speak inspiringly in their respective native language for about 15 minutes, and then abruptly disappear. As a result, Creme finds difficulty in responding to the countless radio, television, magazine and newspaper interviews and speaking engagement opportunities that are requested of him. In a personal interview with Mr. Creme, he conveyed to me that his Master had informed him that millions of people the world over are currently acquainted with the Maitreya story, and privately harbor expectations of its fulfillment.

Close Encounters of the Creme Kind

In packed venues across the globe, Mr. Creme's message is received with rapt attention. I interviewed many who attested to coming away with feelings of awe, emotionally moved, intellectually convinced, and extremely transformed. I found myself concurring with their assessments. I must admit there is something unique and captivating about his public speaking engagements. When I first attended one of Creme's public programs, my experience was no less than astonishing.

At some point in the mid-1980s, with compelling curiosity I took it upon myself to investigate all of this directly by taking a trip to New York City to attend a program and see and hear Benjamin Creme for myself. I had to know the truth. Was this guy just another wishful prognosticator or was there any measure of substance behind his heralding of the return of Christ? The Catholic Church hadn't made any statements to the effect, and, at that time, still hadn't formally released the secret message of Fatima that was scheduled in 1960. Based on that and their known, time consuming manner of researching and confirming incidents of miraculous occurrence, I wasn't confident that the Church would so easily subscribe to Creme's proclamation, and rightfully so. To my knowledge at that time, they still hadn't officially commented on the claimed appearance of Jesus in Nairobi, Kenya, as referenced on the opening page of this book. Despite this, as a Christian and having initially read Alice Bailey's book as well as Creme's own first book on the topic - *The Reappearance of the Christ and the Masters of Wisdom* - I allowed myself to remain open-minded, intrigued but ambivalent, and somewhat optimistic.

What Christian wouldn't admit to secretly yearning for the possibility of such news to be true? Since childhood, we were taught to believe and expect this. In the Catholic mass each Sunday, worshippers proclaim the mystery of faith - "Christ has died, Christ has risen, *Christ will come again.*" Pastors and leaders of Baptist and Evangelical congregations continue to make such assertions based on the interpretation of biblical scripture. Even devout Muslims believe that the Prophet Jesus will return, while Hindu's anticipate the return of the Kalki Avatar.

Like many, I questioned this aspect of my own faith from an early age, going through normal periods of ignorance, doubt, and skepticism. But, as do most Catholics, I have always secretly waited for it to happen, and still believe it can.

My imagined vision of the world as a child had been fairly provocative, with the door left wide open for any number of possibilities to occur. The space age had just begun and television exposed us to everything imaginatively conceivable, from Flying Nuns to domesticated housewife witches; from Star Trek's 23rd century adventures to Uncle Martin the Martian as our friendly suburban neighbor.

In the future, anything might be possible, so why not the return of Christ? In fact, as a child, I'd had recurring dreams of meeting Jesus in person one day. Even at that young age, I instinctively thought it might actually happen in my lifetime. I would kneel at my bedside for long periods of time, praying, making up songs, asking, *imploring* God to appear to me. The dreams I had were always the same, and I can still vividly recall them to this day.

In one recurring dream, I always arrived in ancient Israel via time machine which touched down conveniently near the locale of wherever Jesus happened to be. I repeatedly seemed to encounter Him as He was walking along a road amid throngs of robe and veil clad followers. Jesus would greet me as I stepped out of my time machine, clad in a futuristic, one-piece space suit in the fashion of Will Robinson, wunderkind of TV's *Lost in Space*. The appearance of both my time capsule, a tall glass dome with one part of the wall being an upright control panel, and my futuristic garb would always astonish everyone but Jesus, who was phased by nothing.

In some of the dreams, like Hank Martin in Mark Twain's *Connecticut Yankee in King Arthur's Court,* I would display some artifact of scientific or ingenious achievement, such as - a cigarette lighter! A flashlight! Or *Tang* – the instant orange drink of the astronauts!

Jesus spoke to me in these dreams, yet I can't recall the content of our conversations. They would always end the same way, with Jesus' bestowal of a parting blessing, thereafter leaving me transfixed as he continued his way along a path. The devoted throngs would step around me, pausing only for a moment in curiosity, before following in his wake.

What a day it would be if those dream came true! What Christian in their right mind wouldn't investigate rumors of its actualization? Who wouldn't ponder an apparent, correlating copiousness of miraculous phenomena? Who couldn't wonder what Mr. Creme's story was all about?

The first program with Benjamin Creme's which I had attended was held in the Cathedral of Saint John the Divine in New York City. Taking a seat among the company of several hundred others, I recognized Creme from the photo on his book jackets. Short and stylish with a well-groomed shock of snow-white hair, he possessed a commanding presence, accompanied by a distinguished air and eloquence that was evocative of how I imagined might be that of an ancient Roman Senator.

As he spoke, the slightest hint of a Scottish accent was apparent, and his manner - gentle, clear, concise, quite matter of fact and self-assured. Mr. Creme briefly shared the personal history of his involvement with this work as described herein - how he had been contacted and trained, etc. He then explained the overshadowing process that allowed him to invoke the presence of the Christ. Finally, prior to leading the group into a Transmission Meditation session, Mr. Creme invited all to join him in the recitation of *The Great Invocation*, a prayer with which I was familiar from the Alice Bailey books, and which, he explained, had been given to humanity by Maitreya himself.

We were then given instructions to mentally focus on the *Ajna* center - the psychic center referenced in Yoga that's physically located in the space between the eyebrows - during the tenure of the Meditation. He explained how Transmission Meditation was not exclusively a technique for self-growth, but, in actuality, a potent and beneficial form of humanitarian service. Such Transmissions, he explained, enabled the ascended - and physically manifest - Masters of Wisdom to transmit certain spiritual energies at a reduced frequency that would, essentially, trickle through the meditator. The resulting establishment of outposts, he explained, would aid in healing the world, and help to prepare humanity for the heightened emotional and psychological impact which accompanied the physical return of Christ.

I remember watching Creme after some time had passed, and could not discern whether the church had poor lighting that was affecting my eyesight, or if in fact I was actually seeing a glowing aura around his form. The barely visible aura seemed to emit smoky plumes of light, like wavering flames, reminiscent of film footage of erupting sunspots. I vividly recall the entire church being filled with an effervescent, sparkling atmosphere, alive with energy, purity, and sacredness.

Having been a practitioner of meditation for about ten years up to that point, I was familiar with a variety of common though extraordinary internal experiences, from the visionary and mystical, to simple moments of extreme peace and contentment. As the meditation progressed, I began to experience unsurpassed pulsations of delicate energy coursing through my body. An incredible sense of delicious joy captivated my senses, filling every pore and cell of my form, which was further permeated by a strong and distinct serenity, stillness, and contentment within me and all around me. I felt completely fulfilled, with nothing more I could have wanted.

By that time, I had read many a tale of the extraordinary, superhuman capabilities of legendary yogis and Hindu saints such as Bhagawan Nityananda, Yogananda's Babaji, and the incredible lives and exploits of other great, mysterious, saintly beings of many traditions - such as the uncorrupted corpses of the Christian and Islamic Saints, and tales such as those found in Paramahansa Yogananda's *Autobiography of a Yogi*, or Swami Muktananda's own autobiography, *Play of Consciousness*. I was therefore insatiably curious to see if, perchance, this Maitreya might have magically appeared or somehow divinely manifested - or, even, had simply and physically entered the room - since I most certainly was, without a doubt, feeling an extraordinary presence. I slowly opened my eyes, and, despite the fact that I saw no such unanticipated visitors, to my own surprise I had the recurring, intuitive gut-feeling that the unseen but palpable presence I was sensing was that of Christ *Himself*.

Benjamin Creme in 2006

My yearning for some external, extraordinary display would not, however, be disappointed. Though Creme was still seated alone on the altar/stage in meditation, as I looked on, I perceived an aura around him that was enormous. Pale, soft, milky flames were surging and raging, leaping high into the vaulted cathedral ceilings and extending over the seating area. Was I hallucinating? Was this some sort of trickery? After studying this remarkable wonder for a short while longer, I allowed myself to succumb to the relaxed, meditative drowsiness that prevailed and slowly closed my eyes again, primarily out of respect, to resume relishing the profound inner communion feast I was having. Never in my life had I experienced anything so amazing and unexplainable. This was not a case of Hollywood special effects - this was really happening! Finally, after what seemed to have been not more than a few minutes that passed, the meditation session was concluded. I soon learned, as can be typical of a deep meditation session, that more than an hour or so had elapsed.

My curiosity was further aroused. What exactly was going on here? Though any initial skepticism had been sufficiently shaken, it still, as I would realize with passing time, had not been altogether abated. Part of me was pinching myself, repeatedly asking, 'Is this for real? Did I really see those leaping displays of wafting light?' Could Benjamin Creme's message be authentic after all?

A second visit with Mr. Creme

Many years afterwards, with the memory of that first encounter vividly etched in my mind, another opportunity arose to attend one of Mr. Creme's public programs. A few friends and I caught a train and arrived in New York just as the program was about to begin. What would be witnessed this time, I wondered? Was I expecting too much? Nearly ten years had elapsed since that first attendance, and I wondered if I'd imagined it all.

When we finally arrived at the small Unitarian church, Benjamin Creme was already speaking. Locating an empty pew mid-way from the back, we took our seats and settled in.

Creme's tours are usually broken up into three segments: a lecture one night, a public Transmission Meditation program the second, and a third night which is generally reserved for a less formal gathering of his supporters.

The first portion of Benjamin Creme's talk was comprised of the background information and philosophical origins of the 'reappearance' story. Included were a description of who Maitreya was and how he got here, examples of the sort of miraculous appearances made routinely to either large congregations or individuals, the 'before and after' accuracy of his recent predictions, and his primary message, goals, and mission.

Towards the end of this discussion, Mr. Creme shared some of the most recent and up to then unpublished reports of Maitreya's antics and miraculous appearances. These have always been the stories that intrigued me most, some of which are recounted in the ensuing sections of this book.

After a brief intermission, the final segment of the evening began with Mr. Creme answering the public's questions. Prior to the evening's conclusion, all in attendance were invited to stay and receive Maitreya's blessing, which was to be extended through the overshadowed Benjamin Creme.

Having traveled all this way, this was perhaps the primary reason for my second trip to the program. The memory of the extraordinary sense of presence and the leaping flames of white light I'd witnessed a decade earlier were still etched distinctively in my mind, and I just had to know if it had been real. Had I imagined it all? Had I brought too strong an expectation with me this time? Did others have similar experiences?

I prepared myself to meditate for the duration of the blessing. I gathered that others prepared themselves as well, which was evident by the shuffling, coughing, and sounds of settling in for optimum comfort. After just a few minutes, there was a definite sensation of the accompanying stillness taking on a 'thickness' and I began to feel a conscious drowsiness - I was going into meditation.

At one point when the 'thickness' seemed to have saturated the entire room, I began to feel a heightened euphoria rising within, and the awareness of a distinct and strong presence enveloped me. There was a distinct familiarity, a measure of comfort with the sensation, something that I was recognizing deep within me. Mr. Creme then softly announced that Maitreya was presently overshadowing him, and that the time for the blessing had come. An evident, contagious excitement quietly filled the room, and after a few more minutes had passed, I could no longer contain myself. I had to see what was going on.

As I slowly opened my eyes in the dimly lit room, I anticipated the leaping white flames of light as seen years before, but this I did not see. Instead, I saw Creme facing the crowd with his right arm held aloft, his palm turned towards those in attendance. I surmised that he was 'scanning' the room as he moved slowly back and forth, gazing intentionally and facing his palm at each individual in attendance. Row by row, seat by seat, Creme continued in silence.

Within a few minutes, my opened eyes had adequately adjusted to the dimly lit surroundings, and, after blinking and rubbing my eyes, I was then able to distinctly and unquestionably see what I had thought I was suddenly witnessing - Benjamin Creme was glowing!

I again rubbed my eyes with incredulity, and looked back. The man was radiating an extraordinary aura, the strongest part of which seemed to extend from his body at a distance of 3 to 5 feet in all directions, trailing off thinly from there. The glow around his extended hand was the brightest, and indeed the light from there seemed to be pulsating, radiating. The hue was of a distinctive, soft golden color, like a not-quite-opaque yet softly transparent turmeric.

This was remarkable, I thought, chuckling to myself. There were no spotlights, no fog machines, no projections - this was really happening. As I watched him cast his glance down each row of seats, the direction of his gaze and palm moved closer to where I was sitting, and I began to feel an increasingly pulsating magnetic heat that left me feeling as if my entire being was getting a massage. As his directed palm approached my own seat, I heard an increasingly audible resonant hum, and when he finally looked and faced his palm at me, I instantly closed my eyes with an assumed requirement for respect to relish what was coming.

Suddenly, I felt as if a huge, gentle, almost liquescent, invisible fireball of heat had burst upon and envelope my entire physical form and being. The force with which the 'fireball' hit me was momentarily startling but painless. My heart was enlivened at once by an accompanying sense of joy and delight, with my mind becoming momentarily enraptured and still. The feeling lingered for a short duration.

After the blessing ended and the evening came to a close, those yet in attendance began to stir and depart. I remained sitting in stunned stillness and silence, absorbed in the profound quiet of my mind, and endeavoring to contemplate what I had just experienced. In my mind, I replayed the sources of my understanding gleaned from viewing Christianity through an eastern perspective, which had consistently made an asserted distinction between Jesus and 'the Christ,' and of the same relationship allocated to the Hindu Krishna. Although the words didn't form at the time, I think I was allowing myself to be convinced of the plausibility of Creme's claims. Was it really that simple? Did I really just experience the presence of the historical Christ, the same presence that enveloped the Apostles, disciples, and Saints of early Christianity? Could it all be true - had Christ returned?

The most significant aspect of this for me was the thought that a lifelong dream and prayer may have been unfolding before my eyes. On the train ride home, I reflected on the earliest religious influence of my parents, grandmother, and the years of those early dreams of Jesus. I reminisced about my Catholic upbringing, and contemplated the attested meaning of Baptism and Confirmation. I recalled my initial understanding of what I thought it meant to have the experience of the close proximity to Christ when I'd served as an altar boy at age 11. To my young mind at the time, having such close access and proximity to the Eucharist - the very heart and essence of Catholic practice, the perceived and believed body and presence of Jesus Christ Himself - was a noteworthy achievement that was not to be taken lightly. For me, becoming an altar boy was as equally sacred as the official sacraments themselves. And yes, those infamous Catholic nuns who taught us made certain one regarded it with such esteem - or else!

That event was a seminal turning point in my spiritual path. Having been generally taught to honor and revere Jesus Christ all through my formative years, I'd subsequently developed a yearning to personally know or feel the presence of Jesus in a greater measure. It was then when I most strongly considered the priestly vocation. In the years following, a more liberal, secular alternative presented itself as I investigated the burgeoning 'born-again', *Charismatic*, and 'Jesus' movements in the 1970s. I recalled the richness of the most influential of my high school religion classes, which was entitled *The Search for Jesus*. The class had effectively brought me closer to understanding the spirit and presence of Jesus. There I had developed some enduring high school friendships which so influenced the spiritual direction of my life. In some of those friends I found the same, inner earnestness that considered a life of religious vocation, and actively living the teachings of Jesus. It was they who introduced me to the works of Thomas Merton and other authors and thinkers that had the effect of so transforming my life's focus between the ages of 14 and 16. With them a stimulating debate on the New England Transcendentalists or a philosophical inquiry on the introspective meaning of rock and roll lyrics could while away the hours of an otherwise numbing, bleak, urban teenage existence. Some had experienced the same awe of having been an altar boy as I, and wondered where that inner call would lead us. After just a few short hours with the overshadowed Mr. Creme, I found myself experiencing all those same feelings again. To me, the whole Maitreya thing didn't matter at that point. I had reconnected with my deepest regard and connection with Jesus, and that made it worth all the while.

The shrill of the train's whistle jarred me to my senses. As I then gazed through the window into the serene, night sky, I considered what a fantastic journey had brought me to this point in time. If anything at all had been gained from that evening with Benjamin Creme, it was the awareness that I was now feeling closer to the reality and substance of my personal spiritual ambitions than ever before.

Chapter Four

THE PLAN OF THE MASTERS

> ?"This work of the Masters is proceeding now, and all their efforts are being bent towards bringing it to a successful consummation. Everywhere they are gathering in those who in any way show a tendency to respond to high vibration."
>
> Alice Bailey

To understand or even attempt to conceive of any potential validity to the claims of Benjamin Creme and his predecessors Madame Blavatsky and Alice Bailey, further investigation is certainly required. While the numerous books by all three offer an exhaustive legacy of explanations and/or testimonial evidence, one wonders why three such mavericks operating outside the socially accepted parameters of the existing ecclesiastical institutions which traditionally represent Christ would go to the lengths they do to present their story. In fact, to even consider their views with an open mind, it seems specifically apparent that one may need to look beyond the accepted, taught, and fostered understanding of the traditional concept of Christ. Indeed, the relatively causal aplomb of the Krishnamurti story alone is no doubt shocking to readers maintaining a traditionally accepted perspective. Were the early Theosophists endeavoring to recreate the Christ mythos? In reality, most of Theosophy's claims aren't far removed from accepted theological perspectives. What is evident is that Blavatsky and friends did engineer a plan designed to wrap the world's many diverse religious perspectives into one, which could also appear to be an endeavor to reinvent religion itself. It's almost as if Blavatsky perceived the miasma of theological, metaphysical, and esoteric conjecture - fostered over centuries - as having become unraveled beyond a point of control. Perhaps Blavatsky saw it as her duty - consistent with her legendary prowess as a global adventurer - to lasso and corral these disparate outposts of human consciousness into one, unified school. But what so compelled her? Adopting the stance of a disciple, it was the Masters, she would remind students, who had requested this service of her.

In fact, The Theosophical Society still maintains a written record of Master Morya's admittance to this affect dated 1882.[50]

Though in a position of virtually absolute authority and persuasion, Blavatsky consistently disdained the ecclesiastical structure proposed and ultimately developed by her Theosophical peers and partners. Not until those early pronouncements of Jiddu Krishnamurti do we find a similar, public expression of such disdain.

In fact, it's only after his pronouncement and dissolution of the Order of the Star - perhaps due to Krishnamurti's widely respected status - that we begin to see a potential credence in the reality of the legend of Maitreya and the Masters. Even Krishnamurti himself denounced the ersatz, 'apostolic' power structure at a point when it would have been most opportune for any self-interested man or woman to seize absolute authority. Political despots had done it for centuries, and more and more evangelists were seizing such opportunities at a growing rate at the time. Why not Krishnamurti, who could have landed himself a seat of potentially unprecedented global influence?

According to Benjamin Creme, Krishnamurti's reactionary decision to dissolve the Order of the Star and resign from his designation as World Teacher had, in fact, been made by Maitreya Himself. For the first time in human history, Creme expounded, the Christ elected *not* to work through a vehicle disciple like a Jesus or Krishna after having discerned a way in which He Himself could return in person. Despite this event - a considerable setback of the Theosophical Society's primary mission and canon - the unseen work to unfold this divinely ordained plan of return allegedly continued, with its first phase of culmination arriving in our time.

Benjamin Creme's contention is that the work of Madame Blavatsky, the subsequent grooming of Krishnamurti, and the works of Alice Bailey were only the initial stages of such a much broader, unfolding divine Plan. As claimed by the Theosophical founders, this Plan had been specifically designed to pave the way for the returning Christ - the ancient title accorded to the supreme, hierarchical teacher of teachers, "of man and angels alike." Though defined by various names in differing cultures, the anticipated return of such a superman underscores a widely held belief in a singular awaited event, an advent which would mark the beginning of the reestablishment of the "Kingdom of God" in the realm of mankind. Such an event would herald the erasure of evil from the hearts of humankind, redemption and liberation from the human condition, with a guided course to steer the wandering prodigal

---

[50] Source: "The Founding of the Theosophical Society" by Walter A. Carrithers, Jr.; http://www.azstarnet.com/~blafoun/founding.htm

masses back to understanding their divine origin and experience a direct relation with their creator. It represents fulfillment of a yearning conditioned so far back into antiquity that's it's likely a permanent fixture in the deepest regions of our psyche. Or, as expressed in other, perhaps more accurate terminology - etched upon our soul.

While most philosophers do concur that such issues refer to a psychological goal of spiritual practice, it was Blavatsky's contention that indigenous concepts of attaining the spiritual reward of such a divine kingdom - such as the Judeo-Christian and Islamic *Heaven*, the Norse *Valhalla* or Germanic *Asgard*, - refer to a long-forgotten period of human civilization when the line of demarcation between the divine and humanistic wasn't as thinly defined as in accepted, recorded history. In fact, many of the esoteric, mystery schools hold that this historical, pseudo-physical kingdom had altogether 'ascended' to a non-visible, ethereal plane of matter in an ancient time when 'the dark forces' or, the forces of materiality, essentially gained command and control of our world. Not surprisingly, this very belief, having passed down in oral legend for eons and generations, runs like a consistent string through the very root of the theocratic cultures of ancient Egypt, Greece, Persia, and virtually every known theistic heritage of ancient times.

Associated with the exact moment of separation between God and man in all of these systems are legends of global catastrophes in which the pious believers were saved while non-believers perished. In his book *Fingerprints of the Gods*, author Graham Hancock points out the remarkable similarities of legend found in apparently unlinked corners of the globe. For example, in South America, Northern India, Egypt, Persia, and the Mediterranean can be found the same tale of a pious man instructed by God to build a huge boat in preparation of an anticipated flood that will cleanse and redeem the world. Accordingly, all such ancient records reveal that similarly prophesied cataclysms and other profound, periodic upheavals and events of legend are noticeably punctuated by the presence, appearance, or interjection of some great, 'descended' divine being, a divinely guided prophet - an extraordinarily powerful and chivalrous individual possessing an exemplary degree of wisdom and devotion.

Religious legend and lore have long proposed the concept of heaven, an unseen afterlife, a spirit kingdom wherein the indigenous prophets and saints of all religious legacies reside and continue to operate. Like the variety of heavenly consorts who often assist the primary deity or figure in these ancient legends, the Theosophists and like-minded proponents claim that Maitreya, the so-named returning avatar in our time, will also be accompanied by a celestial entourage. More specifically, they are, in this instance, a significant number of advanced disciples, who, according to all three authors - Blavatsky, Bailey, and Creme - have achieved an equal degree of Mastery in their own right, and are hence referred to as the "Masters of Wisdom."

In his first publication, *The Reappearance of the Christ and the Masters of Wisdom*,[51] Benjamin Creme asserts that some of these returning, ascended Masters have been gradually and physically taking up residence incognito in our world since 1975. They include, according to Mr. Creme, the reincarnated or advanced souls of none other than some of the most illustrious names in history and Christendom, such as the Apostles Peter and John. Mary - the 'Master who was the Madonna' and historical mother of Jesus - says Creme, is not among those who will physically return, but will remain working 'behind the scenes', a view consistent with remarks said to have been made by the Madonna herself after WWII, as referenced in Chapter one of this book. As of the year 2000[52], Mr. Creme contended that there were 14 such Masters actually living among us.

Creme also asserts that, included in this divine advance crew, is none other than the most renowned Christ of all - Jesus - who, now known as 'Master Jesus', acts as one of the principal architects of this unfolding divine Plan.

As dictated by Djwhal Khul, Alice Bailey explains some of the foundation work with which the Masters themselves are involved in her 1922 publication *"Initiation-Human and Solar"*:

> '[Their work includes] First, the work of training their pupils and disciples to fit them to be of use in two great events, one, the coming of the World Teacher towards the middle or close of this present century[53], and the other, the training of them to be of use in the reconstruction of the present world conditions.'

> 'Secondly, the preparation of the world on a large scale for the coming of the World Teacher, and the taking of the necessary steps before they [the Masters] themselves come out among men, as many of them surely will towards the close of this century.'

Note the confident declaration of the time frame in this assertion. It

---

[51] Tara Press, © 1979
[52] When the first edition of this book was initially completed and published.
[53] In response to my permission request for quoting the Alice Bailey material, Sarah McKechnie, President of *Lucis Trust* - publisher of the books - commented: "I note your attempt to pinpoint the timing of the reappearance of the Christ, [citing] references from *Initiation, Human and Solar* and *A Treatise on Cosmic Fire*.....These books were among the first published and before the Second World War and the dropping of the atomic bomb, events which caused a significant realignment of Heirarchy's energies and plans according to what we are told in [other Bailey titles]. This may help to explain why the timing has been "extended" beyond what was foreseen very early in this century."

does leave one to pause and contemplate. She gets more specific:

> 'A special group is forming amongst them now who are definitely preparing themselves for this work. The Master M., the Master K. H. and the Master Jesus will be specially concerned with the movement towards the last quarter of this century. Other Masters will participate also, but these three are the ones with whose names and offices people should familiarize themselves, wherever possible.'

It is interesting to note that she specifically cites the name of Jesus, but only mentions the initials of the other two masters with whom we should 'familiarize' ourselves. In later works by the author, who wrote 19 volumes over 30 years, she reveals the names and identities of these two.

Master M. refers to Blavatsky's own Master Morya, of whom, Bailey says:

> 'The Master Morya, who is one of the best known [at the time of publication] of the Eastern adepts, and who numbers amongst his pupils a large number of Europeans and Americans, is a Rajput Prince, and for many decades held an authoritative position in Indian affairs.
>
> He dwells, as does his Brother, the Master K. H., at Shigatse in the Himalayas, and is a well-known figure to the inhabitants of that far-away village. He is a man of tall and commanding presence, dark hair and beard and dark eyes, and might be considered stern were it not for the expression that lies in his eyes. He and his Brother, the Master K. H., work almost as a unit, and have done so for many centuries. The houses in which they both dwell are close together, and much of their time is spent in the closest association. He acts as the Inspirer of the statesmen of the world, [and] those great national executives who have far vision and the international ideal are influenced by him.'

Of 'K.H.', Bailey says:

> 'Master K. H. is The Master Koot Hoomi, who is also very well known in the occident, and has many pupils everywhere, is of Kashmiri origin, though the family originally came from India. He is a man of noble presence, and tall, though of rather slighter build than the Master M. He is of fair complexion, with golden brown hair and beard, and eyes of a wonderful deep blue, through which seem to pour the love and the wisdom of the ages. He has had a wide experience and education, having been originally educated at one of the British Universities, and speaks English fluently. His reading is wide and

extensive, and all the current books and literature in various languages find their way to his study in the Himalayas. He concerns himself largely with the vitalizing of certain of the great philosophies, and interests himself in a number of philanthropic agencies. To him is given the work very largely of stimulating the love manifestation which is latent in the hearts of all men, and of awakening in the consciousness of the race the perception of the great fundamental fact of brotherhood.'

Of their work together, Bailey explains:

'At this particular time the Master M., the Master K. H. and the Master Jesus are interesting themselves closely with the work of unifying, as far as may be, eastern and western thought, so that the great religions of the East, with the later development of the Christian faith in all its many branches, may mutually benefit each other. Thus, eventually it is hoped one great universal Church may come into being.'[54]

It's also interesting to note how clearly Bailey defines the roles of Masters M. and K.H. What then, is the specific role of Jesus?

'The Master Jesus is the focal point of the energy that flows through the various Christian churches. He travels much and passes considerable time in various parts of Europe. He works especially with masses more than with individuals, though he has gathered around him quite a numerous body of pupils, who are frequently distinguished by that fanaticism and devotion which manifested in earlier Christian times amongst the martyrs.

He himself is rather a martial figure, a disciplinarian, and a man of iron rule and will. He is tall and spare with rather a long thin face, black hair, pale complexion and piercing blue eyes. His work at this time is exceedingly responsible, for to him is given the problem of steering the thought of the occident out of its present state of unrest into the peaceful waters of certitude and knowledge, and of preparing the way in Europe and America for the eventual coming of the World Teacher.

He has stayed and worked with the Christian Church,

---

[54] Considering the date of publication, it's noteworthy to review the unifying efforts and overtures of Pope John Paul II in the years 2000 and 2001. He first extended overdue apologies to leaders of the Orthodox Christian sects; then he traveled to Israel to apologize to Jewish leaders for the centuries of Catholic anti-Semitism; and finally - a first in the history of the church - he respectfully entered and prayed in an Islamic mosque.

fostering the germ of true spiritual life which is to be found amongst members of all sects and divisions, and neutralizing as far as possible the mistakes and errors of the churchmen and theologians. He is distinctively the Great Leader, the General and the wise Executive, and in Church matters he co-operates closely with the Christ, thus saving him much and acting as his intermediary wherever possible. No one so wisely knows as he the problems of the West, no one is so closely in touch with the people who stand for all that is best in Christian teachings, and no one is so well aware of the need of the present moment. Certain great prelates of the Anglican and Catholic Churches are wise agents of his.'

The descriptions suggested above seem to make the Masters sound more like comic book heroes - *Super Friends* - rather than the revered icons they have long been held to be. Has the devotional deification and placement upon exalted pedestals perpetuated an unnecessary, perceived distance between humanity and they?

As far as the comic allegory, I have long thought that the hero figures born from the artist's pen in this century were perhaps the subconscious impressions rendered upon our psyche, if not outright borrowed, from the widely influential doctrine of Theosophy. For example, I'd read once that George Lucas derived the Star Wars saga from impressions gleaned from such ancient legend specifically found in the writings of mythologist Joseph Campbell. Do not the Masters of Wisdom remind us of the *Jedi Knights*? Did we not see Obe Wan Kenobi assist Luke in his post-partem, ascended form of spirit, joined later on by the ascended Yoda and Anakin Skywalker, the former Darth Vader, after his release from the wrangling hold of 'the Dark Force'?

Other examples can be found in the stories of *Green Lantern*, whose mysterious ring unites him with the unseen 'Guardians of the Universe', thus endowing him with super powers. The legend of *Superman* and his 'Fortress of Solitude' recall the legends of the 'supermen' of the Himalayas.

So, in many ways, we have, already imbedded in our popular culture as well as our psyche, images and impressions that allow an opening for at least a small window of belief or latent desire in the possibility of such things as referenced by the esotericists. Perhaps, having been a comic junkie as a kid, this is where my own window was opened.

Otherwise, 'real' history has offered accounts of 'super' men and women who bring the message home all that much more. Consider the fantastic tales of Moses, for example, who parted a sea, turned a river to blood and a staff to a serpent. Or Jesus, who healed the sick, made blind men see, raised a man from the dead, and, after his death - like Obe Wan Kenobi - returned to visit and resume teaching his disciples in an ascended form composed of light. On one such post-mortem occasion at Emmaus, He even dined with them!

Further, there are more contemporary records such as those of the Catholic stigmatist Padre Pio, who is said to have miraculously transported himself at critical moments to those in need, only to be learned later that Pio was seen in two places simultaneously. Or India's Bhagavan Nityananda, who was alleged to also have the similar capability to miraculously transport himself, as well as materialize fruits and sweets, tickets, passports, or fistfuls of money from thin air! Paramahansa Yogananda, in his autobiography, describes similar tales of such beings. But miraculous displays say little about the true work of these beings, who offer such demonstrations solely as an aid to inspire, helping the earnest devotee to see beyond the limitations of the material world.

What will these Masters of Wisdom do when they return? Alice Bailey, once more, offers this explanation:

> "Very definitely may the assurance be given here, that prior to the coming of the Christ, adjustments will be made so that at the head of all great organizations will be found either a Master, or an initiate who has taken the third initiation.
>
> 'This work of the Masters is proceeding now, and all their efforts are being bent towards bringing it to a successful consummation. Everywhere they are gathering in those who in any way show a tendency to respond to high vibration, seeking to force their vibration and to fit them so that they may be of use at the time of the coming of the Christ. Great is the day of opportunity, for when that time comes, through the stupendous strength of the vibration then brought to bear upon the sons of men, it will be possible for those who now do the necessary work to take a great step forward, and to pass through the portal of initiation."

Theosophy contends that Jesus was the Christ of the last astrological cycle - the Piscean age - (hence the fish symbol of early Christianity), yet remains distinct from the person known as Maitreya. According to both Alice Bailey and Benjamin Creme, it was Maitreya, in his role as Christ, who overshadowed Jesus during the period of his recorded public ministry up until the crucifixion. Upon the moment of ascension, the most celebrated event in Christendom and the very event believed to have "burned" Jesus' image onto the Shroud of Turin – the Theosophists believe that Jesus then passed through his own, advanced 'portal of initiation' which led to a culmination in attaining full Mastery.

As illustrated in the New Testament, it is said that Jesus did remain among us after the resurrection, although in a body unlike the ordinary, as previously described. In fact, Benjamin Creme once matter-of-factly stated that Jesus has been residing in the hills outside of Rome since 1984! Why does no one else seem to be aware of this fact? One would assume that it's in fulfillment of the Biblical assertions: "He will come again as a thief in the night" and "In an hour which ye know not, He will come."

Does the Vatican know about this? Mr. Creme asserts that not only are they very aware of it, but at least two of the Pope's key aids in the *Curia* - the Pope's inner circle - are fully conscious, direct disciples of the Master Jesus, and have endeavored to awaken the Pope to the reality of their Master's Hierarchical stature and presence, as presented herein.[55]

Bearing these views in mind, the graphic symbol and slogan for the Catholic Church's Jubilee millennium celebration was most intriguing. The illustration featured an image of the resurrected Jesus with welcoming, opened arms before a two-panel door, accompanied by the slogan *"Open wide the doors to Christ - Stewardship is the Key."* Either someone in the Vatican knows exactly what they're saying, or the slogan is eerily prophetic.

The Theosophical and related perspectives offer that the primary 'stewardship' of Master Jesus, once fully and openly visible to all of us, will be to redirect and reunite all the splintered factions of Christianity, and set the record straight with regard to the many mistranslated, and hence misunderstood, truths of his teachings of long ago.

But, according to Creme, it is 'Maitreya', the traditional bearer of the position, title, or 'office' of 'Christ', who has and will look after the affairs of humanity at-large, and whom is said will do so for some time to come.

Share International and a Master of Wisdom

In the years following my initial introduction to the concept of the returning Maitreya and Masters, I found myself, as previously discussed, continually looking for indicative evidence. I was well acquainted with Benjamin Creme's work and Share International Magazine, and the ongoing, fantastic accounts of Maitreya's apparent presence.

The stories found primarily in *Share International Magazine* were always intriguing and provocative. Each issue offers a section of letters to the editor - Mr. Creme - in which people from around the globe retell of an

[55] Source: Maitreya's Mission, Volume II, by Benjamin Creme, Pg. 224. © 1993, Share International Foundation.

unusual encounter or experience with a strange or unique person, and inquire as to their identity. Mr. Creme, in turn, offers the authoritative confirmation of his own Master, who indicates whether or not the stranger was Maitreya or one of the other returning Masters.

In his own words, Creme's role in this 'Plan' has been to "dot the i's and cross the T's" of the work laid out and paved by Blavatsky and Bailey. He postulates with scant trace of egotism or righteousness, instead presenting his convictions in a manner firm, gracious, and humble, yet colored by a distinct sense of detachment. Unlike some currently popular New Age spin doctors, he makes no profit from his venture, does not live on a ranch or in a deluxe palace, nor dictate his messages from the deck of a yacht. He does not recruit followers or endorse any dogmatic cult or organization. Benjamin Creme is recognizably quite a modest man, albeit one possessing strong conviction in his views. There is something intuitively trustworthy and believable about this fellow.

Interestingly enough, the very stuff most others would find questionable about Creme and his fantastic assertions don't strike me as being all that unlikely. For example, from my own experiences with Indian meditation masters, the concept of telepathic transmission is not only plausible, it's rather routine in the world of Yoga, and scientifically based investigations into the power derived from Yogic practice have engaged countless international universities and government agencies.

Most quality yoga training does address the need to develop the inner capacity to 'hear' the inner voice of one's own conscience. This voice, expounded by almost any work on yoga and related philosophies, is the voice of one's own highest Self - the soul, with that soul being part and parcel of a universal soul. Attaining the experience of unity with the 'Supreme Self' is the goal of yoga, the literal meaning of which is to 'yoke', or enjoin. This moment of unity signifies the goal and very essence of human existence - communion with God.

As development of this intuitive ability grows through practice over time, students of yoga begin to recognize that the true teacher, or 'guru', is right within themselves, *as their Self*. This principal is referenced, in some traditions, as *gurutatwa*, or, guru principal. The inner, intellectual and mystical acknowledgement of gurutatwa allows the yogi to find illumination and fodder for ever burgeoning Self-realization in all things and circumstances, which includes recognition by the student of the evident advanced status and total, conscious establishment in awareness of Self in their teacher, or, Guru. It also allows the advanced student, presuming they've been guided/instructed by such a yoga adept or master, to literally hear the voice of their master instructing them in such moments though the master may be physically situated hundreds or thousands of miles away. Such inner attunement to the inherent, organic, conscious force of nature known as gurutatwa literally aligns the psyche of the master adept and the humble, acquiescent disciple. Hence, it has been this understanding that has allowed me to consider Mr. Creme's telepathic rapport to be genuine and/or plausible, and to remain relatively open to many of his contentions.

As said, I looked for corroborating evidence for Creme's claims. At various times over the years, Share International magazine would print predictions of forthcoming world events allegedly made by Maitreya, and offered via a man simply known then as *'The Associate'*- an unassuming North London pharmacist named Mr. Patel - a self-described disciple of Maitreya. In one of our interview sessions, Mr. Creme informed me Patel has since retired and currently spends his full time in service to Maitreya's mission.

Since the 1980's I had kept notes on these predictions while regularly checking the news, waiting to see if the predictions would manifest. Remarkably, most that I can recall did come to pass. It is intriguing, in hindsight, to review those predictions. For example, Crème's magazine had printed Maitreya's predictions of: the release of Nelson Mandela and the process of détente in South Africa,[56] the resignation of Margaret Thatcher,[57] the Iran/Iraq cease fire;[58] the 1988 Armenian earthquake[59] and the California and China quakes of 1989,[60] the election of a Democrat to the White House in 1982 (Bill Clinton),[61] and numerous other predicted events, such as plane crashes, political skirmishes, and more.

In August of 1987, Benjamin Creme made a special announcement, stating that Maitreya would help bring about a significant breakthrough in international relations. Within a month, negotiations between the Americans and the Soviet Union began, and by year's end, the agreement and plan for a gradual reduction of nuclear arms brought about the previously unforeseeable end of the cold war. Another prediction saw the once mighty and threatening Soviet Union dissolved, opening the door for unprecedented international détente. In 1988, Maitreya had anticipated an international stock-market collapse beginning in Japan. As of August, 2001, Japan was experiencing its most dire economic crisis since the end of World War II, with major

---

[56] Source: Share International Magazine, March 1989.
[57] Ibid, September 1988.
[58] Ibid. June, 1988.
[59] Ibid, November 1988.
[60] Ibid, August 1989.
[61] Ibid, January 1991.

corporations laying off workers by the thousands - a situation the Japanese pledged would never occur. By 2002, western nations, including the US, were witnessing an identical scenario.

According to Mr. Creme, the purpose of these predictions by Maitreya has been to stimulate and reinforce belief, to indicate to people that claims such as those relayed in Share International magazine may be worth heeding, and to remind everyone that God, in some capacity, is ever with us. Mr. Creme and his Master assert that it has been Maitreya who has been primarily responsible for the barrage of what has amounted to the non-stop demonstration of miracles, healings, apparitions, and bizarre supernatural phenomena to which we have all been witness, with the intendment of alerting everyone to his presence, that the awaited one has returned. Even if you ignore the claims of Creme, disagree with the validity of any of and regard it as pure hokum, one must admit, at the very least, something remarkably strange is in the air, and has been going on for some time.

The Plan Unfolds

It is true that most of us associate the term 'Christ' with Jesus. We need to recall that 'Christ' is not and never was a surname. The term derives from the ancient Greek, spelled either 'Christos', or in older usage, with a 'k' - 'Kristos', hence its relation to the Hindu 'Krishna.' The term means, specifically in a personified context: "The Anointed," and originates historically in the Greek translations of both the bible and the newly written Gospels, where the term is found in the Semitic languages as 'mashiah' (messiah).

The ancient Greek philosophers understood fully the magnitude and role of Jesus, the Christ, as did many scientists, philosophers, and sages of antiquity. The influence of the 'Ancient Wisdom Schools' was alive and flourishing, but beginning to wane a bit in the time prior to Jesus' birth, likely due to the dominant expansion of the Roman empire. Hence, it was with great fanfare, celebration, and humility that three graduates of that ancient wisdom curriculum, that is, three 'wise men', also referred to as *Magi* - the title of the high priests of the Persian Zoroastrian tradition - sought to pay homage to the infant that would uplift humanity upon his shoulders. Though the Magi were well-versed in astronomy, mathematics, and other sciences, one wonders how these men were able to find the needle in the haystack that was the humble earthen shelter in the Judean province in which Jesus was born. Precisely what sort of 'wisdom' did the wise men possess? Were they Masters?[62] Did they

---

[62] In the course of our correspondence and interview sessions for this book, Mr. Creme took the liberty of asking this question of his Master. The response was "Yes."

'find' the infant Jesus in the manner by which the Tibetan Buddhists first consult an oracle prior to seeking the reborn Dalai Lama?

It is interesting to note here that philosophers have recognized the distinctive Buddhist flavor of Jesus' Gnostic manner of teaching when compared with the traditional Hebrew canon of his time, and this is why his message stuck out and so outraged the priests and Pharisees. Further, some scholars contend that Jesus actually studied under the tutelage of a Master in the Himalayan region during the so-called 'missing years' of his life, between the ages of 12 and 30. Pursuant to such theory are claims that there yet exists in many remote Himalayan regions of Northern India and Kashmir, evidence of a legendary great prophet, sage, and teacher who long ago worked wonders similar to those ascribed to the biblical Jesus. Some attribute these legends to the forgotten philosopher-sage *Apollonius of Tyana*,[63] a known contemporary of the Apostle Thomas during the period of the latter's ministry in Southern India. Historians assert that records of Apollonius were reputedly squashed by the early Christian Church fathers due his resemblance to Jesus in word, deed *and appearance*, and due to perceived interference in the work of Thomas. In any event, to this day, people of the region still speak with reverence of the great teacher known, alternately, as *'Sant Issa'*, (Saint Jesus), or, *'Hazrat Issa Sahib'* (the Lord, Master Jesus), or *"Yuz Asaf."*

Interestingly, there is a Kashmiri gravesite[64] in town of Srinagar which is claimed by the locals to be the burial tomb of Jesus, which some scholars contend may more likely be the grave of Apollonius. While this assertion conflicts with the accepted tale of Jesus' death and burial as found in the Biblical New Testament, it should be noted that Muslims do not believe that Jesus died on the cross, but went on to live and preach for quite a few years afterwards. What if the Muslim version is correct? Could the tomb actually be that of Jesus?

The Theosophists of our day, like the ancient sages and synchronous popular lore, contend that the Christ has always lived reclusively in a remote Himalayan Valley. It is said that he is an 'immortal', that is, omniscient and ageless, occupying a form not composed of normal human flesh. The Christ was accessible, though not always visible, for he possessed an etheric 'body of light', enabling him to appear or disappear on this plane at will, yet remain at all times in a body composed of a heightened, accelerated, sub-atomic molecular structure. (Yes, these Masters are called just that because they are masters of everything!)

---

[63] A biographical account of Appolonius of Tyana can be found on the Internet at http://www.magna.com.au/~prfbrown/a_tyana0.html
[64] Referred to as 'The Razabal Tomb.'

Readers of Paramahansa Yogananda's 'Autobiography of a Yogi' will no doubt recognize the similarity to his recorded accounts of 'Babaji', whom that author describes as having possessed just such abilities, and whom Yogananda refers to as "the Yogi - Christ of modern India." In fact, when I first started reading about the exploits and antics of Creme's 'Maitreya', I initially surmised that it must be Yogananda's 'Babaji' to which he was referring.

For example, of Babaji, Yogananda says:

The immortal Mahavatar, Babaji as drawn with specific direction by Paramahansa Yogananda for reproduction in his "Autobiography of a Yogi." Reprinted courtesy Crystal Clarity Publications.

'The Northern Himalayan crags...are still blessed by the living presence of Babaji... The secluded master has retained his physical form for centuries, perhaps for millenniums. The deathless Babaji is an avatara. In the Hindu scriptures, avatara signifies the descent of Divinity into flesh. An avatar is unsubject to the universal economy; his pure body, visible as a light image, is free from any debt to Nature.'

Sometime in the mid 80's, my friends and I were discussing Babaji, when one friend claimed that he had been one of Babaji's students. He explained that Babaji had physically manifested for a while, was accessibly in the Himalayas, and was being addressed as 'Haidakhan Baba' so-named after the Haidakhan region of India where he was said to have manifested, lived and taught between 1970 and 1984. I recall our friend having shown us a photo of the saintly Haidakhan sometime afterwards - a photo, he claimed, of the man who appeared to him in the midst of a personal crisis in which he nearly lost his life.

Haidakhan Baba circa 1979, in the photo shared by the author's friend.

It didn't really surprise me. By that point it was a foregone conclusion on my part that such things were possible anyway. Of my friend's suggestion that this 'Haidakhan Baba' and Babaji were one and the same, it was plausible as far as I knew. However, Yogananda had written in the 1940's that:

'[Babaji] has never openly appeared in any century; the misinterpreting glare of publicity has no place in his millennial plans. Like the Creator, the sole but silent Power, Babaji works in humble obscurity.'

In a vein similar to the theosophical description of Masters, Yogananda further offers this:

'Babaji can be seen or recognized by others only when he so desires. He is known to have appeared in many slightly different forms to various devotees - sometimes with beard and mustache and sometimes without them.'

Interestingly, it has been in just such a manner that Mr. Creme has maintained is characteristic of the myriad appearances of the Christ in recent years. However, the similarity stops there, for even more fascinatingly is that Yogananda clearly distinguishes Babaji as a separate individual from 'the Christ.' In fact, in many ways, Yogananda may have revealed or confirmed the reality of this group of ascended Masters who perennially work as a team on humanity's behalf. For, as Yogananda explained:

'Babaji is ever in communion with Christ; together they send out vibrations of redemption and have *planned the spiritual technique of salvation for this age.* The work of these two fully illumined Masters - one with a body, and one without a body...'

'Great prophets like Christ and Krishna come to earth for a specific and spectacular purpose...Other avatars, like Babaji, undertake work that is concerned more with the evolutionary progress of man during the centuries than with any one outstanding event of history.

Such masters always veil themselves from the gross public gaze and have the power to become invisible at will. For these reasons, and because they generally instruct their disciples to maintain silence about them, a number of towering spiritual figures remain world-unknown.'[65]

Here is an essential clue paralleling the assertions of the Theosophical school, of which Yogananda had no affiliation. It had been Yogananda's accounts that served as my initial introduction to the reality of these anonymous supermen, allowing me to be receptive to the concepts proposed by my friend, Sophia, when she first introduced me to the works of Bailey and Creme. I had read Yogananda's autobiography sometime in the early seventies, and it was this work that helped form the bridge between the Western,

---

[65] The entire chapter 33 from 'Autobiography of a Yogi', which discusses the immortal Babaji, may be found at: http://www.crystalclarity.com/yogananda/33.asp

Catholic-Christian tradition in which I'd been raised, and the Eastern philosophical traditions. "Autobiography of a Yogi" had been a regular companion of mine in my youth, and it was a must-bring whenever I went on weekend spiritual retreats which were sponsored by the Catholic order of priests that ran my high school.

It was this seminal work which influenced my decision to embark more earnestly on a spiritual path that was inclusive of a broader philosophical perspective. Yogananda appealed to me as a knowledgeable, spiritual authority. With Benjamin Creme's claims seeming increasingly consistent with those of Yogananda's, it became relatively easy to be initially open-minded to this whole story.

The Thwarted Engagement

Previously addressed was the issue of the Theosophical Society's intentional 'grooming' of a vehicle through whom the returning Christ

Paramahansa Yogananda, circa 1925.

would work. Despite what appeared to be a conscientious objection by Jiddu Krishnamurti, it was instead a conscious decision in partnership with the Christ, who, according to Mr. Creme, had declined to overshadow and work through yet another surrendered disciple, and instead elected to return personally.

It has also been illustrated how much of this theosophical information concerning the return of Christ and the Masters has been disseminated from the Tibetan Master Djwhal Khul through his telepathic agent - Alice A. Bailey - in a significant number of volumes that were written between 1919 and 1949.

It was in Bailey's aforementioned 1948 publication entitled *The Reappearance of the Christ*, where it was formally and conclusively announced that the 'World Teacher', the Christ, had decided as of June, 1945 that he'd physically return again to the world, and much sooner than planned. In the interim, one wonders if this change of plan may have averted some imminent global catastrophe that Our Lady of Fatima had hinted would occur if we did not collectively mend our erring ways.

In 1982, Benjamin Creme publicly announced at a major, internationally represented press conference that the World Teacher had physically manifested as of 1977, and was living in East London "as an ordinary man concerned with modern problems - political, economic and social." For those intrigued journalists who did elect to investigate, finding Maitreya proved to be daunting, largely due to the orthodox Muslim population in East London who thought the idea of the returned Christ, or, for them, the returned *Madhi*, entirely discomforting and unwelcome.

A journalist by the name of Patricia Pitchon had been largely responsible for the leading effort throughout 1984 in the invited search for Maitreya. One evening in 1985, Pitchon was dining at a restaurant in the heart of the Indian community on Brick Lane in East London when she suddenly felt as if someone was watching her from a window behind her.

When she turned to look, she saw a tall, Asian-looking man dressed entirely in white, gazing directly at her. She claimed to know at once that this was the Maitreya that she and her colleagues had been seeking. Yet, as quickly as she had seen him, the mysterious figure moved away from the window. Although Pitchon had thought to get up and go out after him, she remained too stunned to move. For what really enabled her to recognize him was the fact that she had seen the face of this man before.

In January 1982, while attending one of Benjamin Creme's public programs, Pitchon claims to have seen Maitreya's face radiating in a brilliant light that was superimposed over Creme's face during the overshadowing segment of the program. Pitchon's story was carried in *The Sunday Times* in December of 1984, accompanied with an illustration based on her description of Maitreya.

As a result of Pitchon's published testimony,[66] a group of 22 internationally represented journalists from Europe, Japan, and America had planned to meet at the same restaurant at 8:00 PM on July 31st, 1985, with the hope of meeting Maitreya. The specific time and date had been selected largely due to the scheduling availability of one American television representative.

After much planning, set up, financial expenditure, waiting and clock watching, at 9:00 PM, Benjamin Creme announced that his Master had telepathically informed him that the anticipated contact with Maitreya would need to be postponed[67] due to an unforeseen and foreboding interference of "opposing forces." The announcement evoked severe consternation from all in attendance, further entrenching whatever measure of disbelief that may have previously existed.

---

[66] Source: *Maitreya's Mission, Volume 1*, pg. 5. 6. © 1986, by Benjamin Creme, Share International Foundation.
[67] Transcript detailed in *Maitreya's Mission, Volume 1*, pg. 6, Ibid.

The Medjugorje Connection

Benjamin Creme has mentioned that there have been several such incidents of planned meetings in which assorted hindrances had consequently contributed to not only their specific delay, but of the Emergence of Christ and the Masters in general. Recently, while reading the transcripts of the messages delivered by Mary at Medjugorje, it was apparent that there were many segments that seemed quite inconsistent with the average message routinely offered during her apparitions there. It was in these that I found what could amount to a clue as to what sort of interference may have been responsible for the postponements described above.

In general, one may note that Mary's messages repeatedly ask of everyone to pray, change their ways, and convert to a life that incorporates a more spiritual focus - not necessarily a conversion to Christianity or Catholicism. When certain messages are compared with the response of Mr. Creme and his Master for the postponement on July 31, 1985, we begin to see a very different picture. Apparently, there was something of grave importance occurring on the unseen, etheric dwelling plane of the Masters.

In 1985, Mary's messages at Medjugorje were still being delivered weekly, and the transcripts of those messages for the weeks that followed July 31 may amount to what could be interpreted as 'battle reports' from the divine front line.

In fact, all through 1984 and 1985, Mary's messages also make repeated references to a 'plan', just as Blavatsky, Bailey, Creme and Yogananda had, and which are simply attributed to Herself, or God. But she also begins to make references of another kind that seem to escalate in fervor with each passing week. To demonstrate, the following timeline of transcript excerpts are offered:

January 2, 1985: "A part of my plan has been realized. God blesses in a special way all those who are here. You do not immediately understand the reasons."

January 14, 1985: "My dear children, Satan is strong. He wishes with all his strength to destroy my plans. Pray only, and do not stop doing it. I will also pray to my Son so that all the plans that I have begun will be realized. Be patient and persevere in prayer. Do not permit Satan to take away your courage. He works very hard in the world. Be on your guard."

February 17, 1985: "Pray, dear children, so that God's plan may be accomplished, and all the works of Satan be changed in favor of the glory of God."

And here are the 'front line reports' from the weeks immediately following July 31,1985:

August 1, 1985: "Satan has taken one part of the plan and wants to possess it. Pray that he does not succeed because I desire to have you for myself so I can offer you to God."

August 8, 1985: "Dear children; Today I am calling you to pray against Satan in a special way. Satan wants to work more now that you know he is active. Dear children, dress up in clothes of armor against Satan. With Rosaries in your hands, you will conquer."

August 15, 1985: "Dear children; Today I bless you and I wish to tell you I love you. I appeal to you in this moment to live my messages. Today I bless you with a solemn blessing which the Almighty grants me."

August 22, 1985: "Dear children; Today I wish to tell you that God wants to send you tests which you can overcome with prayer. God is testing you through your everyday work. Now pray that you will overcome every temptation peacefully. Come through every test from God more open to Him, and come to Him with love."

August 29, 1985: "Dear children I invite you to prayer, especially now when Satan wants to use the harvest of your vineyards. Pray that Satan does not succeed in his plan."

Finally, after what appears to have an arduous one-month battle beginning around the time of Benjamin Creme's press gathering on July 31, Mary announces the victorious news:

September 5, 1985: "Dear children; Today I thank you for all your prayers. Pray continuously and more so that Satan will be far from this place. Dear children, the plan of Satan has been destroyed. Pray that every plan of God will be realized..."

The suggestion on behalf of all combined views - Mr. Creme, the theosophical school, and Our Lady of Medjugorje - that opposing forces to God's plan exist and counter that plan sufficiently enough to delay the return of the Christ, is disturbing. As a confirmation of the reality of these forces, in 1982 Mary gave a message in Medjugorje of a most profound nature. One must read this passage several times to awake to its import.

Mirjana, one of the young women to whom Mary has repeatedly appeared, informed the Madonna of an apparition in which Satan himself had appeared to her, asking her to renounce her affiliation with the Madonna. Mirjana explained that Satan illustrated how her affiliation with the Madonna would just bring suffering and misery to her, and invited her to instead follow him. In exchange, she would be given a life of happiness and fulfillment in love. With her immovable faith, Mirjana, of course, rejected the offer.

When she had concluded, the Madonna replied:

> 'You must realize that Satan exists. One day he appeared before the throne of God and asked permission to submit the Church to a period of trial. God gave him permission to try the Church for one century. This century[68] is under the power of the Devil, but when the secrets confided to you come to pass, his power will be destroyed.
>
> Even now he is beginning to lose his power and has become aggressive. He is destroying marriages, creating division among priests and is responsible for obsessions and murder. You must protect yourselves against these things...'

Though seemingly naive from an academic standpoint, the weight of that message is profound. "This century is under the power of the Devil" lends credence to the scope and measure of the dire tone of the warnings of Fatima, and even those prior to this century, and the subsequent warnings of the potential fall of civilization.

By whatever name it is termed, - Satanic forces, Forces of Darkness, the Black Lodge, or Brotherhood of Darkness - as opposed to the so-called *Brotherhood of Light* to which Maitreya, Jesus, Mary, and the other Masters are said to belong - its alleged existence helps to shed light not only on the great tribulation to which humanity has been subject in the 20th century, but may serve as the basis for the ancient legends of the battle between light and darkness.

For our time, in addition to the threat of communism, world war, nuclear devastation and the annihilation of religion, a more amazing understanding of the full import of Mary's warnings may be ascertained when enjoined with the explanations put forth by her Master colleague, Djwhal Khul.

The Unknown Battle

In her work *"The Externalisation of the Hierarchy,"* Alice Bailey compiles a series of dictations from Djwal Khul - affectionately referred to as 'DK' - that were issued, published, and disseminated as small booklets between 1934 and 1949. The dictations therein are, essentially, a full, play by play explanation of 'the Plan' as it unfolded prior to, throughout, and immediately following World War II.

In an unparalleled manner of candor when explaining the detailed

---

[68] The 20th century.

activities of 'the world beyond' in the realm of the Masters, DK sheds light on the exact measure and depth of the urgent, critical plight of humanity during those years. When read, one gets the clear impression that we may owe a greater debt to these Masters than hitherto possibly realized. For, in short, the reader is gradually illumined to the fact that World War II may have been nothing less than the biblically predicted Armageddon, that Adolf Hitler is said to have been *'an agent of the Anti-Christ forces'*, and that there was one critical point so dire that humanity faced an almost assured possibility of spending the next millennia enslaved by these 'dark' forces were it not for the extensive efforts and intervention of Maitreya and the hierarchical Masters.

Of this time, DK explains:

'In a way unrealized and underrate of by the average man, the Forces of Evil were in a most potent manner emerging from their ancient lair; they were intent upon seeking those whom they could mould and obsess, and thus hurry mankind towards disaster.

The Hierarchy, foreseeing this, attempted to offset their efforts. They made appeal to the spiritually minded people of the world; Their appeal reached millions and culminated in May, 1936... They struggled to save humanity and to arouse men to their imminent peril; people could not appreciate the true nature of the impending danger.... none appreciated properly the double danger with which humanity was faced: the danger arising out of human selfishness and greed, plus the danger which was nearing the Earth through the agency of the combined forces of evil.'

'In September, 1939, supreme wickedness broke loose upon earth. Because the Hierarchy could not and would not infringe upon human free will, the evil which humanity itself had engendered manifested itself. Rampant evil took possession of the earth through the medium of the Axis nations. The United Nations then began slowly to organize under the impression of the Forces of Light. The war was on.'

"The war," of course, was one that would be meted out on both planes of existence. I've contemplated these points to some extent since having read it many years ago, consequently influencing my thoughts, for example, while watching the D-Day scenes of *Saving Private Ryan* and similar films. In this light, it readily becomes apparent that perhaps the greatest heroic aspect of the veterans of World War II was not only inherent in the fact that they had so valiantly and arduously battled against great odds on *our plane*, if you will, - to vanquish the obvious evil of Nazism, win the war, and secure peace and freedom for millions of Earth's inhabitants - but that they might, quite plausibly, be remembered - if only poetically - as the warriors of Armageddon.

In Philadelphia's Amtrak/30th Street station, there is a marvelous sculpture, erected to memorialize the Pennsylvania Railroad employees who had been killed in WWII, which may perhaps be the best personification of this perception of the war. There, majestically soaring 39 feet into the lofty expanse of the station's cavernous 90-foot ceilings, stands the imposing edifice of Walter Hancock's 'Angel of the Resurrection', which depicts a solemn, masculine angel lovingly uplifting the lifeless corpse of a slain soldier from surroundings engulfed in flames. So awesome was the struggle of the decisive battle, that even the exhausted angels themselves could do little to intervene and prevent such slaughter.

Although the fact that this work stands in a train station may be considered questionable, it may, perhaps, be the most appropriate place, for it was there, like countless other train stations across the American Nation and in the towns and cities of the other Allied nations, that these secular warriors bid farewell to their family and friends, many for the last time.

In this regard, it remains a fitting shrine. Passersby should consider momentarily pausing to contemplate the tale suggestive in the artistic imagery, and offer a gesture of thanks to those who gave their lives - for their respective homelands, and humanity. We literally owe them our existence.

Was this perhaps the true reason for Mary's pleas at Fatima that we pray and repent unceasingly? Repeated warnings were given at that time of 'the great chastisement', whose arrival was ultimately indicated through the ominous Aurora Borealis display of 1938. Had the Madonna, like a true mother, been painstakingly insistent that we wash behind our metaphysical ears and clean up our transcendental act so as to ensure that her children, by doing so, would not only be able to secure the greatest measure of success in life that was, in reality, humanly possible, but who could simultaneously play an unconscious role in the very preservation of humanity and civilization itself? Were the ascended Masters imploring humanity through any number of modes of influence to pray harder and more earnestly, to pray with our fullest love and conviction due to the dire need of which we were so unaware? Had the tears of the families of those whose lives had been sacrificed on the altar of the world wars, let alone the anguished cries of the martyred souls themselves, reached an unanticipated corner of heaven?

In hindsight, provided all of these conjectures are true, a particularly large debt of gratitude would be owed to the Madonna, or, perhaps befittingly, Master Mary. It would seem that this particular Master has appeared consistently in so miraculous and otherworldly a fashion in times of extreme calamity. Endeavoring to inspire human hope to an historically unprecedented level, she also seems to have played a key role in the salvation and preservation of humanity in its grandest sense, in the esoteric context.

Historical testimony claims it was She who has repeatedly returned to warn, admonish, guide and direct us to the correct way of living that would help uplift ourselves from so implicitly dark a future. It's said there is no greater love than that of a mother for her children. There are few examples better than the love so demonstrated and given unceasingly by Mary. For all intents and purposes, the Christian and Sufi views may be correct, that she may as well be the foster mother of all of us - a divine personification of human maternity itself.

Considering these propositions which suggest such a metaphysical magnitude of the war, offered is a clearer understanding of Bailey's assertion that the decision was made for the Christ to return much sooner than planned. In order to aid in the facilitation of this hastening, and in very much the same manner that Jesus gave us the words of the *'Our Father'*, it is said that the Christ offered to humanity a similar ancient incantation called 'The Great Invocation'

Introduced in Alice Bailey's books, The Great Invocation is alleged to be an ancient prayer that at one time in remote antiquity was reserved for use by only the most exalted of spiritual beings and priestly figures, such as Rishis, Lamas, Magi, etc. The prayer is said to have been offered more recently as a gift from Christ, reintroduced for the benefit of beleaguered humanity at the end of the world war, and has been the recommended, prescribed prayer to invoke the Christ's presence and assist in his physical reemergence.

The intention, according to Maitreya and as explained by Mr. Creme, has been to increasingly invite all the peoples of the Earth to repeat this Invocation. Translated from some forgotten archaic tongue, The Great Invocation reads as follows:

'From the point of Light within the Mind of God, let light stream forth into the minds of men. Let Light descend on Earth. From the point of Love within the heart of God, let love stream forth into the hearts of men. May Christ return to Earth. From the centre where the Will of God is known, let purpose guide the little wills of men - The purpose which the Masters know and serve. From the centre which we call the race of men, let the Plan of Love and Light work out, and may it seal the door where evil dwells. Let Light and Love and Power restore the Plan on Earth.'

Suffice it to say, should Creme's views be true, humanity has apparently expressed its overwhelming, heartfelt desire for divine intervention adequately enough to get Christ to return. There now remains one final, potent, collective, and open request needed to enable him to step out into the open for all to see and know him, and for his work to truly begin.

Perhaps due to the presence of Mary at Medjugorje and its resulting ten million visitors; to the response of renewed faith as a result of the incredible abundance of worldwide miracles; and to an overall global growth spurt in human spirituality, it is that Maitreya, little by little, has begun to make himself increasingly known.

According to Benjamin Creme, Maitreya made his first, photographically documented public appearance in 1988 in *Nairobi, Kenya*. Creme asserts that the individual who appeared in Nairobi, despite the proclamations of the witnesses in attendance who claim they saw Jesus, was in fact the theosophical Master of masters - Maitreya, the World Teacher.

Since the occasion of that appearance, it was reported that Maitreya had made countless unannounced public appearances all over the world: to individuals; to world political and religious leaders; and before stunned assemblies and groups of witnesses of all nationalities and denominations. It is

The photograph allegedly of Maitreya, pictured with Kenyan nun, Sister Mary Akatsa. Earlier that day in 1988, Sr. Mary, known as a healer, had announced to the crowd that God had spoken to her during prayer, informing her that her mission would host a 'special visitor' that day. Courtesy Share International Magazine.

further suggested, like the Marian apparitions of Lourdes, Fatima, and elsewhere, that on each occasion, Maitreya had blessed wells and other bodies of water, transforming them into healing holy water. The number of visitors attracted by the legend of these healing wells has grown significantly each day. Throngs of the faithful of all creeds have traveled to Tlacote, Mexico; Nordenau, Germany; Nardana, India, and Maryland, USA, to name but a few.

According to a 1999 edition of Share International magazine, Maitreya had appeared in that year alone, for example, in Annapolis, Maryland on February 7 to an unspecified group of people; to 300 Muslims for 18 minutes in Fes, Morocco on Feb. 14; he spoke for 18 minutes to 150 Christians gathered in Beil, Switzerland on February 21; and on March 7, he spoke to 200 Fundamentalist Christians in Mississippi who sat, awestruck, in stunned silence for 18 minutes. The list goes on and on[69] and the visits continue unabated.

The Press Responds... Sort of

One point that continues to perplex is, if Maitreya has appeared so often to so many, why are the press largely ignoring these events? Are they too fantastic? Will no one believe? Is it a hoax?

An editorial in the November '88 issue of Share International magazine addressed these observations. The comments therein reflect the thoughts of many with whom I've raised the topic:

> "People who take seriously the information about Maitreya's presence often shake their heads in puzzlement, wondering why the media refuse to give this phenomenon more widespread coverage. The relative silence from the media does indeed lead one to ask whether there are no individual journalists at all open to this idea."

Referring to the aforementioned predictions offered by Maitreya, through Mr. Creme:

> "Whenever such a prediction turns out to be correct, as was the case [of the Iran/Iraq truce in the late 1980s], an interest in the source of the information would seem logical. To some extent, this is indeed the case, for a number of journalists have read the various press releases [which were and continue to be periodically issued containing Maitreya's predictions] with the greatest attention. Moreover, they have put them in a desk drawer, and in fascination read them again as soon as they are reminded by events in the world that

---

[69] A more complete but ongoing list may be found in Benjamin Creme's book *"Maitreya's Mission: Volume III."* The list, detailed in chronological order, can also be reviewed through Share International's website - www.shareintl.org.

the releases are, indeed, accurate."

This describes with a fair degree of accuracy what I myself had been doing as well. This was a primary reason why I paid attention to the news for years, looking for related releases, for further proof and other events that might appear in any way associated with Mr. Creme's claims. The Share International magazine editorial further stated:

> "If such an assertion [in routine news coverage of imminent disasters] is belied by events, no one takes the author to task. On the other hand, a prematurely optimistic prediction leads inevitably to loss of face for the author concerned…How dire must be the consequences for stories considered by the media to be 'half-baked' - and the reappearance of the Christ is, for many, just that. As a result, journalists who are inclined to take the story seriously - and there are some - often do not dare admit it openly. For they would certainly lose their reputations and acceptance by colleagues. Thus they prefer to keep silent and to await events."

Guilty here! I too remained cautious about addressing the topic until I felt some evident, verifiable evidence would avail itself. In time, it would occur to me that such tangible evidence might not be the sole criterion for understanding the situation, a notion which is discussed in the ensuing chapters.

The Share International editorial offered the saga of one journalist who convinced his editors that the story was worth investigating, by exposing Benjamin Creme and his supporters as frauds. "[The journalist] himself expected to find "commercialism, money - making, a group of idiots."

To his own astonishment, his meeting with Creme resulted in positive experiences and a positive story - and he had the courage to put it before the editors. Predictably, the reactions were negative. Yet this article was published, accompanied by the following disclaimer:

> "The editorial board would like to announce that they find both the subject and the story entirely ridiculous. We have decided to publish it, though this is a warning that in these dark times even the most intelligent people fall prey to religious mania."

Upon reading this, I was immediately reminded of the influence of the 'Freethinkers' and the cynical atmosphere surrounding the apparitions of Mary at Fatima. One can imagine similar words being used to describe that scenario in 1917. Does this not sound like the typical manner of neutral indifference that has been typical of media coverage of such fantastic claims and eye-witnessed phenomena?

The Share International magazine editorial answered some of my own questions as put forth at the beginning of this dissertation. In fact, it directly appeased my consternation by offering this conclusion:

> "This true story [of the above journalist] may make it clearer what resistant journalists have to overcome, and why the media up to now have reacted as they have. It explains why the media manifest so little interest in so interesting a phenomenon as a man whom thousands instantly recognize as 'Jesus Christ' turning up in broad daylight in Nairobi."

Interestingly enough, if not coincidentally, the Nairobi event referred to had been witnessed first-hand by Job Mutungi, a respected, veteran journalist and editor of the Swahili edition of the *Kenya Times*.

As Mr. Mutungi described the scene:[70]

> "The tall figure of a barefooted white-robed and bearded man appeared from nowhere and stood in the middle of the crowd. He was walking slowly towards the new church building away from the tent. Mary [Akatsa - pastor of the Church of Bethlehem, located in Muslim Village, Kawangware, Nairobi, where the event took place] walked with him, side by side. I stared at the stranger without blinking. Strange, sporadic light wafted on top of his turbaned head, his feet and his entire body."

What clearly struck me was Mutungi's perception of the wafting, sporadic light - an identical description of my own experience at Benjamin Creme's meditation program, when I'd felt and intuitively sensed an extraordinary presence, despite having not physically perceive anyone as did Mutungi, who continued:

> "[Speaking] in clear Swahili, which had no traces of an accent, the strange man announced that the people of Kenya were blessed, especially those who had gathered at the venue that afternoon."

With that, Mutungi quotes the 'strange man' as having said to the crowd:

> "We are nearing the time for the reign of heaven. But before that, I shall come back and bring a bucketful of blessings for all of you."

---

[70] As reprinted in Share International magazine, September 1988.

After the stranger left in a car which had been offered to him in courtesy, Mutungi explained how the driver later claimed that not two minutes into the departing drive, the stranger requested that the driver pull over and stop the car. "On getting out," the driver reported, "he walked a few paces beside the road and simply vanished into thin air."

It sounds like the director's notes on a film script. It reeks of a guest's narrative from *The Art Bell Show*. It resembles a script lifted directly from TV's *Outer Limits*. Yet, according to Mr. Creme, this describes but one of hundreds of alleged such appearances by Maitreya.

As more incidental reports began to increasingly trickle in and word began to spread, many were inspired to take Maitreya up on the offer previously extended to the press when he said: "Those who seek me will find me."

At least one man did just that. A Frenchman, who will remain unnamed, paid a visit to Patricia Pitchon, the journalist mentioned previously. To her he explained his mission of having gone to the White Chapel district of London in search of Maitreya.[71] With a copy of the Nairobi photo of Maitreya as published in The Kenya Times in hand, the man had shown it to everyone in the area whom he encountered, asking if they had seen or knew of the turbaned figure in white. After some time had passed without much luck, the man decided to stop in a teashop and take a break.

While there, he noticed a distinguished looking gentleman of apparently Indian descent who was dressed in a western suit, having tea. Showing this patron the Nairobi photo, the relentless Frenchman asked if he knew the man in the photo. To his surprise, the gentleman told him he did recognize the man in the photo, and that he was often seen attending prayer services at White Chapel Mosque.

After obtaining a schedule of services and accompanied by Ms. Pitchon and her husband, the Frenchman went to the Mosque at the next appointed time for public prayer. Pitchon's husband and The Frenchman were admitted to the main prayer hall, with Ms. Pitchon being escorted to another section reserved for women.

Due to a minor misunderstanding, Pitchon was left waiting in a corridor. Casually glancing through the open door of a nearby office, Pitchon noticed a powerful figure seated inside, and tried to discern if it was the same man she had seen outside the London restaurant. But almost instantly a second man appeared in the doorway, closed the door, and politely inquired as to why

---

[71] Source: Share International magazine, June 1995, pg. 9

she was standing in the hall. After explaining her situation, she was then asked to leave, and wait in a nearby cafe.

When later reunited, the Frenchman shared his observation of "a very tall, beautiful-looking man" standing a few feet behind him with 'fearless' eyes. While this man did not look at him, the Frenchman could not stop looking at him. Ms. Pitchon's husband, who had joined the two on their quest and who accompanied the Frenchman into the prayer hall, said he felt "a very strong energy and an atmosphere of strong devotion during prayers."

Pitchon later inquired with Benjamin Creme, who said his Master confirmed that the man in the office and the man in the prayer hall had both been Maitreya. As an added bonus, the Frenchman learned that the Indian gentleman whom he'd encountered in the teashop and directed him to the Mosque had also been Maitreya!

But why was Maitreya reciting prayers in a mosque? Was this being purported to be the Christ a practicing Muslim? The longer I contemplated and researched a little, the more it began to make sense.

Islam is a highly complex system of belief that remains largely misunderstood in the West. Muslims accept that the Prophet Mohammed, who lived during the 6th century AD, was the final prophet in a long string of chosen messengers of God going straight back to the biblical Adam. Yet, distinct from other religious traditions, Mohammed or the other prophets are not the central figure of worship. In fact, Islam prohibits the worship of any person or deity. Rather, it is the written *Koran*[72] itself which invites the focus of reverence.

As the story has been passed down, we are told that Mohammed, an illiterate yet sensitive, compassionate caravan merchant, grew disillusioned with the corrupt and immoral society that dominated his region of the world, and began to frequent a cave on Mount Hira, located on the outskirts of Mecca. It was there that he found escape and solitude, spending his time contemplating the mysteries of life and the nature of God. After some time had passed, it is said that the angel Gabriel appeared to Mohammed in the form of a man on what Muslims call *The First Night of Power*. In a manner reminiscent of the angelic visits to the three Shepherd children at Fatima, the angel addressed him, repeating three times "Proclaim!" Mohammed, startled and perhaps frightened, initially declined the request of the stranger. By the third time, Mohammed was so overwhelmed by the angel's insistence, that eventually he heeded what was to come.

That which came was the start of a lifelong recitation of the Koran,

---

[72] A transliteration of the Arabic Qu-ran, which literally means 'the recital.'

which, apart from the historic narrative form of all the preceding Judeo-Christian Scriptures[73] as recorded by primarily forgotten scribes, the Koran was said to be, like the Ten Commandments, a verbal recitation from God Himself.[74] From there, the book recounts the tales of the greatest of biblical prophets and key figures from God's point of view. In Islam, it is said that one of the greatest miracles surrounding the Koran is the fact that it had been transcribed by a man known to have been an illiterate merchant. Though the fantastic tales, philosophical conjecture, and charismatic qualities of the prophets were inspiring enough in their own right, it was the perfect form of the writing of the Koran - a feat barely accomplished by even the most learned scholars of the day - that so intrigued and captivated the people in Mohammed's time. Classical Arabic, the vehicle of the Koran, is the most precise and primitive of the Semitic languages, and was the sacerdotal language of the Koreshite tribe of Mecca, whose religious history stems back to the biblical Adam and Eve, and the same tribe into which the Prophet was born. However, what's unique is that Arabic is considered to be a language constructed according to mathematical formulas, a distinction which sets it apart from all other languages.[75]

Therefore, it was the combined aspects of this retelling of the tales indigenous to the old testament in perhaps the original language of the Semitic ancestors, as well as being so composed in a manner that is virtually decipherable in mathematics which so awed those earliest adherents of the Prophet's gospel, and simultaneously astounded scholars. It is significantly more than just a collection of tales. This is the reason the Koran is considered so sacred, and why it is held to be dictated by the voice of God, and, in fact, viewed as an embodiment of God.

Many sects of Islam believe, as do Christians, that the prophet Jesus ascended into heaven and will come again. Other sects assert that Jesus did not die on the Cross, and lived on to the age of 120. Yusef Ali, one of the most respected of Koranic interpreters, points out, that, like the western esotericists:

> "One school holds that Jesus did not die the usual human death, but still lives in the body in heaven." [76]

Like the Buddhists, Muslims simultaneously believe that a great, world teacher, a redeemer of righteousness - the Imam Madhi - will return in 'the last

---

[73] Islam is academically categorized as a Semitic religion. Muslims regard their faith as being inclusive of all Judeo-Christian prophets, beliefs, figures and traditions that precede the Koran. It is, in essence, the sequel and final chapter of the Bible as it exists. That is, it is the continuation of both the Old and New Testaments.
[74] The Arabic name for God, Allah, is, like the term 'God' itself, neuter in gender. For the purposes of this work, I refer to God in the masculine.
[75] Source: The Sufis, by Indries Shah
[76] From 'The Holy Qur'an', translation and commentary by A. Yusef Ali. Originally published in 1934. Page 230, commentary 664.

days.' This aspect of Islamic belief is found in the *Hadith*, a collection of quotations attributed to the Prophet Mohammed as recounted by some of his closest disciples, and upon which many schools of Islamic theological thought are based. Within the Hadith are made numerous references to the return of the Madhi, as well as the return of that well-respected prophet who will work in partnership with the Madhi: *Eesaa ibn Maryam* - or, translated, Jesus, son of Mary.

The Hadith is an extraordinary work for westerners to become acquainted with because so many teachings central to modern Christianity may be found therein. In fact, one could arrive at the assumption that the entire judgement day scenario so fanatically maintained by various Christian sects has its very roots specifically in the Hadith, and within the teachings of Islam in general. From descriptive stories of angels and heaven to apocalyptic references such as 'the mark of the Beast', the appearance of the Anti-Christ, and more, it would seem that Christianity, somewhere along the line, incorporated these quotes of the Prophet into their own creed, but long forgot their original source.

The Hadith is used largely by adherents of Sufism, the mystical branch of Islam, who follow a more Gnostic approach to Islam that is consistent with Vedanta, Tibetan Buddhism, Christian mysticism, and the underlying spiritual foundation of virtually all religious traditions. Sufism fully embraces the core aspect of Islam itself - surrender - which is the very meaning of the word Islam, but with specific emphasis on the hidden meaning - the esoteric nature of Koranic teaching. Historians have discerned that some of the greatest names in the history of western Christian theology, such as Saint Francis of Assisi, had been influenced directly by and ultimately disseminated the teachings of the mystic Sufis[77]. In their own way, each injected the secret Sufi canon into some of the core teachings of Christianity, and others into classics of western literature.[78] Was this, perhaps, the avenue by which the Hadith doctrine found its way west? The source of such teachings could never be revealed by the likes of Francis of Assisi due to the fact that such assertions would be immediately labeled heresy in Christendom, and punishable by death.

In the teachings of the Sunni branch of Islam, the Hadith comments about the Madhi are so numerous that acceptance is a mandatory part of their belief. This collection is classified as *tawaatur*, which means that their sheer volume alone supports their unquestioned validity as truth.

Some such quotes in the Hadith read, for example:

---

[77] Source: 'The Sufis', by Indries Shah
[78] Ref.: 'The Sufis', by Indries Shah, from the introduction by Robert Graves.

> "At the end of the time of my ummah, the Mahdi will appear. Allah will grant him rain, the earth will bring forth its fruits, he will give a lot of money, cattle will increase and the ummah will become great."

> "He (the Madhi) is one of us, behind whom 'Eesaa ibn Maryam (Jesus, son of Mary) will pray."

The Sufis, however, offer a view remarkably coherent with the Christian tradition, and that of Alice Bailey and Benjamin Creme as well. In *The Last Barrier*, author Reshad Feild offers a unique and perhaps obscure insight into this world of Islamic mysticism. The book chronicles the unanticipated journey of Field - a westerner, who is suddenly thrust into the mysterious world of the Turkish *Dervish* sect of Sufism. His escort throughout is Hamid, a London antique dealer of Turkish ancestry who just happens to be a most learned Sheik[79] of Sufism. What begins as a curious inquiry into understanding the Dervish tradition results in an arduous series of tests which ultimately bring about Field's spiritual transformation.

Most intriguing is Hamid's conversation with Feild at the Mary chapel in Turkey, which is a relatively obscure pilgrimage point for Muslims, and which is believed to be the home of Mary after the crucifixion[80] and in her later life[81]. Consistent with Sufi tradition, Hamid explains the virginal aspect of Mary as an esoteric, scriptural allegory for complete spiritual purity and steadfastness, and that an acceptance of Mary is the first requirement for the aspirant in order to awaken that inner spirit that is our personal connection to God. Hamid asserted to Field that what he was seeking, what all seekers, in fact, search for, is the spirit of God. That spirit of God, said Hamid, is one and the same with the inner Christ, the same Christ that comes to redeem to world. That spirit within is the Christ. When recognized internally through spiritual discrimination, the phenomenon referred to in Christianity as "the word made flesh" occurs, and the 'kingdom of God' begins to manifest. In the west, this epiphany is referred to as 'Christ consciousness.' Hamid then concludes with a powerful remark suggesting the importance for each seeker's recognition of this inner epiphany:

> "The eternal messenger is always within, waiting to unfold the moment through the Word, and one day when Mary is recognized again, there will be a reappearance of the Christ, manifested in the outer world."

---

[79]. Teacher; cleric
[80]. Sufis acknowledge the crucifixion, where most orthodox Muslims do not.
[81]. It is believed her tomb is located in Kashmir.

Would this explain why the Madonna apparitions have been so prevalent for the past 150 years? Why one of her most celebrated visits occurred in a village named Fatima, the same name of the Prophet Mohammed's daughter? Why a sustained apparition of her lasted for 8 hours in Zeitoun, an Egyptian town in which peoples of all sects - Muslim, Christian, Coptic, Jew - are respected equally?

The Koran is much different than many of the Hindu scriptures, which not only offer the tales and enduring legacy of Lord Krishna, but also has had numerous avatars throughout the ages. Christianity, of course, had Jesus, but we need to understand that Christian followers invented Christianity, not Jesus. In this light, the Islamic view of Jesus as one of a string of divinely inspired prophets in a specific cultural context would seem a more rational and likely scenario. What is practiced today under the heading of Christianity is more an extension of the interpretations of Saint Paul of Tarsus, and may more accurately be termed 'Paulism.'

Judaism, like Hinduism, offers in the Old Testament one of the best-known records of avatars and prophets of the Semitic tradition with whom we are more familiar: Abraham, Noah, Moses, etc. In fact, the esoteric perspective of the Theosophical school and others is that, the Old Testament is, essentially, a recorded history of Masters and initiates who offered their divine sway and insight for the immediate benefit of those ancient Hebrews and Israelites among whom they lived. Here again the Islamic Sufi view would be consistent.

By the time Jesus arrived on the scene, the Hebrews were so set in their ancient ways that they revolted against the Buddhist flavored message of the Nazarene, and the schism that has defined the two paths of Judaism and Christianity was born. In fact, the Gnostic essence of Jesus' teachings is the very reason Muslims view Jesus as a Muslim and a teacher of Islam, the religion of Abraham the Patriarch.

After centuries of martyring and perpetual warring among the Semitic 'people of the book', the divinely inspired Prophet Mohammed was exhorted by the angel Gabriel to confirm and unite the Judeo-Christian scriptures in that single work that is the Koran. Though Mohammed's legacy of Islam would spread and incorporate a vast portion of the known world, theological differences and misunderstandings, accompanied by political agendas, prevented a full-scale infusion into Christendom in the same manner the Judean world rejected Jesus almost seven centuries before. Mohammed's Islam really is, in essence, a continuation of Jesus' ministry, which had spread significantly since Emperor Constantine's decrees just three centuries prior to Mohammed. With its progressive message of social justice, of humane brotherhood and familiarity, Islam only went so far before becoming corrupted, splintered, and falling into the control of politically motivated rulers, fundamentalists, and Jihad fanatics who misinterpreted the Prophet's intent or adapted the teachings to suit their needs. Like Christianity, it fell into the wrong hands.

Jesus taught a philosophical view that was radical, threatening, and intimidating to his Hebrew tradition. From an esoteric view, the Christ was born in and worked amongst a people who were historically scorned and oppressed. It would make sense, then, that a returning Christ of our time would choose the religious mode of worship which is currently, perhaps, the most scorned and least understood. Scorned only because it's so despicably misrepresented by globally linked Islamic terrorist groups. How tragically ironic in light of the fact that the Prophet's original vision - the very same vision of all the preceding Biblical prophets, which included Jesus - advocated a core, ethical initiative of equalitarian unity, not the divisionism to which humanity has since allowed itself to acquiesce.

Further, in its truest essence, Islam is more of an esoteric, transcendental philosophical system than a religion, which is hard for western civilization to understand, and its best and perhaps most accurate school is precisely that of the mystic sect of Sufism. It is comparable to, say, what the philosophical psychology of Yoga is to the dogmatic aspect of Hinduism. Whereas, the former focuses on attainment of God through one's direct, personal effort and inner experience, the latter focuses on the worship of deified energies, *devas* (angels) and ascended beings in a purely devotional manner. In this way, Hinduism has evolved in a manner similar to Christianity. It remains an enigma that Islam, while having become largely dogmatic itself, has yet retained its core, idol-less principle, that the one true God is completely accessible and available to each of us in equal measure, that a personal unity with Allah is attainable within ourselves. This, of course, had been the heart of Jesus' teachings. It is also similar to mystical Judaism in this manner, which would make sense. The Prophet Mohammed maintained that Islam was simply a revival of the practice of the religion of the Semitic patriarch, Abraham.

Islam has historically served symbolically as the hinge between east and west, and even today this would appear true. If I were a returning world teacher looking for an optimum avenue of expression, what would I choose? It would seem that there is a well-conceived purpose here.

In the case of Maitreya, here we find a being who is said to hold the title of Christ, and is referred to by a name associated with the final incarnation of Buddha. His spiritual intention is to teach humanity the art of self-realization, a process inherent in the Vedantic-Hindu tradition, as well as that of Islamic and Talmudic mysticism, and was found in a Mosque practicing the unifying creed of Islam. In a way, he was communicating through his action that he, too, was a Muslim at the very core of that term's meaning - "one who is surrendered to the will of God." Was He also, then, the awaited Madhi? Is Maitreya the manifestation of the Christ in the wake of the many, worldwide Marian apparitions as asserted by the Sufi teacher Hamid?

It would seem to be an ideal plan. In one fell swoop, this avatar could easily represent the true unity of all faiths by virtue of familiarity to all. Furthering this view is a point addressed by Benjamin Creme who indicated that, at the time, Maitreya had been living with Hindu Swamis in the residential wing of a Hindu Temple. Should anything less have been expected?

Yet, the experience of awakening as described by Hamid does not imply the path of Islam as a prerequisite. One of the most endearing aspects of Sufism is that its philosophy is so universally inclusive. The experience of the 'spirit of God' of which Hamid speaks can happen to anyone of any creed, anywhere, at any time.

Buck and Barbara

Undoubtedly one of the tour de force American visionaries of the Twentieth Century, the futurist-author Barbara Marx Hubbard has been a central catalyst for positive, workable social reform solutions for over 30 years. Raised in New York as the daughter of toy tycoon Louis Marx, she graduated cum laude with a B.A. in Political Science from Bryn Mawr College, studied at the Sorbonne and L'Ecole des Sciences Politique in Paris, and, after raising five children, in the 1960s Barbara dedicated her time to personal, social, and global transformation.

Since 1970, Barbara Hubbard has co-founded several human potential organizations, including the Committee for the Future, the Society for the Universal Human, and the Foundation for Conscious Evolution. She designed and produced 25 SYNCONS conferences - a public think tank and discussion forum - which brought together key representatives and prominent thinkers of all academic, political and social fields to find the means of creating an opening for realizable, socially advantageous solutions. She has made countless television appearances, authored several important and highly acclaimed books, co-chaired summits for Soviet and American citizens in the Gorbachev-Reagan era, and in 1984 was nominated as a Democratic Candidate for the vice presidency of the United States. She also hosted *Potentials*, a television series which she co-produced and featured noteworthy individuals such as Buckminster Fuller, Norman Cousins, John Lilly, and science fiction visionaries

Ray Bradbury and Gene Roddenberry. On the approach of age 90, she continued tirelessly as President of the Foundation for Conscious Evolution in Santa Barbara, California.[82]

In her autobiographical work *The Hunger of Eve*, Hubbard offers several honest accounts of personally transforming moments, but none so compelling as her story of the time she sought retreat from the exhaustive strain of her 1984 campaign tour as a Democratic candidate for Vice President. While driving through the hills around Santa Barbara, California, she happened upon the Mount Calvary monastery, and felt compelled to pay a visit. It was there, while perched upon a stone wall, that Hubbard experienced an "intense light surrounding me."

Barbara Marx Hubbard. Photo graciously furnished by Barbara Marx Hubbard

"It became" writes Hubbard, "the all-pervading living presence of Christ. My attention was magnetized. I turned my inner eyes to face the light and made direct contact. I was electrified. He was real! My heart was flooded with love."

Barbara Hubbard's heart-felt description remains one of the most moving accounts of this experience to date. Recounting the experience, Hubbard recalls the words she heard spoken by the Christ, who said:

"Whenever you feel the rush of warm joy in your heart, it is I - open your heart to the joy."

"I became acutely sensitive," Hubbard continued,

"every cell in my being poised to receive this presence, this relationship with a living being, a full embodiment of God. The stream of ideas [as she describes the 'voice'] continued:"

'My resurrection was a signal for all of humanity's. Why do you suppose I submitted to the calumny of Calvary but to demonstrate that the physical body can and must be transformed...'?

'The resurrection was an early-attraction signal to the human

---

[82] At the time of editing this 2019 revised edition, Barbara Marx Hubbard courageously recognized "her time to leave" and passed away on April 10, 2019 after requesting to be taken off life support. The author is grateful for her support and interest in this project so long ago, and remembers her with great love and respect.

race of what can be done through love of each person as a member of one's own body and of God, above all else. The intensity of that love, the power of that connectedness, is the key to the resurrection which is now known as the transformation... The resurrection was a future forecast of an approaching new norm...What I did alone, all can now do who choose to love God above all else and your neighbor as yourself... That great commandment of pure love combined with the knowledge of God's processes of creation gained by science in the past two thousand years is the formula for victory....'

Barbara Hubbard remained still and silent "for what seemed to be an eternity." "In that instant" she says, "the hunger of Eve was fulfilled. I bowed my head in overwhelming gratitude."

Is that which Barbara terms 'the Hunger of Eve' the same as Hamid's 'recognition of Mary', having recognized this 'spirit of God' as 'the Christ.' So moved was Barbara by her own experience that she wrote almost non-stop for the following six months, filling sixteen-hundred pages with journal entries.

"The most extraordinary insight I received" she wrote, "was that there is now a new dispensation on earth due to the rapid rise of consciousness in so many millions of ordinary people. The violent scenario is not necessary. An alternative to Armageddon is a 'Planetary Pentecost', a time on earth when *everyone who so chooses would hear from within, in their own language, the mighty words of God*. It would be a shared mystical experience for the whole human race, similar to what happened to the disciples in the upper room at the time of the first Pentecost. Each person would be empowered to be a co-creator expressing both their own and God's potential. My life has shifted from within. The presence of Christ has become my living partner."

Barbara could not contain herself, and the first person with whom she thought to share her experience was her dear friend, the renowned architect and inventor Buckminster Fuller. She had a hunch that of anyone she knew, Bucky, to which he was affectionately referred, would understand. So, she mailed to him select pages from her journal.

Later, toward the end of a speaking engagement in Los Angeles, Hubbard saw Fuller in the rear of the room urgently motioning her to hurry, and received a relayed message that "Dr. Fuller needs to speak with you alone." Completing her speech, Hubbard joined Fuller afterward. Sitting intently in a garden outside the auditorium, Bucky took Barbara by the hand.

"I have just read your journal" said Fuller. "I know it is true, because the same thing happened to me. It was in February of 1928 that I had this real and extraordinary experience, the only one in my life that was utterly mystical. I was walking on Michigan Avenue in Chicago when suddenly I found myself seemingly floating along at the center of a sparkling sphere. Then I heard a deep, loud and clear voice, such as I had never heard before, saying:'

'From now on you need never await temporal attestation to your thought. You think the truth.'

'I was directed to the New Testament and began to write, just as you did, almost precisely the same words. But I hid it under my bed. No one has ever seen it."

Then, standing up and embracing Hubbard, Fuller affectionately exclaimed: "Darlin', there's nothing but God, there's only God."[83]

Contact

It was Fuller who urged Marx to run for the Presidency of the United States due to his perception of Hubbard's extraordinary ideas for peaceful solutions to global issues. Hubbard

R. Buckminster Fuller

instead elected to run for the Vice Presidency with the idea that she could accomplish more. She proposed that she should head up the office as an 'Office of the Future', under whose auspices modern methods developed from cutting edge science could be employed to solve intractable pressing social problems.

Hubbard had proposed two planks for the Democratic platform: 1) That the Vice President should be a woman, and, 2) that the Vice President should head up this Office of the Future to plan for and create ideas that work. One outcome of Hubbard's efforts and vision manifested in the popular anthem of the time, "We are the World," which was sung all over the world at large concerts.

With an appealing, visionary agenda, Hubbard's bid for nomination

[83] Reprinted with the permission of Barbara Marx Hubbard.

rapidly gained steam, and she was invited to speak at the Democratic National Convention that year. Her presentation was a rousing appeal far ahead of the routine. The idea fostered by Hubbard for a woman as Vice President did appeal to the Democratic party leaders, and to the American public as well. However, with the rest of her platform deemed too radical for the mainstream, Hubbard was snubbed, and the Democrats instead nominated Geraldine Ferraro as the first female Vice-Presidential candidate in American history.

Barbara Hubbard, as a futurist and visionary, is simply one of those remarkable individuals who live ahead of their time. The intent on Hubbard's part was to infuse some fresh, creative, and bold ideas into the American political process. Had it succeeded, a global influence similar to that of the Kennedy era could have steered the course of America in a challenging new way. But was humanity ready for so progressive an agenda? While it would seem that the obvious answer would be yes, it remains that those who yet wield the global seats of power continue to prevent radical but imminently necessary change. This is nothing new.

In fact, it is precisely this scenario that is addressed in Buckminster Fuller's 1981 book *Critical Path*. Throughout the work, Fuller cites in great detail the key turning points in the history of human evolution, revealing a disturbing pattern of repeated ignorance at times when soluble opportunities which could have advanced humanity significantly had presented themselves. Hence, the work's title is in itself a summarized statement declaring that if humanity fails to wake up and pay attention, we are doomed to repeat the pattern once more. But due to the obvious advances in modern times and particularly during the twentieth century, the situation is much more dire than at any other moment in the history of human civilization.

Fuller addresses the question "What are we ignoring here?" before the question is yet posed. He explains that our traditional, conditioned tendency when reviewing published, academically accepted history is to continually search for the *invisible power structure* behind the historically visible kings, czars, presidents, etc., as well as the underlying, hidden causes of specific wars which tend to contrast with the published explanation and/or and popularly accepted causes of such wars.

He cites as an example the era of the 6th Century, BC, and suggests an overlooked significance in the fact that two of history's most brilliant, perceptive, and inspired individuals - Pythagoras in Athens, Greece, and Buddha in the Orient - lived at the same time, and yet remained completely unaware of each other. In the meantime, those in power quarreled and warred to no end, while a succession of highly influential biblical prophets in the

Judean province were inspiring great segments of the population with their teachings while their scriptures and teachings traveled far. In short, the known, civilized, human world was being educated in arts, letters, science and spirit to such a degree that right then and there existed all the right conditions for the flowering of a renaissance unprecedented in the history of man. So enormous was this opportunity that an opening for the utter emancipation of humanity - a complete and perfect world - was at hand. The combination of philosophical and spiritual revelation and mathematical tools then taught still remain indispensable to human development and civilization. But perhaps, most importantly, people were reminded of their direct, personal inner hotline to the creator, and with the advanced knowledge being cultivated they could actually envision, plan, and gradually discard the old, warring ways and form an ideal society based on ethics and sharing of resources: A vision of a socio-democratic culture of self-realized, enlightened people in every facet of society.

Fuller explains how the 'warlords' and leaders of the era who then held the reins of power did not initially notice the significance of all of this. Yet when they did take notice, the threat was imminent, and for the following two centuries it would become a universally accepted, primary issue for those in power who had the most to lose. A method of controlling the individual hotline to God needed to be set in place.

This man-made 'power structure' of which Fuller speaks henceforth guided and controlled humanity in a domineering fashion throughout our known history, until now, as we bear witness to its steadily crumbling edifice. Fuller lived with the conviction that the fulfillment of his earnest vision was on the threshold, firmly believing, as previously asserted by Gandhi, that in humanity itself lay the key to the global changes it wished to see manifest. Imagine a world with the likes of Buckminster Fuller, Jiddu Krishnamurti, of Pythagoras and Buddha, of Jesus and Mohammed at the helm. Such a world, and such an opportunity, he then asserted, is upon our doorstep once more.

The reappearance of a being of such stature as ascribed to the Theosophical Masters as Maitreya could find wide appeal from the standpoint of religious tradition, and this knock at the door in our time once again poses that very opportunity which history presented in the likes of Buddha, of Jesus, and others. But, just as it was received in their respective times, it simultaneously is interpreted as a threat today. Even so divinely appointed a plan would require the leaping of that other, perhaps more critical hurdle so central in each of the recorded or attributed sagas of those avatars and prophets of old. That being the "invisible power structure" of our time - the indigenous agenda of the world's varied and frequently opposing powers of government - an area which any returning world teacher will unquestionably need to address in a very direct and diplomatic fashion in today's world.

In December of 1985, after the 'mild turbulence' that disrupted the imminent meeting with the press on July 31 of that year had settled (as indicated in the Medjugorje transcripts), Benjamin Creme suggested that Maitreya took advantage of this 'favourable period' and decided to approach the British press himself.

Without question, the media contacts with whom he met immediately recognized him as a most remarkable holy man from the East, but were hesitant to agree with the contention that he was the Christ, and further reluctant to risk their professional credibility by promoting him as such. However, a happy medium was arrived at, and it was agreed that a brief, simple statement would be issued, suggesting, as Benjamin Creme put it:

> '...that a man claiming to be the Christ lives in London; that he is a member of the Pakistani community but presents himself as a World Teacher for all groups, religious and otherwise; that he wishes an opportunity to meet members of the press and media from all lands and peoples in order to establish his credentials; that if invited to do so he would welcome an opportunity to address all mankind through the linked TV channels in a way that will convince the world of his true status.'

With the exception of the British press, the worldwide response was mild. Though many articles issued forth, few were given broad attention. Phrased in such a manner by that initial media contact, no wonder the statement just fizzled into obscurity. Had the press once again dropped the ball? The lackluster response resulting from the inadequate press coverage would not impede 'The Plan.' A greater measure would need to be taken.

According to Benjamin Creme, an unpublicized, top-secret conference was organized in April of 1990 at which Maitreya was to preside. The objective was to enable the many international world dignitaries to whom He had appeared in prior years to join together under one roof, to share and discuss their individual experiences, and collectively meet Maitreya once more.[84]

Two hundred are said to have accepted Maitreya's invitation, and in attendance were Ambassadors and other diplomats, members of British Parliament, religious representatives, a king and members of various royal families, professors, scientists, industrialists, and journalists. Major print and broadcast media representatives from around the globe were invited to attend

---

[84] Ibid, June 1990.

as observers only, but only a token number of the British press accepted the invitation.

During the conference, it was said that the man known as Maitreya spoke of his role as a humanitarian advocate, and as the head of his group of highly advanced teachers - the so-called hierarchy of Masters. He confessed to have been the primary instigator behind many of the unexpected, remarkable twists in human affairs that had already transpired, such as the end of the cold war, the release of Nelson Mandela, the end of apartheid, and much more.

It was said that Maitreya encapsulated his mission at this time in history as one of focusing on sharing and international cooperation. He indicated his top priorities as facilitating the end to the pathetic persistence of needless human hunger and starvation. He proposed the initiation of a program bent on offering adequate housing and food supply for all the peoples of every nation, and asserted that universal healthcare and education were fundamental rights deserved by all.

On several occasions throughout the two-day event, Maitreya demonstrated his command of the laws of physics by displaying carefully selected *siddhis* - supernatural powers - such as disappearing then reappearing before the astonished guests, just as he had in Nairobi two years prior. He explained the plan of his eventual Emergence, how it would partially rely on the cooperation of those in attendance, and invited them - at the right time - to share their own experiences openly. The anticipated result, according to Maitreya, was that humanity, upon hearing the endorsement and verification of his existence from such eminent, recognizable world leaders, would realize the apparent truth of His presence and petition him to step forward.

Maitreya was said to have then addressed how the team of Masters abide by a fundamental law of nature that prohibits an infringement on human free will. It was explained to those in attendance that these Masters relied solely on the resulting demand fostered by the sharing of the presented facts through the anticipated, subsequent media coverage, which, in turn, would have the effect of laying out an apropos welcome mat. He concluded by indicating that the proverbial ball was in their court of free will.

During the intermissions, the attending journalists were allowed to mingle with and interview those in attendance. The atmosphere was said to have been exhilarating, as all agreed the event was most engaging. Overall, it was considered by Maitreya and his group to be a great success.

Yet, despite these facts, there was virtually no international commentary specifically about the event. An American tabloid, *The National Examiner*, reported the following week that a Catholic Bishop close to the

Vatican was quoted as saying, "There is overwhelming evidence that Christ's return has already taken place and that an announcement of this only awaits a final decision by the Pope."[85]

Due to the public's general indifference towards tabloid announcements as a credible journalistic outlet, the statement was largely dismissed. Considering that I had tracked the Emergence information for almost 10 years at that time, I was not even aware this conference had transpired until I was engaged in summarizing my research for this book nine years afterwards!

Once, while watching a news update on the Kosovo Crisis of 1999, I was quite moved by the tales and video footage of the harrowing reality which then prevailed. Unmarked, mass graves dotted the landscape; hundreds of abandoned vehicles used to transport fleeing and returning refugees sat silently askew, riddled with bullet holes, doors flung open, personal possessions strewn about, like ghosts whose ominous presence yearned to tell a grave tale. There were stories: of young men who'd been shot without question or hesitance in an obvious attempt on the part of the aggressors to prevent the birth of future generations; of young women, rounded up and herded off to camps to be repeatedly and brutally raped, then slaughtered, and discarded.

In the same newscast, it was noted that yet another series of threats of potential, unannounced bombings and attacks worldwide were issued by fanatic Islamic Jihad terrorists. How clearly contradictory is their message of destruction, terrorism, and desires for bloodshed worldwide - without question a message so antithetical to the heart of Islam itself. Without question, so anti-Christ. It is clearly the fault of such militant fanatics for continuing to give Islam a bad reputation, which instantly leads to a persistent, mass misunderstanding on behalf of the rest of us while perpetuating distraction and division.

Further still, on the very same broadcast was news of escalated quarreling between Pakistan and India over the question concerning the fate of Kashmir - a region with an historically sacred reputation comparable to Jerusalem or Mecca - and which, ironically, had been dubbed by the press "the most dangerous place on earth." While many fear the emergence of a third world war and a very definite threat of nuclear exchange does exist, there is at least one reassuring affirmation which issued from the Madonna at Medjugorje: "There will be no third world war."

If this is so, what are we witnessing then in these small pockets of

[85] Share International magazine, June 1990.

horror, darkness, and evil that seem to be erupting around the globe? From hostage situations in our schools, theatres, and other public venues; a rise in sexual perversion and psychological imbalance amongst our clergy; to maniacal murder sprees and bombings in shopping malls and discotheques, it would seem that darkness is seeping out from every remote, unheard of crevice and corner of the globe. Is this perhaps, the expunging of the "last dregs of God's wrath" of which the Madonna forewarned at Marionfried in 1946?

It is difficult for us to have any measure of faith in anything, let alone aspire towards hope in light of such happenings that seem to stain the pages of our morning newspaper with blood. Have we lost faith? Are we in such pain that we are unable to hear about the upliftment and miracles in other people's lives? Have we turned a blind eye to our ancestral faith in a God at all? Would God let such things happen? If Christ were here, would he let such things happen? How are we to hear the words of a man like Benjamin Creme when our bleak existence renders us feeling powerless and uncaring? Or, perhaps we do care - yet feel compelled to focus on the need of our own survival. It almost seems like a dark, engineered plan to distract us from aligning with our better nature. Would this explain the ages old legend of the battle between dark and light forces?

Have our leaders - governmental, ecumenical, social, etc. - failed us by not informing us of the Christ to whom they were introduced in 1990? If so, what about us? Does it take a government or some ecclesiastical structure to decide whether such news would be harmful or beneficial? Frankly, it seems indicative that the wrong individuals may be at their respective political and religious helms.

On the other hand, perhaps it has not exclusively been the fault of our leaders. It is quite easy for us to point our fingers and blame another, and by doing so perpetuate the lingering atmosphere of hatred, enmity, and indifference that continues to foster war, selfishness, and ill-will toward our fellow man. For repeatedly punctuating the works of Djwhal Khul, Bailey, and Creme has been the indication that the Christ will only step forward when we will have collectively invited him to do so. The ball, in the end, seems to be in *our* court.

To help us along, we have been given 'signs and wonders' - those instances of miraculous occurrence and unanticipated social transformation that are found in the news. Otherwise, we might not believe.

During the very same newscast on which I'd seen the items mentioned above of dark and troubling, life-threatening crisis around the globe, at the very end was a filmed report of a church in Kansas in which a statue of Mary, the Blessed Mother, that was visibly crying actual tears. It struck me as odd in that the evening news kind of served as a form of thrill park entertainment. Topping it off were tales invoking fear, worry, concern, then an interlude addressing daily business and weather. Then finally a concluding tale instilling wonder, hope, and relaxation. We could now go to bed in peace. Truthfully, it was a very nice capping touch, I thought, to an overall rough day for all of us.

Was the crying Madonna statue a reminder that we are not alone, that we need not fear? From Fatima to Medjugorje with the constantly offered presence of Mary, accompanied by crying icons, the transformation of rosaries to gold, the phrase 'Allah is here' composed in melons and other foods; the crosses of light and miraculous healings and stories of 'angels' intervening to aid and assist us, it would seem that we have been incited precisely to stand in wonder.

In her message of October 24, 1981 at Medjugorje, the Madonna exclaimed: 'All of these signs are designed to strengthen your faith until I leave you the visible and permanent sign.'

Are these occurrences due to the claims of Christ's presence among us? Has Christ returned? Are such signs suggestive evidence or divinely ordained hints?

As I departed church after having attended Catholic mass one Sunday, I picked up a small, illustrated card bearing the title *Our Lady of the Millennium*. It featured a profile image of the Madonna, dressed simply in humble peasant garb, kneeling in a simple, earthen-floored room, enlightened by the golden light of a simple lantern before her. It is, curiously, a distinctive departure from the usual image of Mary typically distributed by the Catholic Church. This is not a deified, heavenly icon, with magic rays of light issuing forth from her palms and form. Gone is the added visage of the bleeding, thorn-encrusted, exposed 'immaculate' heart. Gone is the torso length rosary, and gone is the image of her standing atop a miniature globe as Queen of the world.

Here was a simple woman, a loving mother, gently cradling the unseen but obviously present infant Jesus. The captured moment suggests that He is already born, and with the artist's depiction of Mary in the process of lifting one of her arms, one is given the added impression that she is ready to reveal her child to us, represented by the radiant glow emanating from her obscured lap.

Behind her is a window revealing the star-filled night sky, with the frame trimmed by the accent of a pale warm light as that of an approaching dawn. Though the night has been long, the new day will surely arrive. The lantern suggests that there has always been a glow of hope in the permeating but temporal darkness.

On the reverse side of the card is printed the Marian Prayer of Pope John Paul II. There, in one stanza, we find the following words, and another possible clue:

> "To you, Mother of the human family and of the nations, we confidently entrust the whole humanity, with its hopes and fears. Do not let it lack the light of true wisdom. Guide its steps in the ways of peace. *Enable all to meet Christ*, the Way, the Truth, and the Life."

Are we being told for what we should prepare and expect? If the Pope's words aren't convincing, then the artist's depiction may be. All aesthetes and artists will tell you that art is a pictorial language, the same language first used by primordial man in its infancy, and the same language of the ancient seers, shamans, and Rishis used to reveal and teach the ancient mysteries.

If these and the words of Benjamin Creme, Djwhal Khul, and the other theosophical proponents are still not enough, we need only turn again to Mary, our constant guiding maternal companion. For in her apparition of November 25, 1998 at Medjugorje, she offered us this message:

> 'Dear children! Today I call you to prepare yourselves for the coming of Jesus. In a special way, prepare your hearts.'

Finally, we find yet another indication in the works of Alice Bailey, where, writing for Master DK in her 1925 publication *Treatise on Cosmic Fire*, it says:

> "When He comes at the close of this century and makes his power felt, He will come as the Teacher of Love and Unity, and the keynote he will strike will be regeneration through love poured forth on all. This He will demonstrate in the formation of active groups in every city of any size, and in every country, which will work aggressively for unity, co-operation and brotherhood in every department of life - economic, religious, social, and scientific."

What might we expect? What will it be like, to live in a world beginning anew under the guidance and tutelage of humanity's world teacher? How will we be regarded? Are we to be fearful of wrath, admonishment, and punishment? Or can we anticipate upliftment, an end of barbaric and self-interested behavior, a time of sharing and cooperation, a time of healing, a time of 'life abundant'?

But what are we to think about a most confusing aspect of the scenario presented, which asserts that the Christ and Jesus are, on this occasion, distinct from each other? Perhaps the answer is offered by a most extraordinary boy living in Argentina.

In its December, 1998 issue, Share International Magazine reported on five-year-old Gabriel Moyano, and his demonstration of a remarkable ability to heal and cure. Laura Fernandez, a Share International correspondent from Spain, was visiting relatives in Argentina and decided to investigate.

Here, in Ms. Hernandez' own words, is her account of the experience.

"On a recent trip to Argentina to visit relatives, my family and I decided to visit the house of Gabriel Moyano, the child of five who acquired healing powers after a visitation from the Madonna. We had the opportunity to talk with Gabriel and his parents, Dora and Carlos, who live in the western province of San Juan, in a humble village of modest houses and unpaved streets.

We had to arrange an appointment, since people come from all over the country to see the 'miracle' child. At first Dora and Carlos received us distantly, since the media and the church have taken mixed and contradictory positions regarding the truth of their son's powers.

"Who are these people from Spain, bringing a magazine called Share International? How do they know about Gabriel and what do they want?" were the questions we saw written on their faces.

"Before Gabriel saw the Madonna in the repair-garage wall, we never imagined anything like this," explains Dora. "First, I didn't want my child to do what he is doing, I wanted to protect him since he is such a young boy. But then I realized he is more intelligent than I am. He can differentiate between his life in the school, his life as a normal child playing with others, and his 'mission', as he calls it. He doesn't invent what he says and does, and he is not crazy. We are not afraid, although the church doesn't approve of what he does, and even says - without having talked directly to us or Gabriel - that we are making money with this, which is false." (As we would confirm later, the Moyanos do not charge any money for their child's activities, nor do they accept presents or donations.)

Gabriel receives a visitation from the Madonna every night, Who shows him the people he can heal at home and others whom he has to visit to cure them. A couple of brief sessions is all that he needs. The boy places his little hand and a rosary from the Madonna on the patient's head, mumbles some words and says: "That is it! God heals where He can!"

Many people have been healed in this way, as witnesses and

patients can report: from diabetes and bone-fractures to cancer and heart problems. Doctors cannot explain why their patients' tumors or fractures disappear, although there has not yet been any clinical report certifying these miracle cures.

"If you want to receive some healing," said the boy's father, "come on Monday, Wednesday or Friday at three o'clock. You will have to queue, since about 100 people come around. I know it is very hot at that time of the day, we have told him to leave it until later, but all he says is: "Daddy, the Lord is not a supermarket where you open according to season. He heals at three o'clock." [Laura Fernandez interjected here, adding: "We found this a striking coincidence with Maitreya's blessings, which he always gives at three o'clock local time."]

Dora also told us that some time ago a woman (who apparently is telepathically sensitive) came to their house and told them that Gabriel was a reincarnation of Brother Martin de Porres or, as he is often called - "Brother Broom." A celebrated Saint in Argentina, he was renowned for his healing powers and because he always wanted to perform the most humble tasks, mainly sweeping, in the monastery where he lived. Dora and Carlos had not heard of the Saint, but they laughed because their son's favourite toy was a broom.

Some days later, we came across a pharmacy called 'Saint Martin de Porres.' We asked the owner if she had some pictures or images of this saint, and she very kindly gave us a little 15cm statue which she wrapped up as a present. We returned to Gabriel's house, where the boy was giving his healing sessions that afternoon. After queuing for some time, we came into the house and my husband placed the wrapped statue on a table. Dora told us they could not accept presents, but we explained that maybe this "present" had something to do with their son's past. Gabriel then came into the room and treated my husband, who had strained his leg. The little boy placed his rosary on my husband's head, said a prayer and then placed his rosary again on his 'working table', full of pictures, flowers and candles. He appeared to be absent, as if listening to an inner message.

Then he turned and went straight to the table where we had placed the wrapped statue. He had to stretch his arms to try to get it as he is short and could hardly reach it. When he finally picked it up, he exclaimed: "Oh, I wanted to know what I looked like!" But Gabriel did not waste any time, as many people were waiting for him.

Dora, having become more forthcoming and relaxed, asks an

astonishing question after seeing Share International.

"Tell me, do you know why Gabriel always talks of two different individuals, the Christ and Jesus, as if they were two different people, I don't understand anything. Does my son know what he is saying?"

Then we show her the photograph of Maitreya in Nairobi, we explain what we know about the Reappearance of the Christ, tell her who the Master Jesus is, and talk about the existence of the Spiritual Hierarchy. She listens attentively, then talks about other matters. Then, suddenly, she stops and says, holding Maitreya's photograph: "Let's see if Gabriel can recognize the man in this photo, because he always talks of a 'Man in White.'"

She calls her son, who is playing in a backyard with other children. He comes in and Dora shows him the photograph, asking him lovingly:

"Look at this man in the photo, look at the robes he wears, his beard and this kind of hat, it is very strange."

The boy, who is very short, throws a naughty look at his mother and smiles, not surprised by this question: "Yes, I know him."

"And who is he, do you know?" she asks.

"Mum, He is the Christ!" says the child with an extraordinary confidence.

His mother appears somewhat confused, but cannot stop inquiring:

"But where do you know Him from?"

"From heaven, Mum, when the Madonna takes me with Her, and They talk to me."

Chapter Five

SCIENCE, SAINTS, AND SIDDHAS

"Thousands of people used to come to see my Gurudev Shri Nityananda. They would sit very quietly and in silence while he played in the ecstasy of his own inner love. He would not speak, yet people would receive something just by watching him and would say, 'I feel contented and happy.' This is the effect of a Siddha's company; this is why God can be attained through the grace of a Siddha."

Swami Muktananda

Our time has been witness to an extraordinary growth of the human potential movement, of religious revivals, and widespread interest in all things spiritual, metaphysical, or under assorted alternative banners such as 'the new psychology', etc. It's only logical that associated therewith are many charlatans, rogues, pseudo-gurus, false prophets, misinformed clerics, and 'half baked' teachers. It poses difficulty and confusion for soul seekers and those desirous of an enriched, fulfilling way of living to sort through the varied methods and approaches, innumerable books, audio therapies and enrichment seminars, let alone their authors and prognosticators.

Even the once celebrated Madame Blavatsky had been denounced in her later years by critics who claimed that many passages from her debut work *Isis Unveiled* had been blatantly plagiarized from earlier academic works. But it should be noted that all such popular movements of the day were, as they often are now, debunked by strongly opinionated naysayers who subscribed to the political, academic, and scientific social order of the day. Many spoke out to win support of peers, to specifically achieve acceptance into a higher social rank, or to further a cause or movement of their own. Case in point: Frederick Engels and Karl Marx, while wagering their socialistic idealism in defense of

German migrant workers in mid-nineteenth century industrial England, specifically cited the then emerging Theosophy movement and spiritualism in general as just another example of how the European Aristocracy and the American wealthy were attempting to dull the minds of the masses[86].

Rumor mongers have always had something to say about even the most respected teachers. Swami Vivekananda, for example, who had achieved worldwide respect after his speech at the World Congress of Religions in Chicago, in 1893, was subject to an onslaught of slanderous, derogatory, and racist campaigns, largely due to bigotry and prejudice. Paramahansa Yogananda, the name perhaps most associated with yoga and eastern thought in the west for the better part of 50 years, was also maliciously referenced.

One of the most extraordinary spiritual teachers of the latter 20th Century was the late Swami Muktananda Paramahansa. Widely hailed as an authentic yogic adept, Muktananda's Siddha Yoga mission and teachings had a global impact far beyond any extent achieved by any previous teacher of his kind. Acknowledged in his day as 'the guru's guru', the late Swami Muktananda was esteemed by many respected leaders of the human potential movement as a premier fountainhead from which genuine Self-knowledge could be gleaned. One through whom direct access to the long sought inner experience of God could be obtained.

The legends surrounding Muktananda's omniscience are numerous. There is one famous story, for example, told by Richard Alpert, the former Harvard professor and contemporary of Dr. Timothy Leary, Aldous Huxley, and Alan Watts - all pioneers in consciousness research in the 1950s and early 1960s. Perhaps best known as Ram Dass - the name given to him in 1967 by the Indian guru Neem Karoli Baba - Alpert has played an acknowledged key role in integrating eastern and western spiritual philosophy, following the footsteps of Vivekananda and Yogananda. As author, lecturer, psychologist, and humanitarian, Alpert has served tirelessly.

Once, Alpert paid a visit to Muktananda in his Ganeshpuri, India, Ashram. Alpert appealed to Muktananda for aid in acquiring a heightened level of spiritual experience. Muktananda responded by giving Alpert very specific instructions for meditation, including a time and location. After finding the assigned private, sound-proof room known as 'the meditation cave', he settled into a meditation posture. Alpert explained how he first experienced a physical sensation of lightness, which was then followed by an awesome out-of-the-body experience. Though he remained physically seated in the small meditation

---

[86] Source: SIMPOS: Netherlands foundation for information on social problems and occult tendencies; "Marx and Engels on Spiritualism and Theosophy" by Herman A.O. de Tollenaere

room, he soon felt that he was 'flying', higher and higher, faster and faster, combined with an extreme state of bliss filled ecstasy. The experience seemed to be timeless and without end. The euphoria Alpert experienced was beyond anything he'd known up until then. Finally, after a considerable time had passed, Alpert witnessed his spirit plummet rapidly back into his body.

Afterwards, while still relishing the 'high' of his experience, Alpert was somewhat astonished when he next saw Muktananda. Sporting an impish grin as he peered playfully over the rim of his glasses, Muktananda asked Alpert: "Did you enjoy flying?"

In his autobiography, *Play of Consciousness*, the classic life of a spiritual seeker in the Indu-yogic tradition is revealed through Muktananda's stories of the challenging stages one experiences in their quest for truth, from youthful idealism, earnest study, contemplation, and questioning, to descriptions of remarkable visionary experiences through the process of yoga and meditation, and the stories of his inspiring encounters with extraordinary, God-realized, fully enlightened and super-human beings. In his lifetime search to know God, Muktananda literally walked around the entire continent of India, from southern Madras to the Himalayas, seeking the company of revered and legendary saints and holy men.

Called *'Siddhas'* in the yogic tradition, these beings are renown for mastery of life in all regards - spiritual, psychological, and physical. They're also know for possessing profound psychic powers called *siddhis*, such as clairvoyance, clairaudience, and telepathy. Such 'divine' attributes as the ability to heal illness and manipulate physical nature still invoke wonder from the devout of all sects.

Often having strange personal habits and curious mannerisms, to the uninitiated these beings were rationally dismissed as madmen, and were generally treated as such. But to the devout, religiously humble, and those who sincerely sought to know God like the young monk Muktananda, it was clear that such external representation was only a facade - the exhibition of a harmless psychological posture which Carlos Castaneda's Yaqui Indian sorcerer Don Juan referred to as "controlled folly," a master's manner of concealing the true depth of their omniscience.

In his autobiography and other writings, such as *Secret of the Siddhas*, Muktananda frequently discusses these unique qualities of Siddha masters. While they may appear foolish or strange in behavior and appearance, he points out that they are truly perfected masters, possessing a highly advanced inward intelligence, an extraordinary depth of scholarly knowledge, and flawless discrimination. Muktananda understood that these beings live with total independence. Free of expectation or desire, they exhibit perfect detachment and renunciation from the yogic standpoint.

Some of the Siddhas with whom Muktananda spent time are legendary in various regions of India. Consider *Hari Giri Baba*, an eccentric being who appeared to be virtually oblivious to everyday life. His controlled folly was to appear noticeably outlandish by walking about dressed in a princely turban and several layers of clothing simultaneously, while demonstrating what appeared to be trivial behavior, such as speaking to pebbles he'd find and inform them of their preciousness. But Muktananda explained that this was all part of the Siddha's carefully planned facade.

There were times when Hari Giri frequently admonished Muktananda for following him around when the young monk sought to learn from the sage. On the other hand, there were times when Hari Giri regarded Muktananda with boundless compassion, and would embrace him with an unfettered love as if he were a parent or grandparent. For example, at times when the young monk was feeling depressed, uninspired, or having difficulty in understanding things, Hari Giri would suddenly show up out of nowhere, offer solace or give apropos advice without having any apparent foresight, then spontaneously leave.

Though Hari Giri and other Siddhas whom Muktananda had met, such as Zipruanna, Siddharuda Swami, and Sai Baba of Shirdi, were equally unique in that they were all arbiters of an exalted depth of wisdom, devotion, and omniscience. Though Muktananda saw them as potential gurus, virtually all of them urged Muktananda to move on, hinting that his teacher was to found elsewhere, had yet be encountered, or, specifically, could be found in Ganeshpuri, a small rural area situated about 200 miles outside of Mumbai. It was there that Muktananda would reunite with a being that he'd met in his youth, and whom is claimed as the source of his initial inspiration to become a monk and begin his spiritual path.

Muktananda would thereafter settle down and search no further, knowing that he had finally arrived at the culmination of his lifelong quest, having found one of the greatest saints/masters of modern India. It was here that he would begin a humbler monkhood, maintaining study and yogic practice under the guidance of the renowned sage, Bhagavan Nityananda.

Unquestionably a Siddha and yogic master of the highest caliber, Nityananda was one of those rare, extraordinary beings that are oft alluded to when discussing the mysterious abilities of India's saints. Incredible, miraculous tales surrounding his lore have been well documented by eyewitnesses. There are numerous testimonies, for example, of Nityananda burying himself completely in a grave-like pit, where he would remain for as long as three hours. When he would later emerge and be questioned of his behavior, Nityananda would simply explain himself with playful, teasing retorts such as "I had some work to do in Delhi." These incidents were often substantiated when, in the weeks that followed, visitors would arrive at his residence, claiming "the Master visited us in Delhi," or elsewhere, though those closest to him knew he'd never left the area at the time indicated.

After another such instance of his unknown whereabouts, three Muslims arrived to have his darshan[87] upon return from their Hajj pilgrimage to Mecca. When asked by Nityananda what they had seen, the three responded "We saw *you* there, Swamiji, and hence we are here to pay our homage." His closest disciples knew Nityananda had been in Ganeshpuri the whole time.

Such exploits are not exclusive to Hindu lore, however. There is a comparable story told by General Luigi Cadorna, General Staff Chief of the Italian army during World War One. After a humiliating defeat of his forces by the Germans in Slovenia in November of 1917, Cadorna sat in his tent, forlorn and despondent, fingering his revolver and contemplating suicide. Suddenly, a Catholic monk appeared out of nowhere, admonished Cadorna with the words "Don't be so stupid!" and then vanished!

Years later, long after the war, the General visited a church in Foggia, in central Italy. There he saw a monk whom he immediately recognized as the one who had appeared long ago. Cadorna stared in astonishment, when, as the monk walked past, he glanced at the general and said, "You had a lucky escape, my friend!"

The monk was the Catholic Capuchin Friar Padre Pio, well renown for such clairvoyance, miracle working, and for possessing the *stigmata* - the involuntary, supernaturally borne wounds corresponding to those of the crucified Jesus. Pio's life was extraordinary. For 50 years he endured the stigmata, losing one cup of blood per day. A life-long devotee of the Blessed Mother, when once asked if the Madonna ever visited him in his room, Pio chuckled and replied "Why not instead ask me, does she ever leave my room?" When asked if the Blessed Mother appeared to him while conducting Mass, Pio responded by explaining that the Blessed Mother accompanied him always to mass, and remained at his side throughout.[88] Pio was canonized as a Saint of the Catholic Church in September, 2002 by Pope John Paul II. Many other tales associated with Padre Pio are remarkably similar to those attributed to Nityananda.

For example, sometime in the 1920s, a Monsignor Damiani of Salto, Uruguay was so taken by the sincere piety and miraculous nature of Pio that he

---

[87] The customary manner in Hindu culture to have audience with a Saint.
[88] Source: The Padre Pio Foundation of America.

insisted on dying in his presence. "You will die in your native land," the monk responded, "but do not be afraid."

Some 20 years later, in 1942, the Archbishop of Montevideo was awakened in the middle of the night only to find an unknown monk standing by his bedside, urgin the Archbishop to visit Damiani at once, and then vanished.

In compliance, the Archbishop traveled to Salto, and, upon his arrival, had found that Monsignor Damiani had died. Sitting beside his comrade in mourning, he noticed a slip of paper on the floor next to the bed. It read: "Padre Pio came."

Seven years later, when the Archbishop finally had the occasion to personally meet Padre Pio, he recognized him at once as the monk who had appeared at his bedside.

Tales of beings such as Nityananda, Padre Pio and others dot the landscape of all cultural and theistic traditions, further reinforcing the notion of a conscious, hidden, sphere of activity, which is particularly revealed when it comes to matters of God. It is reassuring, when viewing such legends, to know that down through the ages, we have been blessed with the influence and presence of some divine agent or another, often with greater frequency than we realize.

A young Padre Pio circa 1910, with stigmata wounds clearly visible

The extraordinary yet basic humanness of a Padre Pio or Nityananda is more tangible, when contrasted with, say, the ethereal/spirit form of the Blessed Mother apparitions. Such phenomena literally introduce us to a whole other dimension. It's amazing enough to consider such remarkable feats by the likes of an extraordinary being like Nityananda, who seemed to possess the ability to actually manipulate physics at a level that enables such a being to produce real items from thin air. But to also consider that one can actually *reproduce their own form* as well is another story. One question arises here - if such advanced beings, presuming they've theoretically attained the highest conscious state possible by a human, can perform such miraculous deeds while alive, can they do so after they consciously leave their corporeal forms, after death?

Additionally, if such beings have proven that they can perform such deeds, it follows that they would likely be the obvious suspects responsible for the sort of worldwide miracles that have been occurring, precisely as asserted by Mr. Creme.

Scientists scratch their heads in the endeavor to explain such phenomena. What of these quasi-corporeal apparitions, or the manifestations of oil and tears emitting from photographs and statues or the disappearance of milk with Hindu icons? What explanation can be offered for the elimination or healing of diseases and other health afflictions? What about the paranormal transmutation of natural elements, such as the name of Allah appearing in Arabic script in melons, tomatoes, and other foods? Or the Catholic Eucharist wafers that change from bread into flesh and seep blood? How are the many 'crosses of light' formed through some unexplained manipulation of the molecular composition of glass windowpanes?

Such phenomena would indicate a visible bridge between the world of the seen and tangible, and that which is traditionally thought to be beyond - the unseen, the afterlife, the other world, the intangible. Are the Saints, Adepts and Masters - examples of beings who've attained a great measure of self-mastery within an average human life span - demonstrating how human beings innately possess the potential to manipulate and utilize physical matter in its most refined state?

Yogic science, as an ancient, methodical technique of conscious, personal development and evolution, precisely indicates that we do have an innate capacity to gradually accelerate the sub-atomic components of our physical bodies, transmuting them into a form composed of a refined and enhanced material nature.

Traditionally eastern occult techniques such as those found in the yogic sciences also begin to awaken a fuller understanding and appreciation for such western religious mysteries as Catholicism's *'Transubstantiation.'*

Transubstantiation is the term used in Catholic Doctrine to describe that moment in the Catholic mass when the *Eucharistic* bread and wine are offered to Christ for His blessing. While commemorating Jesus' breaking of bread during the last Passover supper prior to his arrest, Catholics believe that upon this moment of invocation of Christ, these normal foods are consecrated and changed into the 'mystical' body and blood of Jesus. They then become sacred, holy food.

To the Yogis of old, such ritual is routine practice, and this is one of the reasons Jesus is so highly respected in the East. The Yogic sciences offer a direct glimpse beyond the realm of belief - it offers an explanation and opportunity for direct personal experience. Does this reduce the awesome, humbling impact of the miracle suggested in such a ritual as Transubstantiation? On the contrary, it provides an opportunity to truly know, understand, and accept the metaphysical reality of the incorporeal. It offers an opportunity to fully embrace the event, and suddenly, it is plausible to conceive that a true miracle can actually occur during such ritual.

If such theories aren't enough, there have been several documented instances, as mentioned, of Eucharistic wafers that literally transubstantiated, such as the eyewitnesses in New Orleans who claimed a communion wafer and wine physically changed into human flesh and blood! Incredulous? A 1998 episode of the ABC network television news program *20/20* - which highlighted the incredible, miraculous activities[89] surrounding the life of a then 14-year-old American cataleptic, Audrey Santos - offered viewers a close-up inspection of several such wafers exhibiting the same phenomenon.[90] Is somebody up there trying to convey a message?

Through this, we are able, perhaps for the first time, to truly grasp, understand and practically touch the tales of Jesus, especially those after the post-crucifixion ascension. In fact, we can perhaps begin to understand the ascension itself.

The Ascended Jesus

Is it possible that what happened in the tomb after Jesus' burial was the transubstantiation of his own physical body into a body of radiant energy? This has been offered as the explanation behind the impression left on the *Shroud of Turin*. As Jesus' body transformed into an accelerated mass of biophotonic matter - light infused organic matter - it passed through the burial shroud's fibers and ascended heavenward. More aptly said, Jesus' form metamorphosed into ether, and merged within the refined, sub-atomic, biophotonic makeup of the physical universe.[91] Was this a demonstration of

---

[89] Such activities include medically inexplicable healing, and an unexplained, copious emanation of oil from countless Christian icons, statues, and photographs. In one instance, an authorized Catholic review panel, sent to investigate the claims, brought with them a previously determined, uncorrupted statue of the Madonna. Upon their entry to the Santos household, their own statue began to spontaneously emit the same, mysterious healing oil.

[90] The program originally aired on 10/05/1998. Transcripts or video can be obtained by accessing: http://more.abcnews.go.com/onair/2020/transcripts/2020_santo981005_trans.html

[91] Physicists have actually concurred that the nature of the image on the Shroud of Turin has qualities only found inherent in modern X-Ray technology. For example, one physicist took note of certain shadows appearing in the center of the image of hands on the Shroud. Having conducted a series of tests, it was concluded that the shadows were an X-Ray image of the subject's thumbs. Physicists have also concluded that such an image could only have been produced by a sudden burst of radiation taking place *after* the formation of blood stains, which is consistent with the Gospel's version that Jesus lay in his tomb for 3 days prior to the ascension. One physicist has taken the research one step further by openly asserting that it is his belief that the physical subject in the Shroud had, in fact, 'disintegrated' in a very short amount of time.

God or a greater, supreme being's power to transform the event into a spectacular miracle that would become ingrained in the memory of civilization for the subsequent two millennia? Or was it the conscious work of the now ascended great master Jesus himself?

Mystics and scientists can no longer remain disparate entities. The two disciplines need to be acknowledged as simply two representative human approaches of discerning the mysteries of nature. For the former, the human body and consciousness are their laboratory. For the latter, analyzing the physical universe in a petri dish is their cup of tea. Enjoined, with mutual respect, the two could feasibly open a door that can catapult human evolution into an unprecedented golden age of endeavor and achievement.

For each of us, the nurturing of both qualities - scientific/intellectual and devotional inquiry - is key to establishing a balanced, active engagement in one's personal and collective evolution. This is the science of yoga in a nutshell. Establishing such a balance is not easily accomplished, yet inherent in the striving for this goal is found the inner strength and equipoise that creates the groundwork of Self-mastery. With this balanced groundwork having been lain, moments of enlightened inspiration then become the vanguard of one's life. These heightened sensory, uplifting moments provide the literal ignition spark that fuels the drive of the aspirant. It is here that the necessity of balance becomes crucial, for one confronts the danger of becoming polarized - obsessed and attached to one or the other modes of being. One could become a cold-hearted, atheistic scientific eccentric, or a charismatic, narrow-minded, over-zealous religious fanatic. In the scope of the human psychological make-up, both qualities cannot ultimately remain mutually exclusive. It would seem that self-mastery via a steadfast, cautious but joyful approach to the path is the *Camino Real* for the human species. In other words, we cannot deny our respective destinies as potential enlightened Masters.

So, it would seem that those already regarded as 'Masters', upon achieving full mental and spiritual enlightenment, full 'Godhead', obtain the added benefit of their physical, molecular structure having also become 'enlightened.' Every conscious atom of their forms is at once transubstantiated into increasingly accelerating generators of energy, until finally they are spinning at the speed of light. This light then dissolves into light itself, yet retaining the identity of their former, gross materialistic counterparts. The existence of this 'memory' of form has already been virtually proven, for example, by Kirlian Photography, and in studies conducted on amputees who report to still 'feel' their missing appendages.

The Gospels suggest that Jesus the Nazarene understood his destiny, from the moment of his teaching in the temple at age 12, on the occasion of his baptism by John the Baptist, to the last, private moments in the Garden of Gethsemane. His life was one of pure sacrifice, complete and unparalleled surrender. The writings of Djwhal Khul offer the view that Jesus' life was one of progressively improving and evolving degrees of self-mastery. Even as he gasped his last breath on the cross, his level of mastery was achieving the zenith of human existence and potential, as painfully he renounced and relinquished any remnants of attachment to his gross human form. It was at that moment - death for the stoic, the beginning of new, true life for the pietistic - that Jesus achieved the highest degree of trans-human, conscious mastery – *Mahasamadhi*,[92] the first step toward full oneness with a great being's subtle form of light and spirit. A form fully liberated from the conditions of nature and average human existence, a form that doesn't gain weight, doesn't require physical sustenance or sleep, doesn't age, yet containing endless energy and aliveness. Such describes the form, or vehicle, of 'ascended' Masters.

It could be concluded, then, that it has been in this form through which Jesus has appeared since His ascension, casting a new light on the gospel story of the supper at Emmaus and similar tales. We can also now look at His appearance at Fatima in a new light. It wasn't just a spiritually projected image Lucia was seeing in 1917, or whom she heard in 1927. It was Him!

---

[92] Literally, "great resolution." Sanskrit in origin, the term is used in reference to describe the master yogi's conscious shedding of the physical human form. The root word is samadhi, which refers to the practicing yogi's attainment of full conscious unity with the Absolute, a.k.a. - the Self, the Soul, God, etc., which is the goal of yogic practice. Though viewed by the layman as death, for the master yogi, who omnisciently knows the hour of his passing beforehand, Mahasamadhi marks the final meditation, the permanent communion & merging with the conscious essence of his soul, of the Absolute.

Chapter Six

JESUS ON THE MAIN LINE

> "In Nicaragua, quite a stir was caused when people stated they had met Jesus. Some of them claimed to have been healed of illnesses. In several Nicaraguan news publications, Rosalia, a market stall holder, gave an account of her experience: one day while she was at work on her stall a man came up to her and introduced himself with the words:
>
> "You wished to meet me. Here I am. My name is Jesus."
>
> The man went home with her where he cured her sick child. Another stall holder recounted how Jesus had visited her home and from that moment on her three alcoholic sons were cured of their addiction."
>
> Source: Trouw (Netherlands)[93]

One of the most intriguing aspects of researching for this book was the surprising number of testimonies attributed to the apparent ongoing antics of Jesus. There are so many such tales offered by a variety of sources and authors that even the fiercest skeptic is likely to succumb to their magic. One can really glean a sense of the enormous amount of compassionate, caring, and, when appropriate, mischievous love the man had - *and has*. When adding a tally of all the contemporary reported incidents of his physical materialization, one gets the impression that he is quite an accessible fellow.

Perhaps accessible is an understatement. I found the above referenced story of the Nicaraguan market stall keepers both hilarious and inspiring. In a manner similar to when he made himself known to the unassuming men who became his Apostles nearly two thousand years ago, Jesus just walked up to

---

[93] As reprinted in Share International magazine, June 1992.

these 20th century women, introduced himself, then tagged along home with them to heal their children. Can it be any simpler?

All four of the Gospels reference Jesus' post-death manifestations, with Luke and John offering the most extensive descriptions. While there is much debate over the historical accuracy and authorship of the Gospels, for argument's sake readers are asked to consider the prevailing interpretations widely maintained by the world's Christian population.

In Luke, we find the extended story of two unspecified disciples who were walking along the road to Emmaus, discussing and debating over all the events of Jesus' arrest, crucifixion, etc. I had heard this scripture read one Sunday after Easter during Catholic mass. I was both delighted and enthralled at how it readily paralleled many of the tales of encounters with Jesus, Maitreya, angels and other Masters as reported in Share International and other venues, such as the account featured on the opening page of this chapter. I recall contemplating the notion that "He never left! He did it then and He's doing it now." I wondered how many of those gathered in the church that day really knew just how 'real' the story could plausibly be. For all anyone knew, Jesus could have been sitting in the pew next to any of us.

Luke explains how Jesus himself, probably in another guise, drew near and began walking with the two men, though they didn't recognize him. Jesus then inquired: "What are these words of sadness you exchange?" Surprised, the two retorted by questioning why the stranger could have been so out of the loop.

"Are you the only stranger in Jerusalem who doesn't know what things have transpired around here?" Jesus, no doubt amused by the effectiveness of his disguise, replied, teasingly: "What things?"

After the two recounted the entire saga, the disguised Jesus said: "Come, come, now - Were not all these things foretold in the scriptures?" Jesus then pointed out every scriptural passage that referred to him and what had occurred. Impressed with the degree of knowledge and understanding this stranger seemed to possess, the two invited him to join them for dinner upon their arrival in Emmaus. It was there, as Jesus himself broke the dinner bread, that he finally revealed who he really was, and then, as the story is recounted, *vanished into thin air*!

The two then ran to join and tell Peter and the rest of the Apostles, who, according to scripture, had already heard a similar account from Mary Magdalene. Despite these corroborating accounts, the Senior Apostles yet remained skeptical. (Yes, even the Apostles themselves harbored doubt as to the credibility of such things!) However, while the debate grew more heated,

Jesus appeared before his astonished students at that instant. He admonished his old friends for not believing it was really He, and resorted to displaying his crucifixion wounds to convince them.

A week later, according to St. John's version of the story, the Apostle Thomas arrived, was told the story, and responded by refusing to believe the stories until he saw and touched the wounds for himself. Shortly thereafter, Jesus appeared once more, and invited Thomas to examine the wounds. Upon doing so, the astonished Thomas only then believed.

In Luke's version, we are told that, as if to further prove he is really with them, Jesus asks if they have anything to eat, and is subsequently served broiled fish and honeycomb. Luke's rendition seems to offer a more humanistic interpretation of Jesus, wherein one can almost begin to detect the personality trait of a good-natured person who is no doubt experiencing sheer delight in the whole situation. While playfully toying with the incredulity and seriousness of his apostolic friends, He simultaneously provides an advanced teaching in a manner as had Buddha, Krishna, or other great teachers of preceding ages.

St. John offers an appendage to the above story, continuing where Luke's version leaves off, informing us how "Jesus manifested himself again at the sea of Tiberias." He describes how several of the Apostles had gone on an all-night fishing excursion, but had caught nothing by the time dawn approached. As they closed up shop and rowed their boats homeward, to their surprise Jesus was then seen standing on the shore. After Jesus instructs them to cast their net once more, the reluctant, despondent Apostles comply, then reel back the net. To their astonishment, they find the net heavy and miraculously overflowing with fish. After hauling in their unexpected bounty, the Apostles then go ashore to greet and have breakfast with Jesus. Still astonished by yet another experience of his posthumous presence, some dare not speak for fear of being scolded again for doubting. St. John then reminds the reader that "This is now the third time that Jesus appeared to the disciples after he had risen from the dead."

John concludes his gospel with this cryptic assertion: "There are, however, *many* other things that Jesus did; but if every one of these should be written, not even the world itself, I think, could hold the books that would have to be written."

Behold, I am with you all days..."

In my office/studio I have an assortment of photographs and icons of Saints, Siddhas, great beings and deities from a variety of religious traditions. Among them, I have a copy of what is alleged to be an actual *photograph* of Jesus.

In the late seventies, two of my brothers had returned home after a lengthy stay in Texas. During that time, they shared the story of an extraordinary photograph they saw in the home of a teacher with whom they studied. It was purported to have been an actual image of Jesus. I first saw this remarkable photo in the background of a snapshot they'd brought back, and was instantly awestruck by its visual potency, its potential authenticity, and, most of all, the extraordinary legend behind it.

The story goes that at some time during the early part of the 20th century, a group of Christian missionaries had set up an establishment in a remote South American village. The native people, having never heard of Jesus, took some time to embrace the message and claims of the missionaries. They were, however, sufficiently open-minded as many of the stories were reminiscent of similar legends extant in their own culture.

After some time had passed, the natives began to inquire. "Where is this Jesus?" they would ask. "You say he is with us all the time but we never see him. When can we see him?"

In their efforts to appease such confrontation, the missionaries simply responded, "If you really want to see Jesus, you must pray very hard. If you truly believe, he will come." Little did the missionaries realize with whom they were dealing, for the natives had a much greater degree of faith than had been assumed by their foreign, would-be redeemers. As a result, a vigil was begun, and for weeks on end, prayers were said without cease in the little chapel. Day and night, 24 hours a day, the villagers would take turns, praying in shifts, wholeheartedly believing in what they had been told.

Soon, word had spread to other villages in the area of the extraordinary vigil being kept in anticipation of the arrival of Jesus. Many came from all around to see for themselves, and soon word caught the attention of a photographer from a prominent magazine that was doing a shoot in the region. It is said that, shortly after the photographer arrived, and to the astonishment of the missionaries, Jesus did indeed then appear. The photographer was able to take the shot, and the image has circulated ever since.

Once having heard this tale, I was smitten with the desire to obtain a copy of the photo. Having seen the image in the snapshot, I had an idea of its extraordinary power. If, in fact, it was genuine, I had to have a copy - a larger copy. My recollection of the image would haunt me for several years to follow. Up until then, the only image of Jesus of which I was aware that came remotely close to a photograph was that of the Shroud of Turin, the authenticity of which continues to be a subject of debate.

For years afterwards, I occasionally shared the legend of the South American missionaries with many friends. Most had never heard the story, nor were they able to tell me where I might find a copy of the photo. Then, while I was studying with Swami Muktananda's in his upstate New York ashram in 1981, I did manage to meet someone who had heard the story, and, in fact, informed me he had a copy of the very picture back home "up North." Though he was a stranger, I asked if he'd mind sending me a copy, to which he replied "Sure." I gave him my address, and added "Or, you could send it here (to the Ashram)."

I then went back to the Ashram kitchen to do some *seva*, which is a slotted time of selfless, volunteer service, which all ashram guests are asked to contribute for a reasonable period of time each day. In an Ashram, everybody pitches in. The idea is to take the lessons of community effort, team cooperation and, above all, an unconditional giving of self, back to one's life upon leaving the ashram.

On that particular day, I had been bussing tables and refreshing dish-drop stations with empty bus pans. While performing this seva, I'd mentioned to a few friends about having met this fellow who was to send me the legendary photo of Jesus. As I continued tending to my chores, I stopped suddenly at one point and did a double take when I saw a five by seven-inch copy of the very photograph lying in the bottom of a bus pan. Shaken, I was astonished at what I was seeing. Was this a coincidence? Did someone overhear me? Did one of my friends place this there? That didn't seem possible as the timing was much too fast unless someone just happened to have one with them. Or, was it some sort of small miracle? I asked my supervisor, Bhimi, if the photo belonged to anyone. Bhimi glanced at it, saw it was in a bus pan, and told me to help myself as it was assumed to be discarded trash. I could not believe my good fortune. Curiously, I never did receive anything in the mail from the stranger I'd met. In fact, I never saw him again. I've treasured the photo ever since.

It is natural to question the validity of the South American story of Jesus' appearance, but it does lend plausibility to the Nairobi, 1988 story. And why not? Did Jesus himself not say, after his resurrection, when some doubted the reality of his living form before them:

> 'All power in heaven and on earth has been given to me....
> Behold, I am with you all days, even unto the consummation of the world.'[94]

[94] (Mark 28: 18)

Sister Anna

In the mid 1990s, European media, including broadcasts on Italian and French TV, reported on a press conference held in Rome at the behest of an African Archbishop Emmanuel Milingo. Milingo introduced the Kenyan nun Sister Anna Hadija Ali, who made the remarkable claim of having had weekly meetings with Jesus on every Thursday since the occasion of the first such visit in August of 1987. On each Wednesday prior, it was explained, Sister Ali's face would begin to swell and inflict excruciating pain for her, culminating with her weeping tears of blood! It is an atypical case of Stigmata, but Sister Ali substantiated her story by then offering as evidence of her encounters two photographs of Jesus that were said to have been taken in 1987 and, one of which, taken in 1988, also weeps tears of blood itself! Doctors have testified that her experience is an "absolutely inexplicable phenomenon from the scientific and human point of view." One physician testified that, during the stigmata, Ali seems to exude what he termed an "extraordinary aroma of freshness," which was referred to as "the perfume of the Christ."[95]

The South American photo of Jesus found in a bus pan by the author

What particularly moved me was seeing just one of the two photographs. Without question, I immediately saw the same face, though with a slightly differing pose, as the person in the South American Jesus photo I'd found in Muktananda's ashram seven years earlier. At the moment of first seeing Sister Ali's Jesus photos on the Internet[96] I was stunned. "Oh my God!" I thought. I promptly turned to the photo in my office, and said aloud: "It *is* You!" While the thought occurred to me that Sister Ali was somehow capitalizing on use of the South American photo and claiming it as her own, the medical testimony surrounding her stigmata served in her defense. Any glimmer of doubt that I might have had in my own Jesus photo began to rapidly melt.

[95] Source: Share International magazine, April, 1994
[96] Internet users may find the Sister Ali's photo at http://web.frontier.net/Apparitions/da.jesus.gif

Ali experienced her first such encounter with Jesus at 3:00 AM on September 8th, 1987. As she describes the situation:

> "This time I was not asleep and I was not praying. I just had my eyes closed in the dark. I heard a pitiful voice near my ear saying: "Be attentive to what I am telling you." I opened my eyes and from outside I saw a ray of light; through it I saw the Lord kneeling on the right side of my bed."

The verbal appeal then allegedly offered by Jesus - the first of nearly 200 since that night - is quite reminiscent of the sort of rhetoric ascribed to the Marian apparition messages of the past 100 plus years, with references most affiliated with Catholicism.

With poignant overtures of warning, requests for prayer, contrition, and heeding of the countless number of given signs, miracles and messages, presented is nothing less than an impassioned plea for acknowledgement of the reality of His presence, of the reality of the existence of God, and dire need for humanity to get its collective act together.

For example, in one of the sterner remarks, Jesus is quoted as having said:

> "I have seen My Eternal Father looking severely at the earth and saying these words: "In a few minutes I will destroy this earth of mire, blasphemy, scandal, infamy, sacrilege and insults. I will destroy everything if the world is not converted."

But such comments are assuaged by reassurances such as:

> "Tell mankind to abandon evil ways. Devote yourself to prayer, meditate in the silence of recollection and listen to the voice of My mercy and love. I want to save you."

> "My mercy is immense. I ask for faith, intimacy and confidence. My daughter, humanity does not want to listen to Me."

> "My Mother has given continuous messages. These are not now simple words but rather an afflicted and painful appeal to all mankind."

In June, 1988 - curiously enough on the day Catholics celebrate the Feast of Corpus Christi[97] which recalls "the Real Presence of the body of Jesus Christ in the Eucharist" - Jesus came again to Sr. Ali, crying, as she described,

---

[97] Lit. - 'body of Christ.' With roots as far back as the 3rd century AD, the Feast Day became a papally sanctioned, annual practice by the 12th Century. The occasion is celebrated to this day with the saying of Mass featuring hymns and theological text as composed by St. Thomas Aquinas (d. 1274) as requested by Pope Uban IV. Catholic legend holds that so compelling was the mastery and poetic beauty with which Aquinas expressed his doctrinal perspective on 'the Real Presence', that the figure of Jesus allegedly descended from a crucifix and declared to him "Thou has written well of me, Thomas."

"tears of blood." Ali explains:

"[He] came with His own light. He was enveloped in light, which was of the same hue of the sky when it is deeply blue. His presence illuminated the whole room. He wore a [blood red] tunic, with wide sleeves. He has shining dark hair. He gave me a message and, on His instruction, I started writing down the messages…"

On the subject of the Eucharistic in particular, Jesus explained:

"My Divinity is present in the Consecrated Host, in every small particle. Day and night I have abundant blessings in My Tabernacle, ready to give to anyone."

But some of the more interesting quotes address the many, worldwide sightings and encounters with Jesus, offering - if true - what amounts to a first-hand explanation of not only current apparitions, but those post-crucifixion occasions as recorded in the Gospels.

"My daughter, after so many messages with painful events, they [humanity] remain indifferent as if it were an idle call. What more can I do for mankind? All are silent, paralyzed as if the Almighty does not exist. I want My Voice full of affliction to fly to the very ends of the earth, saying over and over again: Be attentive…the time to settle accounts has arrived! Let them all know … everyone, prepare yourself, wake up from your apathetic slumber! Let them know clearly that 'blessed are only those who listen to My Voice and prepare themselves.'"

"I make this known to souls. I give many communications so that My messages and those of My Holy Mother will defeat the resistance of mankind to repeated calls."

"What I now make known to [humanity] is My sacred mystery. I stay in the glorious triumphs in heaven while still on earth. In this mystery I give Myself not to mankind as a whole, but to each and every individual in a simple way."

"I love mankind and I make myself visible in order to give my warnings of mercy."

"Listen to me. I am above this earth. I allow myself to be seen after many warnings."

"I make myself visible in order to bring back souls."

"Many do not listen to me because they do not believe in my reality."

Many, like Sister Ali, have offered their own alleged messages or evidence of intimate contact with Jesus in recent years, posing further difficulty and confusion for those sincerely interested. Books such as *He walks with me: True encounters with Jesus*, by Brad and Sherry Steiger, Betty J. Eadie's remarkable *Embraced by the Light*, and *I am with you always* by psychotherapist G. Scott Sparrow offer hundreds of documented cases which feature Jesus with a persona and approach varied and seemingly relative for those to whom he appears.

Jesus is said, for example, to have saved people from auto accidents, death by poison, heart attacks, and other impending afflictions. Some of the tales claim he simply appeared, or offered words of reassurance.

Share International magazine offered an incredible story as originally published in a Japanese edition of *Newsweek*, which highlighted such an experience by no less than the immutable South Korean President, Kim Dae Jung. Harassed, imprisoned, exiled, hunted and almost killed numerous times for his tireless efforts for Korean democratization, in 1973 Kim was taken from a Tokyo hotel room by six men and brought aboard a ship which then sailed to sea. Once having arrived miles away from shore, Kim's captors tied him to a board, attached to which was a concrete anchor. Kim says that at the moment he realized his life was about to end, he claims to have then seen "Christ standing near me." Reaching out and grabbing the sleeve of His garment, he pleaded: "Please save my life! I have so much work to do for the people of Korea!" Without explanation, Kim's captors abruptly pulled the board back on deck, and untied him. Kim's life was spared.[98]

Others have claimed that Jesus has visited them in the aftermath of earthquakes, by their hospital beds, or in dreams. But many of the stories purported to have been visits from Jesus aren't quite as 'heavy' as the above stories, and instead suggest, as demonstrated previously, that Jesus seems to have quite a sense of humor.

Radio talk shows, magazines and newspapers from across the globe have routinely offered tales of Jesus, an angel, or other unknown visitor who would appear then mysteriously vanish. There have been many accounts, for example, in Newspapers from New Zealand, Holland, the United States and elsewhere, of someone picking up a hitchhiker[99] who, shortly thereafter, would say something like "Christ is in the world!" or "You know, Christ is coming back soon, don't you?" and then promptly vanish[100] whether from the passenger seat of a moving car or from the back of a motorcycle. In one such instance, when reported to the police, a highway patrol officer remarked

---
[98] Source: Share International magazine, April 1998.
[99] Source: Share International magazine, issues: 1991 - Jan., April, July; '92 - Oct.; '93 - Sept., Oct.; '94 - April, May.
[100] Source: Share International Magazine, May 1994.

"That's the 16th time I've heard that story." When one woman realized that she was speaking to Jesus, she asked him "How can I reach you again?" to which he replied "I'm in the phone book!"[101]

The stories are countless, having been published or recounted in some form throughout this century, but particularly in the past twenty years.[102]

Many of us, when reading such fascinating tales, may ask, "Why doesn't anything like that happen to me?" But the truth of the matter is that it's more likely that such accounts confirm incidents we ourselves may have had but were too aloof or modest when it came to talking about it. The sharing of such stories might, for example, be typically preceded by - "You may think I'm nuts or something, but...."

Nonetheless, I think my own obsession with the topic stems from not only marveling at such tales since childhood, but primarily due to a significant number of incidents of unexplained phenomena that have transpired in my own life. All routine visions and heightening of psychic sensory perception through the practice of meditation aside, there are some things that remain a mystery, and others that seem to convey some import.

For example, I've already discussed the repeated dreams of meeting Jesus that I had as a child, which I have always resolved with several hypothetical explanations. First, due to my personal acceptance of the reincarnation theory, I have pondered the possibility of having met him in a previous life, an encounter of such profound impression that my collective subconscious memory would most certainly continue to recall it. Second, it may be that my psychological and emotional desire has been so strong for such an event to occur, that my mind conjured up an incredible looking version of the story and replayed it during sleep. Third, I have always held an earnest wish, desire, prayer and/or belief that the dream was somehow prophetic, that I would meet Jesus in the future, either while living or most certainly in the hereafter. Based on some of the stories I've been reading, I realize it could have already happened. In fact, there was one mystifying, unforgettable incident that occurred when I was between the ages of three and five that I've never been able to shake from memory.

At some point when I was old enough and able, I discovered my ability to perform the daredevil stunt of climbing onto the edge of my crib, brace myself against the wall, and then step atop the crib's headboard. Having mastered the simple climb, I then discovered how to reach around the wall

---

[101] Source: Share International Magazine, December 1993.
[102] Curious readers are again invited to check out the website of Share International (www.shareintl.org) and assorted link sites, where they will find a virtual library of miracle reports, book titles on these topics, etc., as the overwhelming abundance of them are far too numerous to reprint here.

from my crib, and grab onto the moulding atop our closet door. With my grip firmly affixed to the closet moulding, I'd then release my feet from the crib, and swing in and out of the closet. Then I'd let go, jump to the floor, climb back in the crib and do it all over again. My poor brother James used to petition me to stop before I got us both into trouble with our parents, who thought we were both long asleep.

On one such night, as I clung to the moulding and swung in and out of the open closet, I was suddenly surprised and completely alarmed by the sight of a pair of deep, dark, penetrating eyes glaring right back at me from a distance of no less than a foot away from my face from within the dark closet. So startled was I that I shrieked loudly, lost my grip, and fell to the floor with a loud thud. My brother got up to ask what was wrong and before he could get to the light switch our parents had already arrived on the scene. In complete fright, I told them of the eyes I'd seen, but they assured me after checking for themselves that there was no one or thing in the closet at all. "It must have been the light reflecting on the hangers," they offered. I looked again to see if one of my other brothers had somehow played a trick, but they were in their own room down the hall. Needless to say, I don't think I ever swung on the moulding again.

As time passed, I tried to figure out what exactly had happened. What remained most unexplainable was the position of the closet, its interior and specifically the area where I saw the eyes. There was no possible way anything could have reflected. The only window in the room was to the right side of the closet's protruding wall, and the door to the room, which had been closed at the time, was on the opposite end of the room. Nothing faced that closet door opening but the darkest corner of the room across from my brother's bed.

No one seemed to ever believe this story and always tried to dismiss it somehow or another, but eyes I did see, and can still see with ease when I think about it. It would not be until I first saw the South American Jesus photo in the late 1970s that I began to entertain stauncher notions. And it probably was the cause of my initial receptivity to similar accounts in Share International Magazine, to which I was introduced just a few years afterward.

It took me quite a long time to recover from the initial incident, and I know I didn't sleep well for the longest time. For years I wondered whose eyes they might have been. Given the limited extent of my understanding of the supernatural at that tender age, there was only a marginal selection of possibilities from which to choose. Had the eyes belonged to Jesus? An angel? One of the saints? I reasoned that it certainly couldn't have been a ghost - the visage was way too powerful for that. No, the eyes clearly belonged to someone of significance. For as frightened as I was, there was a sense of harmlessness about the incident, that somehow it was communicated to me through those eyes that no harm was intended.

The experience was difficult to speak of, and though I kept it private for a long time, there had been at least one person in my youth who *did* listen and allow me the benefit of the doubt. I found that person in my fiercely devout Irish-Catholic grandmother.

Born Nora McCarthy in Newcastle West, County Limerick, Ireland, and having emigrated to America while in her teens, Nora's life of unswerving faith, devotion, and uncompromising fear of God served as the foundation upon which her future family would be raised in her new American home. Always clutching a rosary and maintaining a murmur of prayer on her lips, she was a beacon and direct inspiration to four subsequent generations of descendants.

Well respected by both the Protestant and Catholic Irish who'd also emigrated and settled in the Philadelphia neighborhood in which we'd been raised, Nora had earned a reputation for being one of the best examples of true, Christian living in her day. Always charitable, generous, welcoming, and kind, Nora would liberally share her simple provisions, offer shelter to a neighbor's visiting relative, or simply lend an ear to any 'poor soul' needing consolation.

When neighbors, friends, and relatives had a family member on their deathbed, it was not the local parish priest they'd call, but my grandmother instead. Toting along a portable *Extreme Unction* kit for the administering of last rites, Nora would light candles aside the bed of the dying, anoint them with holy water, and lead the gathered family members in the saying of the rosary.

For all intents and purposes, to those people, Nora might as well have been a priest. People recognized in her an inherent depth of reverence that few others possessed. Today, it remains that this sort of deep-seated spirituality inherently possessed by my grandmother is what people seek and desire, both in their clergy or in themselves. It's no doubt a characteristic we could all use.

Nora simply practiced a perfect Catholicism. Through such examples as cited above and by her attendance of Catholic mass every morning while physically able, she transformed the practice into a yoga, that is, a lifestyle founded on daily, conscious, spiritually focused activity. Everything she did, from making the beds to chopping firewood, was offered to God or accompanied by prayer.

Her lifestyle was completely harmonious with the true Christian canon. As such, as well as in accord with the precepts of yoga, Nora attained the goal of her practice. Her reward was not external, material, or monetary, but rather she was blessed with a life in constant communion with God, complete with visions and dreams of her chosen deities. There was a quality about her that instantly attracted the respect of all who met her. In later years, even school friends of family members would affectionately adopt her as a second grandmother, dropping by to pay a visit as they would a member of their own family.

Between caring for the needy, visiting the sick, or volunteering for church fundraisers, Nora raised four children on her own by meager means after the sudden death of her husband, Patrick Delargey, in 1933.

Long before the era of American desegregation and the civil rights movement, Nora and 'Paddy' regularly welcomed into their home the African-American coworkers Paddy had befriended, and for whom Nora would daily prepare a generous lunch. This non-egoic, simple gesture, in a time and place when it wasn't a readily acceptable practice, was demonstrative of their non-prejudicial manner of thinking, consistent with the Christian teaching of "Love thy neighbor." By doing so, Nora and Paddy acknowledged and lived by the codex of true, human equality and brotherhood.

Respectable yet boisterous, Paddy would return home from a hard day's work in jovial spirits, playfully endeavoring to elicit a kiss from his bashful and modest young wife, who would always dismiss such attempts by exhorting him instead to wash his hands for Dinner. After his death, each night before retiring Nora would take her bedside picture of Paddy and lovingly kiss it, saying "That's for all the times I never let you kiss me."

For our family, our 'Mom-mom' would always be regarded as the exemplary, saintly, family matriarch. Not a week went by when one of her children or grandchildren wouldn't call and ask her to say a prayer for one thing or another. It could have been a request for a prayer to her self-described 'best friend' - Saint Anthony of Padua - to aid in finding something that was lost; or, to any icon of the Catholic pantheon to pass a school exam, succeed in a medical operation, or for one of our CYO football teams to be victorious. All of us felt as if we had lost our closest, reliable connection with God and His cohorts in December of 1984, when Nora passed away at the age of 91.

My grandmother had been one of the few people I ever told about the eyes in the closet incident. Her sole, compassionate acceptance of my harrowing story was probably the source of my ultimately healthy ability to reason and attempt to resolve the mystery of the incident. However, one thing that enabled her to offer such support and compassion and which indeed contributed to my sanity, transforming the initial fear into wonder, was the fact that she, too, had an unexplainable experience of the supernatural in her own youth while still in Ireland. While many dismissed or refuted our respective tales, both of us believed that our experiences, though confusing and relatively inexplicable even to us, were genuine.

In 1978, while in my senior year of Catholic high school, I interviewed my Grandmother for a religion class project. In those days prior to video cameras, my best friend and I went armed with a 35 mm camera and a cassette tape recorder to ask questions of her as a living witness to the events of the first half of the twentieth century, and as an 'old school Catholic' witnessing the modernization of the Church.

She shared with us the tale of a remarkable occurrence that happened to her in 1905, while sitting on the front step of her home Knockane Road in Newcastle West, County Limerick. Here, from that cassette recording, is Nora's tale as described in her own words.

"I remember sitting on the step, ...and I told this to many people...there was a stone outside of the house... and I sat on that stone and I used to look up to heaven, and I'd be talking to God. And this night, a man came and tapped me on the shoulder...Now this is as true as I'm lying in this bed [she was sick in bed at the time of the interview] ...and there weren't a soul on the street, not a soul around, I was by myself. My father and mother were out. The man tapped me on the shoulder, and he said to me, "Do you know who I am?" I said "No." "I'm God," he said, and he'd pat my shoulder and patted me [on the head] and disappeared.

'And that's the truth! And he had the beard on him and was dressed in clothes like...like a regular man. I don't know where that man come from, he couldn't come from nowhere because there were fields around there and he couldn't jump the field and there wasn't a soul on the street and he came right out of nowhere...tapped me on the shoulder."

Though on a cassette recording, one can detect a shift in her voice intonations when, as she uttered that last phrase, you could tell that Nora was recalling the incident as if it were recurring at that very moment. I recall when I was with her at the time, her awareness became suddenly self-absorbed, as she paused, looked up and out the window, then uttered: "tapped me on the shoulder." You could tell she wasn't making it up, and she was probably used to people not believing her, responding with pat answers, scoffing outright or perhaps politely changing the subject. But quickly she gathered herself from her momentary reflection, and continued.

"That's as true as I'm here! I told my mother about it, but she said 'Aw...you slept. You must have dreamt it.' She wouldn't believe me but it's true. I was only a little girl around seven years old. But I always talked up to God when I was a kid."

This and other marvelous stories that my grandmother shared always invoked wonder and it was her tales that firmly entrenched in me a belief in all things mystical and in the life hereafter. Just knowing that someone else, let alone the revered matriarch of our clan, had also experienced such things created an opening of normality for me, and no doubt sowed the seeds of my quest for understanding that continues to this day.

The mystery of the 'eyes in the closet', however, remained definitively unsolved. By 1978, though having by then seen the South American Jesus photo, I was still uncertain of their owner's identity. It was around then that I saw another photograph which offered a potentially alternative explanation.

On the cover of a book authored by a renowned, Southern Indian Yogi was a photo of the book's author featuring deep, penetrating eyes which bore a chilling similarity to the eyes I had seen in the closet. The book was "Play of Consciousness," and its author was Swami Muktananda. Hence my life-transforming saga with him began.

But in the interim years since having eventually met Muktananda, and entertaining the possibility that the eyes I'd seen had belonged to him (Countless practitioners of Muktananda's Siddha Yoga offered similar stories of their own), I left the door open with regard to the true identity of the eye's owners. Having since seen the Nairobi Photo of Maitreya, and the Sister Ali photos of Jesus, I remained open to other possibilities. Somehow, none of these 'answers' seemed to be just right.

I had a curious experience of Jesus which occurred just after Easter, 1999. As an alternative to giving just chocolate, jelly beans, and stuffed bunnies to my two-and-a-half-year-old daughter as the traditional Easter thing to do, I had the desire to do something non-secular so as to begin exposing her to what Easter was really all about.

Since she was having monster nightmares at the time, I purchased a small plastic statue of Saint Michael the archangel - the demon slayer - along with a laminated flashcard of a guardian angel protecting two children; a jigsaw puzzle of Jesus greeting three young multi-ethnic children in a meadow; and a similar flashcard of Jesus bearing his 'Sacred Heart.'

I assured my daughter that now that Saint Michael was in the room, no monsters would get near her since he and our dog Pooki were both in the house. I also comforted her with stories of guardian angels and Jesus as 'always being around, and in your dreams to protect you.' This was reinforced by my suggestion that she keep the laminated cards with her in bed. She would hold and study the pictures carefully, asking me questions about them. Indeed, the nightmares eventually stopped.

But on one such night, my daughter's frightened crying awakened me. When I went to her room, she first told me that a monster had been in her room, and then that a lion had been trying to hurt her. Trying to calm her down, I kept only the nightlight on, and gave her the Jesus flashcard. "Here you go," I said, "Jesus will look after you." She took the card, and I took notice that she needed a diaper change. Due to the dim light, she then said insistently "I can't see his eyes, I need to see his eyes!" which she repeated several times.

I turned on a small lamp to fulfill her request, which I thought was quite an interesting one for a two-year-old. For one thing I had learned through Muktananda, and which is often repeated by other saints and enlightened teachers, is that the eyes of a Saint or agent of God are one of the means by which they bestow grace, blessings, power, or initiation on the devout. I had no problem with my daughter's request to see the eyes. In fact, if anything, I probably assumed Jesus wanted to calm her down Himself in this way, and who was I to argue with the manner in which He handled it!

Despite my assurances, my daughter refused to sleep alone for the remainder of that night, so I decided to lay down beside her until she fell asleep. After settling in, I was kept awake by her fingering and flexing of the laminated Jesus card, which she continued to study earnestly via window light. I suggested she put it under her pillow, and that way Jesus would be in her dreams, which she did. Shortly thereafter, I felt movement under my own pillow. I lifted my head, and, turning to see what was going on, found that my girl was putting the Jesus card under my pillow. Thinking it was such a sweet gesture, I thanked her and kissed her on the forehead. It was then, as I closed my eyes while putting my head back on my pillow, that I saw, uninvoked and born of its own volition, a crisp and very real vision of Jesus wearing the crown of thorns.

In dark hues and bearing deep, penetrating, possibly blood-soaked eyes which gazed directly at me, I saw only the head and face of a beleaguered, sorrowful, and admonishing Jesus against a background of soft, neutral, tones, which gave me the impression of classic renditions of Veronica's veil. It then disappeared just as fast as it came. Deeply moved, I lay awake for some time groping for an understanding. What elicited such a vision? Was it addressing karmic retribution for some past transgressions (i.e. sins), or was it some sort of subconscious reminder of the great suffering Jesus had handled, which, when compared to my own, made my whining and complaining seem utterly meager? What was equally profound was the fact that the eyes of this vision evoked an immediate comparison to those I had seen in the closet so long ago, most likely jogged to memory by my daughter's expressed need to see the eyes.

Such experiences only fueled my curiosity in waking hours. Did anyone else have these sorts of things happen to them? Through the years, I had heard many stories of people's encounters with saints, yogis, angels, etc., which I found plausible due to my own experiences. But rarely did I recall having anyone personally tell me of encounters with Jesus, specifically. When I eventually set down to work or the purposes of this book, I endeavored to *personally* speak or interview anyone who might have had such an encounter.

It didn't take long very long at all to find many people who were willing to openly share some story that they felt held intrinsically personal meaning, even if it had only been a dream or visionary experience. But for that type of story, I initially didn't have too far to look to get started.

While reviewing the taped interview with my grandmother with the specific intent of relaying her previously mentioned account, I listened nostalgically to the rest of the tape, hearing again that wonderful, Irish-brogue accentuated voice for the first time in more than ten years. Much to my surprise, towards the end of the interview, 'Mom-mom' shared a dream that was profoundly moving for her.

She prefaced by explaining that across the street from her American row-home, there had lived a certain neighbor - a young mother of nine children. Having married at age 13, the young woman's husband and she enjoyed a relatively healthy marriage for several years. Then, apparently, the woman began to acknowledge the affections of her husband's best friend, resulting in an extramarital affair. This must have gone on for some time, until one day when the woman went to Nora distraught over the fact that her husband had abandoned her, and was nowhere to be found.

Crying uncontrollably, the woman confided in Nora the truth of her errant behavior, and that she had not attended Catholic Mass in five years, which was not something you told Mom-mom unless you were prepared for the inevitable. In a manner both typically Irish and inimitably her own, Nora lovingly scolded the woman as if she were her own child, saying:

> "You get yourself over to [the church] and show yourself to the priest, and get confession and communion, and go to mass each

morning and pray until your husband will come back. And lock your back and front [doors] and don't let that [other] man near the house."

The young mother took the advice, and went to mass penitently each morning. In the meantime, Mom-mom pulled a few strings of her own. She explained how she herself had prayed, on behalf of her neighbor's plight, a nine-hour novena to the Infant of Prague, saying: "I prayed every hour on the hour, and on the ninth hour I got my prayer answered."

My grandmother swears that at the hour of the ninth novena, the young mother received a telegram from California inquiring if she was the wife of a man who was being held in custody for vagrancy. She wrote back, and a few days later the man was returned home. The couple converted their ways, began attending Catholic mass regularly, and both he and his wife lived a fine and proper life thereafter.

"But that night that I brought her back to church," Nora related, "I dreamt. I was out on the top step, and the sky opened, and our Lord and the Blessed Mother and Saint Joseph appeared with their arms stretched out to me. And I screamed... I hollered 'People, people - come and see!' and I woke up hollering 'people.'"

While on a roll, in the interview Nora went immediately into another, similar tale, though it was not clear whether this experience was a dream or not. With my grandmother, you just never knew.

"Another time I was going down the street, and I looked up and the sky opened, and the Blessed Mother, [along with] her mother, Saint Anne, walked down [a set of] steps, turned the knob on the door [of her home] and walked in. I saw the two of them walking, in the sky. Now that's as true as I'm here, I'm telling you."

I had not recalled these tales at first, but the more I thought about it, I vaguely recall them being quintessential 'Mom-mom' stories of my youth. When I was once explaining how parts of this book dealt with people's personal experiences of the miraculous and supernatural, a young Muslim friend with whom I was acquainted responded by telling me about a legend in Islam which claims that, on one day out of each year, God selects one deserving person to whom He will reveal heaven. My friend was uncertain of the specific source of the legend, but claimed that a similar tale has been passed down in his own family about one of his maternal grandparents, who allegedly was granted the vision one year.

Both accounts bore a remarkable resemblance to this report as published in a September, 1983 edition of Share International Magazine:

'Five hundred children from Emilia Aguinaldo elementary school on the island of Luszon, the Philippines, witnessed a vision in the sky. On the afternoon of 19 November 1982, a ten-year-old girl was sitting in the playground of the school. When she looked up at the sky, she saw three angels, Mother Mary with a baby in her arms and an old man standing next to her. Other children saw the same vision in the sky. They described the vision to a reporter in great detail: Mary was wearing a gown and a gold crown on her head; the angels had golden hair and wore long flaming gowns; one of them had a key in her hand. One teacher who had seen the vision told the reporter that she felt an awesome force making her kneel down.'

Almost everyone with whom I raised the topic of miracles had some relative story of similar lore in their own family. It was unbelievable! Whether it had been their own or that of a parent, grandparent, aunt, uncle, or cousin, someone they knew had a tale to tell.

For example, I had casually shared many of the amazing stories I'd unearthed as well as my quest to personally interview such people with a co-worker of mine. In turn, she began to share a virtual watershed of stories from her own family lore. She had so many stories that I often teased her and suggested she write a book herself.

Antonio's Dreams

My friend told me two fascinating stories which originated from her father. As a child in the Calabria region of Italy, her dad - Antonio - endured many of the hardships associated with war victims during the Italian campaign of World War II. There, he witnessed first-hand the effects of Allied bombing campaigns, which had reduced most of the buildings around his home in the village of Montauro to rubble. With his own father off serving in the military, young Antonio quickly had to learn to fend for himself. Impoverished, homeless, shoeless, and withstanding hunger for days on end, he slept many nights throughout the war in fear and isolation, wondering about his fate. On repeated occasions, Antonio often had dreams of Jesus.

In particular, he recalls one recurring dream in which he found himself helping a fallen or injured compatriot along the side of a road. While assisting, Antonio would look up and see Jesus, riding atop a donkey, slowly approaching from over a little hill off in the distance. His features became gradually more defined as he drew nearer, and when he got very close, Antonio claims, Jesus would give him the most beautiful smile he ever saw, which seemed to be accompanied by a strong sense of peace. The young boy was elated by his good fortune, filling him to the brim with joy and happiness. In the morning, despite any previous hunger or distress, Antonio awoke feeling refreshed and enlivened with a renewed sense of hope.

The image is evocative, of course, of Jesus' 'triumphant' and celebrated entry into Jerusalem on Palm Sunday, an image often associated with peace and spiritual victory. After having this dream several times, Antonio recalls the great sense of elation he felt on the day he saw a truckload of American troops pass through his town. He particularly remembers when, as the truck rolled by, an American soldier sitting at the rear of the truck gave him what he thought to be a most beautiful smile, reminding him of Jesus' smile from his dream, and which made him feel incredibly happy and hopeful. To this day, the grown man says he will never forget the smile and face of that one anonymous American soldier.

Antonio had yet another powerful dream encounter. Having eventually emigrated to America, marry and raise a family, Antonio struggled to make ends meet as many do. Beleaguered by stress, Antonio's growing uneasiness contributed to a particularly difficult period in his life when a great deal of animosity with his own paternal siblings developed. Feeling isolated and alone in his adopted homeland, Antonio's anxiety was further accentuated by a persistent unavailability of steady employment and other related problems that seemed to have no end in sight. For some interminable length of time, Antonio experienced all the heightened symptoms of severe stress - tightening of the chest, panic attacks, sleeplessness, constant worry, etc.

Then one night, He had a marvelous dream. He found himself afloat in the center of a huge body of water. No matter how much he tried, Antonio felt unable to move himself or swim to the surrounding land which, though visible, seemed unreachable. Just as he was about to give up, Antonio saw, standing on the shore and waving to catch his attention, a beautiful, solitary woman dressed in common peasant garb, whom he instantly recognized as Mary - the mother of Jesus.

Struggling to swim in her direction, Antonio recalls that Mary yelled out to him

> "Don't worry, you're going to be alright. You're not going to drown, everything will be alright."

When he awoke, Antonio explained that he 'felt saved' by the woman in the dream who was unequivocally Mary, and thereafter, the stress that had permeated his daily life markedly dissipated. Antonio tackled life from then on with a renewed vigor.

The Amazing Tales of Mickey Drake

Perhaps the most profound and colorful personal interview I'd conducted was with Mickey Drake, a youthful 76-year-old semi-retired nurse from Boulder, Colorado. Her lifelong series of incidents and visits are so amazing that at one point during the interview Mickey informed me she had been urged to send her story to Share International at the solicitation of Benjamin Creme himself.

Raised a Catholic, Mickey grew up a playful, mischievous urchin whose favorite pastime was to challenge church and school authorities - and God - in every possible manner.

"I taunted God and tested Him all the way," Mickey explained in a phone interview. "I would go to confession and lie to the priest, and tell him that I did all these awful things like stealing and lying."

Though having not really done any of these things, Mickey would receive penances that were unusually extensive.

"I [was told I had to do] a thousand 'Hail Marys' at one time. Then I'd come out and sit in the pew and I'd talk to God, and I'd say 'I'm not gonna do this, I'm not saying any penance, and what're ya gonna do? Are you gonna punish me? What're ya gonna do to me?' And every time that would happen, I would feel this tremendous love. One time I almost felt like He'd patted me on the head!"

I wish my grandmother had lived to hear that one. It's remarkable that I can say I now know two amazing women who both had the experience of God patting them on the head.

Mickey continued telling tales of how she would go in the church after dinner and light every one of the offertory candles, which are traditionally lit to represent a petition made to a chosen Christian saint, accompanied by a small, monetary donation. Afterwards, she'd challenge God again: "Well, I didn't pay for any of these - what're ya gonna do to me?"

After once discovering the location of the switch which opened the Monstrance where the Eucharist wafers were stored, Mickey removed the chalice and ate all the wafers, intentionally chewing them since that wasn't then permissible according to church law. After returning the empty chalice, she went and sat in a pew and once more said to God, "Ok, what're ya gonna do?" Once again, Mickey claims, she felt an invisible but definite sensation of being patted on the top of her head.

After some years had passed, at 19 years old Mickey succumbed to an unexplained illness and was hospitalized in critical care. With a relentless, untreatable fever of 105 that persisted for ten days, a paralyzed throat resulting in an inability to speak and accompanied by an overwhelming weakness, Mickey lapsed into a coma. She recalls being totally cognizant of the presence of a number of nursing residents and doctors who had gathered around her, working fervently to help save her.

It was while in the coma, Mickey recalls, that she had what amounted to a classic OBE - an 'out of the body experience.' She recalls witnessing herself hovering over her body, which was lying in the hospital bed surrounded by her peers. "I don't know why anybody is afraid to die," she remembers thinking, "This is wonderful, I'm free of pain!"

After multiple efforts to resuscitate her, Mickey, still hovering over herself, recalls hearing the doctor finally say, "She's gone," at which point she was officially pronounced dead. Despite the overwhelming sense of joy and freedom from suffering she had experienced while out of her body, Mickey recalled being alarmed by the finality of the doctor's edict. Filled with the same indignation and feistiness toward assertions of authority that'd irked her in her youth, Mickey wouldn't allow herself to be controlled by the decree of anything or anyone outside of herself, even in death. As the doctor asserted "She's gone," Mickey's immediate, audacious response - as she shared with me - was "You son of a bitch, I am not!" at which point she 'felt herself' zoom down back into her body.

After a three-month recovery, Mickey resumed a normal life and ultimately graduated nursing school in 1945, pursuing her career. Was Mickey's unexplained illness due to some sort of retribution, a chastisement in response to her earlier taunting of God? Or was it a blessing in disguise? Regardless, it would seem that it took no less than her illness, clinical death, and recovery to bring about a sufficiently balanced view of things that would mould her attitude for the rest of her life.

A caring, loving, and respectful demeanor has characterized Mickey's personal life and professional career. Accordingly, Mickey would exhort her fellow medical professionals to treat comatose patients with the same care, dignity, and respect as that administered to the average patient, knowing all too well that they indeed knew what was going on around them. In her own experience of helping such patients in this manner she claims to have been able to "literally feel them smile" when she spoke to them. She could sense their relief and delight that helping them was someone who understood.

Some years later while employed by a medical group in Maryland in the early 1950s, Mickey would routinely eat lunch in an outside park with a co-worker she'd befriended. On one such occasion, Mickey's friend suddenly recalled that she had an appointment for which she had failed to draw up the necessary paperwork. Excusing herself, the friend rushed back to work, leaving Mickey sitting alone to finish her lunch.

She noticed, at one point, an attractive, well-dressed man in a business suit walking towards her. She was taken by his beautiful smile and a playful twinkling in his eyes that seemed to harbor a mischievous sense of humor.

"He came over and asked if he could sit down, and I said "Sure! Sit down." The man then remarked "You know, I read palms - do you mind if I read yours?"

Curious yet fascinated, Mickey replied "Sure," and held up her hand for him. As he was holding her hand, the stranger looked into Mickey's eyes and said, "You know, you're not even supposed to be here." Surprised, Mickey recounted the story of her near-death experience to the man.

Then he pointed to another break across the 'lifeline' of her palm, and told her to expect another serious illness later in life, adding "but you'll get through that alright." Indeed, sometime in the late 1950s or early '60s, Mickey was later diagnosed with severe Rheumatoid Arthritis by a Rheumatologist in Denver, and told she would probably expect to be confined to a wheelchair within a year. Responding with that same, feisty resistance toward authority, Mickey asserted to the specialist: "Not on your life will I be in a wheelchair in a year!" "So, I went home," Mickey recalled, "and dumped all my pills in the toilet." Thereafter, Mickey changed her lifestyle, adopted a macrobiotic diet and within 3 months was running 2 miles a day. The arthritis cleared up and Mickey has been active and healthy ever since.

When the palm reader had finished, he stood up and smiled as Mickey thanked him. Then, Mickey says, "He walked away and just disappeared right in front of me."

"Suddenly" Mickey continued, "I became aware of cars going by. All the time he was there I realized there had been no sound - no cars, no nothing!"

Mickey sat dumbfounded by what she had witnessed. In the meantime, her coworker returned, and, noticing Mickey's unusual pallor, asked, "What's wrong?" Upon recounting her experience, disappearance and all, Mickey's friend simply responded by saying, "You have the weirdest things happen to you!"

Despite the fact that having already been introduced to the works of Alice Bailey and Djwhal Khul, the theosophical teacher Lucille Cedercrans,[103] her study of esoteric Buddhism while in college, and practicing meditation at a

---

[103] For more information on Lucille Cedarcrans, her publications are available through: http://www.wisdomimpressions.com/home/wihp2.html

time when such things simply were not commonly spoken of, Mickey made no connection that her experience may have been a bonafide encounter with a Master of Wisdom. It would not be until years later, after meeting Benjamin Creme, that she was told via Mr. Creme's Master that the palm reader had been none other than Jesus!

In fact, Mickey was told that on at least two other occasions she had unknowingly met Jesus again. In one instance, which took place years later while visiting her sister in Manhattan, the two women took a stroll through Washington Square Park. While walking, they stopped to watch a few men who had been playing a board game. As they stood watching, Mickey looked up at a tall man whom she suddenly noticed standing next to her. The man smiled and told Mickey that he was "from out of town," and asked if she knew the name of the game the men were playing.

"I don't know," Mickey responded, "but I think it's Mah-jongg." He smiled, thanked her, and then walked away.

Attracted by a hubbub of activity that had drawn a large crowd a short while later, Mickey and her sister walked closer to investigate. As they approached, Mickey noticed the same man to whom she had just spoken, his head sticking out high above the rest. Despite everyone else's interest in what was going on, the stranger "was looking back at us with that same smile, and I couldn't take my eyes away from him." Her sister took notice and remarked that she thought the man was trying to pick Mickey up. "Let's invite him up for coffee," said the sister, but Mickey exhorted her to stop talking, now knowing that the man was someone special. "He had those wonderful eyes, again, with the humorous look." Mickey probably dropped her jaw when she then realized, at that moment, that the man she was looking at was the same attractive, smiling fortune teller in the pin stripe suit she had seen almost 10 years prior. Shaken by this, at the moment of her recognition, once again, the man suddenly vanished.

Having been open to idea of the imminent return of the Christ since her initial exposure to Alice Bailey's writings in the late 1940s, it was easy for Mickey, from the onset, to recognize the sincerity of the claims made by Benjamin Creme, whom she first met in the 1980s. Possessing an intellectual understanding of the theory of a spiritual hierarchy comprised of a body of highly evolved Masters of Wisdom enabled her to accept the notion that her visitor was the Master Jesus. It also enabled her to accept the assertion that this was apparently being verified by one of the Masters themselves through Mr. Creme. Who better to have known than an apparent peer of Jesus himself?

Mickey shared another fantastic encounter with a mystifying being whom she would recognize from a photo many years later, yet she was also aware that it wasn't the same individual whom she knew to be the fortuneteller.

As recounted in the June, 1996 issue of Share International magazine, Mickey, her two sisters, her daughter and grandson were driving en route to Las Vegas from their California home one day in 1986, when "We were driving along and pretty soon this [white, stretch] limo started to pass us and drive right up alongside of us." Mickey explained. What struck them as peculiar was the fact that, on the two-lane highway in the middle of the desert, where no other vehicles had been seen for miles, the limousine seemed to come out of nowhere. Though the sight of a limousine was not an unusual occurrence when en route to Las Vegas, its presence no doubt elicited a mild curiosity, especially when they noticed, the man sitting in the passenger seat, who, sporting facial hair and a white turban appeared to be Arabic or Middle Eastern, was investigating them.

"He looked at each and everyone one of us, and it was like it was in slow motion. He kept looking, and he kind of smiled at my grandson, and then all of a sudden my sister said 'Gee whiz! Look at Him, He's staring at us!"

But Mickey was noticing something else altogether.

"You know what?" said Mickey, "There's no driver in that car!"

At that point, Mickey added, "All hell broke loose"

"Oh my God..." her sister exclaimed, "there isn't! Do you think that's Maitreya?"

Whoever it was, Mickey noticed that all during the hysteria that had erupted in their own car, the passenger in the driverless limo bore a prankish smile. Then the limo passed, pulled in front of their car, "and disappeared right in front of us. The whole thing disappeared."

Several years later, Mickey attended a conference in Colorado, where someone showed her the photograph of the purported appearance of Maitreya in Nairobi, Kenya, in 1988.

"I almost passed out when I saw [that photo] because it was so real to me...and I had the whole [limo] experience all over again. He had that beautiful face and his eyes were just tremendous. *That* was Maitreya!"

Indeed, the extraordinary man referred to as the elusive Maitreya had already been the subject of numerous eyewitness testimonies and accounts which had been confirmed by Benjamin Creme and his Master to have been

Maitreya in some disguise or another by the time the Nairobi photograph was taken and released in 1988.

After Nairobi, which is allegedly Maitreya's first known documented public appearance, a voluminous flurry of accounts began to regularly pour into the offices of Share International from all corners of the globe. Many of the descriptions were similar to Mickey's 'Arabic' car passenger, or the "man in white" described by Gabriel Moyano: An unknown visitor dressed in a long white tunic and matching turban, who would allegedly appear suddenly and unannounced before large, astonished groups of people of all religious denominations, speak for approximately 18 minutes, then disappear just as fast as he came. From Catholics in Mexico to fundamentalist Christians in Mississippi, from Buddhists in Japan to Muslims in Morocco, it seemed that this once questionable being named Maitreya was making appearances with an increased regularity.

The Many Faces of Maitreya

Aside from the listed 'group' encounters, many individuals already familiar with Benjamin Creme's work, both in print and on the lecture circuit, have written to him about encounters with a captivating individual whom they've suspected to have been Maitreya or one or another of the Masters. Representatives of Share International magazine told me that such queries are only published if Mr. Creme's Master confirms their authenticity.

From all over the globe, questions are routinely confirmed and printed. For example, one person wrote to inquire about a 'princely' figure she encountered while on a class break in Regent's Park, London, in 1989. Her description, as published in the May, 1999 issue of Share International magazine, went something like this:

> "To my left sitting on the grass was a prince out of The Thousand and One Nights! He was dressed in a splendid emerald green silk robe and turban similar to the ones worn by the moguls in old Indian miniatures - he was absolutely breathtaking. Spread out on the ground was a circular piece of cloth in the same material and colour of his robe. His gold slippers were placed neatly in front of him. There were precious stones and gold adorning the robe, and on his turban a huge deep purple stone. His hair was thick and wavy black, His complexion warm golden. He was clean-shaven but otherwise, in hindsight, very much like Maitreya as He appeared in Nairobi in 1988.
>
> None of the above were as extraordinary as his huge, dark and luminous eyes: the love that shone in them flowed from his entire

being. He held me in his gaze a brief moment until I must have looked away. [After attending an appointment] I rushed back into the park but of course he was gone."

In another instance, a German couple described a unique individual they encountered while on a trip to Brussels, Belgium, who was also confirmed to have been Maitreya.

"...we passed a dark-skinned man wearing a turban who strongly attracted our attention. We could not directly see his face yet he appeared to be drunk. He was stooped over, trying to retrieve something that looked like his wallet, which he had dropped. As he rose, something else fell from his shirt pocket. There was something very funny about the scene and even though drunk he seemed to be under control, so much so that none of us thought of helping him and walked on.

After a short while we realized we were lost and went into a hotel to get directions. On leaving the hotel, to our surprise we once again saw the man with the turban directly in front of us, holding himself up against a car. We wondered how he could have got there so quickly."[104]

Or how about this one sent in from an American woman from Atlanta, Georgia, while en route to a meeting about hunger and poverty relief:

"As I came to the end of the ramp at my freeway exit, there was a healthy-looking, attractive black man with a full beard sitting on the guard rail - he looked very much like the Nairobi photograph of Maitreya without the headpiece. He was holding a cardboard sign that said: "A little help goes a long way." I came up on the intersection too fast to do anything but read the sign and glance at him, but as I went by he looked right at me with a friendly look and waved casually."[105]

Many individuals also commented that their encounters were accompanied by similar inflections of encouragement. Another couple from Columbia, Missouri, inquired about an experience they had while performing music for a large audience in Kansas City in 1983. They wrote:

"After the program, when the group was disbanding, an elderly gentleman approached me and thanked us for singing, saying something like: "Keep up the good work - it's more important than you know." I was astounded at his presence, the depth of his focus

---

[104] Recounted in the May, 1999 issue of Share International magazine.
[105] Recounted in the June 1999 issue of Share International magazine.

and his love. He had plain, dark, ordinary clothing but an incredible rosy glow and a healthy, simple beauty I had never seen in anyone of any age. I was speechless, my eyes welled up with tears and my heart with joy. I turned to see if [my husband] was nearby so that he could meet this man. When I turned my head back (maybe two seconds later) the man had vanished!"[106]

Numerous accounts of an "extraordinary beggar," "rather disheveled individual," or, simply a "drunk" have all been confirmed by Creme's Master as having been Maitreya in some variation of the disguise. Conversely, many of the sightings offer, like Patricia Pitchon's Frenchman, a description of a man resembling the Indian or Asian 'gentleman' in the London tea shop: poised and distinguished, neatly trimmed hair, with or without a beard, and dressed elegantly in a western style men's suit or casual attire.

Whether in a park, an art museum, or at an outdoor festival, all accounts remark on the extraordinarily attractive presence surrounding the individual, who possesses a riveting gaze of unfathomable compassion and love.

According to Creme, Maitreya has said: "Those who know me will recognize me." Creme has added that though he may appear in assorted disguises, it will always be in "a form that inspires recognition."

A group of people in Amsterdam had gathered to discuss their skepticism about the Emergence of Maitreya and the Masters, when a casually dressed man walking a dog was suddenly seen peering through the window. Those gathered claimed to have simply 'felt' that the man was Maitreya, yet remained uncertain.

As the meeting adjourned, the man with the dog stepped across the threshold of the door and stood inside the room. In a teasing, playful twist, the man said to those exiting: "Now this dog is not Maitreya. Even if Benjamin Creme or His Master tells you otherwise, it isn't him."

What struck those in attendance is that there were no means by which the stranger could have known the topic or contents of the group's discussion, as it was not publicized, there were no posters displayed in the window or outside, nor could the discussion be heard outside of the room. Mr. Creme's Master would later confirm the man had indeed been Maitreya.[107]

A Question of Faith

It is my firm conviction that, in accord with many philosophical assertions, the Masters and Saints use dreams as a primary means of contacting

---
[106] Ibid.
[107] Recounted in the May, 1999 issue of Share International magazine.

us. Many would say that it's just a matter of interpretation. It's also likely that many people have a tendency for ignoring such dreams altogether, dismissing them in the same manner as they dismiss the stories and legends of paranormal, metaphysical phenomena.

It does indeed boil down to a question of belief, yet many may tend to think that having belief is a self-generated illusion. Even in those cases where the issue of faith is outwardly unquestioned, those who consider themselves believers still yield with caution when it comes to entertaining associated paranormal notions.

My take on the matter is that belief is the core teaching underlying all such experiences, or more appropriately, the lesson we are being asked to learn. Think about it. From the dreams and tales detailed herein, right on down to unexplainable miracles and phenomena such as the image of the Madonna visible in a subway puddle, or the crosses of light, etc., it all points to belief. Why else are such things manifest in so mysterious a manner? Why are all apparitions so temporal, so fleeting? Why don't these saints and Masters just appear and stay?

I believe, if you will, that we are being reminded of the essence of the concept that is human faith - an inherently unique capacity. It is distinguishable from, say, the faith a dog has that its owner will return home from a day at work. Faith is the hallmark of our humanly spiritual journey, whose ultimate destiny is Gnosis - knowing - our true nature in its totality; knowing our Soul, and living consciously as a soul. It is fitting that, through the plethora of incredible demonstrations, Jesus, the Madonna, and others have so generously revealed themselves in an effort to awaken us, to remind us.

Once, as the New Testament informs us, Jesus was asked by ten lepers to heal them. Instead of laying his hand upon them, he told them to go and show themselves to the priests. As the lepers complied, they discovered after walking a short while that their leprosy had vanished. But of the ten, only one, a Samaritan - the equivalent of an 'untouchable' in Jesus' day - returned and threw himself in prostration before Jesus' feet in gratitude.

Noticing the absence of the other nine, Jesus commented:

"Were not the ten made clean? But where are the other nine? Has no one been found to return and give glory to God except this foreigner?" He then said to the man, "Arise, go thy way, for thy faith has saved thee."

Again, it would seem that the efforts inherent in the explosion of personal, spiritual experiences and miracles are all geared to re-instill the essence of belief and faith. What to do when such external, miraculous phenomena are encountered, or even experienced in a dream? Western psychologists influenced by the Trans-personal trend in thought and research have acknowledged that such experiences are not only genuine for the individual to whom they've occurred, but represent for that individual a personal invitation to 'the path.'

It is fascinating that Western psychology is arriving at this conclusion in our time since this has been the acknowledged meaning and substance of such experiences for thousands of years in the East. Whether a Christian dreams of Jesus, a Catholic of Mary, or a yogi of their guru, the result is highly personal. We seem to need the respective, divine personalities and their demonstrations of superhuman characteristics to attract us. Their 'light' unveils the 'truth', and when we, attracted like moths to flame, gaze at that light, their job at that point is to show us the 'way.' It could truly be said that the Master is then servant to the student as their guide.

For when we see evidence of the divine, when we see 'proof', our belief is instantaneously entrenched, but, being the creatures of habit we tend to be, we immediately start slapping our faces and dousing ourselves with cold water to help us 'wake up.' Interestingly, according to the traditions of yoga and Buddhism, such efforts to 'wake up' are actually putting us back to sleep, bringing us back under the delusion of materialistic existence, of our own conditioned reflex to resist and renounce such awakenings. Eastern philosophical systems contend that the only true reality is the one we don't see every day, and that the human life as we know and presently live it en masse is in its infancy, just beginning to scratch the surface of all that can be learned, that can be known. To them, faith and belief are just the first toddler steps. Once firmly learned, we advance closer to our fullest potential, to knowing our true selves - our souls - by leaps and bounds.

Therefore, if miraculous occurrence acts as a form of divine invitation to seek, to walk the path, then our resulting response at the moment of acknowledgment and acceptance, manifesting in the form of acquiring sound belief and faith, could be viewed as an early moment of initiation. On this, both western and eastern psychology agree - the twain does meet.

For the first time in human history, east and west are enabled to see eye to eye, the multi-lingual Tower of Babel now has a common language. Furthermore, humanity is now enabled and empowered to initiate right human relations - the barriers are gone. Most of us could acknowledge that barriers to right human relations are indeed illusory. With this in mind, we can begin to understand the eastern contentions that not only are such things illusory, that they are transitory and fleeting, but that they are our own creation. To many, this notion may seem presumed, which is a strong indication of just how far we've come. Yet, it wasn't that long ago that the Berlin Wall was torn down. What more ludicrous and symbolic an example of our self-imposed boundaries and limitations than that? When that wall came down, a barrier for all humanity was torn down with it. A huge, collective, evolutionary step was taken forward, closer to unity, to oneness. According to the eastern traditions, unity in oneness - with the spirit of creation, a.k.a. God - is the goal of the human being, of the human species.

It has been suggested that our innate sense of this divine kinship is genetically and psychologically imbedded in our make-up. No less than one of modern philosophy's most influential proponents of rationalism, the eighteenth-century German philosopher Immanuel Kant, in his *'Critique of Pure Reason'*, expressed it this way:

> "No [philosophical] system yet propounded [that he then knew of, in the west] can, in view of the essential purpose of metaphysics, be said to really exist, [leaving] everyone sufficient ground for doubting as to its possibility.
>
> Yet, in a certain sense, this kind of knowledge [re: natural science] is to be looked upon as given; that is to say, metaphysics actually exists, if not as a science, yet still as natural disposition. For human reason, without being moved merely by the idle desire for extent and variety of knowledge, proceeds impetuously, driven on by an inward need, to questions such as cannot be answered by empirical employment of reason, or by principles thence derived. Thus in all men, as soon as their reason has become ripe for speculation, there has always existed and will always continue to exist some kind of metaphysics."

As we know today, however, there were, in Kant's time, quite a few philosophical systems that were in accord with his theories, yet to which he must not have been aware.

Such a system, for example, is the recondite doctrine *of Kashmir Shaivism*.[108] In just one of that system's texts - the *Vijnanabhairava* (vid-yan-na-by-ra-va), which scholars concur was written in the seventh or eighth century, can essentially be found a manual of mystic practices. A handbook, if

---

[108] Shaivism (shave-ism) has, as its root, the term Shiva, a name for the destructive aspect of God. The name philosophically refers to the destruction of anything that interferes with or obstructs the aspirant's awareness of his innate unity with God. The name is also given to describe the transcendent state of one's direct experience of conscious union with God. The Shaivism of Kashmir is noted as being relatively progressive when compared with other traditional systems of yogic thought. For example, where traditional doctrine might advise complete renunciation of association with the things of average, material life, Kashmir Shaivism suggests that complete indifference isn't necessary, provided one learns the means to see and experience Shiva even in those same things of everyday life, in which God is also manifest as a part of His creation.

you will, designed to teach students of self-mastery some proven methods for taming and merging the limited-egoic self into the Universal Self. In other words, it offers a simplified, methodical approach to experiencing oneness with God. In the philosophical view of Shaivism, all creation as we know it is considered an expression of God's spiritual energy or thought forms, which is known as *Shakti*.[109] Since we are made "in His image and likeness," it follows that our own relative worlds, our immediate existence, is largely colored by the way we view, interpret, and think about things in our everyday life.

So far, nothing is inconsistent with any western theological system. For example, if someone spills a drink on our lap, do we: a) get upset with them and get a towel and seltzer to blot out the stain, or, b) forgive them and get a towel and seltzer to blot out the stain? With such an inherent capacity to 'create' cause and effect, the concept of being made in his image and likeness is less heretical. It is simply a matter of 'as ye sow, so ye shall reap.'

Shaivism, like most theological modus operandi, contend that such petty experiences are perfect fodder to learn a lesson, or, perhaps more appropriately, evolutionarily propel and advance us towards mystical union with the divine. For example, several verses from Vijnanabhairava not only illustrate the theory of the banal springboard, but also very closely address Kant's aforementioned assertion of 'Natural Disposition':

> 'Wherever the mind goes, whether towards the exterior or towards the interior, everywhere there is the state of God. Since God is omnipresent, where can the mind go to avoid Him?
>
> On every occasion that the consciousness of the Omnipresent Reality is revealed through the sensory organs since it is the characteristic only of the Universal Consciousness, one should contemplate over the consciousness appearing through the sensory organs as the Universal Consciousness. Thus [the seeker's] mind will be dissolved in the Universal Consciousness.
>
> [Then, to offer an example of the above:] At the sight of a land [as from a boat], when one lets go all thought of the remembered objects [and concentrates only on the experience which was the basis of that memory] and makes his [psychosomatic] body supportless [that is: free from all residual impressions associated with that memory], then the Lord appears.' [That is: mind will be restored to its inherent, pristine form of pure consciousness, of pure experience, or, as Kant calls it, 'natural disposition'.]

---

[109] Shakti (shahk-tee), the power of God, is designated as a female principle. In Hindu mythology, this principle is represented by characterizing Shakti as the 'wife' or consort of Shiva.

What is being described here is what we know in the west as 'the zone.' For example, remember when you were a child swinging on a swing in the playground. At first you start out slowly, swinging to and fro, and you delight in this experience. As you grow older, you learn how to accelerate your swinging with the use of your feet. Gradually you learn to swing higher and higher, and then you push yourself to see how high you can make yourself go. Then, there is that exhilarating moment when, after many years of practicing your swinging, you make it to the highest point, almost leveling your body with the bar from which the swing chains are suspended. In that moment of exhilaration, your joy of accomplishment – in that instant – supplants all awareness of other external matters. Your mind and breath stop and your bliss of achievement knows no bounds. What the sage-author of Vijnanabhairava is suggesting here is in that instant of exhilaration can be experienced the transcendent state of unlimited consciousness beyond the everyday state of limited self-identity. He is simply suggesting that if you observe, witness and meditate on the experienced state of being in that moment of exhilaration, then one can initiate the process of shifting their consciousness into that joy-filled state as a permanent state, and thereby experience the unity consciousness that is the goal of all yoga practice. Many have referred to that exalted experience of union oneness with God.

So, what about those of us who simply prefer to practice devotion to God, to a saint or deity? Kashmir Shaivism acknowledges devotion as not only a valid practice, but also serves as a means of attaining the state of divine union. One verse describes how basic devotion is transformed into an advanced yogic practice by means of the simple alteration of perception. It says:

> 'The sort of intuition (a.k.a.-*mati*) that emerges through the intensity of devotion in one who is perfectly detached is known as the Shakti of Shankara.[110] One should contemplate it perpetually. Then he becomes Shiva Himself.'

Of this one verse alone the book's translator and commentator, Dr. Jaideva Singh, offers a brilliant elucidation on the full scope of its meaning and implication. Further, he summarizes how this one technique alone can enable the aspirant to achieve union with the divine. Singh explains:

> "One who is perfectly detached, that is, not attached to sensuous pleasures and is devoted to God develops mati (divine intuition). The mati is full of beneficent power that can transform and

---

[110] Shankara is another name for Shiva - God to the Shaivites.

consecrate life. That is why this technique recommends contemplation on mati.

There are four steps in this technique. (1) One's value of life has to be totally changed. He should be completely detached from sensuous pleasures and trinkets of life. (2) He should be devoted to God. (3) Through the above two, the mind of the aspirant will become purified, and then will emerge mati which is spiritual intuition full of the power to transform life. She[111] can remove all obstacles in the path of the aspirant. (4) The aspirant should perpetually contemplate on this mati (as it's perceived). She will completely transform his life, and then his mind will be dissolved in Shiva. [Here, devotion] means viewing God in all life and dedication of oneself to the Divine in word, thought and deed."

The passages describe the attainment of the "Buddha-nature" to which Buddhist's refer, as well as the state of "Christ-hood" or Communion in Christ in Christianity. As stated before, this state of achieved union is that to which Jesus referred when He said: "I and the Father are one." As it was said: "Unto them He gave power to be called Sons of God."

What I found particularly beautiful in Dr. Singh's commentary is how routine and natural the four steps are. I noted the similarity, for example, to the experience a Catholic might have when offering a candle and sincere prayer before, say, the statue of the Madonna in a church. Though many people of faith are unconscious of the fact in such instances, the presence and opportunity to experience unity with the divine is right in the palms of their clasped hands.

For example, I had given a photocopy of the South American Jesus photo I'd found in the bus-pan to a friend. She decided to share it with her 85-year-old grandmother, a lifelong, devout Catholic. When the grandmother - whom my friend called *Nonna* - was shown the picture, she was visibly shaken, physically awestruck. The woman practically fell back, as she was instantly transfixed in wonderment. "That's Jesus Christ!" the grandmother declared with conviction. But what is more awesome is to read between and around her remark to examine what she *wasn't* saying. What her body language and emotion related was more like: "That is Christ and I am Christian. He is mine and I am His!"

Consistent with Shaivism, Buddhism, Gnostic Christianity, and a host of other esoteric, mystical paths, Nonna's mind momentarily stopped - and in

---

[111] Here, 'She' refers to mati - spiritual intuition - as a form or expression of Shakti, the female energy principle.

that instant she had experienced, though unconscious of the fact, that state of oneness, of unity, of yoga, that is the goal of all theistic traditions. It was through her experience, that she was subconsciously introduced to the personal Jesus. The photo does have a way of doing that to you, which is exactly what I experienced prior to finding it in the bus-pan.

So, we've seen that no matter what our religious affiliation, Muslim, Christian, Jewish, etc., powerful things are happening in ways we will recognize as aids in instilling belief, faith, and hope. Whoever our respective deities may be, they come in visions, dreams, etheric apparitions or in the flesh, in ways that put us at ease, that make us feel comfortable with their presence in our lives.

Chapter Seven

THE DIPLOMAT

"Until philosophers are kings, or the kings and princes of this world have the spirit and power of philosophy, and political greatness and wisdom meet in one, and those commoner natures who pursue either to the exclusion of the other are compelled to stand aside, cities will never have rest from their evils, - no, nor the human race, as I believe, and then only will this our State have a possibility of life and behold the light of day."

Plato, The Republic

The name Wayne Peterson had been brought to my attention several times over the course of many months. I had received a number of such references of people who were said to have had incredible experiences of Maitreya and the Masters. Mickey Drake's story was but one. Having completed the first draft of several sections of this work, Wayne Peterson's name was again brought to my attention. "You really should get in touch with Wayne Peterson," said Buddy Piper, a nationally known media personality whom I had approached to inquire about scheduling an interview after one of his public lectures. "He has an incredible story."

Piper himself had an incredible story. A veteran theater and television actor who had appeared on *The Red Skelton Show*, had hosted the children's show *Winky Dink*, was writer, producer, and co-creator of *Classic Concentration* - television's longest running game show, and a director of public information programs, this 70 year old dynamo continues to inexhaustibly travel across North America delivering enthusiastic lectures and doing radio guest spots in which he discusses the phenomenon of miracles - and the emergence of Maitreya and the Masters. Averaging about fifty such gigs per year, Buddy still finds about an extra hundred hours a week to perform volunteer community service.

He shared with me a number of tales, first about his own encounters with Masters, then about his interviews with a group of church board members in Tennessee who'd witnessed Maitreya and two other Masters parade up and down one of the church's side aisles while the puzzled onlookers had gathered to view and discuss the unexplained, massive crosses of light that had suddenly and miraculously appeared in the church's windows. The board members were even more astonished when the three strangely dressed visitors suddenly vanished into thin air before their very eyes.

Buddy had graciously faxed me a sizable volume of pages filled with a variety of similar experience stories that he felt would be fitting for this particular book. Among them was a brief mention of Wayne Peterson, which simply described him as a US Foreign Service Diplomat. That fact alone intrigued me, and I immediately wondered if such a government official had any inside knowledge of the 'secret' London conference of 1990. At the time, however, it wasn't my focus, so it was buried under other pressing issues.

It would not be until I had been discussing this book with a friend that I seriously considered inquiring about Peterson's story. When I mentioned certain concepts I had in mind, it was my friend James who filled me in on some additional details about Wayne Peterson.

"Wayne Peterson's story" he told me, "is really incredible." "This man" James said, "has met with world leaders who know about Maitreya. He even knows people connected with the Vatican who know." Mesmerized, I listened intently as James, who had once worked for a high-profile government leader, told me about Peterson's diplomatic affiliation and other extraordinary details.

I tried to contact Mr. Peterson first through Buddy Piper, but, due to the man's unyielding schedule, I was unable to reach him for some time. A second attempt was made through Lon, an acquaintance affiliated with the Rocky Mountain Transmission Meditation Group in Boulder, Colorado. I knew Lon was relatively acquainted with Peterson, and it was Lon who had put me in touch with Mickey Drake.

Eventually I contacted the volunteer staff at Share International USA, the non-profit public relations and distribution arm for the work associated with Benjamin Creme. In response, I was sent an e-mailed press packet which included an intriguing autobiographical sketch of Mr. Peterson.

As fate would have it, I later learned from my friend James that Peterson was preparing to embark on a speaking tour of the Eastern United States, with my own town of Philadelphia as one of his stops, which James had volunteered to host. I told James about the biographical information I'd received, and in turn, was then told more details about Peterson's story as published two years prior in the December, 1997 issue of Share International Magazine.

On Christmas Eve of 1944, three-year-old Wayne Peterson watched with bewilderment as his family made all the usual festive and extravagant preparations associated with the celebration of Christmas.

"I remember not understanding why so much effort was being made for someone's birthday," Peterson wrote.

> "While my mother arranged the small Italian statues of the holy family with figures for the manger scene under the Christmas tree, she explained, as best she could to a three-year-old, that the [celebration of the] Christ child's birth was to remember how God came to earth as a human."

Contemplating his mother's words, young Wayne played with the manger figurines, which included biting off several of the figure's heads. In the months following Christmas, Wayne had been quite ill and was taken to the doctor on several occasions, but each time nothing could be medically detected to explain his condition. On Good Friday of 1945, just one week after his fourth birthday, Wayne felt severe stomach pains. Having told his mother, the boy was placed on the living room sofa to lie down as dinner was served to the rest of his family in the kitchen. As he lay there staring at the ceiling, he heard what sounded like "the swishing sound that a silk or fabric makes as it is rubbed against itself."

He discerned that the source of the sound seemed to be coming from the top of the stairway. Concluding it must be a guest, this puzzled him since he had not been informed that anyone was visiting. As he lay watching the staircase for this unknown guest to descend, he saw a white satin or silk slipper come in view on the top step, followed by a long white flowing gown which was also silken in appearance. As the figure began to descend, he watched until the figure stopped at waist view.

> "At that point, a young lady bent forward until she could [see] me. Strangely, she knew exactly where I was in the room and looked directly at me with a warm friendly smile while continuing down the stairs. I was fascinated by the clothing she wore...so different from what my mother or her friends wore. Half way down the stairs I became aware that the blue veil covering the back of the head and flowing down to the hem of the dress was identical to the one worn by the Christmas statue of Mary.
>
> As she walked...toward me I began to sense that this was no

ordinary house guest but in fact must be the real Mary, mother of the Christ child..."

Mary then proceeded to kneel beside young Wayne and inform him that his life was in danger, and that he needed to convince his parents to contact a doctor that night or She "would have to return for him." However, Mary told Wayne the choice was his, to which Wayne replied that preferred the idea of going with her. Mary lovingly suggested to Wayne how sad his parents and family would be if he had to leave them, yet Wayne insisted on going with her.

'I noted something like frustration on Her part at my decision. Her eyes rolled toward the ceiling and She was quiet for a moment. As she looked back down toward me Her expression appeared more serious. She said: 'I am going to tell you a secret that few now know. If you stay with your family, you will see the Christ because He will come to live with the people of the world.'"

Excited by this, Wayne attempted to sit up, yet was pushed back on his pillow. "When will He come?" he asked Mary, to which She replied the event would occur when he was much older, and that Wayne would be among the first to recognize Him. Again, however, Mary gave Wayne important instructions with regard to his illness, requiring him to rehearse precisely what he needed to say. When She was satisfied, Mary tenderly tucked the blankets around him and departed. Afterwards, Wayne managed to convince his parents of the urgency of his predicament.

"My father finally agreed to call the doctor at his office even though it was late afternoon on Good Friday and almost everything in our small town was closed. Much to my father's surprise, the doctor was in and requested that we go directly to the hospital since he had an emergency case there. My swollen appendix was removed just as it was about to rupture. I awoke at the first sign of light on Easter Sunday morning."

Wayne Peterson credits the Madonna's warning with having saved his life. In the years that followed, he kept the story to himself, telling no one save for a few close friends, perhaps for the same reason I kept my own tale of the eyes in the closet and other experiences to myself. Who would believe him?

As he grew older, his experience had instilled in him a strong faith, believing first hand in the stories surrounding Mary's appearances at Fatima, Zeitoun, and elsewhere, and with the understanding that such saints and great beings *do* communicate and intercede with humanity on rare occasions. But in the deepest recesses of his being, from time to time Wayne would wonder about the promise made to him by Mary. When within his lifetime would he see the returned Christ? How would the Christ make Himself known?

The New Frontier

The early 1960s in the United States was a period of contagious optimism, spurred by the promise envisioned by President John F. Kennedy's 'New Frontier' socially oriented political agenda. Gone was the dark specter of 'big brother' McCarthyism, and the pseudo-military style government of the Eisenhower administration, an apparently beleaguering but necessary evil in view of the post-World War II threat of Stalin's Soviet idea of expansionism. Kennedy embodied, if only in convincing rhetoric, all that was realizable in the ideal democracy. "Ask not what your country can do for you, but what you can do for your country" was the rallying cry of the first wave of the baby boom generation, and the resulting spirit of altruistic public service provided the ideal conceptual funnel for the enthralling euphoria.

To actualize the ideals, the Kennedy administration inaugurated a host of government sponsored programs which empowered all American citizens - and the youth in particular - to become acknowledged player/participants in the creation of a brave new world and bright new future which would not just benefit US citizens, but people of all nations. Hunger and poverty could end. Health care, education, and housing were equitable, inalienable rights. Compassion, respect, dignity, and justice were the birthright of all. In Kennedy's view, a virtually perfect world was just an effort away, an effort which simply required mutual civil cooperation, and a sharing of abundant resources.

Designed to serve as a secular, humanitarian missionary team, the US Peace Corps was fostered during Kennedy's watch to render altruistic service and good will in assisting the plight and development of America's foreign neighbors. It was this enthusiastic, unifying spirit which colored Wayne Peterson's college years at the University of Wisconsin. After being approached and recruited in his graduate year by Peace Corp volunteer and then president of the Chase Manhattan Bank David Rockefeller, Wayne consented to join the Peace Corps.

A new US government administration in the wake of J.F.K.'s assassination brought with it a host of varied political influences and changes, and by 1966, Wayne Peterson had grown dissatisfied with unanticipated, imposed limitations in his Peace Corp work. Having written and sent a disheartened letter to his parents back in the states, on the day the letter arrived and was read, his parents happened to be hosting Congressman Melvin Laird, who would go on to become the US Secretary of Defense during the Nixon administration. Lending a sympathetic ear to Wayne's plight, Laird opened a few doors that allowed Peterson more freedom in choosing a preferable diplomatic position with the US Foreign Service Corps. Within two months, Peterson became a regional cultural attaché´ for the US Embassy in Brazil.

With his aspiration and optimism rejuvenated, Peterson employed, in his first two years of service, the first, privately funded public welfare program in Northern Brazil. *The Society of Social Work*, or, *SOS*,[112] as the project was called, virtually eliminated the endemic begging which then plagued cities there. The program was so successful that within two years of its 1964 inception, the program spread nationally, and is still in effect to this day.

Over the course of the ensuing 13 years, Peterson would serve in a similar capacity during assignments in Southeast Asia, Africa, and Latin America. In the late 1970s, Wayne settled in Washington, DC, taking a post as a Director of the Fulbright Scholarship Program, a position which he manned for the next 17 years, the duration of which made Wayne an internationally respected figure, as the scholarships are routinely administered through foreign US embassies.

It was during his tenure as Fulbright Director in 1982 that Wayne Peterson caught his first glimmer of what was to have been the fulfillment of the Madonna's promise in his youth. While in Washington, Wayne happened to be watching *The Merv Griffin Show*, when a conversation between Merv's guests intrigued him. Author Gore Vidal and a then relatively unknown British author - Benjamin Creme - were discussing the extraordinary subject matter of Creme's first book, in which "a group of very advanced men, perfected men" were said to engaged in guiding brilliant technological advances and helping humanity from behind the scenes.

"Hearing the story of Maitreya," says Peterson,

"made me suddenly recall again the vision of the Blessed Mother I had when I was four years old. As I viewed Mr. Creme on that TV show, I knew instantly that this was the message I had been waiting to hear. Following [this], I immediately purchased [Mr. Creme's] book *The Reappearance of the Christ and the Masters of Wisdom*."

Having read the book, a series of coincidences led Wayne to a Transmission Meditation session in Washington, DC, where he learned that Benjamin Creme would be in town the following week to give a public

---

[112] SOS is the abbreviation of the *Society of Social Work* in the Portuguese language.

program. It would be at that program that Wayne finally arrived at destiny's doorstep.

With little exposure to the esoteric precepts of Theosophy or Eastern mysticism, Wayne attended Mr. Creme's lecture with the intention of gaining further insight on the imminent return of Christ as predicted to him in childhood by the Madonna. Wayne listened with a combination of interest and skepticism, weeding through propositions that perhaps interested him little.

> "As Mr. Creme explained the overshadowing process that was about to take place by [Satya] Sai Baba for a blessing upon completing the evening lecture," says Peterson, "I became incredulous."

Peterson was not only dubious of Mr. Creme's claim to be overshadowed, but with the sudden introduction of Satya Sai Baba into the program, Wayne felt the inclusion was simply a patronizing gesture on the part of Sai Baba devotees, and that it took away from what he felt was the more important focus of the *Emergence* story, which had spurred his initial interest to attend.

Wayne sat defiantly as Creme began the overshadowing, until he noticed Mr. Creme drop his hands and actually stop the process. The audience grew confused as Mr. Creme scanned the room as if he were looking for someone. Spotting Peterson, Benjamin Creme kept his attention fixed on him as he walked closer to the side of the room where Peterson was seated. From a distance of more than ten feet, Benjamin Creme raised his hands to face Peterson.

"Suddenly," said Peterson,

> "Mr. Creme...thrust his hands toward me. At first I did not realize what had happened. Something very solid and very real hit me, [pushing] me with such force that the chair upon which I sat slid away from my row, [crossing] a narrow aisle and slammed me against the wall."

Readers will note how similar Mr. Peterson's account is to my own earlier recollection of the force of the overshadowing, when I experienced 'an invisible ball of fire' burst upon me with similar force, though not enough to knock me across the room.

Despite the intensity, Peterson refused to acknowledge that the unusual force had anything to do with Satya Sai Baba.

"I looked at the windows thinking perhaps a huge storm had blown open a window causing this sensation like a strong wind," said Peterson. When he finally accepted that the force must have been coming from Sai Baba, with humility he inwardly prayed for it to stop. Instantly, the intensity of force subsided, and Benjamin Creme averted his focus to the others in attendance.

The event was just the beginning, and Wayne soon learned why he had apparently been singled out with such force. Within several months of attending this lecture and overshadowing, Wayne Peterson met with the most unanticipated occurrence of all when an associate of Maitreya Himself contacted him, and extended an invitation to join Maitreya and the Masters for a meeting, the purpose of which was not immediately revealed. Peterson agreed, and was told he would later be contacted.

A short time after that, Wayne had traveled to the home of friends for an informal gathering. No sooner had he arrived than he noticed a globe of golden light about the size of a volleyball floating about the crowd (which is reminiscent of eyewitness descriptions of similar phenomena which occurred during the Fatima apparitions of 1917, as discussed in chapter one). The orb of light was then followed by a second, then a third, which all then united, linking like a string of pearls, and maintaining a steady speed as they encircled the room. None of the other guests seemed to notice this phenomenon, and when the astonished Peterson attempted to inquire with two others with whom he'd been conversing, he found himself unable to speak. After several such repeated, unsuccessful attempts, Peterson collapsed to the floor, simultaneously hearing a distinct voice from within himself say: *"Do not tell anyone in the room what you see."*

After being helped to a seat and reassuring his friends that he'd be fine, Wayne sat in silent awe as he watched the golden glow steadily increase until it filled the entire room, the other guests oblivious all the while.

The globes of light had multiplied and began to spin around Wayne at a terrific velocity, forming about him a vertical tunnel of golden light. People were interacting with Wayne as if nothing of the kind was occurring, and he assumed he was hallucinating for no known reason. After a few moments, Wayne found himself lying next to an opening on the floor. Peering down, he realized he was on the other side of a tunnel which he describes as having been composed of 'golden light', and he was now situated far above the room in his friend's home. (Could Wayne's tunnel have been the 'Portal of Initiation' as described by Master Djwhal Khul in chapter two?) As he studied this strange environment, from behind an illumined panel a male figure emerged who then introduced himself as Wayne's guide. Wayne was offered the option of returning to the room with his friends with no memory of the globes or anything that had transpired, or, the guide would escort him to join the Masters for the previously appointed meeting.

Wayne quickly agreed to go with the guide, and apparently blacked out once more, for when he awoke he found himself standing only with the aid and support of two unknown men, one on each side, who each held an arm. Though he then heard a voice say "You can stand on your own now," the two men continued to support Wayne, apparently yet unable to stand on his own legs.

They helped Wayne join a large gathering of others dressed in short white robes, and, looking down, Wayne noticed he, too, was inexplicably dressed in a similar manner. Looking behind, he noticed that the two men who had assisted him previously were wearing longer robes, as were others nearby.

"I assumed they were Masters," said Peterson. How similar is this description to Krishnamurti's own account of the Masters Koot Hoomi and Djwhal Khul when escorting him on the occasion of initiation? "One 'sponsor,' (which Peterson termed his escorts)

"... appeared very friendly as he motioned to me to step forward alone into the circle. Suddenly there was an instant flash of light as gigantic doors, [which he describes as being about 20 feet tall], at the far end of the huge room were pulled open. Light flooded in and revealed a scene of many men in long robes forming rows with a wide path for the entering human figure. He was bathed in white light and wearing white robes. I knew this must be Maitreya."

As the figure approached where he stood, Wayne inquired to verify if this was, in fact, Maitreya, to which one of his 'sponsors' replied yes. Without further delay, Maitreya himself then addressed Wayne, saying:

"From time to time the Masters and I invite members of humanity here whom we believe are prepared to assist us in our task. Do you wish to help us?"

Wayne responded affirmatively, and was asked by Maitreya if he would consent to an examination to determine what manner of service would be most suitable. He was told that he would not remember any of the questions and answers posed to him, and when he had concern about giving wrong answers, Maitreya laughed, having read his thoughts, and assured Wayne no such concern was needed.

For a period, which he later estimates to have been approximately an hour, Peterson says "Time did not exist; I thought years might have passed." In that time, he was able to answer the questions and go through a sort of 'spiritual examination', conversing with Maitreya all the while.

The sense of timelessness is reminiscent of Mickey Drake's

description in her experience of the time she met the 'palm reader' in the park, whom she was later informed had been Jesus. As for the details of Peterson's 'spiritual examination', reference to Krishnamurti's account in Mary Lutyen's book may help fill in the blanks. Mr. Peterson published his own book in which his experiences are recounted, and further details may be found there.[113]

As his sponsors were leading him away, Wayne requested more time to ask Maitreya some questions. Uncertain of what was fully going on, Peterson asked if he was physically still alive in the 'real' world. Maitreya laughed, then paused in thought, and asked: "What is it that so attaches you to the physical world?"

Peterson responded, "Nothing."

Maitreya then led Wayne to a blank wall, and, as Wayne describes, 'with a wave of his hand, a window to the world below was opened before him.' At first, Wayne saw the sun rising over the horizon and began to estimate his geographical position. Maitreya exhorted him to look deeper, and, as Wayne recounts:

> "He then touched me, and I floated into many...channels of consciousness viewing the wonders of man's achievement in high culture..."

Wayne explained that he then understood the lesson of attachment to his small life in the big picture. "I would go back and complete your incarnations for you," Maitreya teased playfully, "but I am not allowed," thereafter telling Wayne that he had to go back and do it himself.

After this, his parting moment with Maitreya, the next thing Peterson knew he was back in the room with his friends, all of whom, he noticed, were now asleep. Undoubtedly dazed by his otherworldly experience, Wayne attempted to slip out of the house. But, as if having been in suspended animation, his friends suddenly became reanimated, resuming the party as if nothing had happened, unaware that an hour or so had slipped by unconsciously.

"After that experience," says Peterson,

> "I became accustomed to being awakened at 4 AM as if being startled by something. At times I saw figures... [but] I discovered that I tended to awaken at the moment of a Master's departure. I can only confirm to others that the Masters do indeed teach us at night while we sleep."

---

[113] The title of Mr. Peterson's book is Extraordinary Times, Extraordinary Being: Experiences of an American Diplomat with Maitreya and the Masters.

In the aftermath of Wayne Peterson's meeting with Maitreya, he claims to receive repeated visits from Masters or representatives who instruct him in the art of Self-realization. Wherever he may be traveling in the world, *someone* appears on schedule at about 3:00 am and says "I am here to give you your lesson for the day."

He's also encountered 'familiars' of Maitreya. Once, for example, at one of Mr. Creme's lectures, Maitreya was disguised as a woman toting a huge bag filled with bottles of water. Wayne noticed that only one other man in attendance recognized this woman for who she really was, and watched as the man approached her, asking for one of the containers of water. According to Peterson, Benjamin Creme claims this very man later wrote to Share International Magazine, declaring that the water had cured his friend of AIDS.

In his professional capacity as a Fulbright program director, Peterson found his experience was not unique, encountering numerous individuals and dignitaries who not only had similar experiences, but openly spoke with him about Maitreya.

"In private meetings and dinner parties," says Peterson,

"I was able to discuss Maitreya with personal friends of the Pope, important businessmen close to the [US] President, foreign government leaders, Catholic priests and Protestant ministers, and those involved directly with the miracles at Medjugorje. All knew the story of Maitreya the Christ, and many offered to tell me their special experiences with the Masters, which they had mainly kept to themselves for fear of being ridiculed. All, however, knew that when the time was right they would come forward and openly fulfill the promises they made to Him to support His work of changing the economic and political structure of the present world.

A friend that heads an international organization [had] read [a copy of Mr. Creme's book on Maitreya] and was so impressed with Maitreya's teachings that he immediately included the ideas in his speech.

Immediately after his presentation, he received a note from the reigning monarch of the country [which hosted the conference where he spoke], inviting him for lunch at the palace the next day. Upon arrival he was surprised to find himself in the company of a variety of world political leaders who questioned him about his speech, [who nodded in approval when they learned it was inspired by Maitreya], and gave him the names of other political leaders in various countries already working with Maitreya's ideas. Just as Maitreya has promised, He already has many leaders prepared to follow Him into a New Age."

When Peterson stopped in our town for a speaking engagement, I found it refreshing to hear many key points addressed in person. Here was a man whom I understood to have met Maitreya personally, who knew significant world figures that had as well, and who was clearly an inside player on a global level with regard to the Emergence. He spoke quite matter-of-factly of the whole ordeal throughout the evening, mentioning things that seemed to add substance to much of the research presented in the initial chapters of this book.

For one, he mentioned issues surrounding the involvement of the Masters in World War II. Though I'm told the following is relatively common knowledge, I was unaware that Franklin D. Roosevelt had regularly consulted with Helena Roerich, a Russian aristocrat and esotericist, who allegedly had established communication with the Masters in the first half of the Twentieth Century. Peterson contended that correspondence between the two is well documented, and can be found both in the Roosevelt archives, as well as in a book distributed many years ago by a European publisher. Apparently, according to Peterson, there are documented references which suggest that Roosevelt had been given a special medicine created by the Masters which literally kept him alive until a major hurdle was overcome in the waning years of the war.

With regard to more current issues, Peterson remarked on Benjamin Creme's suggestion that Mikhail Gorbachev had been mentally stimulated by the Christ, that this stimulation had resulted in the development of the Soviet Glasnost and Perestroika policies, and that Gorbachev personally believes that Christ has returned to the world.

"I believe," explains Mr. Creme, "[Gorbachev] thinks the Christ is working through him; that the visions which he has are of the Christ. He is a man open to the possibility of a Christ being in the world. Just how much he is aware of his relationship to the Christ, in terms of inspiration, I could not say. You would have to ask him that."[114]

Gorbachev's own, open declaration of having been a Christian since his youth was big news around the time of his closing days as Soviet President, with coverage of the topic found in most major news journals at the time.

In a more recent television broadcast of Sunday, October 22, 2000, Gorbachev spoke with veteran religious broadcaster Robert Schuller at the

---

[114] Maitreya's Mission, Volume II. © 1993 by Benjamin Creme. Quoted courtesy Benjamin Creme.

famed Crystal Cathedral in California.

Gorbachev began by saying that "the revival of the Russian Orthodox Church is one of the most important gains of Perestroika" and openly discussed the presence and practice of Orthodox Christianity in his childhood home. "There can be no freedom without spiritual freedom," Gorbachev said.

Schuller repeatedly pressed Gorbachev throughout to openly voice his own faith, to publicly 'witness' in the evangelical Christian sense. After politely evading the issue each time, Gorbachev finally responded cryptically by saying "There will be a time when we will *really* talk about this with you." Was Gorbachev cryptically referencing his views of Christ returned?

As the interview concluded, Schuller recalled having been privileged to observe a private meeting of world leaders who spent 24 hours together analyzing the end of the Cold War. Sponsored by George Herbert Walker Bush and moderated by veteran newscaster Jim Lehrer, those in attendance were Bush, Gorbachev, François Mitterrand, Margaret Thatcher, and Brian Mulroney. Schuller pointed out that after Lehrer wrapped up the meeting, it had been Gorbachev who added the final word by saying "And we must remember Jesus Christ!"[115]

In response to the question of Maitreya's delay in going public and the close-mouthed policy of world leaders, Wayne Peterson claims they have been instructed to do so by Maitreya, who asked of them to bring about a specific measure of peace into the world before He could appear on global television.

Additionally, Peterson surprisingly informed the audience that the Chinese government was also quite aware of Maitreya's reality, and were taking gradual steps in making changes as best they could while handling a billion or so citizens. Further, in a comment that was incredibly reassuring, Peterson remarked that Maitreya has not only predicted but affirms that Tibet will be independent in the very near future.

The majority of those in attendance at Peterson's Philadelphia lecture were mesmerized by the information, and questions reflected their interest in areas of global politics and spirituality as well. Peterson told an extraordinary tale about an acquaintance of his, a well-known, prominent world figure, whom he declined to identify. "If I even told you his profession," Wayne later told me, "you'd know who it was immediately." Suffice it to say, Peterson told me this man developed a project of great import for which he lobbied heavily but came against all measure of opposition. Uncertain of where to turn next, the unidentified man surrendered the project to providence.

Then, late one night, this man was awakened with the suspicion that

---

[115] Source: Christianity Today, October 20, 2000.

there was someone in his home. As he began to check around, he noticed a brilliant glow of light coming from the guestroom. Quietly entering, the man was stunned when he saw three men dressed in martial attire, yet who were radiating a brilliant aura of light. Uncertain what to say or who the angelic-like men were, he finally said "What are you doing in my guest room?"

One of the three spoke, reminding him that several weeks prior he had prayed for help with his project, and that they were coming in response to his prayer. Incredulous, the man asked why they were dressed in such a manner, to which one of the three replied, "We are ready to fight for your cause."

When later asked by an audience member if the three were identified, Peterson replied that the three were Maitreya, Jesus, and the Master who was the Madonna.

As the program concluded, I spoke with a man visibly shaken, his eyes filled with tears. Wayne's account of the three Masters in the guestroom had moved him considerably, he explained, for it had offered possible closure for an incident that occurred nearly forty years earlier in his own life.

"When I was sixteen years old," he explained, "I was going to commit suicide. I was in my room, when all of a sudden three men appeared to me who told me it was not my time to leave this world. They told me that I had some important work to do, and when the time came I'd know about it. Then they disappeared and I never had a clue about who they could be until I heard [Peterson's] story tonight."

As I shared my awareness of thousands of people globally who have had similar experiences, myself included, the man sobbed with a combination of relief, joy, and hope. It was extraordinary.

Another woman shared her experience of the Madonna, whom she claimed had appeared to her several years prior, but about which she'd never openly spoken. A fellow Siddha Yoga student whom I'd invited shared that once, while attending a lecture given by Swami Muktananda, she saw Jesus appear right next to him. "Jesus appeared out of nowhere, and just stood there next to Baba" my friend exclaimed. "He was just hangin' out and smiling and lookin' around while Baba talked, and then a few minutes later, he disappeared."

After the lecture, an informal reception was held in which a sizable number of people eagerly attended to learn more. The occasion afforded this smaller group a chance to speak more casually with Peterson, during which some key points were further elucidated. For example, the gentleman to whom the Masters appeared dressed in uniform was, according to Wayne, heading up a program which he claims is "Maitreya's top priority."

I shared with Peterson my finding a correlation between Djwhal Khul's discourses in the Alice Bailey books, remarks made by Benjamin Creme, and the transcripts of the Medjugorje Madonna apparitions. As a Catholic himself, Peterson acknowledged that these findings were not only accurate, but that he had spoken with several individuals associated with Medjugorje whom, he claimed, are well aware of Maitreya and the Emergence. Among those was one of the Medjugorje visionaries. Wayne told me he once mentioned Maitreya to the visionary, who replied "Then you know the last secret," referring to the cryptic messages which the Madonna instructed the visionaries to keep secret until the proper time arrived, similar to the secrets of the Fatima visitations.

I asked Wayne if he attended the secret conference of 1990 in London at which Maitreya presided. He had not, and could not comment further. He did, however, reiterate, as he had in his lecture, how the press at the time made note of world figures converging on London. For example, the *New York Times* and *Washington Post* reported that King Hussein of Jordan and Yasser Arafat were among those in London, fueling speculation of secret Middle Eastern peace negotiations. However, Wayne claims, the press also trailed Mrs. Hussein, who had gone to New York that same weekend. When interviewed Mrs. Hussein dispelled any notion of such rumors.

The Vatican also sent two representatives to London that weekend, according to Wayne. The following week, one of the two was quoted in an article published in the Vatican newspaper in which it was stated that it was the author's conviction that Christ was in the world. As of this writing, I was unable to find this article in archival research.

I later asked Peterson if he had a copy of that article, or knew how I might narrow my search. Though he didn't have the Vatican newspaper, he told me he recalls that one of the tabloids at the time had picked up the story (referring to the *National Examiner* article mentioned earlier).

Tabloids again. They haunt me. I couldn't help but imagine how the tabloids handled the story, which was only further substantiated when Wayne told me that they added their own twist to the facts by asserting that Christ had been cloned from DNA extracted from the Shroud of Turin!

Oddly, on the very night I'd spoken with Wayne, I later happened to be channel surfing and came across an episode of *The Outer Limits* television program, which featured a science fiction retelling of the Nativity story in which the Christ-child had been cloned with DNA extracted from the Shroud of Turin!

While Peterson and I had earlier joked about the tabloid spin, I later considered the upbeat, inspirational handling of the same material by the fictional TV program. Were not both achieving the same end, I thought? Though having created a fantastic exaggeration in the obvious interest of revenue, did not the two sources, unintentionally perhaps, renew interest in the Biblical Christ tale, as well as the potential reality of Christ returned? How could I really criticize either when artists have been doing the same thing for two millennia?

The brief but potent time spent with Wayne Peterson, along with the later telephone conversation clearly confirmed the measure to which the Emergence has already influenced world events. Wayne Peterson himself perhaps offered the best summary by saying:

> "I believe that the world crisis which is affecting us all is about to shift dramatically for the better...I can assure you: the future is bright."

I certainly hope so. As each day passes, just when it seems that peace and international cooperation may be on the horizon, something goes awry. Through Peterson's story, it certainly becomes clear that the time has arrived for those who have long been working behind the scenes to finally step forward. We certainly could use the help right about now.

Chapter Eight

SUPERNAL ENCOUNTERS CONFIRMED BY A MASTER

> "Jesus could materialize his form anywhere he wished. And he still does...I went to the Masters in India for training, and they taught me about Christ in a profound and loving way as never I heard in the West. I saw Christ in their company. They talked with him. Did St. Francis lie to us? He saw Christ every night. Lord Jesus Lives! I have seen him. When you are behind a screen you see everyone else outside, but they can't see you. So the saints and the angels can see you, but you can't see them - unless you practice yoga."
>
> Paramahansa Yogananda[116]

There were several points in Wayne Peterson's story that most engaged me. On one hand, some evoked pleasant childhood memories. For example, when Wayne described how he played with the family manger figures, I instantly recalled playing with my own family's manger figurines as a child, having also bitten or chewed them. In fact, I was flooded with memories of all the religious items I too had played with that I had long forgotten. One year, for either Christmas or Easter, I was gifted with a book of heavy paper punch-outs of the town of Bethlehem which could be assembled to create a 3-D environment, and included were paper representations of the holy family. For the longest time, one of my favorite toys was the paper figure of the boy Jesus. I endowed Jesus with super-powers I thought befitting such a lad as I understood him, such as the ability to fly and perform miracles. I would drive him about in my toy cars, engaging him in interaction with toy animals and action figures. Among them was a red toy rubber frog which, for some reason, I had designated as Jesus' regular companion, like Robin to Batman. I

---

[116] From "Man's Eternal Quest" by Paramahansa Yogananda. © 1975 Self Realization Fellowship. Courtesy Self Realization Fellowship.

used to help the frog fly with Jesus by placing him in a 'space ship' that I had fashioned out of the transparent shell of a pencil sharpener. With my memory jogged by Peterson's story, I wondered if this was the root of, or inspired by, the 'time-travel' dreams of Jesus in my own youth.

Another more general issue was Wayne's encounter with the Madonna as a child. In that alone I was curious how he had processed so remarkable an experience based on my own 'eyes in the closet' event. There were few secular individuals I was aware of who had openly shared such a tale. It was here that I saw a personal parallel in our stories, in that Wayne, too, kept the story private for most if not all of his life, while privately seeking understanding and closure. Like he, it was not until Benjamin Creme's announcement of 1982 that things started to gel. As time would pass, others I would meet had very similar tales to tell - of a profound experience as a child that all seemed to lead them to this same point in time.

But one aspect of Wayne's account[117] was actually somewhat chilling for me when I first came across it, for it offered the first potential clue to what had been a most profound yet inexplicable, similar experience of my own.

During a particularly stressful period in my life, I was consumed with financial concern as I simultaneously worked two to three jobs at times just to barely make ends meet to help support my family. Working 60 to 80 hours a week or more - at an accelerated pace with the aid of a generous, never ending supply of coffee and cigarettes - I began to experience, and ignore for many months, all the classic warning symptoms of stroke or impending heart attack: A tingling numbness of the extremities, particularly in my left arm and leg; an inability to walk reasonably short distances or up a flight of steps without feeling complete exhaustion, heaviness in my legs, and/or loss of breath; non-stop heartburn to the point where antacids were literally a daily staple; increased heart rate and perspiring; chest pains, headaches, and more marked my routine day.

The level of anxiety during this time was so great that I could not sleep with regularity. It got to a point where I was actually afraid to let myself fall asleep, certain that I would have a heart attack and die, never waking again to see my then infant daughter. I couldn't die, I'd think. I had too many goals, too many ambitions. I had worked so hard for so long - I couldn't stop now. Just a little longer, I'd tell myself. Just another few months, or just another year, if I could just hang in there, I might achieve some measure of success that was consistent with my envisioned goals.

Simultaneously, it was during this same period that I was heavily

---

[117] Share International magazine, December 1997.

reading - in my *spare* time - quite a number of spiritually oriented books. These were another means of sustenance in my view. Such writings inspired me, kept me going, and offered solutions that helped take the edge off of my excessive state of stress and anxiety. Among those were the Alice Bailey books, which, quite remarkably, always and consistently seemed to offer, through the astute words of Master Djwhal Khul, some amazing morsel of information that satisfactorily explained my precise condition. Feeling reassured that certain conditions were a routine part of a day in the life of a yogi or spiritual aspirant, I would then feel just enough comfort to relax a little, endeavor to pray and meditate a bit, and then drift off to sleep.

I suppose, however, that I was really looking for a miracle at the time. I had read so many astonishing tales of the miraculous and supernal encounters of others through the years, that I just knew there had to be help of some kind out there. That's what enabled me to plow through and hang in there. I knew there was light at the end of that arduous tunnel. By this point in time, I was cautiously becoming relatively convinced that there might be some conclusive reality to all of this talk about the alleged supernatural presence of ascended Masters. I had faith that help was out there regardless, and my go-to prayer sources were Jesus, the Madonna, and other saints of the Christian tradition, who were being categorized as Masters anyway.

There was one particular night when my fear of falling asleep anxiety prevailed, when it would appear that all of those prayers were answered concurrently. Though anxious, I eventually fell asleep at some point, but I soon found myself waking around 4:00 am with a feeling of incredible pressure around my heart. Within that instant I immediately assumed I was having the oft-dreaded heart attack that I believed would get me in the end. My life began to quickly flash before my eyes - I thought of unaccomplished ambitions and goals, of friends, family and loved ones, and of my daughter. But these thoughts were interrupted when I sensed the distinct presence of other people in the room with me. I heard motion, and then felt repeated, pounding, forceful pressure being applied to my heart, accompanied by a sensation of 'fiddling' or 'tooling around' the attached ventricles, which led me to believe I was having heart surgery performed on me. After a short time, I heard a male voice say "He's starting to come around."

As I was quite drowsy and disoriented, I thought at first perhaps I was in a hospital emergency room, but when I attempted to open my eyes, I found myself unable to do so. In fact, I noticed that my entire body felt paralyzed, and the effort required to even attempt the act of opening one eyelash was enormous. I reasoned that this must have been due to a substantial amount of anesthesia still circulating through me.

Continuing to feel the pressure around my heart, I continued to strain to move and open my eyes, until finally I managed to open them just a sliver. To my astonishment, I saw, standing over me, three beings composed entirely of brilliant, lively, scintillating, pale blue light. My vision was hazy, and I was unable to make out any discernible visual details such as distinct facial features. Though they were completely composed of light, with no shadows cast beneath what were otherwise obvious to me as arms, chin, etc., it was apparent that they were people, and that at least two were male.

To my immediate left was the one responsible for the pounding and fiddling around my heart, and I could tell the one standing at my feet had been the one directing the 'operation', and had made the announcement of my waking up. The third being to my right seemed to be just observing, but I don't recall if he or she was doing anything or not.

Then, almost by the force of some unseen, silent will, my eyelids seemed to be forcibly closed by a power greater than my will. After a short while, I felt the presence depart and the room filled with a detectable silence and stillness. My body relaxed and when able I immediately opened my eyes, only to find myself lying in the darkness. As I lay there, still feeling a slight tingling pervading my body and my mind completely still and refreshed as it often is after a good meditation, I noticed a complete change in the condition of my heart. Any pain seemed gone. My anxiety was gone. My body felt completely rested, refreshed, and rejuvenated. I realized that these unknown, divine surgeons had healed me in some urgent yet mysterious manner. From that point on, all the symptoms I had prior never recurred afterwards, and medical examinations since show no evidence of damage to my heart of any sort. Twenty years after this incident when I did a series of stress tests during a hospital stay, the head heart specialist overseeing my case informed me that I had the heart of a thirty-year-old man, that it was in remarkably impressive health for my fifty-six years of age, and I needn't be concerned in that department.

For some time afterwards, I frequently recalled the event and wondered who those beings were. I would even question if the whole thing were real. One thing I was absolutely certain about was that it had not been a dream. I'd intuitively probe my subconscious with the hope that I might discern if they had been angels, Masters, or whatever!

Just as I had been doing, I scoured books and websites of all kinds, looking for anything similar. One such account I'd come across was associated with the Islamic Prophet Mohammed, who, at the age of four or five, is allegedly said to have had "two men dressed in white" appear to him, throw him down to the ground, open his chest, and 'stir their hands about.' As recorded in the Islamic *Hadith*, the Prophet, when asked about the incident later in his life, explained that the men were angels who had come to purify his heart of original sin by washing it with snow.

Hmm. Had my visitor's been angels? I read on. In Alice Bailey's *A Treatise on Cosmic Fire*, I found an interesting, correlating explanation as offered by the reliable Djwhal Khul, as follows:

> 'There is a definite occult reason, under the Laws of Electricity, behind the known fact that every initiate, presented to the Initiator, is accompanied by two of the Masters, who stand one on either side of him. The three of them together form a triangle which makes the work possible.
>
> The force of ... [initiation] is twofold, and its power terrific. Apart and alone the initiate could not receive the voltage ... without serious hurt, but in triangular formation transmission comes safely. The two Masters Who thus sponsor the initiate, represent two polarities of the electric All; part of Their work is therefore to stand with all applicants for initiation when they come before the Great Lord.'

Now, this explains the 'sponsorship' described by both Krishnamurti and Peterson in a context for them that seemed more plausible. But did this explain my own experience?

It was several years after this when I read Wayne Peterson's stories. I immediately saw the age parallel between his own Madonna encounter and the Prophet Mohammed's angel encounter. What struck me was that this was also the approximate age when I saw the mysterious 'eyes in the closet.' On this particular common aspect, Djwhal Khul purports that at the age of four to seven is the time of life when the "hitherto overshadowing" soul takes possession of its nurtured, physical 'vehicle.'

But it was Wayne's 'visit to the other side' - like Krishnamurti's - for his meetings with Maitreya and the Masters which I found most intriguing, and led me to wonder if my nocturnal 'heart surgery' was the tail end of my own, unrecalled, overwhelming visit somewhere. I had to wonder: Were these experiences of what the esotericists refer to as initiation? I didn't want to be so presumptuous. On the other hand, book after book after book I'd read explained such mystic phenomena in some similar, relative way.

Or, had it been simply an unprepared introduction, spurred on by sincere, prayerful invitations, with a miraculous, life-saving RSVP. How could I know if it really happened? On the other hand, how could I doubt the reality of so amazing an experience? It was quite real. There was no reason for me to doubt the potential plausibility that the three attending 'surgeons' had, perhaps, been some of the very Masters referenced herein.

As I replayed the scenario over and over in my mind, I thought it was quite possible - due to my state of health at the time - that I actually *had* died in my sleep, and that I'd been graciously revived, either solely due to the intense fervor of my prayers, or because I had some unfinished business remaining. For thereafter, not only did I begin to experience a gradually noticeable improvement in my health, but my life then became flooded with many marvelous events of a similar nature, and my personal, spiritual growth seemed to swing into a new, accelerated direction, as if some major obstacle had been removed.

All of these things yet intrigued me, especially when they literally seemed to be happening first hand more and more. By the Spring of 1999, I had already mailed an early draft of this book to Benjamin Creme for review and quote permission, and in anticipation of securing another personal interview. I was aware that he'd likely be in the United States for his regular summer lecture tour. Having read so many accounts of confirmations by his Master, I'd hoped, if personal contact with Mr. Creme was established, that the opportunity might avail itself to inquire of his own Master's view on this experience, as well as a series of strange incidents and encounters.

After some time had passed, I received a response from Mr. Creme, his letter having arrived just a few weeks shy of his scheduled lecture in New York. I recalled how amazing my experiences had been in previous years - the forceful ball of golden light, the leaping wafts of light, the golden glow during the overshadowing. I was also aware that, as Wayne Peterson indicated, that Maitreya himself is said to routinely make a brief appearance, although generally in disguise. Nevertheless, I wanted more than anything to investigate my recollection of that incredible energy, the extraordinary, undeniable sense of presence.

On to New York

Upon arriving in New York, it was just a short walk to the Hotel Pennsylvania, where Mr. Creme's lecture was to be held in the Skytop Ballroom. Adjacent to the ballroom entrance was a showcase displaying a montage of vintage black and white photographs of the Glenn Miller Orchestra. Having seen the old film version of *The Glenn Miller Story* with Jimmy Stewart and June Allyson countless times, the connection about Miller's song *'Pennsylvania 6 - 5000'* never occurred to me until right then and there.

This very Ballroom had been one of the swing era's most jumpin' joints, and the thought of sitting in a room so historically integrated in popular culture was fascinating.

The room itself gradually filled with sparse groups and singular attendees who trickled in right up to the two o'clock start time. As I looked around it seemed apparent that more than likely everyone else had also heard the stories about Maitreya's alleged tendency to appear in disguise at Mr. Creme's lectures, as many seemed to be looking at others with suspect, sidelong glances. I too found myself taking note of any outstanding, eccentric qualities in others.

Dismissing the notion, I turned back to face the front. A quiet, breathless atmosphere of expectancy pervaded the entire room as Benjamin Creme took the stage. After a few minutes were extended for stragglers to enter and seat themselves, Mr. Creme began to speak. Just as I remembered him, Mr. Creme had a gentle, commanding presence, speaking with casual conviction. Dressed in a camel tone suit and tie, his demeanor was simultaneously authoritative and relaxed.

"I believe that what I'm saying is true," Creme began, "but I present it to you this evening for your consideration only, not as dogma. If it appears logical and rational, by all means accept it, otherwise not. All I ask is that you keep an open mind." His words and mannerisms reflected an inherent respect, cordiality, and consideration of all in attendance.

Much on what he then spoke was background information with which I was quite familiar, yet it was pleasant to hear it anew. Mr. Creme accents his lectures with frequent injections of dry wit and common sense. It would be the sort of talk you might expect from Benjamin Franklin - down to earth, practical, yet addressing issues of global social, political, and economic concern in the same breath. "No nation can stand alone," said Creme. "Competition is antithetical to cooperation." He explained at length why the established political and economic systems do not work and cannot survive and ultimately face complete collapse.

He outlined and offered illustrative examples of where established systems had already collapsed, indicating the role in those changes played by Maitreya and the Masters. He discussed the point addressed by Wayne Peterson - how Maitreya had allegedly *appeared* before Mikhail Gorbachev, the influence of which saw the advent of Glasnost in the Soviet Union, and the ultimate demise of the cold war. He offered that Maitreya had also influenced Nelson Mandela while the latter was still a political prisoner, and that it was Maitreya who inspired Mandela to write to the South African President, requesting a meeting. Creme said that Maitreya then appeared to the South African President (whether it was De Klerk or Botha was unclear), and had a little chat with him as well. The rest, we know, is incredible history.[118]

As to the exact hour of Maitreya's formal public Emergence, Creme explained, even Maitreya himself cannot answer that question. It would require a prevailing, ideal set of circumstances that created a comfortable opening for him to step forward, but paramount was adherence to the key 'prime directive' - that it did not infringe on human free will in any manner. He also addressed the issue of an imminent television interview with Maitreya that had already been arranged with a major American television network, and which is said to be on standby until Maitreya gives the word.

Creme then humorously offered various examples of other lecturer's and author's suggested signs and ways in which Christ would return, such as that certain mathematical formulas gleaned via the Great Pyramids of Egypt were held to reveal the precise date of His return, etc.

As intermission commenced, I wondered if the opportunity to speak with Mr. Creme would avail itself, but the emcee then requested that the audience refrain from approaching him. Respectfully, I detached myself from further concern to speak with him.

While chatting with some acquaintances, I heard my name called from behind. Turning, I noticed my friend James walking in from the lobby, followed by Benjamin Creme.

James then introduced me to Mr. Creme. Vigorously clasping Mr. Creme's hand, I insisted that the pleasure was mine. James explained that Mr. Creme, long acquainted with James and aware that he lived in Philadelphia, had recalled my mailed manuscript segment and expressed a desire to meet me.

Mr. Creme began by mentioning a young Sufi teacher I'd written about in the original manuscript, and remarked that he'd been familiar with his work since the late 70s.

I laughed, and commented on how he'd told me more about the young Sufi than the Sufi himself had revealed.

"Well," Creme replied playfully, "I asked how much *I could* say."

He was referring to telepathically asking his omniscient Master, who apparently had filled Mr. Creme in on relatively confidential details about the Sufi. As we chatted, I took notice of others standing nearby who wished to speak with him. I knew this just wasn't the right time to get into any requests of his Master's confirmation. So, I thanked Mr. Creme, shook hands, and

---

[118] Attempts were made by the author to contact both Mr. Gorbachev and Mr. Mandela with the hopes of securing an interview for the purpose of verification of these alleged encounters. No response has yet been received.

expressed my wish to speak again soon. I then gravitated back to my seat as the intermission ended, for the best was yet to be.

The Overshadowing

As the program resumed, Mr. Creme fielded questions from the audience that had been prepared in writing during the intermission. The questions ranged from inquiries about Maitreya's latest appearances to understanding the direct consequences resulting from his anticipated public debut. Creme's answers, as expected, were informative, sometimes inspiring, frequently provocative and occasionally humorous.

As the question and answer session concluded, Mr. Creme announced that the time had come for Maitreya's blessing. He also mentioned, that, since the Indian saint/avatar Satya Sai Baba had been mentioned in the final answered question, that his presence had been invoked. Thus, it was explained, that Sai Baba would first overshadow and bless the audience, followed afterwards by Maitreya. We were asked to get comfortable as if preparing for meditation.

Benjamin Creme also adjusted his seated posture, after which he abruptly raised his right arm, as though prepared to swear an oath, his palm faced outward to the crowd.

Shortly thereafter, I detected an audible hum such as that which I had experienced in previous years at these programs. It resonated very much like the primordial mantra of all mantras - Om. Though no recording of any specific sound was played, there was a distinct change in the atmosphere. The 'hum' seemed to shift in pitch in cyclical stages, gradually increasing in potency. Simultaneously, though the room was flooded with daylight, I was awestruck to see an increasing white aura around Mr. Creme. The room was then saturated with energy so thick that it seemed like an invisible, electric gel had filled all the open space in the room. The very air particles seemed denser, almost weighty.

I started to feel my *ajna* center (third eye) throb and undulate as if an impatient worm had just awakened between my eyebrows. The sensation increased gradually but rapidly, until it felt like a basketball was being dribbled between my eyes.

As I watched Mr. Creme, the aura of white light around him had become brilliant, practically silhouetting his form. I looked on as I saw the light around his head pulsate in unison with the throb of my ajna center. The light grew more brilliant until finally it seemed as if his head had dissolved and disappeared, replaced by a munificent glowing orb of scintillating white light. When I could once more see his face, I noticed that Mr. Creme's gaze had come to my seat in the row, and I noticed that he now had both hands raised.

As our eyes met, the throb between my eyes was so forceful that it truly felt like some alien creature would burst out of me at that instant. Though fiercely racing like an accelerated heartbeat, I intuitively knew there was a harmonious order and rhythm that was harmless and safe, so rather than fearing it, I remained calm and relished it.

The glowing orb that seemed to replace Mr. Creme's head again began to transmute, and I then saw emerge a pale, light-infused version of Satya Sai Baba, replacing Mr. Creme's head first, then his whole form, his suit replaced by a long white robe. It was now Sai Baba who stood thus dressed with his hand extended. I was amazed, yet my consciousness at the time was not in a position to think mundane thoughts. I was too transfixed on what I was seeing.

But then the translucent visage of Sai Baba dissolved as well, and a pure light of golden milk bathed the front of the room. At times, I thought I was seeing various forms and other people - historical figures - but wasn't sure if this was just an imaginary experience resulting from the intense drowsiness brought on by the potent energy pervading the room. The radiant light originating from center stage continued to resonate and saturate the entire atmosphere, and all throughout, I could not perceive Benjamin Creme. It was as if he had completely dissolved into light. Inwardly, I was amazed, on the edge of complete humility, for it wasn't just the reaction to such a remarkably powerful visual spectacle, but an absolutely fulfilling experience of unconditional love. This was not imaginary or a psychological projection of some deep-seated yearning or desire. There was a presence as close to my concept of God or the divine that just made my heart melt. It was a feeling of coming home, of being welcomed without haste, without judgement.

The resonant presence remained palpable for some time. I didn't want it to end. All external sensation and perception aside, I was feeling closer to the goal of my personal sadhana - my spiritual practice and pursuits - than I had in a long time. I felt as if my very heart had become sacred ground - the holy of holies, and there was little I could do but inwardly pranam in acknowledgement.

When the program concluded and Mr. Creme took leave, I sat still, relishing the aftermath of yet another extraordinary experience. The point between my eyebrows continued to noticeably throb, but at a greatly reduced rate, pulsing rhythmically like a normal heart rate. This overshadowing was by far the most powerful that I'd felt in all the occasions of attending Mr. Creme's programs.

As we departed the Hotel, I glanced at a "Crusade for Christ" banner sprawled across a vast expanse of Madison Square Garden, which was directly across the street. Though I'd noticed it earlier, I now thought how ironic it seemed in light of the incredible experience I'd just had of the very epicenter of focused energy and love of what was asserted to have been the Christ Himself.

As our small group of friends joined together outside the hotel on Seventh Avenue, our friend James informed us that an invitation had been extended to join some others at an informal reception for Mr. Creme in Brooklyn that evening. That would be great, I thought. For many years Sophia had shared about having joined Mr. Creme in such an informal fashion in years past and had often expressed how delightful it had been. She'd told me that Creme had frequently communicated with his Master in such instances, to answer the questions or inquiries of the guests, and to confirm various experiences. I wondered if this would be the chance to inquire about the experiences that I'd had. I'd seen him confirm various things at his public programs, and I was always struck with the casualness with which he handled it. I did like this aspect of Creme's personality. He wasn't a fanatic at all. At the very least, I did have one small objective - I had to know the view of Mr. Creme's Master about the eyes I saw in the closet as a child.

After taking a series of connecting subway cars, we arrived in Brooklyn, and, walking a short distance from the station, we arrived at the apartment of some of Mr. Creme's supporters. I recognized a number of those gathered, perhaps 25 in all, who had attended the program. As the apartment was long and narrow, the small group of people made for quite an instantly cozy atmosphere.

As I looked about, I saw, seated on a wooden chair in the center of the living room was the saintly bard himself, Benjamin Creme. Seeing that he was surrounded by a small group of people engaged in conversation, I again surrendered at once the notion of discussing personal matters. He seemed to be enjoying his meal, and I realized the guy needed a break, decided it was best to leave him alone to enjoy the company of his friends, and instead enjoy myself in the company of those who were immediately around me.

I soon found myself speaking with visitors from various parts of the United States, and at least one fellow from China who'd participated in the 1989 Tiananmen Square protests. I listened eagerly as others shared their own experiences of how each came to hear of Benjamin Creme, or had received confirmation of their encounters with Maitreya or the Masters, of the type of which are frequently found in each issue of Share International magazine. We talked about art and politics, religion and spirituality, idealism and social activism, and the impact of the work of various people and organizations at a grass roots level.

After a while I noticed an empty seat near Mr. Creme and decided to venture closer to listen. Mr. Creme was telling amazing stories of his own experiences, of others he'd met on his various world tours over the years, and he was confirming the experiences of encounters with Masters with some of those present.

One woman explained that she had been running late earlier in the day, arriving at the Hotel Pennsylvania well after Mr. Creme's lecture had started. As she hurriedly rushed up the Hotel steps, she was taken aback when she noticed Benjamin Creme walking past her in the opposite direction, exiting the hotel. She expressed how shocked she was since she knew the lecture had started some time before, and was puzzled as to why Creme was leaving. She was even more baffled when she then entered the Skytop Ballroom and found Mr. Creme already lecturing.

Compounding her story was the interjection of another woman who explained that she too had seen Mr. Creme leaving the hotel. Mr. Creme meekly laughed, and, ever in telepathic rapport with his Master, explained that both women had seen Maitreya in one of his favorite and frequently used disguises - that of Benjamin Creme.

Those already familiar with the playful capabilities of the Master of Masters gasped in delight. All listened intently as one person after another offered some experience for Mr. Creme's Master to confirm. Mr. Creme either made light of his Master's reply, or offered a sincere, comprehensive, and respectful explanation, depending on the disposition of the individual whom he addressed. There were all sorts of stories, of meeting Maitreya in the middle of an intersection, at a bookstore, in a library, at a church. All of them were intriguing.

As I didn't know anyone personally, I listened politely to the interchange without wishing to be intrusive. Then, at one point, a man who had been sitting in the chair to Mr. Creme's immediate right got up, turned, and motioned for me to take the seat. While preferring to be modest, I graciously seized the opportunity, uncertain of where to begin.

An Unexpected Guest

After waiting a few minutes for a lull in the conversation, I handed Mr. Creme a photograph that I'd brought with me. It had been taken at the birthday party of a Muslim friend a few months prior. In all of the photographs there appeared either a hazy green streak or smudged orb of white light, or a combination of the green along with a streak of white light. They had the appearance of something moving very fast just as the shutter was released. In this particular photograph of my friend and I, the green light was present, yet around my head was a distinct, perfect, thin, crescent-shaped arc of light which resembled an artist's depiction of a halo. I wanted to inquire about the light since Share International Magazine had printed similar light-streaked photos, which Mr. Creme's Master had confirmed as having been caused by one of the Masters.

While closely analyzing the photo, Mr. Creme asked me when and where it was taken and what the occasion was. Having informed him, Mr. Creme said, "I'm not sure about the green light, but this one (pointing to the white, halo-arc) was caused by the Master Jesus" further explaining that the Master Jesus had been present but invisible.

I was fairly astonished to hear Mr. Creme's assessment. On one hand, Mr. Creme's words served to validate the known depth of my relationship with Jesus. I often feel He is with me. So, in this regard, it wasn't all that earth shattering, but having it captured in a photo was pretty cool. It was also consistent in that the common ground of conversations with my incredibly devout Muslim friends was our common belief in the sacredness of Jesus and Mary. It was one area that formed a foundational bridge for communication despite our differing respective religious and national backgrounds.

On the other hand, Mr. Creme's words may have indirectly confirmed another experience. I couldn't wait to tell my friends who were with me that evening. At one point while dancing at the party, I had an exceptionally profound meditative experience of my heart filling with an unusually heightened and overwhelming feeling of joy. I recall, that, accompanying the sensation was the feeling that an extraordinary presence was in the room. In those days, while I was engaged full swing into the research on divine apparitions by Jesus, Mary, Angels, and then, in the esoteric context - Masters, I recall there were times when I seemed to almost be able to sense when such a thing was happening, as if I was getting unseen, heavenly assistance with this book, as if these alleged unseen Masters *wanted* their story to be shared.

During the party, I then turned to my Catholic friend who was standing on the edge of the dance floor. She had been a primary assistant while I was engaged in the research for this book from the beginning. "Do you feel that?" I asked. "Can't you feel that?"

My friend wasn't sure what I meant at first, but then her eyes lit up, and she slowly acknowledged - "Yes... Yes, I think I can feel what you mean. It's like the energy level in here changed. Feels more positive or something. What do you think it is?"

"I don't know" I replied. "I have to wonder. Could it be one of the

Masters Mr. Creme talks about?" My friend beamed and rolled her eyes. I continued: "If I didn't know better, I'd swear one of them is here. Or an angel, or something."

I'd had experiences like this before, but never so potent and had never quite summarized it like this. Years before, I used to consciously practice club dancing as a form of yoga with the goal, like the whirling dervishes of Sufism, of exercising dance as a means to get into mindless, meditative ecstatic states. Part of my reasoning was then based on my study and practice of the tenets of Kashmir Shaivism which declare that everything can be used as a tool for experience of the divine. These sensations were particularly heightened when dancing to a song that I would interpret as having some spiritually themed content, such as *'Express Kundalini'* by the band Love and Rockets, *'Invisible Sun'* by The Police, or *'Heaven'* by The Psychedelic Furs. The whole experience was a complete meditation. It wasn't until more recently, after reading scores of accounts such as those herein, that I started to try and distinguish the Shakti felt on certain occasions as possibly being the presence of 'an other.'

In fact, in those years, as I increasingly read so many testimonies of individuals having such incredible encounters, I found myself comparing their stories to quite a few of my own personal encounters with individuals that had definitely stood out from the rest of the pack and made my 'spider-senses tingle.' Though I'd pass, encounter, sit next to, behind, or in front of any number of people on any given day, there was occasionally that one individual who seemed to possess an uncanny power of attraction, leaving me at times to wonder if I was intuitively sensing the presence of what the esotericists defined as a Master.

As discussed earlier, such heightened sensitivity is referred to as *mati* - a by-product of meditation practice. But since initiating the first stages of this work, from a concerted review of the research to beginning the first few pages of writing, it seemed that the number of such instances began to occur with greater frequency. The strange or inspiring things that had occurred only further begun to transform my once cautious belief into a willing open-mindedness. It was these instances that I wished to run by Mr. Creme.

The Dynamic Duo

Once, my friend Sophia and I were discussing some of the 'confirmed sightings' in Share International Magazine. In particular, we were quite amused at how playful Maitreya and Jesus seemed when encountered together as a duo. I commented in particular that, like a comedy team, Maitreya seemed to always play the 'straight man', while Jesus behaved quite humorously, which prompted me to say, at one point: "He's the wacky one!"

The following day, while cleaning the inside glass on the front door of a shop where I then worked, I noticed a short, Mexican or Native-American looking fellow in a red baseball cap walk quickly past very much like Groucho Marx, while simultaneously grinning, crossing his eyes and making hilarious facial expressions at me.

Immediately following was a taller, distinguished looking man with greyish hair and who appeared to be of Northern Indian or Pakistani origin. As he walked into view, he also looked directly at me while pointing with exaggeration to his goofy friend with one hand and simultaneously twirling his other finger around the temple of his head making the 'crazy' sign. I unassumingly translated this gesture to mean that the first man was 'the wacky one.'

I immediately wondered, since I'd been discussing this only the night before, if I had just encountered the dynamic duo of Maitreya and Jesus. Since there was a wall on either side of the door that prevented me from anticipating them in the first place (or they, me), and seeing the direction in which they headed, I turned to put down the bottle of glass cleaner and paper towels, and opened the door and check them out a bit more. But in the brief time it took to put my things down, open the door, and look down the sparsely crowded sidewalk - no more than 10 seconds - they were gone. If it had been them, they must have certainly found my comment amusing.

When I shared an abbreviated version of this with Mr. Creme, his Master confirmed that the shorter 'wacky' man had indeed been the Master Jesus, and the second, taller man had been Maitreya.

Reunion on South Street

Another time, my friend and I were discussing the experience presented in Share International magazine of a woman who'd encountered a curious and bizarre, African American street person in the New York Public Library. In that encounter, the street person exhibited curious behavior after laying out neatly before himself a selection of books opened to pages featuring scriptural references to the second coming, several periodicals with highlighted selections, some sheet music, and a set of grooming tools with which he proceeded to carefully trim his hair and beard. He also had, lying on the table, a silver flute, which he picked up and mimicked playing yet emitted no sound. The woman later commented that the flute reminded her of similar images of

Lord Krishna, as found in the Bhagavad-Gita.[119] Benjamin Creme revealed that the flute player had been Maitreya.

A few days after this conversation with Sophia, my wife and I went to Philadelphia's famed South Street, where there was then a used book store that has been a favorite of mine since the mid 1970s. I had planned on purchasing a copy of Alice Bailey's *Externalization of the Hierarchy* for additional research, and for several days I felt as if something kept compelling me to check out that particular bookstore first. It was with some degree of surprise, therefore, when my wife suggested, out of the blue, that we take a jaunt to South Street, a trip we rarely take together.

No sooner had we parked our car and began walking in the direction of the bookstore, that I noticed, on an adjacent corner, a neatly groomed African-American man playing a silver flute. I was amused by the coincidence of his presence based on the fact my friend and I had just discussed the New York Library story.

I watched curiously since, by that time, I'd read virtually hundreds of encounter stories in back issues of Share International magazine. The man's eyes possessed a deep sweetness that seemed to dance with every note of his flute. As my wife and I passed, I noticed his instrument case propped open for donations from passersby, so I paused to dig into my pocket for some change to put in the case.

I pulled out a few coins, and, as I leaned down to place the money in the case, the flutist began to bend, leaning down with and towards me, and gazed right at me. Sensing this while still hunched over, I looked up to see the flutist's face right before mine, and when our eyes met, he briefly stopped playing and said to me, "Nice to see you again," then immediately resumed playing.

Nice to see me? I'd never seen the man before. Or had I? Doesn't this guy always play around town? The flutist rolled his twinkling eyes heavenward, then back down in my direction, the whole while sporting a mischievous grin. I was puzzled, yet humored. Shocked at the idea of who I thought this could be, I grinned, childlike, as I slowly straightened myself up. My thought at the time was, if it were, in fact, Maitreya, the comment was simply confirming the previous encounters I'd wondered about. In addition, I did find an old, battered copy of Bailey's 'Externalization....' in the used bookstore. When I completed sharing this, Mr. Creme said his Master informed us that the flutist had indeed been Maitreya.

---

[119] This entire encounter was videotaped by the woman, and is available through Share International Foundation.

A Wayward Soul

I recounted another incident that happened while en route to a wedding. Along side of a small cafe where the ceremony was to take place was a rear service alley where I temporarily parked my car to let out my wife and daughter. After they went inside, I drove around the block to find a place to park. The only space I found was one street over and virtually diagonal from where I had just stopped temporarily. To save time, it made sense to walk back through the same alley.

As I walked around a bend, I saw a short, stocky, disheveled-looking woman emerging from the opposite side of the alley. She wore a crocheted hat and held a brown paper bag that I assumed was camouflaging a bottle of beer or wine. I began to check my pockets for change, which I often do when in anticipation of being panhandled. Sure enough, the woman asked if I had any to spare.

"Sure," I said, smiling at the woman. She seemed sad and weary, quite down and out, revealing that it wasn't likely that she took very good care of herself.

"Now you are going to use this to get something to eat, right?" I asked as I counted some change. Sheepishly, she nodded and mumbled something in response, yet I noticed that she spoke with an Irish brogue, which wasn't all that unusual since the area where I live is heavily populated with Irish immigrants. Being of Irish extraction myself, my heart went out to this broken, fellow kin. As I placed the money in her hand, I clasped it between my own hands. "What's your name?" I asked her.

"Bridget" she replied promptly.

"Well," I said with surprise, "that's my daughter's middle name, and it was my Great-grandmother's name. She was from Limerick."[120] 'Bridget's' eyes lit up with joy, sensing the familiarity. "Where are you from?" I asked her.

"County Galway!" she exclaimed with a smile.

"Ah," I said, "That's where my father's family came from, but a long time ago." She listened with interest as I still held her hand. I looked at her with compassion, making sure she was looking into my eyes. "Are you taking good care of yourself, Bridget?" I asked. Her eyes began to well with tears as she mumbled something in response. I asked her to what parish she belonged - the quintessential question between two Irish Catholics on the occasion of first meeting. After telling me the name of her church, I said to her, "Now listen, Bridget. I'm sure if you get yourself over to church and say some prayers that

---

[120] Referring to the County by that name in Ireland.

things will turn out better. Will you do that, Bridget?" The woman nodded in agreement, so I then shook her hand between mine, preparing to part. I smiled as I looked into her eyes, saying "You take care of yourself, Bridget, Ok? God bless you."

With that, I continued on to the cafe. Glancing back, I saw Bridget's desperate loneliness manifest in her posture, holding her crumpled brown bag more firmly than before, and I noticed she had begun to weep. I thought how nice it must be for her or anyone in such circumstances to be treated with kindness for a change. I wondered about what sort of difficulty had transpired in her life to bring on such dire straights.

After recounting the tale, Benjamin Creme then said, "That woman was the Master Jesus."

The 'Eyes' Confirmed

Everyone in the small living room was by now listening with great interest, much as they had while listening to the sharing and confirmations of those who spoke to Mr. Creme before me. Concerned that I might be 'hogging' his time, I looked about to see if there was someone else who wished to speak to Mr. Creme, but as there was a brief lull and no one spoke up, I seized the moment for one more.

"Ben," I began, "there is one experience that I've been wondering about all my life." I then explained my mischievous habit of climbing around my childhood bed room.

"When I was a child, somewhere between the ages of three and six, I used to climb on the edge of my crib and swing from the molding atop my closet door. One night, as I clung to the molding, I saw a pair of eyes in the closet. My parents insisted I had seen a reflection, but there was no way anything could have reflected in that part of the room."

Mr. Creme smirked. "And who do you think it was?" he asked.
"Well," I replied, "at that age I wasn't sure, but I've always thought it had been Jesus."

Mr. Creme nodded respectfully, "That *was* the Master Jesus whose eyes you saw."

The moment was personally quite moving. For over thirty years I have recalled that incident of the eyes in the closet, wondering if I would ever learn to whom they belonged. Mr. Creme's confirmation brought complete closure, along with an innate sense that this was the truth. I recall getting a lump in my throat.

"What did this mean?" I thought. I contemplated with conviction the awareness that many of my hunches through life had certainly been true, that the eyes were Jesus', that it was Jesus who guided me to Baba Muktananda and other teachers, but more overwhelming was the thought in totality that Jesus had been looking after me all my life. I felt extremely blessed. It didn't matter that no one in my entire life had believed me, what did matter was that I knew, and that knowing had just been acknowledged. Any remnant of doubt that had been born in external criticism and humiliation just melted away. I felt a lifetime of emotional scarring over the rejection I'd encountered begin to heal right then and there. A feeling of tremendous love filled my heart. The lifelong wait had ended.

Sophia's Angel

My friend Sophia inquired with Mr. Creme about an experience she once had back in the early nineties. It was mid-winter, and Sophia was heading home in the pre-dawn morning hours from her work as a restaurant manager. After arriving at an intersection near the bridge that would take her from Philadelphia to her home across the Delaware River in New Jersey, her car suddenly stalled. Contemplating her options, she decided to persevere through the bitterly cold wintry winds to find a policeman. The streets were desolate, and finding no one, she then made her way back to her car. Still, Sophia was concerned, for the city streets in that section at 4:00 am are not really an appropriate place for a woman to be alone.

Having returned to her car, she noticed a late 1980s model burgundy 'Crown Victoria' model automobile pull up alongside her as if out of nowhere. "What's ironic" Sophia later explained, "it looked sort of like the car I'm driving now."

She then described how "A large guy, with very dark skin - a tall, very big, 'round' person, with kind of a gentle nature to him" got out of his car and asked if she needed assistance.

"I was very cautious of interacting with someone at four in the morning, but I felt at ease. I felt there was a softness to this person," who then helped her push the car off to the side of the road. The man asked her what she was gonna do, and Sophia mentioned that she would need to use a phone. In those days before cel phones were a thing, the man asked if she knew where the closest pay phone was, and Sophia indicated she thought it was just a few blocks away.

"He offered to drive me up and it was freezing outside," she continued, "so, I was kind of hesitant because of safety, but I felt it was ok. So, I got in his car and he drove me up to the corner. I got out of the car and the entire time I was on the phone he kept the car running and stayed at the corner, kind of protecting me, and sure enough, every once in a while, there'd be some weirdos who'd drive by and yell stuff out the window to me. I was on the phone for a good half hour, periodically getting in his car to warm up so I didn't freeze, between trying to get through to someone and make arrangements for a tow truck to meet me. We got the situation handled and he proceeded to drive me back to my car, and it took a little longer because there were all these one-way streets."

As they drove, Sophia thought about how she could repay the man's kindness, and wondered how she could break the ice and broach the subject.

"So, I asked him at one point, "What are you doing up so late?" He said he had just gotten back from church, which didn't faze me at the time, but later I wondered, "What church is open at three in the morning?" I told him I worked at a restaurant and asked if he would like to come in so I could treat him to dinner or whatever in repayment, and he responded by saying no, that he and his wife don't go out or drink. I then told him that I'd like to repay him in some way but I didn't know how."

"He said 'The way that you can repay me is by turning around and doing something good for someone else. That's enough in itself.'"

"And then I got out of his car and off he went. The sun was then coming up so I just sat in my car and waited for the tow truck. I'm not sure whether I verbalized this to him or not, but I definitely recall thinking 'You're like a guardian angel who's come to help me.' If I didn't say it to him that's how I thought of him whenever I would later tell the story to someone."

All of us in the small room listened attentively to Sophia's story. Sporting a confident grin, Benjamin Creme then said to Sophia, "And who do you think it was?"

"I always thought it was an angel," Sophia responded, "but now I'm not so sure."

"That," said Mr. Creme, "was the Master Jesus who helped you."

Shortly afterwards, Sophia, James, and I decided it was an appropriate time to leave. After thanking Mr. Creme, our hosts, and bidding farewell, we went to catch our train, and all during the subway ride back to Manhattan we spoke enthusiastically about our mutual revelations. James shared a number of similar experiences he'd had confirmed in the past, and all of us discussed the profundity of the evening's occurrences.

When we arrived in Manhattan, we agreed on finding somewhere to get a nightcap and a bite to eat, so James escorted us through Times Square, which was teeming with lively nighthawks and tourists. After working our way through the crowd, we arrived at the Marriot Marquis Hotel, settling ourselves in a sofa lounge on the expansive mezzanine, where we continued to share stories and wax philosophically into the early morning hours.

Transmission at Grammercy Park

The following morning, Sophia and I stopped for a quick breakfast before going on to the Sunday Transmission Meditation session which Mr. Creme was to host.

Shortly after arriving at the Grammercy Park Hotel, I sat down to write out some thoughts and questions for Mr. Creme with regard to some pertinent, confidential issues relative to this book which I found perplexing at the time. I had planned to offer these in the form of a letter since I wasn't sure if I'd have another chance to speak with Mr. Creme in person.

As I sat writing in the rear of the small conference room, Benjamin Creme entered, and was immediately besieged, albeit at a relaxed pace, by a barrage of individuals and couples who engaged him in conversation. I wasn't sure if I wanted to bother him and then assumed it unlikely that I would be able to speak with him. Having completed my letter, I planned on simply handing it to Mr. Creme and extend a cordial farewell and thanks in advance. While a small group of people around him had thinned out, I took my place off to the side as he spoke to the last of the group, and then I approached him.

Extending my hand, I thanked him and expressed my pleasure in meeting and conversing with him. Mr. Creme acknowledged my sentiments in kind, and I then presented the envelope. "When you have a chance," I said, "I've written down some questions pertaining to issues raised by the young Sufi man that I thought you could help clarify." I noticed, that, instead of placing my letter in his bag as he had done with envelopes handed to him by the others, he immediately began to open the envelope and run his fingers along the page as if he were reading it telepathically. "What is it regarding?" he asked.

As I explained to him the details of the letter's contents, he expressed interest in some of the points. Then Mr. Creme then made some interesting, *specifically detailed* remarks on certain points which he had no way of knowing. Only a few close friends knew some of those details, and only I knew one or two others. Instantly, it was then when I became convinced that Mr. Creme's telepathic rapport with his Master must indeed be genuine.

Mr. Creme's Master explains telepathy as follows"

"As understanding grows of the nature and source of consciousness, a truer picture will emerge of the status and function of the brain, as the focal point for the infinite variety of impulses reaching it from higher principles.

For many, too, the mind is the man. They see themselves, through identification, as mental beings, capable of thought and action, completely autonomous and separate, whose very existence stems from the ability to think and measure. This, likewise, is but a shadow of the true relationship existing between man and mind.

Man's mind is an instrument, a body, more or less sensitive, depending on the person, by which the mental planes can be contacted and known. The plane of mind, the mind-belt, is infinite in extent and serves as the conduit for all mental experience.

When men realize this, they will understand how telepathy is the natural result of this relationship, and a new era of mutual communication and understanding will begin."[121]

Benjamin Creme further elucidates:

"A mother often has a close, telepathic contact with the child: if something is harming the child, the mother will know. Telepathy as described by the Master and as known and used by Hierarchy is of the same nature but of an altogether different order.

The Masters do not use speech. They might if they came before a disciple physically but the normal way for a Master is by telepathic contact. The Masters train their disciples in telepathy and form, if necessary, a telepathic link, if the disciple has the ability. We all have it potentially, but a disciple who already has the ability can be contacted. This faculty can be developed, trained, and becomes a powerful instrument of contact. Of course it saves the Master from having to visit a disciple and make an actual verbal contact. He can flash an impression or a thought and He knows that the disciple...will carry out the Master's wishes."[122]

When Mr. Creme had concluded his remarkably insightful comments, I was mesmerized. I knew his response was coming from a source beyond himself and I can only relay to readers that it's something to be experienced for oneself to fully comprehend. I wasn't sure that I completely understood it, at the time, but it was definitely apparent. I smiled and shook his hand.

"Please ask your Master if I might have His blessing," I said, to which Mr. Creme replied, smiling and sporting a loving twinkle in his eyes, "You always have blessings."

---

[121] Source: 'Maitreya's Mission Volume Two', by Benjamin Creme; Chapter 12, page 3
. Originally published under "the Growth of Consciousness" in Share International Magazine, September, 1992.
[122] Source: 'Maitreya's Mission Volume Two', by Benjamin Creme; Chapter 12, page 386.

A Bit o' Heaven on the Frankford El

After meditating with the group for several hours, I took an early leave as planned, and caught a taxi to Pennsylvania Station. On the long train ride home, I sat and reflected on all the things that had transpired on this most marvelous of weekends, recording some of the events in my journal. When I finally arrived in Philadelphia in the early evening, I caught a connecting commuter train on the Market-Frankford elevated line to the suburb where I live.

This same elevated train had been made famous by a popular song in the late 1960's called "You can't get to heaven on the Frankford El." Yet, ironically, I would later learn that one of heaven's representatives had actually joined me on that El trip homeward.

I was sitting in the very first car of the sparsely populated train, when I noticed a dark figure appear in the window on the outside of the door of my car. While the train was still moving and jerking along, the door opened, and I saw a very dark-skinned black woman enter. She was wearing a black T-shirt that said something about Jesus printed on it in white, sported a backwards turned black baseball cap, blue jeans and sneakers. As she entered she approached the person sitting closest to the door, shouting maniacally at the top of her lungs,

"IN THE NAME OF JESUS CAN YOU SPARE TWO DOLLARS FOR SOMETHING TO EAT?!"

The passenger ignored her. She went to the next person, then to the next, and finally to a young man who was seated diagonally across from me, each time shouting her request. I noticed the man across from me was wearing a Catholic League basketball T-shirt, and upon closer examination, noticed that he had been reading the Bible. When the woman asked this man for the $2.00, he also declined her request. Then she turned to me.

Having returned from a weekend of miracle confirmations as I just had, from the minute the woman walked in I just had to wonder if this was going to be another one of those freaky encounters with a Master. Amused with her mannerisms and dress, I wondered if I could intuitively guess her real identity. Bear in mind, in each of those experiences I had confirmed by Mr. Creme's Master, there had been a curious sense of familiarity apparent. I was feeling that same sense with this woman. As she asked me "In the name of Jesus can you spare two dollars for something to eat?" I took noticed of her deep, dark, penetrating eyes, which seemed so familiar. She was also wearing, around her neck, a string of white plastic rosary beads, which led me to initially wonder if this might be the Madonna, perhaps, in disguise.

I smiled at the woman, and knowing I only had a few dollars that I'd likely need for bus fare, I said to her "I can't spare two dollars but I can give you some change." She verbally acknowledged that as acceptable but I can't recall the exact words. After I handed her the change, she thanked me and walked past, going behind my back.

The young man who was reading the bible took notice of our transaction and called the woman back as he dug in his own pocket for some change. When the woman returned, she stood with her back to me as I smiled, examining the white rosary and still playfully pondering which Master this might be, again, based on this inner, instinctive sensation that I'd felt in each prior incident. I thought I'd experiment this time and see what might happen. In my mind, I telepathically said to her "Who are you?" at which point, while the young man still dug for change, the woman turned back and looked right into my eyes, holding her gaze steady for what seemed longer than the brief time it had been. There was a serenity about her and a deepness to her eyes that I could have plunged right into. I detected an inspired, obscure sense of love spontaneously well up within me, while simultaneously perceiving what appeared to be a faint, barely noticeable, *Mona Lisa*-like smile from the woman.

After the man handed her some change, the woman walked behind me toward the front of the train. Gleeful over the whole affair, I commented to the man, referring to his Catholic League T-shirt, "I guess twelve years of Catholic School taught us something after all."

Looking down at his shirt, the young man replied, "Oh, I'm not Catholic - just a practicing Christian." And with that, he folded his Bible shut and stood up to get off at the next train stop. When I arrived at my own stop and got off the train, I looked about both within the car and among the group of passengers coming from the front of the car, but the woman in the black T-shirt was gone.

Sometime afterward, I spoke again with Mr. Creme by telephone. I explained my 'gut instinct' at the time, an intuitive feeling that I began to refer to as a 'sense of presence', which is what had led me to inquire of each instance. "That woman" he had his Master confirm "was the Master Jesus."

I can still see, vividly etched in my memory, that woman's eyes as if she were before me even now. Remarkably, they do match the eyes in the closet I had seen as a child so long ago.

Chapter Nine

SENSING THE PRESENCE

"Entering my heart unbidden even as one of the common crowd, unknown to me, my king, thou didst press the signet of eternity upon many a fleeting moment."

Rabindranath Tagore, Gitanjali

I could have spoken with Benjamin Creme for hours that night in Brooklyn. There were so many experiences I'd had and wondered about that stood out from the routine dating back to adolescence. Though I did maintain contact and correspondence for a number of months afterwards, I endeavored to restrict the discussion primarily to book related business with regard to quote permission, etc, and occasionally if a window presented itself, as was the case with the woman in black T-shirt, I would discuss some more personal issues. However, I knew the man was unceasingly busy, ever travelling the globe giving lectures and interviews and Transmission Meditation sessions. In fact, many times Mr. Creme repeated that the sort of phenomena his Master confirmed for me was not just happening to me, but to many, many people - countless thousands, perhaps more - around the globe. Though I still retained a balance of cautious skepticism, I allowed myself to keep an open mind with Mr. Creme, and his answers to my questions began to instill a sense of trust in me. I found that he had no hidden agenda and wanted nothing from me. Again and again, he simply asserted that he was doing the work asked of his spiritual Master.

The one fascinating revelation that I contemplated as a result of the confirmations of Mr. Creme's Master was this 'sense of presence.' In each confirmed instance, it was evident that I somehow sensed a certain, distinguishable air of peculiarity to a sufficient enough measure to have me recall both the person and the occasion again and again. All of them were unshakable impressions, with the strongest of these having been not only the eyes in the closet, which engendered a strong enough impression to have it stay fresh in my memory for over 30 years, but a recollection of the dynamic personality that seemed to accompany them.

While engaged in the research for this book in the two years prior to meeting Mr. Creme, the number of such occurrences seemed to be more frequent. But it dawned on me that it wasn't really an increase of activity at all. Rather, what had shifted was an intuitive awareness within me. I had noticed a pattern of development in this inherent ability of tuning into these psychic-spiritual impressions, and I knew that such abilities were one of the naturally unfolding, ultimate by-products of yoga and meditation practice. Patanjali speaks openly about it in his *Yoga Sutras*. It later occurred to me that perhaps my semi-regular participation in local *Transmission Meditation* sessions had so nurtured this ability in such a hastened and dynamic manner.

One such pattern of development I noticed was in hearing distinct, subtle shifts in a high frequency pitch that I had previously concluded was a case of tinnitus acquired by attending countless deafening rock concerts and live music shows in small clubs in earlier years. For several years prior to that point, I started to notice what sounded like changes in pitch and frequency. My typical response was to jokingly remark that I was able to 'hear' when my neighbors were changing their television or radio stations.

I had not consciously tried to attain such an ability through my yoga or meditation practice. In fact, I'd consciously rejected signs of any such heightened sensitivity for years. This development just seemed to be happening on its own. I could be reading, writing, watching TV, or doing just about anything, when suddenly I would hear and sense a shift in both decibel and atmospheric pressure. It was always a strange occurrence. Sometimes it would be brief, and other times sustained.

More often than not, I hear these audible shifts while meditating, and almost always when meditating with a group of people. Through yoga I eventually understood these varied, audible pitches to be what is referred to as "the music of the spheres." There is one system of yoga, *Shabd Yoga,* which specifically focuses on what is referred to as 'the audible sound current'.

The premise of Shabd philosophy is that, just as a lot of contemporary metaphysical and New Age genre publications focus on the spiritual 'light', it is popularly overlooked that the light has a corresponding sound. While a lot of yogic systems suggest focusing on the 'light in the head' while in meditation, the Shabd path suggests focusing instead on the audible sound current, specifically in relation to the system of chakras. Both systems meet the same end for the yogic practitioner, and in reality, are intermeshed.

The light is the light of the sound and the sound is the sound of the light. It's as if there is a corresponding 'ringing' to the varying degrees of light's radiance.

Likewise, in physics, the molecular rate of the cells of each form of matter in nature produces a corresponding degree of energy. Within this energy is a corresponding degree of generated light, the velocity of which creates a resulting, corresponding sound.

Metaphysicists assert that the mineral kingdom - rocks - are essentially a form of living organism with a molecular rate that generates at an appallingly slow speed. Nonetheless, there are whole schools of thought that agree on the inherent electromagnetic faculties and resulting effects and benefits those faculties have on humans. Within this scientific detection of electromagnetic fields in minerals can be found the very emission of light and sound which is being discussed. The best-known example of this in the mineral kingdom is uranium, and we have seen evidence of the amount of light and sound that one mineral alone has stored in just one atom.

This same principle when applied to the plant kingdom is why it is widely believed that plants grow and thrive when spoken to by humans. In yoga, the power behind the conscious employment of the spoken word is called *Matrika Shakti*. While the term Matrika infers affiliation with the power of letter and word, it translates as "the little unknown mother." We know her better as 'Mother Nature.' Matrika Shakti is the power of Mother Nature, the power of word, or, 'Logos.' The science of sound is the philosophical reasoning behind the yogic tradition of mantra repetition. Mantras are essentially recipes, or more accurately, prescriptions, composed of Sanskrit 'ingredients.' The Sanskrit language is actually a system of highly complex sounds based on recreating those features that were detected in the audible sound current by the ancient yogis. Mantras created with Sanskrit sounds have a reverberating effect on the entire human nervous system, as well as the molecular particles in the atmosphere, enhancing and balancing the health and 'well-being' of both. Hence, there are yogic systems based on such premises.

The physics behind all of this is why saints are able to heal someone who simply comes in contact with the hem of their garment, their chair, etc. They are charged with Shakti - walking, talking, breathing lanterns of charged molecular particles. The reason we are able to 'hear' the 'presence' of a great being is due to the sound generated by their accelerated molecular rate.

The essence of advanced spiritual adepts of all traditions, whether termed Avatars, Masters, Sadgurus, Qutbs, etc., ascended or not, is to use any means necessary to teach, guide, and advance the students in their care. The whole world of external, material phenomena is their cache of teaching aids. While the great ones have the ability to disguise themselves when visiting or appearing to us, it is then, if you will, that perhaps we receive our examination, on which our 'grade' is based. Reflect for a moment on the stories surrounding Padre Pio discussed earlier.

It is understandable that entertaining the notion of certain individuals as disguised manifestations of Masters would be subject to scorn, but it has been so through the ages when all such legends came forth. People no doubt viewed such tales about Bhagavan Nityananda or Padre Pio with initial skepticism, but as more eyewitnesses have stepped forward, the rumors acquired credibility. It has only been through the shared experiences and eyewitness accounts of those who've had such things occur that I'm in a comfortable position to consider these experiences as naturally occurring events, another facet of natural phenomena.

There have been times when I've had undeniable experiences of an unseen but palpable presence. Sometimes in these instances I would think of a deceased love one like my grandmother or my father and wonder if this was how they would let me know that they were still with me. There was one night, for example, as I sat in front of my computer reviewing a segment of this very book, when I felt a presence as if it were standing behind me. I didn't bother to turn around to look, and instead kept working. Then suddenly, I felt a discernible sensation as if I was being patted on the head, which I found a bit humorous since I had recently written the segments on Mickey Drake and my grandmother. I had wondered what their experience of a divine pat on the head must have felt like.

Then something fantastic happened. In almost as brief a duration of time as was the pat and accompanying thought - a matter of seconds - a brilliant flash of light flooded the whole room, as if a camera flash went off. This is difficult to describe, but I internally saw the flash of light originate from the top of my head, which, according to yoga, is the premier center of spiritual activity - the *crown chakra*. Though it may sound incredulous, I also thought I saw the light flash and emit through my own eyes, as if they were small flashlights. The experience seemed soft, silent, harmless - and ecstatic. It only lasted a few seconds or less, but it was extraordinary. The thought occurred to me that I might be having a psychotic episode and should consider visiting a doctor post-haste. But the peaceful, reassuring feeling I felt associated with it, and mindful of such things as the routine residual effect of yoga practice, I just smiled and thought to myself "Now, *that* was cool!" and resumed working.

That experience was only further heightened when, the next day, my friend Sophia called to ask if I had any unusual experiences the night before. "Why?" I asked before answering, though somewhat expectant of what she might share.

"I had this experience that somebody was in the room with me last night, but nobody was there" she said. "It happened a few times. I would keep waking up, thinking someone had been there, but like they had just left. I felt as if somebody was standing over me, looking at me. I had the impression that there might have been two people, but I'm not sure."

We talked about it for a while and when I told her my story it didn't surprise her all that much. Both of us knew, as we had for a long time, that this sort of thing happens with yoga practice, but, more so, was indicative of the sort of thing happening to people all over the world.

There was one time when I sensed this while in a seaside amusement park with my wife and daughter. It was so strong that I happened to casually bring it up once when I was having a conversation with Benjamin Creme. The most remarkable aspect of that one, however, were two men with whom I had a conversation about my daughter who were standing next to me one instant, and after briefly turning to check on my daughter who was on an amusement ride to my left, I turned back but the two men had vanished. Mr. Creme responded by telling me that his Master confirmed that the two men had been Maitreya and the Master Jesus.

In another instance, after getting in from work quite late one night and taking some time to wind down, I went to bed finding that at some point in the middle of the night, my daughter had climbed into bed with my wife. Looking lovingly at the two, I nudged my daughter over as I took my place next to them. As I sat up arranging the blankets, I heard the familiar shift in the sound pitch, and the sensation of 'presence' was immediate. The feeling was so strong, however, that, this time, I actually looked around the room in the dark. As usual, I saw no one, but the feeling of a presence was so considerably heightened this time that I sensed whoever it was hovered or stood just a few feet in front of me and slightly to my right.

I laughed to myself, and dismissively said hello as I laid down and closed my eyes. But then, almost as if in response, I felt a strong, loving pulsation and surge of joy fill my heart. I opened my eyes and looked around. Was this a ghost? What was this about? At that point, without words, I got the impression that this presence I was feeling was trying to communicate with me, drawing my attention to my sleeping wife and daughter. Inwardly, an unpremeditated thought entered my mind - "They're beautiful." I was amazed.

This was a first. Is this what telepathic communication was like? I wasn't sure what to do. I was mildly frightened, and yet, intuitively I sensed harmlessness. While glancing over to my wife and daughter I thought "Yes. They are beautiful, aren't they?" Immediately the surge in my heart increased to a physical sensation of fluttering. Was this an acknowledgment of my awareness of this presence and what seemed to be a confirmation of communicating?

Then, the feeling dissipated and everything felt normal. I laid in bed for a short while and wondered about what I had just experienced, about who this visitor might have been. Was it Jesus? The Madonna? A guardian angel? Was it the ghost of my deceased father or Grandmother?

I simply accepted the experience as a blessing, uncertain, once again, if I'd ever know the identity of this invisible friend. Smiling, I pulled up the blankets and shut my eyes, feeling completely safe and secure, having the knowledge that all was and would be all right with the world while it lay in the hands and under the watchful gaze of those invisible ones who are always near.

An Unseen Visitor

One cool summer night as my wife, a close acquaintance, and I sat outside enjoying some beer, a conversation on the topic of miracles arose, and our guest disclosed to us an experience she herself had, having previously shared it privately with only her husband and closest friends.

Our friend had been afflicted with Multiple Sclerosis for a number of years, and at the time she'd been admitted to the hospital to deliver her first child, there was concern that her post-natal period could exacerbate a permanent debilitation. One night after delivery, while our friend lay in her hospital bed, she awoke with the sense that someone was in the room standing next to her, applying forceful pressure to her chest. As she turned to look, she saw only the hospital curtain lift and furl as if someone had just left her side. She glanced at the clock and recalled noticing that it was around three or four in the morning. Our friend had requested that she not be awakened for the standard four o'clock nursing due to her condition, and so no attending nurse had been scheduled to check in at that time. Puzzled, she abruptly got out of bed, went to the door to her room, quickly opened it, and stepped into the hallway. She looked in both directions down the corridor, only to find no one there. A few hours later, she inquired with the first nurse who checked in on her, who knew nothing about any visitor, and verified that no one had been scheduled to check on her at that time.

"I still don't know who it was," she told me, "but there was definitely somebody there. Maybe it was an angel."

Our friend continued, informing us that in the weeks that followed the birth she did develop accentuated MS symptoms. Despite the diagnosis that permanent incapacitation could have been imminent, to her doctor's surprise, her symptoms took an about-face, and within a year our friend was completely healed. Her doctor could offer no explanation, and later confided that he had been preparing for the worst. Unsure of how to recount the tale of her nocturnal visitation, our friend explained to her doctor that she felt it was prayer that healed her, a prognosis which the physician sympathetically accepted. Several years later, the symptoms have still not returned. Our friend has since enjoyed an active, healthy lifestyle. She still believes there is a connection, though, between her mysterious visitor and the improvement in her health.

When our friend and I later discussed details, I couldn't help but see the comparison with my own, previously mentioned experience of applied pressure to the chest, and an unexplained, consequent healing.

There have been countless experiences shared by many along this line. Yes, it is somewhat unnerving to think that unseen visitors, whether you want to call them angels or whatever, may visit when we sleep or when we least expect it. But each person who has shared such an experience has explained that ultimately each incident has proven to be so pleasant and harmless that it's actually a pretty cool phenomenon to have happen.

My wife, our friend and I continued to sit on the porch, discussing various cases of miraculous phenomena. Since we were all Catholic, the topic mainly centered on the Marian apparitions, encounters with Jesus and angels, and the aforementioned recollections of my grandmother, which my wife was hearing for the first time.

I shared with both of them a number of the stories of Jesus and Mary encounters that I'd read in Share International magazine and elsewhere. Though their response was expectedly skeptical, there was definitely an opening for consideration on their part since the lore of Catholicism and Christianity is overflowing with accounts of the miraculous, and our own experiences had ingrained in us an acceptance of the undeniable existence of the divine.

At one point, I excused myself and returned with the photograph of Jesus that I'd found in the bus pan. Without explaining what it was, I asked what they thought. Our friend well knew of my long interest in yoga, gurus, and things Eastern, and though somewhat mesmerized by the photo, concluded that it was some foreign or Indian guru, mentioning that 'there was something about the eyes.' I then shared the background story of the photo, about the South American tribe and missionaries, et al. I then showed them the Sister Ali photos of Jesus that I'd downloaded from the Internet, and pointed out the apparent similarities. Was it possible that such items could actually serve as evidence to support the countless tales of the miraculous?

The Case of the Miraculous Medal

After we talked about the issue for a while, I then shared with them the story of a more recent personal incident, which I believe had been a little miracle.

Several years ago, my car had been vandalized in such a way that it seemed like an intentional attempt or prank to cause me to get into an accident. Sparing specific details, there was strong evidence to support my suspicion that a disgruntled coworker of mine had done this due to an incredibly petty misunderstanding. At the time, I was both angered and concerned since it could have been potentially life threatening.

My first act of recourse was to pray. This was around the time I had been experiencing the aforementioned health problems that I believed were all stress related, and I had been praying for relief or healing of that on a regular basis. The vandalism incident just further aggravated the stress, and my anger left me uncertain as to how I would confront those whom I suspected as having been responsible. As I prayed that day for physical healing, I blessed myself with some holy water from the Marian shrine at Lourdes that a friend had given me. Pausing to reflect on my emotional state, I further prayed to the Madonna for healing, and asked for help to diffuse my anger, and to enable me to forgive the vandalism suspects, which I knew was the proper thing to do, and the only way interpersonal healing could be initiated. This, I realized, was the only way I would be able to confront my irrational coworkers. I then surrendered the situation to the Madonna, leaving it in Her hands. When I'd concluded praying, I sat briefly to meditate as I always do, but for the added purpose of endeavoring to diffuse the anger, and allowing the prayer to fully be acknowledged.

With the anger abated and feeling assured that my prayer had been heard, I left for a scheduled appointment at the police station in order to file an incident report and submit the physical evidence for review. Having entrusted the situation into the Madonna's hands, I had faith that the situation would be resolved in the best possible way.

Upon arrival, I was escorted from the main lobby to a small, enclosed briefing room which contained only a small desk with a telephone, two chairs, and a short set of shelves with stacks of assorted crime prevention pamphlets. I was given an incident report to fill out, and instructed to wait there until a certain officer who was en route in his car came to question me. Having filled out the form, I sat for some time waiting for the officer. I then got up out of boredom to peruse the various pamphlets that were on the shelves on the other side of the desk.

While leafing through one of the pamphlets, the door opened and a policeman came in. I thought he was coming to see me, but instead following him was a short, thin, elderly yet spry, grandmotherly looking woman with neatly coifed grey hair, who wore wire-frame glasses, a nylon print blouse and a pair of light-colored casual slacks and loafers. The policeman pointed to the phone on the desk and said to the woman "Here you go, you can use this phone." for which the woman thanked him. I noticed as the woman was taking her seat that she kept glancing at me over the top of her glasses. I turned to the officer, was about to ask him a question, when he said to me, "She just needs to use the phone, I'll be right back to talk to you in a minute." Looking at the woman, we smiled at each other, then I resumed looking at the pamphlet in my hands.

As I stood there I could sense that the woman continued to glance at me, and perceived this out of the corner of my eye. I then looked back towards the woman, who was ruffling through her purse. "I'm sorry," I asked her, "Would you like some privacy?"

"No thank you," she replied. "I just need to get something out of my purse."

At that same moment, a second door opened behind where I stood, and a police officer invited me to his office to review my report. Having picked up my paperwork from the desk, I smiled at the woman as I took leave, who smiled in kind.

After spending a very brief time with the officer and answering a few questions, not more than five minutes at most, I was escorted back to the small room again and asked to wait a few more minutes. Upon entering, I saw the woman had gone.

As I stood waiting just on the other side of the door from which I had entered, I gazed with a blank stare as I contemplated the whole, trying ordeal. It was then that I noticed a small, oval shaped metallic object next to the phone on the desk. Having sat there to fill out my paperwork, I knew it hadn't been there before. Perhaps it was something the elderly woman had accidentally left there after rummaging through her purse. From a distance, the shape seemed familiar, and my immediate thought was that it was a 'Miraculous Medal', a popular religious medallion worn by Catholics. I reached over and picked it up to confirm whether it was or not. It was, and just as I thought of giving it to a policeman on the other side of the glass door to return it, the thought occurred to me that the woman had intentionally left it for me, and intuitively the phrase "This is for you" popped into my mind. Even if I was imagining the latter, I thought it was an awfully remarkable coincidence.

I sat down, fingering the medal, analyzing the small image of the tunic and veil clad Madonna, her arms outstretched in blessing. I deciphered the small, barely visible inscription, which read "Mary conceived without sin pray for us who have recourse to thee."

It was then it hit me. I had a crystal clear, intuitive sense that this was a material response to the prayer I had offered to the Madonna just prior to my arrival at the station. I sat stunned, half-doubting yet half convinced that this medal had indeed been intended for me. The realization deeply moved me, as I not only realized my prayers were convincingly heard, but that my concerns for safety at work were also addressed, and I felt assured I'd be fine.

Just as I concluded that the medal was intended for me and stuck it in my shirt pocket, the police officer entered the room and told me he was finished, and that I could go. From there I went to work, filled with humble gratitude. I worked my shift and interacted with my suspected co-workers as if nothing had ever taken place. The anger was gone, and my act of forgiving them had removed all trace of animosity within me.

After recounting the tale to my wife and our friend, I took the medal from my pocket and showed it to them. Though they were dubious of the 'miraculous' nature of this particular medal, I proposed to them that what mattered in this situation was the same which mattered in everyone's miraculous experiences. That is, what I believed was so for me. Whether it had been a materialized gift or an incredible coincidence, it certainly was nature's way of serving as a confirmation for me.

When I later recounted this tale in one of my continuing conversations with Benjamin Creme, he informed me that his Master confirmed that the

The Miraculous Medal. Said to have been designed and first manifested by the Madonna Herself on November 27, 1830 to the Parisian nun Sister Catherine Laboure, who had experienced frequent visits from the Madonna. Then Mary spoke to Catherine, instructing: "Have a medal struck upon this model. Those who wear it will receive great graces, especially if they wear it around the neck."

elderly woman in the police station had been the *Master who was the Madonna*, and that the miraculous medal had indeed been left by her as a gift for me.

Marian Minstrel

In the September, 1999 issue of Share International Magazine, I'd read a particularly moving story which shed a wonderful light on my experience of the Madonna. An American Peace minstrel named James Twyman had gone to Yugoslavia to support the student protests against the Milosevic regime. It was there that he encountered what he described as "the most beautiful woman I had ever seen" who seemed to know everything about him. She said to him,

"Don't trust whatever appears before your eyes, for the truth lies behind this sight. Look beyond appearances and you will receive something which is closer to the truth."

She told him he'd see her again soon, and then disappeared.

A few days later Twyman was on the 'Hill of Appearances' in Medjugorje, when he heard footsteps behind him. As he turned around, he saw the same woman he'd met a few days earlier. In an apparent parallel to my own experience of 'the presence', Twyman remarked "I felt the same overwhelming sensation as during our first encounter. Then I realized what was really going on." Twyman knew it was the Madonna, whose presence is so prevalent in Medjugorje.

Seeing Twyman's apparent surprise at this revelation, the woman asked why he was so surprised, and reminded him of something he'd said at age 12.

"You were outside the church waiting for your mother," the Madonna said. "You said you gave yourself to me and you wanted to be used to bring people to God. You forgot your promise, but I didn't."

Twyman noted that the woman appeared different from the more familiar form for which the Madonna is known, which the Madonna immediately addressed by saying,

"God always works in ways we can understand. To Croatian children who only know their catechism I appear as the Queen of Peace with a rosary. But the message is always the same. The form is not important, the energy is."

Twyman met the woman whom he believed to be the Madonna again on the following day. She foretold of the imminent genocide in Kosovo and mass deportation months before these atrocities even occurred or were seen on global news telecasts. The Madonna concluded by saying:

"Only know that the Light has come into the world, and the night is almost over."

I Stumble Upon a Master

Twyman's account sent a few chills, albeit reassuring ones, up my spine when I reread his story. Just several days before, I had gone to Philadelphia's Cathedral of Saints Peter and Paul, where the relics of Saint Therese of Lisieux were on public display as the focus of veneration and as part of a brief, rare US tour. I had heard several profound stories from people I knew or met who claimed St. Therese had miraculously intervened in their lives, and had since investigated that legacy which is well documented. At this point, I didn't doubt any such claims.

The Cathedral was quite crowded, and when I entered, a lecture was being given by Bishop Patrick Ahern of New York, a well-known author and world-renowned expert on St. Therese. I decided, that, rather than go through the center doors, I'd enter on the side to my left.

Upon entering I immediately noticed situated among a section of folding chairs adjacent to the Cathedral's shrine *to Mother Katherine Drexel*,[123] a young Asian woman who was kneeling on the marble floor, her hands leaning on the chair in front of her. On the chair was an 18-inch plaster statue of the Madonna, and leaning on that was a tall piece of cardboard which bore tattered pictures of the Madonna, Jesus, St. Therese, Padre Pio, and one other, possibly Saint Francis of Assisi.

No one was sitting in this section, apparently wanting to avoid association with her. I thought it was interesting that such an obviously devout woman would be socially rejected due to an external appearance of religious fervor. The world could use a few more people like this, in my view. After watching a number of people so avoid her, I decided that I preferred to sit near this eccentric devotee, no matter what people might think.

I found it most interesting to watch the reactions of those entering the Cathedral when they passed this woman. They weren't too bad, yet, even if polite, they still did not want to get too close. As I studied her, with her huge, overstuffed backpack which she wore while praying, her manner of devotional fervor, and the portable, makeshift shrine that was set up in front of her as she prayed, I thought to myself how much, in many ways, she resembled myself.

---

[123] Mother Katherine Drexel (1858 - 1955) was born into one of the wealthiest families on the Philadelphia Social registry. Renouncing her wealth, she instead became a nun and founded the order of *Sisters of The Blessed Sacrament*, whose mission was dedicated to the welfare of under-privileged African and Native Americans, for which Drexel worked passionately and without prejudice. Drexel has been beatified by the Catholic Church due to a number of documented, miraculous cures attributed to her intercession which, curiously enough, all deal with problems that involve a lack of hearing. She was elevated to the official status of Roman Catholic sainthood in the Fall of 2000.

Like her, I too carry my conceptual baggage about, even though I think I'm not wearing my spirituality on my sleeve. Could I be that obvious, I wondered?

I sat for a short while thoroughly enjoying Bishop Ahern's lecture, which was quite inspiring and full of power. He was commenting on the mystical passion for which St. Therese was known, and reminding all that the key to a fulfilling personal relationship with the divine could be found by following the example given by St. Therese. "The human being," the Bishop said, "by nature is a mystic. We were born to make love with God." Yes! That's the kind of spiritual rhetoric I like to hear. The man was quite on target. I recalled a remark made by Barbara Marx Hubbard in her work *The Hunger of Eve*, who noted that 60% of Americans claim to have had mystical experiences yet were too embarrassed to discuss it, and, as such, America is largely a 'nation of repressed mystics.'

Here I was, sitting in the rear of the Cathedral with a woman who was following the example of St. Therese. I thought it interesting how society, even religious communities, tend to scorn those who choose to follow the example of the extreme devotion of those deemed saints. The Pope himself had commented that the true test of devotion lay in imitating, for example, the virtues of Mary, the Blessed Mother. Privately, I wished I had it in me to have such a measure of devotion as I saw in this woman.

I smiled in acknowledgment of the Bishop's words, and closed my eyes to meditate and relish the Shakti of St. Therese. Not long after doing so, my 'third eye' began to pulsate vigorously, and I knew there was an exceptional spiritual energy in that church. After a short while, I noticed the sound of the muted 'clicking' of the oriental woman's rosary beads, and I then realized that the inner pulsations I was feeling were synchronous with the Asian woman's rosary repetition. I thought, perhaps, that I was picking up on the Shakti - the very power - of her prayers. I opened my eyes and looked at her, wondering if, perchance, there was more to this woman than was meeting the eye.

I wanted to acknowledge this special woman in some way. Just watching her had enabled me to reflect on my own measure of devotion and consider how I could improve myself. After contemplating for a while how I might approach her, it came time to move to the front of the church to get in line to see the reliquary. Standing up, I went to her side, and, leaning down, I tapped her on the shoulder.

"Thank you for your prayers." I whispered, "We need all the help we can get."

She looked at me and nodded in agreement. I smiled in kind, then leaned to her ear once more, saying, "You should know that they will be answered very soon."

Excitedly, the woman's eyes practically bugged through her glasses, as she enthusiastically thrust her thumb up in acknowledgment, remaining silent throughout. She then pointed her finger up, gesturing for me to wait a minute, and dug into her overstuffed backpack, eventually producing a holy card featuring a picture and prayer of Saint Therese.

"These are from the Monastery," she said, referring to the local Carmelite monastery that housed the nuns of the order to which Therese belonged. The reliquary was only in Philadelphia for three days as part of a nationwide tour, and had been at the monastery for two days prior to the Cathedral day.

She then motioned for me to come near, and started whispering in my ear. "Because you have thanked me for my prayers, I will ask Mother (her name for the Madonna) to give you special blessings." I thanked her, and she continued, but I couldn't hear very well due to the activity in the church. She motioned for me to wait as she once more dug into her bag. I sat down again as she then handed me a piece of paper and pen and asked me to write down my name. After doing so, she explained that she would submit my name in some manner for the special blessing.

She looked at me curiously as she then rattled off a long string of Christian sectarian names, asking to which I subscribed, saying, "What are you, Dominican? Marian? Augustinian? Franciscan?" After listening, I responded that I considered myself none of these, and as an after-thought, I said in jest that I was just an American. But then she said some wonderfully profound things that at moments caught me by surprise.

The Lesson of Thomas

"What is your name?" the woman asked. I had already written my name on a piece of paper for her, so my obvious response of "Thomas" seems to have been anticipated. As I leaned my ear closer to her mouth in order to better hear her, she immediately responded in a manner that I at once perceived to be personally quite profound.

"The lesson of Thomas" the woman explained "is about learning to see with the heart and not with the eyes. Thomas doubted in Mother's son until he touched the wounds to see for himself. This doubting is also the lesson of the crown of thorns."

I instantly shot my head up and looked at the woman. "Who are you?" I internally asked. Her words pierced me to the core. Not only had I been recently contemplating this very issue of seeing with the heart, but the minute she mentioned the meaning behind the crown of thorns, I immediately recalled the vision of the crown of thorns I'd had the previous Easter. Wondering if this was a Master speaking to me in disguise, she motioned again for me to listen closer as she whispered in my ear. She then went on a lengthy but engaging discourse about 'going beyond the form', and 'seeing without the eyes', much in the manner described in James Twyman's account of his encounter with the disguised Madonna in Medjugorje.

The woman then spoke about 'harvesting wheat' and how the wheat does not yield much fruit. Sadly, though I remember still being very moved, it was somewhat distracting and difficult to hear in the church. I didn't recall all that was said, but I recognized certain key, symbolic references that were used by Jesus in the gospels. Despite her inspiring dialogue, I still wasn't quite sure if this woman was just an eccentric devotee or someone special in disguise like the old woman in the police station.

Having been challenged by my rational mind, I wasn't quite prepared for so profound an encounter. The age-old internal conflict of rationality versus faith compelled me to then move on. Was I frightened? For a brief moment, the woman and I gazed into each other's eyes. I sensed she could see deep within me, and though I knew there was nothing to fear, I was shaken, and needed to reflect upon what had just happened. I then clasped her hand and thanked her, proceeded again to the front of the church, and got in line to view the St. Therese reliquary.

After moving slowly through the line and eventually having a brief *darshan* with the reliquary, I walked back around to the left side of the church and found myself facing the huge tile mosaic of the Madonna gracing the front altar. All Catholic churches have a separate altar dedicated to the Madonna located to the immediate left of the main, central altar. While slowly approaching the mosaic, I thought of all that had transpired, of the old woman in the police station and the Miraculous Medal, of the countless stories of encounters with Jesus, of my own experience of 'the eyes', and the perspective of Mr. Creme's Master. I considered all the accounts of Marian apparition and miracles I'd read of and researched. Was it all really happening? Could all of this really be true? Was the promise of answered prayer in such a marvelous manner really that simple and so accessible? Was this being called Maitreya really the Christ returned? If so, what a marvel, what wonder ignited my spirit at that very moment. What a world we would live in. What salvation would be brought to those who need it most.

I then thought deeply of Benjamin Creme's fantastic assertion that the woman in the police station had been She, had been the Madonna herself, and the Miraculous Medal, a gift. Gently grasping and fingering the medal, which I still wear on a chain around my neck, I studied the mosaic with wonder, and bore witness to a subtle surge of heartfelt gratitude and humility. Again, my more rational side yet continued to question it all: Had all of this - all these deeply personal, miraculous events - really been true? The answer was all too apparent.

I knelt to pray. Inwardly, as I remained transfixed on the image, I addressed the Madonna with simplicity, as if she were a dear friend, and thanked her. What a profound thought to consider that the Madonna of all humanity, the very soul who was the mother of Jesus, the same Mary who listened to the prayers of humanity for close to two millennia, revered by Christian and Muslim alike, had given me the time of day to acknowledge a prayer.

Lingering for a short while longer, I began to take leave and walked towards the rear of the cathedral. The Asian woman, who hadn't been there when I'd approached the altar, motioned for me to come near. I watched as she dug in her stuffed bag once more, from which she produced a small card with the name 'Jesus' printed on it in red ink. On the reverse were instructions, interestingly enough, to place the card beneath my pillow. She then handed me a second one, saying, "Give this one to a friend." Fingering the cards while pondering the coincidences, I grinned, and looked at her curiously.

As I exited the Cathedral and walked to my car, I contemplated this remarkable encounter, endeavoring to recall and make mental note of her many profound remarks, such as the 'wheat and fruit' comments, the references to 'eyes that see', etc. When I got home, I immediately poured over the entire four gospels. As the hours slipped past, I flipped back and forth to compare, to bookmark those terms and quotes she said that I did recall. Then, having weeded through, I read, reread, and contemplated the specific verses the woman had quoted.

In the Gospel of John, I found a great deal of insight into what the woman had been saying. In Chapter 4, Jesus says:

"Do you not say, 'There are yet four months and then comes the harvest?' "Well, I say to you, lift up your eyes and behold the fields are already ripe for the harvest. And he who reaps receives a wage, and gathers fruit unto life everlasting, so that the sower and reaper may rejoice together."

But I may have been more moved by what I read in Matthew, Chapter 13, in which Jesus spoke to a crowd along the shores of Galilee. It was there that Jesus told the famous parable of the sower and the seed, i.e., "And other seeds fell upon good ground, and yielded fruit...He who has ears, let him hear." His disciples asked Jesus why he spoke to the crowd in such parables, which were obviously veiled references to the truth. Jesus replied:

> "To you it is given to know the mysteries of the kingdom of heaven, but to them it is not given. For to him who has shall be given, and he shall have abundance; but from him who does not have, even that which he has shall be taken away. This is why I speak to them in parables, because seeing they do not see, and hearing they do not hear, neither do they understand. In them is being fulfilled the prophecy of Isaiah, (who said): 'For the hearts of this people have been hardened...and they have been hard of hearing, and their eyes they have closed; lest at any time they see with their eyes, and hear with their ears, and understand with their heart, and turn to me ...I will heal them.'
>
> But blessed are your eyes, for they see, and your ears, for they hear. For I say to you, many prophets and just men have longed to see what you see, and hear what you hear, and they have not..."

This is what the woman had said to me. It was as if I was guided to read these words. Little by little, my understanding of many of the events that had transpired in the previous year - accompanied by the research up to that point - had further coagulated and clarified in that moment. Never in my life, as I reread those passages, had I felt as if Jesus - Master Jesus - was speaking directly to me, that somehow there was a connection to understanding these passages, his appearance to me as a child, and everything that was transpiring in the present. My heart just crumbled with humility and gratitude.

Encountering the various Masters as confirmed by Mr. Creme and being knowledgeable of their presence seemed then to have become just a matter of course. But this passage, and perhaps what this unique Asian woman was telling me, was that it was further confirmation that I was walking the correct path, that I was sufficiently heeding the lessons of my Christian faith, of my yoga teachers and those of other faiths, and finally and perhaps most importantly - through the inner prompting of my own soul - the way of 'understanding with the heart.' As a result of persevering in faith, I had been enabled to see and hear, but I was only beginning to comprehend any of it.

> "Hear, therefore, the parable of the sower... the one sown among the thorns is he who listens to the word but the care of this world and the deceitfulness of riches choke the word, and it is fruitless. The one sown upon good ground, that is he who hears the word and understands it; he bears fruit and yields..."

I understood that the 'seed among the thorns' - those who 'heard the word' but continued to allow themselves to be distracted by the conditions of everyday, material life - represented the majority of us. Jesus explains that disciples like his hear the word, may revel in the joy for a short while, but when pressured to bear witness, many of us coil in retreat - through embarrassment, through the psychological need for social self-preservation. By doing so, we fail to 'reap the fruit' of our experience and allow the very essence of religious or spiritual practice to fully encompass our being. This is the shortcoming of religious practice in the world today. The most painful aspect of this reflection was the personal need to admit that I had fallen into this category for most of my adult life. Though I remained intellectually and consciously aware of spiritual teachings, my practice had been, for many years, 'half-hearted.' It has only been in recent years, and specifically since the 'near death experience' of my heart trouble and nocturnal visit and/or surgery by the three beings of light, that I re-engaged myself in a more sincere spiritual pursuit. To consider that all of these experiences had resulted simply from focused, sincere prayer and a deepened spiritual effort is a point that instills great hope, and indeed strengthens faith.

"The kingdom of heaven," Jesus continues,

'is like a man who sowed good seed in his field, but while men slept, his enemy came and sowed weeds among the wheat, and went away....[The householder said] 'lest in gathering the weeds you root up the wheat along with them, let both grow together until the harvest; and at harvest time, gather up the weeds first and bind them to burn, but gather the wheat into my barn.'

'He who sows the good seed is the Son of Man. The field is the world; the good seed - the sons of the kingdom; the weeds, the sons of the wicked one...But the harvest is the end of the world, and the reapers are the angels...Then the righteous will shine like the sun...He who has ears, let him hear.'

'The kingdom of heaven is like a treasure hidden in a field; he who finds it hides it, and in his joy goes and sells all that he has and buys that field..."

Perhaps, I thought, this is why so many people around the globe are fearful of sharing their mystical experiences of sensing divine presence. Perhaps their visions are of such a profound, personal nature that they are reluctant to let go from fear of losing it. As a result, we tend to bury our 'treasure' until we've invested everything we have upon its truth. It's the only sure gamble. But now, a time for sharing has dawned, and the 'landlords' of the kingdom of heaven open the gates of their field for all to enjoy.

Yes, there was a great lesson in these verses from Matthew which the Asian woman had shared. After further contemplation, about the harvest of wheat and fruit, about the lesson of Thomas, about the crown of thorns, and how she had repeatedly referred to the Madonna as 'Mother', I began to wonder if there had been more to this Asian woman than perhaps I had initially perceived.

I recalled one of the very first thoughts I had while examining her, about how I thought she resembled myself in her devotional manner. The statue of 'Mother' and the accompanying, tattered cardboard altar, which she had set before her facing the Madonna in the church, was a sort of exaggerated analogy, I thought, to how I prayed. It seemed as if there was an implied message, that, when I pray - when we all pray, whether it be internal or ritualistically expressed, such as the clinging to my Miraculous Medal, or even going to mass - all were as a sort of costume or shield, like it was all a spiritual facade, a uniform worn when I knock on God's door, wearing my icons like an identifying medal. I wondered if I'd been lugging around my own, overburdened backpack loaded with conceptual spiritual baggage, like I felt a need for this to ensure my admittance through St. Peter's gate.

The implied lesson, I thought, was that such things are demonstrative of being attached yet to the external form, of ritual and dogma, of signs and miracles, of the personalities of God's saints and messengers. In truth, such things are ultimately hindrances to the full experience of God. This was the lesson of the Prophet Mohammed, and of Islam, that worship or deification of form, of a messenger or saint is fundamentally unnecessary, and that true, spiritual life is transcendent of form. In fact, when I looked at the measure of pure, spiritual surrender inherent and lived by this woman, it occurred to me, that, though a declared Marian Christian in every sense, the woman was clearly Muslim in the fullest context of that term.

I understood then that this is the reason that these Masters are said to frequently appear to us as unrecognizable 'familiars', for in almost every recorded instance, the familiar represented some concept held in one's own mind, such as the man who perceived Maitreya as "a prince right out of '1001 Nights,'" or how Jesus represented himself to me as 'the wacky one' when I was washing windows. In some way, the familiars will always be a reflection of ourselves, of our contrived, limited perception and understanding. The 'lesson of Thomas' was really the lesson for all of us, for we all need to acquire the key to 'seeing with the heart', seeing beyond the form.

With her makeshift shrine before her facing the altar as she prayed, her overstuffed backpack filled with a ready supply of holy cards, religious paraphernalia and God knows what else, this Asian woman, I felt, was lovingly but unintentionally mimicking me, mimicking all of us. The purpose of such demonstration is to shake the aspirant out of his or her self-imposed limiting stagnation.

Because I had 'ears that would hear', because I was willing to greet her with respect and listen to what she offered, she whispered to me the secret of seeing, which was not with the eyes but with the heart, to look beyond the form and instead see the essence.

Every nuance of our encounter led me to wonder, at the time, if this woman had been a Master. I wondered if she could possibly be the reincarnation of some saint or disciple from church history, such as in the case of Gabriel Moyano. Then there were the similarities to James Twyman's encounter with the Madonna in Medjugorje. "Look beyond appearance," She had said to Twyman, "The form is not important."

Was *this* woman the Madonna? Was she a Master at all? I later shared with Benjamin Creme my story about the woman. In doing so, I referred to the woman as a possible 'familiar' - a temporal apparition like the old woman in the police station. Mr. Creme simply said, "This was not the case." I gathered that there was little else Mr. Creme *could* say at the time, but sensed there was more that he might say, so I inquired further with specific inquires, and concluded by asking "Was the woman anyone?"

"It was not the Madonna, nor the Master Jesus," Mr. Creme informed me, "but it was another - an American Master - whose name is not yet being revealed." And that had to be perhaps the most fascinating response from Mr. Creme's Master that I'd heard yet. I would not begin to understand this for another two years.

What was I to make of all these marvelous events? How was I to anticipate that the writing of an investigative report on Maitreya, Masters, miracles and mystics would instead become my own Magical Mystery Tour? How was I supposed to understand or verify the potential authenticity of Mr. Creme's remarks? All of the described incidents had, after all, been colored by an uncanny sensation that left me recalling and pondering each indigenous situation. It was kind of wondrous that Mr. Creme was someone who offered the first semblance of an explanation. Though non-clinical and unmeasurable, and certainly unorthodox by conventional standards, but a potentially plausible explanation from the standpoint of spiritual or religious experience. Was it possible that what Mr. Creme offered could be true? There were other incidents, too, that impressed me as seemingly miraculous events with no real explanation. I had not initially inquired about these. Many remained unexplainable, such as several occasions when I was spared serious injury from car accidents. They were of the sort that are often reported in news items as an unexplained intervention of a guardian angel.

Once, for example, while en route to pick up my daughter from daycare, I was driving with difficulty through the torrential rainfall of Hurricane Floyd on September 16th, 1999, when a minivan suddenly pulled out of a driveway obscured by both rain and traffic, and rammed with full force into the driver's side of my car. The force of impact was so great that my car was laterally pushed off the asphalt and onto the sidewalk, and instantly I found myself unable to control the vehicle as it plowed head on toward the angled corner of a concrete wall just a few feet away. I witnessed this, gripped with wide-eyed fear and the full expectation of being launched through my windshield on impact. Suddenly, it felt as if time itself had stopped, my engine shut down and my car abruptly stopped dead just an inch or two before impact. An inch! I recall sitting stunned for an undetermined amount of time, just staring at the concrete wall, witnessing nothing but the sound of my own breathing, the pound of my adrenaline-flooded heart, and the heavy rain on the roof of my car. This frozen moment in time was concluded when a stranger - in the pouring rain – suddenly knocked on my window, asking if I was alright.

In another instance, also during a heavy downpour, I was steering around a corner which had become obscured by thick, overhanging brush that sagged from the weight of the heavy rain. With my own car equally obscured, the driver in a car on the other side of the bushes was looking in the opposite direction in order to turn. Though attempting to avoid collision, I veered away and instead found myself hydroplaning into the oncoming traffic lane, with the likelihood of a three-way collision seeming inevitable. Remarkably, my car had hydroplaned to the left just enough so that the turning car literally stopped about one-quarter of an inch from the side of my front fender. Simultaneously, as my car was about to slam head on into an oncoming vehicle in the oncoming traffic lane, the engine of my car, again, abruptly shut down for no explainable reason, and the hydroplaning stopped just in time to avoid a collision within inches. The three of us who were driving sat in stunned silence for what seemed like a timeless void. Then, gathering my senses, I turned the key in my ignition, and the car started right up. After proceeding through the space between the two vehicles, I pulled over to park, take a deep breath, and consider what had just happened, or, rather, what had *not happened.*

Then there was the time my wife and I were lost in Amish country of Pennsylvania's Lancaster County, when a stranger had suddenly appeared to help us. What was most curious about this incident is how I had pulled our car onto the edge of a cornfield, which completely obscured us from traffic in the 'T' intersection just ahead. I got out of the car first to look if there was any way to see above the corn stalks to define any nearby roads. In those pre-GPS and cell phone days, I unfolded our roadmap to try and determine where we were. Out of nowhere, it seemed, a small blue car pulled to a stop in the intersection just in front of us, with its driver immediately inquiring if she could be of any assistance. It was if she knew to find us there, and, further, how did she know we were lost? Well, the unfolded map would have been a give-away, but she couldn't have seen it below the top of my car door. She got out of her car, stepped closer to ours, and, after offering what seemed to be an endless, exhausting and almost humorous variety of alternate direction options, the stranger - a tall, plain woman dressed in a long, white linen dress with a pale blue cornflower pattern - abruptly extended her arm through the open, driver's side window of my car, poked me sharply in the chest, and said "And *you* watch out for those Buggies," referring to the horse drawn carriages of the Amish people.

Hours later, after finding our way and having spent the day at a family amusement park, my wife, child and I were driving back through the Amish area towards home. Having had little sleep the night before due to a double work schedule at the time, I inadvertently grew sleepy, and unconsciously dozed off at the wheel while driving. Suddenly, I was jolted out of my slumber when I again felt a sharp jab in my chest in the same spot where the woman had poked me earlier. As I opened my eyes, I saw, immediately ahead, a horse drawn Amish Buggy emerging from the tall, obscuring corn field that lined the road. Slamming on my brakes while the buggy driver simultaneously pulled back his horse's reigns, a certain, potentially deadly accident was averted. The jolt woke my wife, who had also fallen asleep.

For the remainder of the ride, I marveled at the prospect of who that clairvoyant stranger might have been who'd poked me in the chest. Had it been a guardian angel? How could such an abrupt interaction with a Buggy have been anticipated? I pondered all the nuances of our encounter. At one point, after she had poked me in the chest and stood up, she glanced in the back seat at our daughter, asleep in her car seat, and asked "Is that your little one?" Since I was engaged in researching for this book, I recalled that the comment immediately brought to mind many of the 'messages of Maitreya' relayed by Benjamin Creme over the years in his magazine, in which it is claimed that

Maitreya repeatedly refers to humanity - his flock, if you will - as 'my little ones.'

Could the stranger have been Maitreya? A Master? A guardian angel? Was it possible that the poke in my chest was the insertion of some sort of divine, metaphysical alarm clock that I felt hours later and saved the lives of us, the horse, and the buggy driver? Do I need to ask such a question in light of the remarkable timing of my waking in the car? Whoever it was, something miraculous happened that day.

With regard to my last inquiry to Mr. Creme, I again met the Asian woman in Philadelphia's Cathedral on two more occasions. In each further incidence, my friend Sophia had been with me. She was familiar with the confirmation from Mr. Creme's Master, so consequentially we found ourselves studying her with curiosity as we conversed with her. How was it that this woman, who shared with us that her name was Kathy, could be a Master? She didn't *seem* to possess any of the attributes of at least my own, limited academic understanding of a Master. However, she certainly did demonstrate an unprecedented, exemplary measure of not only devotion, but a complete and utter surrender to her faith.

We witnessed, for example, on Christmas morning of 2000, as Kathy bowed with clasped hands before a chapel alter, and, in complete submission, walked on her knees to the front, side entrance, without ever allowing her back to face the altar. The year before, also after the midnight Christmas service, we chatted with Kathy and gave her a ride to the home of a family in South Philadelphia where she had planned to perform an all-night prayer vigil. We declined an invitation to join her, mindful of our mutual Christmas morning family obligations. I couldn't help but question Creme's assertion of this woman being a Master, but, simultaneously, I was also aware that a hint had been given to some other, unrevealed aspect. Could Mr. Creme have been implying that, when I first met the woman, she had, perhaps, been overshadowed at the time? Was she such a pure vessel of devotional surrender that she became, in essence, a channel through which "Mother" - the Madonna - had worked?

I observed as young Catholic seminarians who knew and respected the woman, seeing in her a spiritual quality they perhaps sought or latently possessed, ask tenderly that she keep them in her prayers. The woman would respond without a trace of vanity or inhibition, instead exhibiting an enhanced, pure enthusiasm at the pliant opportunity to pray even more. This woman was by far one of the most intriguing individuals I think I may have ever encountered in Philadelphia, aside from visiting lecturers and others. Was she a

Master? How could I know? When I first saw her, she was sitting just next to the shrine of Mother Katherine Drexel, who was canonized as a Saint by the Catholic Church in October of 2000, and then she told me her name was Kathy. Hmm. An American Master. Could it have been? In any event, I thought it most likely that anyone who takes the time to receive her with sincerity, compassion, respect and graciousness, is unlikely to ever forget the permeating influence of her displayed measure of faith.

Among all these fantastic personal experiences, it was those eyes I'd seen as a child which captivated me for so long. No matter how much skepticism I allow myself to muster up, that singular incident had been undeniably real. It's the one I never forget. Inwardly, as mentioned, I had always suspected it had been Jesus, but dare I consider such a thought in this age of scientific rationalism? No, with Mr. Creme's assertion of it having been Jesus I could not dispute. Something powerful and remarkable happened that night in my youth that would mould my spiritual inquisitiveness for a lifetime to come, and Mr. Creme's comment became as a catalyst for both a culmination of the event, and a now, heightened perspective from which to reflect upon it. For if he is correct, then this author is firmly convinced of the 'naturally disposed,' metaphysical disposition of the creation we live in. In other words, my faith is galvanized by what allegedly amounts to an 'eyewitness' first hand encounter. The implied double entendre would, after all, be consistent with aforementioned references to Jesus' sense of humor. How could you not want a guy like that to return and teach the world?

Looking back on many of the events and tales shared herein continues to instill marvel: the interrelated, insinuated links found in book after book after book; the jolting, ponderous claims of Wayne Peterson, and, lastly, both the recollection of the amazing, initial encounters at Benjamin Creme's public programs so many years ago, as well as the sentiments of his Master about the curious encounters I've had. What other reasonable explanation could there be? Thousands upon thousands of people around the globe were having - and continue to have - similar miraculous events and encounters in their own lives. All controversial conjecture aside, all of this spurious activity *must* amount to something; there must be an explanation. Whether one's view is spiritual, scientific, philosophical, political, psychological or even atheistic, it's evident that something's abuzz, something's happening. What's going on? Where is it all leading?

Chapter Ten

FAITH AND RATIONALISM

"Now when Jesus had risen from the dead...He appeared first to Mary Magdalene. She went and brought word to His disciples. And they, hearing that he was alive and had been seen by her, did not believe it. After this [Jesus] manifested in another form to two of them, [on the road to Emmaus], and they went and brought word to the rest, and even then they did not believe. Finally, Jesus appeared to the eleven Apostles and upbraided them for their lack of faith and hardness of heart, in that they had not believed those who had seen him after he had risen."

Gospel of Mark, Chapter 16, verses 9-15

The human debate between rational thinking and faith is *older* than the hills. The possession of an unwavering faith has always brought on its bearers the judgment of pragmatists who saw such individuals as lunatics, fanatics, and even menaces to civic order. The faithful, the visionaries, and the mystics have endured derision, persecution, and even martyring, from being thrown to the lions in ancient times, to being labeled as witches and burned alive, crucified, drawn and quartered, exterminated in the Nazi death camps, and, more recently, gunned down in their place of worship or beheaded by deluded fanatics. It's hard to believe that such cruel, sadistic acts are still being enacted on earnest adherents of faith, all because they live with spiritual hope, and believe or experience the reality of the existence of the subtleties of the kingdom of God.

Each religious denomination has embraced a select representation of these, bestowing upon them their respective official stamps of 'beloved', 'saint', 'blessed', and other such titles. Yet, such designations can contribute to further removing the reality of the readily accessible close proximity of God from the lives of everyday people. Due to the dogma and cultishness associated with such labeling, most people first assume the notion that only the worthiest and most pious of humanity live that rare life. Modern civilization, at least in the west, suggests that pursuit of mystic experience is an impractical pursuit in life. However, mystics themselves, as well as teachers, guides, and adepts of all traditions consistently assert otherwise. The truth of the matter is, each of those beings called 'saint', etc., would probably have wanted nothing to do with being labeled, canned, and processed for wholesale consumption. This was an important aspect of Krishnamurti's experientially based philosophy. The experience of the grace and presence of God is not based on divine bias. It is available to all of us, at any and all times.

In fact, grace comes in ways that are completely opposite that view, and it's for this reason many of us don't recognize it. As an omnipresent, omniscient, intelligent life force which is part and parcel of our inherent pure being, grace is completely aware of our shortcomings, which are primarily self-created.

It's important for us to recall and reflect on the utter humanness of Jesus' Apostles. More than being selected as suitable representatives for future evangelistic work, Jesus must have omnisciently known that the human element of their story would be a key aspect when viewed in the light of history.

At the Last Supper Passover meal, Jesus revealed that he knew even then that one had been selected whose role was to bring him down - Judas. Reflect on the particular temptation which so blinded Judas - pieces of silver, greed - material want. Judas needed to play this role in demonstration of the distance one will go when just one basic transgression of the essential human code of law consumes one's heart and mind. Blinded by the glitter of silver, Judas' gaze was distracted from the divine light right in his midst. His story is analogous to modern living.

Likewise, Peter, 'the rock' upon which Jesus planned to build his church, lied and completely denied his affiliation with Jesus three times to avoid arrest and persecution, and later, as referenced, he still refused to believe Mary Magdalene or the other two about the post-crucifixion apparitions.

Virtually the whole of the New Testament gospel narrative is in itself a parable about faith versus skepticism. From his youth, Jesus invited scorn from the Temple elders, and as his ministry began, miracles were his mainstay to help instill belief in the existence of the unseen to a simple people. He wanted the truth of reality made known, not just about Himself, but as the legacy of all humankind.

"There is nothing concealed" Jesus said, "that will not be disclosed... What I tell you in darkness, speak it in the light; and what you hear whispered, shout it from the rooftops!"[124]

Jesus openly exhorted those who followed him to specifically not simply worship him. Repeatedly it is expressed throughout the gospels that his teachings are to be used, to be lived by, adhered to in action. The goal of which, Jesus reminds us, is to make us all like him. 'Like him' means in *every* way. Otherwise, why teach if the teachings will be ignored?

> "But why do you call me 'Lord, Lord' and not practice the things that I say?"[125] said He. "No disciple is above his teacher, but when perfected, everyone will be like his teacher."[126]

The connotation does not imply becoming a Christian as it's been somewhat translated through the ages. The great prophets, the Mahatmas, have always exhorted what Saint Paul described as "sober truth."

In Chapter 26 of the New Testament's Acts of the Apostles, the imprisoned Saint Paul is given a chance to speak in his own defense. Paul recounts a summary of his life story, informing all that in his youth he endeavored to live up to the standards of being a Pharisee, the biblical archetype of the rational skeptic.

> "I then thought it my duty to do many things contrary to the name of Jesus," said Paul. "Many of the saints I shut up in prison, having received authority to do so; and when they were put to death, I cast my vote against them; and oftentimes I punished them and tried to force them to blaspheme; and in my extreme rage, I even pursued them to foreign cities"

It was on such a pursuit while en route to Damascus that Paul, who was then called Saul, recalls the famous occasion of his transformation;

> "At midday...I saw on the way a light from heaven brighter than the sunshine around me...[I] fell to the ground, and I heard a voice saying
>
> "Saul, Saul, why dost thou persecute me? It is hard for thee to kick against the goad."
>
> I said, 'Who are thou, Lord?' and the Lord said, 'I am Jesus, whom thou art persecuting. But rise and stand upon thy feet, for I have appeared to thee for this purpose; to appoint thee a minister and a witness to what thou hast seen, and to the visions thou shalt have of me. [To the peoples of all nations] I am now sending thee, to open their eyes that they may turn from darkness to light, from the

---

[124] Matthew 10: 26-28
[125] Luke 6: 46
[126] Luke 6: 40

dominion of Satan to [that of] God."

How uncannily reminiscent are these words of those spoken by the Madonna at Fatima, Lourdes, and Medjugorje? Further, it offers an uncomplicated explanation for everyone: it's just important to share one's personal, spiritual and mystical experiences and visions, to serve as a way of inspiring others, to plant seeds of hope. The truth is, as Barbara Hubbard had asserted, most of us really are closet mystics.

After explaining to his jailers that it was while engaged in this work requested of him by Jesus when he'd been arrested, Paul reminded them that there was nothing he said that hadn't already been prophesied by the Old Testament prophets. Paul was then interrupted:

"Paul, thou art mad," Festus said with a loud voice. "Thy great learning is driving thee to madness."[127]

Paul, in his defense, respectfully responds by saying:

"I am not mad, excellent Festus, but I speak words of sober truth."[128]

The struggle with personal acceptance and understanding of mystical experience boils down to an internal conflict. Fear and clinging to what is safe, familiar, and rational only perpetuates a lack of faith. It is this sort of thinking, for example, that allows hunger, poverty, and other gross injustices to persist in a world of wealth and abundance. Jesus said "Seek ye first the Kingdom of God..." and "The Kingdom of God is at hand." He wasn't kidding. It's right here, all the time, accessible whenever we want. Personal, unanticipated, mystical experiences are like television commercials or divine public service announcements issued from '*The* Producer.' When we acknowledge and accept this naturally ordained mystical side of human life, when we have sought and found this inner link to the 'Kingdom of God', then we're in the groove, we're tuned to the right channel, going in the right direction, etc. Things in our personal lives begin to almost magically fall into place. Conflicts are resolved, emotional scars are healed, inhibitions vanish, and our personal suffering ceases to be. When we embrace this aspect of our life, our relationships with others are transformed for the better, and it is from there that we will be able to finally, and permanently, establish right human relations on a personal, familial, communal and global level.

How do we truly entrench the 'Kingdom of God' in our own lives? Yes, prayer, meditation, and the practice of our preferred theology and dogma

---

[127] Acts 26: 24-26
[128] Ibid

are all valid. If the theological approach is not your cup of tea, then simply an ethical approach to empirical living will do the trick. One thing that fully balances all such active efforts is sharing and selfless service. Service is a naturally ordained function of being human, just as it is in neighboring animal and insect kingdoms. Bees together build their hives, collect and provide sustenance for all members of their dwelling. Animals of many species herd together, share waterholes and grasslands, and communally nurture their young. Humanity can learn much by observing them. This is precisely how our ancestors did learn, and, in fact, many

Hatha Yoga postures so popularly practiced by countless people today were created by ancient yogis after observing animals in the wild. The names of such postures yet retain the animal name that inspired their origin, such as the Lion or Cobra poses. By serving each other altruistically - by giving of self - we enable each other to uplift ourselves. While engaged in such activity, as confirmed by the Kashmir Shaivite Sutras, a door to the Self is opened, and when we are awake in such moments, enlightenment or epiphanies occur instantly. Until we learn to do that, as long as we perpetuate our blindness to the hidden truth, we truly do serve only darkness.

Jesus' request of Paul was a simple one. After the life transforming experience on the road to Damascus, He essentially said to Paul, 'Now that you've seen this, my demonstration of the light, go and tell others what you've seen.'

"It is hard for thee to kick against the goad." Jesus said to Paul. Stubborn denial or harboring one's experience due to a fear of social criticism or verbal persecution serves no one, and least of all, ourselves.

The Big Question

As stated, personal incidents of miraculous occurrence instill faith and remind us there is something unseen in which we can believe. Encounters with the form or presence of alleged ascended Masters or living adepts seems to suggest that there is a higher goal to strive after, that we can have a better life than we think is possible. They act as guides, as stewards, reminding us to simply practice what has been preached, to live the teachings of our respective religious creeds.

They exhort us to detach ourselves from our lower nature, to "see beyond the form." To transcend our inherent, materialistic, animalistic bodily tendencies and the resulting psychological composure, and instead strive towards manifesting our inherent, organically ordained divinity by gradually learning to recognize the true reality and presence of our souls, our true Selves, our Atman.

Upon manifesting our soul life, we, by choice, begin to personally play our role as co-creators in manifesting the legendary 'Kingdom of God' through our lives and onto this plane of existence. All the great teachers of antiquity and of our own time have given us the means on a regular basis. They are relatively simple rules:

"Love one another as I have loved you." (Jesus);

"Be chief among the charitable." (Muktananda);

"Never boast of your wealth, friends and youth. Time may steal away all these in the twinkling of an eye." (Shankaracharya);

"Those who are seeking the way of enlightenment must always bear in mind the necessity of constantly keeping pure their body, lips, and mind. To keep the body pure one must not kill any living creature, one must not steal, nor act immorally. To keep the lips pure, one must not lie, nor abuse, nor deceive, nor indulge in idle chatter. To keep the mind pure, one must remove all greed and anger in false judgment. If the mind becomes impure, deeds will be impure; if the deeds are impure, there will be mental suffering, so it is of the greatest importance that the mind be kept pure." (Buddha)

"Don't worry, be Happy." (Meher Baba)

They are all there. Every means to proper and fundamental living has been given to us over and over and over again. Why do we ignore them? They are simply offering helpful suggestions. Even if enlightenment isn't desired, even if your system of belief prohibits you from accepting an assertion that you could attain a state like, say, that of Jesus, and you just would like to live a good life, then what remains are simple, sound tenants of down to earth advice.

Great teachers have always acknowledged practical life. It is not expected that everyone cast aside his or her daily responsibilities and run to a mountain cave to pray, fast and meditate. From all accounts discussed herein, these spiritual Masters are, first and foremost, one of us, having lived lives like ours, and knowing intimately all of life's pitfalls. They simply offer assistance, guidance, and counsel. They have been there, done that. As the old saying goes: "To know the way ahead ask those coming back." That, in a nutshell, is why they are referred to as Masters. They've mastered the challenges we deal with daily.

A number of years ago, I was given the following poem by the principal of a high school where I then taught. I've always felt that it describes what all experienced elders offer.

"The Bridge Builder" by W. A. Dromgoole

An old man going a long high way, Came at the evening, cold and gray, To a chasm vast and wide and steep, with water rolling cold and deep.

The old man crossed in the twilight dim, the sullen streams with no fears for him; But he turned when safe on the other side, and built a bridge to span the tide.

"Old man," said a fellow pilgrim near, "You are wasting your strength with building here. Your journey will end with the ending day, You never again will pass this way. You've crossed the chasm, deep and wide, Why build you this bridge at eventide?"

The builder lifted his old gray head. "Good friend, in the path I have come," he said, "There followeth after me today a youth whose feet must pass this way. The chasm that was naught to me, to that fair-haired youth may a pitfall be;

He, too, must cross in twilight dim - Good friend, I am building this bridge for him."

Do we not seek advice or counsel from those perhaps more experienced than we? And then some! In fact, we seem to routinely seek help from anybody these days. We seek 'magic' aid through store-front fortune tellers, dialing psychic hotlines, logging on to psychic chat rooms, writing queries to newspaper advice columnists, seek therapy or counseling, all perhaps out of an avoidance or inhibition of becoming or being labeled too spiritual. For those of us that like to feel spiritually guided, we seek the company of people who pray and/or speak to God often, i.e., our rabbis, sheiks, ministers, priests, imams, swamis, or other respective clergy. In either case, both our behavioral patterns of seeking as well as our very need for help may stem from an understanding that we have somehow, lost our way.

Unconsciously, we are seeking to touch the cloak of God by proxy. We bless ourselves with holy waters, light candles to assorted deities, patron saints and icons, asking blessings even for our lottery and horse racing tickets. Finally, we seek the company or proximity of others who have been said or that we may perceive to have been touched by God themselves. Not all of these are necessarily wrong or misguided things to do. A true master, an enlightened adept, could utter a statement that may profoundly move you to reconsider an unconsciously harmful action that you might have been contemplating. Conversely, if what is needed is support or blessing for a desired endeavor that is noble, practical, or worthwhile, a master adept might wholly acknowledge it and even pad it with some extra advice to steer you in the right direction.

In fact, there are more examples of master adepts giving practical advice than there are tales of a miraculous nature, although the latter appear to be giving them a good run for their money. For example, as a youth, I had contemplated becoming a Catholic priest or join a monastic order. Though I felt a call to serve God, I wanted to have a family, which Catholic monastic life prohibits. Hence, like countless others no doubt, I sought a comparable but inclusive spiritual fulfillment elsewhere. For a number of years, I wrestled with my decision, remaining unclear as to whether I had made the right choice or not.

It was not until I once asked Swami Muktananda, himself a monk of the Saraswati order of Shankaracharya, for guidance. His response was simple. "You should seek a relationship, and when you're old enough get married."

Muktananda's advice was always pregnant with meaning, if you will. Though his words were often confirmations of correct choices, as illustrated above, or appeared to simply answer a question or address a particular issue at hand, the true lesson, the true value in heeding his advice would only become gradually apparent years later. While he'd offered a few answers that would appease my mind for the time being, Muktananda understood that the path of relationship was the most suitable direction for me to create an essential balance in my life.

Perfecting relationships is a fundamental teaching in the yogic tradition. How we relate to each other is what creates our civilization. By observing, correcting, and consciously and lovingly contributing to our relationships, we support each other and help relieve the strain of living. Though arduous and difficult at times, the 'heat' of the moment in relationships serves as a forge, which molds the seeker into the best individual he or she can be on the outside, in one's external life. Our partners provide assistance to the foundation required for rising to any occasion that arises in the external world. This external forging process (in the fullest sense of the word) of a relationship helps to mold the inner character, and in the silent acknowledgment of our partner's invaluable contribution and their intrinsic role in our life, true love issues forth.

Whether externally handling things at face value or inwardly contemplating a situation with composure, what I've ultimately discovered is that it's been the acquisition of an internal, straight and narrow perspective which seems to be the more vital of the two. Internal discipline is what allows one to experience a life of joy, contentment, and a resulting fulfillment that colors all our thoughts and actions, and enables us to give that joy back to our family, our friends, our environment, our world. It is this joy and fulfillment which energizes us sufficiently to tackle the mediocre tasks of everyday life with a smile.

In the end, the practical aspect of spirituality is what remains most beneficial. Coupled with a simple adherence to the golden rules and pearls of wisdom that have been offered by the mentors, prophets, and teachers of our respective ancestral or chosen religious paths, we can all find ourselves well on our way down our own respective straight and narrow to balanced and fulfilling lives.

It has been my experience and understanding of the practical side of enlightened teachers and masters that has allowed me to be relatively open to acknowledging their presence, and their importance in other people's lives as well. Many friends and acquaintances have shared similar stories of the help received from teachers, mentors, and gurus that they have encountered in their own journeys. Some have met teachers of great fame and respect, while others have raved about someone I may have never heard of. There are always recognizable, consistent hallmarks of masters and great beings that allow one to know and understand that those people are being taken care of in their own way.

With regard to their more fantastic and miraculous abilities, we need not fear the presence of the alleged immortals in our midst. By dedicating their lives in service to God, by virtue of God's love and care for us, they seek only to serve and uplift us to live the most abundant of lives.

Of the gradual emergence and presence of so-called ascended Masters among us, the words of Benjamin Creme's Master Himself explains it thusly:

> "Now, waiting in the wings, the Guides of the race stand ready to serve advancing mankind. *From the ranks of men* the Masters have come; to Their ranks they beckon and welcome us.
>
> That Their task will not be easy they know well. Long centuries have conditioned Them to work unseen and unannounced. Now, in the full light of day must They guide the destinies of men, leading them consciously to the mountaintop. Men, from their divine free will, dictate the rate of progress and response. Only thus can the sons of men become the Sons of God.
>
> Men await the coming of the Christ yet know not that He is here. So blind are they to the reality of life that they see not the Promise in their midst. Not alone the Christ but the vanguard of His group are now among you, awaiting the call to enter the affairs of men. Soon will They take up Their willing task and shepherd men into

the fields of Knowledge and Love, Sacrifice and Service, Justice and Brotherhood.

Thus will men avail themselves of the higher knowledge of their Elder Brothers, and create with Them a civilization worthy of the name. Thus will men come to know that they are not alone, have never been so, nor will ever be. Always are the Masters at hand when help is needed; on that may men depend. Now in full measure will that help be forthcoming, given openly for all the world to see."[129]

---

[129] Source: Share International Magazine, July/August, 1988.

Chapter Eleven

A MASTER EMERGES IN INDIA

"Now it is not merely for Dharma samstaphana[130] that I have come. I have come to give mukthi (liberation) to mankind, and inaugurate the Golden Age."

Sri Bhagavan

Years had passed, and my intense endeavor to fully grasp the potential reality of the many assertions put forth herein had brought me back to the very same place - one of uncertainty, of longing, of prayerful hope and yet a suspect concern that some aspects of the Emergence story remained somewhat questionable. Mainly, where were these Masters?

With all its subjective plausibility, I found myself included among countless others who are familiar with the story, yet able to grasp or accept only its most tangible aspects. With mixed emotion, I wondered if my rational judgement was too sacrilegious in nature, or if I was denying a basic, innate logic.

With many aspects of this discussion I maintain a firm, unyielding belief. I am convinced miracles have, can, and do happen, and, for me, my own mysterious events and experiences stand as my very own proof of this. Whether or not anyone else believes me or not can't be my concern. I know what I experienced, know the circumstances surrounding each instance, and most of all, recognize how it registered within me, in my complete sense of body, mind, and heart. Understanding a reason behind it, what lesson it might engender, and discerning whether such incidents are true emanations arising from the soul or subconscious, or self-produced mental imaginings borne of spiritual longing, desire, resolve - from some personal, emotionally stimulated

---

[130] Establishment of *dharma* - the path of righteousness; to steer mankind back to a spiritually based civilization

want - that was the question. Were thousands, millions, perhaps, deluding themselves into believing? Psyching themselves into manifesting an illusion of healing, of apparition, miraculous phenomena, or visits from beings of divine origin? Or has our modern world generated such disbelief, callousness, and insensitive indifference that we simply don't recognize an organic, a priori component of our DNA that our ancestors knew well and knew how to cultivate and accordingly live by?

One aspect of all such conversation that still holds water is the actuality of contemporary, flesh and blood god-men and women - those living, breathing saints and sages who have abilities that seem to defy the physics of our reality. With this view, I have never had an argument with Benjamin Creme's perspective on the presence of such immortals, nor with his claims to have an established, personal relationship with such a being. Such incredible men and women have always been with us, as history has testified. All esoteric explanations aside, the plausibility of extraordinary, spiritual mentors remains unquestionably true. It's just that, throughout the writing of this work, and indeed in the many years of research preceding, I often wished I could find just one that didn't maintain a habit of disappearing just as they were recognized.

In September of 2001, *Share International Magazine* published the miraculous account of a Hindu saint whose photographs were said to have produced streams of honey issuing from the saint's extended hands. What caught my attention was the fact that the accompanying photograph was of a *living* Hindu spiritual teacher by the name of Sri Mukteshwar Bhagavan. More amazing was information offered in the caption beneath the reprinted photo, in which the editor noted that Sri Mukteshwar was *a Master* - one of the very sort of Masters to which Benjamin Creme had been referring for over 20 some years. Mr. Creme's own Master, of course, confirmed the declaration.

In the course of my research spanning many years, Mr. Creme had never openly attributed the title 'Master' to any flesh and blood person before, at least to my knowledge or recollection. Creme had always explained that his own Master instructed him to never reveal the esoterically defined "evolutionary status" of any individual while they were still living. Yet, here, at long last, and so casually referenced, was the sort of link I had sought.

With minimal effort, I was able to find some basic information on the internet, and by email I was able to contact one of Sri Mukteshwar's representative teachers in the US. After exchanging a series of emails that were quite helpful, the teacher emailed a note offering that one of her colleagues, named Dasaji, would be on the East Coast in a matter of weeks, and that, if I could assemble a small group of interested people, Dasaji would be delighted to stop in Philadelphia for an evening between her scheduled workshop engagements.

Dasaji was the primary representative for Sri Mukteshwar then teaching his techniques in North America, Canada, South America, Australia and New Zealand through lectures, advanced meditation programs and Raja yoga workshops designed by Sri Mukteshwar himself, under whose tutelage Dasaji had been personally trained.

After contacting Dasaji by phone, she spoke freely with me for more than an hour from her Northern California home. At that time, it was only several weeks after the tragedy of September 11th, 2001 had passed, and like most Americans, I was preoccupied with a more concerned and serious frame of mind desirous of answers and solutions to the insanity that seemed to be embracing the world. Because of this, I had developed an urgent desire to arrange an interview with this Master, provided, of course, that he was just that. From preliminary research, I'd arrived at the conclusion that, Master or not, Sri Mukteshwar was indeed one of those rare, extraordinarily potent saints of the Hindu tradition, ranking right up there with the great Bhagavan Nityananda, the legendary Babaji, or the peerless Sai Baba of Shirdi, who, I would later learn, had a direct affiliation with Sri Mukteshwar.

Among the first emails I had received was the transcript of a prior interview with Sri Mukteshwar. With a relative, jaw-dropping fixation, I read one too many parallels between prophetic remarks

The miraculous "honey picture" of Sri Mukteshwar Bhagavan. This photo was taken while honey inexplicably streamed forth from the saint's hands in the photograph. Small cups are seen at the base to catch the honey. Photo courtesy The Foundation for World Awakening

made years ago by my own teacher, Swami Muktananda, and just as many that were remarkably consistent with the writings of Madame Blavatsky, Alice Bailey, Benjamin Creme, and Krishnamurti.

For example, in that interview, Sri Mukteshwar freely discussed the state of the world, and what to expect in the next 20 or so years. On the topic of mystical experience, He says "By the year 2002, everybody will have mystical experiences." On the impact of his own mission: "By the year 2006 I'll give Mukthi (liberation) to 60,000 people. That is, I'll liberate them from their sufferings. By the year 2012 everyone should attain Mukthi." On the state of the world, he says "Don't worry, everything will be fine by 2010."

On the overall topic of humankind's direct experience with the divine, Sri Mukteshwar explained:

Taken in another home, this photo of Sri Mukteshwar Bhagavan shows an abundance of the sacred Kumkum powder used in numerous Hindu religious ceremonies miraculously flowing freely from the saint's extended hands. Photo courtesy The Foundation for World Awakening.

> "Ancient man had very good communication with God. He has not lost that communion due to civilization, but due to other factors like the [cycle of Yugas, or cosmic ages] and civilization was born after losing the communion. These could be the movement of the earth, the solar eclipse, the various planetary configurations. The energies of all these fall on the earth during their course of journey, by which the bond of God and man became far. There is nothing like good or bad in the society. If you are suffering, it is not due to your

mistake. By the year 2023, everybody will be enlightened and at that time there will be no question of [separation]."

Here, I thought, might be the real McCoy. This certainly *had* to be one of the long-awaited Masters anticipated for more than 100 years. As Dasaji and I continued our conversation, some of her remarks seemed to correlate with assertions made by Benjamin Creme, though she was completely unfamiliar with any names or books associated with western esoteric tradition. As she shared the details of Sri Mukteshwar's life story, a picture began to emerge that seemed to serve as evidence that the hundred year wait begun with Madame Blavatsky was drawing to close, and that the much-discussed Emergence of living Masters, may, in present actuality, be underway.

A Bhagawan is born

In many ways, Sri Mukteshwar's biography reads like a textbook case of any of the great saints of India. Born on the 7th of March, 1949 and given the birth name of Vijaykumar, he was the first child of a humble, middle-class couple residing in the small village of Natham, Tamil Nadu State, India. His birth was without fanfare, pretense, or prophecy, as normal as any. His legend began shortly thereafter, when many would remark that the infant seemed to possess a divine air, with eyes that appeared to radiate a deep, inner brilliance. People claimed that just being in the infant's presence would make them feel better, uplifted, and enabled to forget their worries. Soon, talk attracted the attention of the entire village, with many wanting to meet this child for no apparent reason. While highly flattered, Vijaykumar's cautious parents endeavored to raise their child in an essentially average manner to the best of their ability with the aid of his maternal grandparents, in whose home the family lived along with an aunt.

As the boy grew, Vijaykumar - whom we'll refer to as Vijay henceforth - developed a deep love for his grandmother, and her passing when he was 5 years old proved to be a moment of devastating loss for him. The event triggered, as recalled by family and friends, an accelerated period of intense psychological development. He tried, as best a five-year-old could, to understand the mysterious cause of his beloved Granny's abrupt departure. His sorrow turned to fantasy, and in his mind the notion was conjured that a very bad person was responsible, prompting him to go to sleep each night with fearful expectation of the responsible person's return, leaving him ready to reap revenge on the malicious fiend who took his grandmother away.

While grappling with emotional anguish, young Vijay endured the entire range of human suffering - despair, anger, confusion, hopelessness, and helplessness - until his obsessive quest brought him through that dark tunnel into an awakening of clarity, redemption, hope, then joy and ecstasy, right on through to full enlightenment. Vijay's thorough contemplation had awakened a very mature clarity of mind for a five-year-old. From his own experience, he understood personal, internal suffering, and reasoned that others must experience similar suffering. By the time he was seven-years-old, he understood that his grandmother's death had perhaps provided the opportunity of the greatest of blessings, that his questioning enabled him to realize the modus operandi of the mind, and one's personal ability to control their respective, psychological state of well-being.

By the time Vijay had begun school, the family - now with three added siblings - had resettled in the town of Perambur, where Vijay was enrolled in a Christian convent school. Highly sensitive and perceptive, Vijay maintained a continually developing predisposition for lofty contemplation and heightened imagination, extracting wonderment and fascination from all that he was taught and perceived, a trait he would retain into adulthood. His mind was as the proverbial sponge - enabling him to increasingly become a theoretical authority on any topic - from the history and knowledge of the game of Cricket (though he never played a single game) to a comprehensive understanding of the laws of physics. From the very start, he demonstrated excellence in academic studies with minimum effort. He was notably a brilliant child, possessing a piercing intellect and flawless memory.

Vijay was puzzled by the average things that interested other children. His parents - Varadarajulu and Vaidharbi - also took note of their child's inherent, special qualities. His focus even at that tender age was a compassionate concern for what he perceived as the suffering of humanity. Young Vijay began to demonstrate an unshakable religious and philosophical depth, openly voicing his yearning to find a way to end such suffering. Though developing tendencies that would normally lead a young Hindu boy to consider the life of a renunciant, Vijay made a very conscious decision not to renounce the world and become a monk or sannyasin, but rather, to instead live through and experience life like anyone else. He reasoned that by so doing he would share human suffering first hand, thus providing a hands-on insight to the psycho-spiritual effects of the trials and tribulations of daily living. In turn, he could know intimately the correct approach for aiding humanity's means to liberation. This was before he reached the age of eleven.

His mature spiritual development grew increasingly evident at a very rapid pace. One memorable example cited by family friends was the time his parents took young Vijay to the family temple. While engaged in the Hindu practice of *pradakshina* - walking clockwise around an effigy or statue of a deity - a statue of Lord Krishna in this instance, Vijay remarked to his astounded parents, "Why am I going around *myself*? Why am I worshipping myself? It's me who is in the idol!" A living testament to the goal of Hindu practice, he was identifying with the essential soul of the deity.

Like the story of young Jesus amazing his parents and teachers in the Temple, Vijay's remarks of this kind led his parents to wonder if they had borne more than just an above-average student, or even a candidate for Hindu monkhood. They wondered if they had been raising a saint.

Thoughts and remarks such as those expressed in the temple incident also proved distressing for the boy. While his inner conviction would confirm his experience as a oneness with divine consciousness, he would simultaneously question his experience, asking Shiva - his closest friend and confidant - if he was being too arrogant to think such thoughts or feel such feelings. Reviewing the psychology of his circumstances thoroughly, he would, again, eventually reason through to a new height of enlightenment.

In a provided transcript, his friend Shiva reveals much about Vijay's extraordinary boyhood qualities, and offers perhaps the first evidence of Vijay's more exalted divine identity and life's purpose even then. Referring to the time when Vijay was just eleven years of age, Shiva wrote:

> "[Vijay] first approached me and said, 'I have a mission to change the world. Will you help me in this mission?' I was not shocked or surprised. I immediately accepted and believed this mission also. We were in the same grade then, although I was one year older. I ran to tell my mother of all that had happened that day. I was so excited and told her that my friend was enlightened and that I was going to help him in his mission."

Remarkably, at that tender age, Shiva recognized and accepted Vijay as his Guru. Without saying much, Vijay simply assumed the role, a natural ordination in Southern Indian culture. It gradually became apparent to Shiva that his close friend must be much more than just another enlightened spiritual guide. He understood him even then to be an *Avatara* - a bodily incarnation or manifestation of divine consciousness. Shiva enthusiastically recounted how his friend had once remarked:

> "My mission is greater than Krishna's. [Krishna incarnated for *Dharma samstaphana* - establishment of *dharma* - the path of righteousness; to steer mankind back to a spiritually based civilization.] Now it is not merely for Dharma samstaphana that I have come. I have come to give mukthi (liberation) to mankind, and inaugurate the

Golden Age."[131]

By the time Vijay had reached high school, his closest friends were well aware of the child prodigy in their midst. While all of his teachers didn't necessarily subscribe to the suggestion, they were fascinated with Vijay's ability to breeze through tests on virtually any subject with ease, despite sparse study beforehand. An avowed fan of Albert Einstein, at age nineteen, Vijay authored a brilliant dissertation on Einstein's theory of Relativity. Vijay not only expounded liberally upon every nuance of Einstein and the details of his work, but also celebrated the fact that Einstein himself was a practitioner of Hindu/Yogic arts, and, specifically, that he used to recite the *Gayatri Mantra* - a beloved, classic Hindu prayer invoking God's guidance of intellect and the development of wisdom. The precise translation from the ancient Sanskrit is as follows:

> Oh God! Thou art the Giver of Life, Remover of pain and sorrow, The Bestower of happiness, Oh! Creator of the Universe, May we receive thy supreme sin-destroying light. May thou, Almighty God, illuminate and guide our intellect to lead us along the correct and righteous path.

The scholarly explanation of the Gayatri Mantra is that it was purposely composed and engineered by the ancient *Rishis* to inspire wisdom. The Rishis - the god men, sages and seers of antiquity in the Hindu tradition - are said to have carefully selected specific words and syllables of various mantras and arranging them in such a manner so that they not only convey meaning but also generate specific power when spoken. In other words, their very utterance invokes the energy of God to enable the manifestation of the prayer's intent.

The asserted meaning of "May thou, Almighty God, illuminate and guide our intellect to lead us along the correct and righteous path" is supported by the Yogic philosophical view that all personal problems are solved if a person is endowed with the divinely ordained gift of righteous wisdom. Once endowed with a flawless, piercing, far-sighted wisdom, a man is neither entangled thereafter in calamity or suffering, nor will he walk an *adharmic* or personally inappropriate and non-righteous path in life. The wise man finds the solution to all outstanding problems. Utterance of the Gayatri Mantra is

---

[131] A reference to *Satya Yuga*, or, in the Hindu-Vedic context, the next cyclical age of enlightenment. Each Yuga - four in total - lasts thousands of years for a total of one complete cycle being 24,000 years. These cycles have recurred time and again during Earth's history. While an exact time frame is hotly debated among Hindu and Vedic scholars, the main philosophical view of Mukteshwar is that our time marks the end of the cyclical age of *Kali*, or, *Kali Yuga*, a 2400-year period wrought with a decrease in overall spiritual inclination, and an inclination for warring, selfishness, hedonistic behavior, etc.

believed to remove any mental or emotional deficiency that would hinder the manifestation of wisdom and clarity[132].

The 1913 Nobel Laureate Bengali poet Rabindranath Tagore visits 1922 Nobel Laureate Albert Einstein at the latter's home in Caputh, Germany, July 14, 1930. Einstein's fascination with esoteric eastern philosophy was a lifelong passion that influenced his theories and genius.

Perhaps we have stumbled upon the secret to Einstein's brilliance. "The most beautiful and profound emotion we can experience" Einstein wrote,

"is the sensation of the mystical. It is the source of all true science. He to whom this emotion is a stranger, who can no longer wonder and stand rapt in awe, is as good as dead. To know that what is impenetrable to us really exists, manifesting itself as the highest wisdom and the most radiant beauty, which our dull faculties can comprehend only in their primitive forms --- this knowledge, this feeling, is at the center of true religion."

In any event, Vijay certainly had grasped, as the explanation of the Gayatri Mantra summarizes, at least one key aspect of his latter core teachings.

In his college years, Vijay was already thoroughly familiar with the political viewpoint of Mahatma Gandhi, and took it upon himself to seek methods and solutions for political and socio-economic reform of his native India. He sought ways to combine scientific and technological achievement and rural, agrarian development to produce a sound foundation for both immediate and long-term sustainable development to benefit the future of India. He aspired to see India discover its inherent greatness, and rise from and shake off its own self-induced mire and backwardness without sacrificing any of its cultural and social legacy. His peers convey how he would discuss such topics with a fervor that had no precedence, leaving them to conclude he was being overshadowed by some supreme, existential intelligence. When pressed, for example, to produce a paper on the topic of rural development with little more than a day's notice, Vijay not only addressed the topic in the expected manner, but discussed it with full ideological and sociological relevancy. In an excerpt from that particular work, Vijay offered:

[132] Reference: "The Great Science and Philosophy of Gayatri" by Shree Ram Sharma Acharya, Shanti Kunj, Hardwaar, Uttar Pradesh, India.

"Rural development is a 'must' not only to remove rural poverty but also to lay at rest the all-consuming demon of exponential growth let loose by the conventional model of economic management. It should ultimately lead to the emergence of a new form of human society that is more enduring and in which man's role vis-a-vis nature shifts from one of parasitism to symbiosis, exploitation to nurture, dissipation to conservation. India is perhaps much better placed than the other countries of the world to make this breakthrough on the rural front. Our national ethos, combined with the vision of men like Gandhi and Vivekananda, sets us apart among the comity of nations for this role."

Such broad-minded thinking evolved as a standard of greatness steadily recognized by all who came in contact with Vijaykumar. Shiva's parents also recognized his special qualities, and introduced him to the writings of Krishnamurti. With continual urging and correspondence spanning a number of years, Vijay completely absorbed and internalized the teachings of Krishnamurti as he'd done with the life and work of Albert Einstein. To Shiva, Vijay once wrote:

"Is it not a shame on the world that there isn't another like [Krishnamurti]? Should there not be ten like him, to burn the heaps of rubbish and to dispel the darkness?"

This period would prove to be a definitive turning point in Vijaykumar's life. He continued to openly make cryptic remarks alluding to his vision of his life's work. At one point, he told his parents that he saw no need to finish his collegiate education, instead wanting to pursue his inner ambitions. Recognizing his parent's despair and disappointment with his decision, out of compassion he changed his mind and persisted through graduation.

While he knew his parents only wanted to see him succeed materially, Vijay also saw how his parents were simply subjecting themselves to a needless, self-imposed human conditioning. To Shiva, he would explain,

"My parents suffer because they seek. To postpone is just another trick of the mind for its security. To postpone is the height of hypocrisy. To postpone is to be denied of freedom forever."

Having honored his parents, he completed college with a degree in Mathematics. After graduation he became gainfully employed and earned a reputation as an exceptionally hard worker. He refused to accept any form of monetary assistance from anyone while struggling in the same way most college grads do when entering the workforce for the first time. Yet despite this struggle in those early years, many recall that he openly shared all he had - his home, money, food - everything.

After working for some time, Vijaykumar had met, courted, and married Srimati Padmavathi on June 9, 1976. Known for possessing deep spiritual and devotional qualities from a young age, Padmavathi - now lovingly referred to as *Sri Amma* (Mother) - had often prayed for the man she would marry to be a holy man - one who would share an equal measure of religious conviction. She had been raised in a very orthodox Hindu family in the nearby village of Sangam, having regularly attending morning prayers at the local Temple, and had undertaken numerous religious vows while still living with her parents.

Having received the wedding invitation when he was a working professional in Mumbai, Shiva recalled:

> "I wrote back to Vijay, asking him whether Padmavathi knew very well whom she was marrying. For all I knew, Vijay was no ordinary mortal."

Shiva recognized Vijay's response as completely consistent with his friend's world-view. He explains:

> "All these diverse kinds of worldly tasks [referring to Vijay's roles as working man, husband, father, etc.]...were preparing Vijay... since it was his destiny to be more or less involved in the world in a [leadership] capacity...[and] a wide variety of experiences and educative lessons...would [eventually] prove so indispensable for the actual work of dharma samsthapana."[133]

Vijay, self-aware of an imminent, greater role, continued his ambition to live as anyone else and experience the human condition first hand. He wanted to be completely familiar with all the trials and tribulations, joys and sorrows, pleasures and sufferings. Shortly after their marriage, Vijay and Padmavathi brought a child into the world and named him Krishna. Considered an equally gifted child, Krishna would one day become widely recognized in India as a compassionate, enlightened teacher.

In July, 1984, Vijay, Padmavathi and young Krishna moved to Kancheepuram, a rural area in the state of Tamil Nadhu, where he cofounded Jeevashram - a private school established in the ancient Hindu tradition. Known as a *Gurukula*, the school would offer not only the standard curriculum, but an enhanced focus on the personal development and spiritual

---

[133] Ibid: establishment of *dharma* - the path of righteousness; to steer mankind back to a spiritually based civilization

growth of the individual student through ardent application of the yogic arts.

With solid financial backing, Jeevashram offered academic excellence from the start, and in due course of time, both students and parents would realize that their spiritual education was not just another routine yoga class at the YMCA. Among those benefactors and early supporters was Dr. N. Sivakamu, a close associate of J.D. Krishnamurti.

Originally a school for boys, Jeevashram added a girl's section in 1987, which was headed by Mukteshwar's wife Amma Padmavati. Just two years later, one of those first young girls to attend Jeevashram would have a spiritual experience that not only transformed her life, but launched an unpredictable spiritual movement that would spread around the globe.

With all the naivete expected of a child his age and a casual aplomb similar to that of his father in his youth, Vijay and Padmavati's son Krishna went to his father one day to explain that he had had an extraordinary and transforming mystical experience. Krishna asked his father if he could 'give the [same mystical] experience to a fellow classmate. Vijay explained that he could and granted his consent.

Not long afterwards, Krishna's friend reported having a similar dramatic experience while home for summer vacation in July, 1989. The classmate described her experience of a golden *ball of fire* entering her, settle, and unfold within her *Brahmarandhra* - the highest chakra of the kundalini process. What was so exceptional about this experience is its alleged rarity in yogic lore, and is among the goals of yoga practice itself. Yogis of old would have spent a lifetime practicing arduous austerities, the uttering of countless, perfectly pronounced Sanskrit mantras, years of guided meditations under the watchful tutelage of a perfected yoga master, and a lifetime of personal contemplation, insight, and reason. With nothing further to attain, the experience resulted in nothing less, it is claimed, than virtual instantaneous enlightenment for the Jeevashram student.

While witnessing the internal ascent of the energy through the chakras - spiritual nerve centers corresponding to key hubs along the spinal cord - the young student saw the form of Mukteshwar - Krishna's father - beyond the paramount chakra. She knew at once that the "golden ball of divine grace" she had witnessed had originated from Mukteshwar himself, and the vision revealed to her that Krishna's father, the director of the Jeevashram, was someone with a very close relation to Parabrahma - God itself.

Accompanying her experience was an immediate, heightened consciousness, with comprehensive, expanded knowledge and understanding.

She knew without a doubt that Mukteshwar was one of the rarest of great beings.

What I found remarkable while reading this student's 'golden ball of fire' account is how evocative it is of experiences shared throughout this book that have transpired across a span of nearly 100 years. Witnesses at Fatima, for example, claimed to see a bright orb of light around the time of the apparitions of Mary. J.D. Krishnamurti described a similar experience around the time he experienced visits from the Masters, as relayed by Mary Lutyens and those eyewitnesses who were with him. Wayne Peterson offered a similar description of his experience during the gathering at his friend's home. For me, the ball of fire description immediately jogged my memory of the "invisible ball of fire" that I'd experienced during the overshadowing of Maitreya at Benjamin Creme's lecture.

After word had spread through the school about their classmate's experience, the others initially began referring to Vijaykumar as *Sri Bhagavan Ishwara*. Thus, the establishment of the current, affectionate reference to him as simply 'Sri Bhagavan.' Gradually, each of the students began to have their own, equally profound, transforming experience. Though at an average age of fourteen to fifteen years of age, these young devotees began to expound philosophically in a mature manner typically associated with the most advanced of scholars. They had extraordinary mystical experiences, visions, heightened understanding, and some even claimed to see God. In her recorded account, Krishna's friend also added that students as young as seven and eight-year-old had developed the surprising ability to travel in their subtle body, known otherwise as astral travel.

> "Different students began to have divine experiences about Sri Bhagavan...Children who were not inclined towards spirituality whatsoever began to have mystical experiences and they could reveal when it came upon them. This phenomenon initially began with Bhagavan's own son, Krishnaji. It broke loose there and later it came to the other students. It just happened spontaneously that Sri Bhagavan manifested within Krishnaji and from there Sri Bhagavan moved out to others where children began to move to altered states of consciousness. They used to see divine beings, have thundering revelations about the universe, its natures, its laws, and they also had death experiences. These were [students] in the 9th and 10th grade. Children [in] 2nd or 3rd grade used to go astrals[134] to their homes and

---

[134] Referring to Astral travel - conscious, out of the body experiences. Identical to those described by Jiddu Krishnamurti earlier in the book.

see what their parents were doing and come back. All that they would do is to sit in front of him & feel the connectedness within them and say 'I want to see my parents.' Even as they would ask it happened to them.'

'Then the phenomenon took another leap [when] Bhagavan had healed a Mongoloid child who had a problem with his genes and was mentally [handicapped] and couldn't do anything. The mother of the child was very sad and approached Sri Bhagavan and asked for his grace and he told her it would be all right. Then she went home and asked for his grace and the child was healed. And then from her house the phenomenon started where from his living picture honey, milk, and water began to flow. Once it began in one house, it started happening in thousands of houses. Today it has become an ordinary phenomenon in ordinary houses and people report saying- 'Sri Bhagavan came to my house', 'he gave honey in mine', 'He came out of my picture', and 'Sri Amma is cooking in my house.'

Today Sri Amma & Sri Bhagavan have begun to manifest *physically* in people's houses. At that time people began to call him Sri Bhagavan. Til today he never claimed that he is a Bhagavan - it is people who call him that. It means- 'A Being who descended from the higher loka (plane of existence) to transform the Consciousness"[135]

The experiences prompted explanation from their Bhagavan, and the resulting teachings formed the foundation of transforming Jeevashram Gurukula to *Satyaloka Monastery*.[136] Bhagavan then spent a period of time training the small group of student monks to conduct workshops for the purpose of helping others find a means to alleviate personal suffering, and to teach the means necessary to experience a natural, mystical connection with God, and with their own spiritual Selves. They then began to travel initially throughout Southern India offering Sri Bhagavan's teachings in a series of workshops and retreats. Their process offered the same experience as the student monks, with an ultimate goal of establishing the groundwork for attaining the state of enlightenment.

Many attendees at these early workshops declared their own lives had been transformed in practical ways such as increased income, improved relationships, and a deepened, authentic spirituality. As word of the phenomenon spread throughout the region, many started making claims that Sri Bhagavan was the *Kalki Avatar* - the 10th incarnation of Vishnu - whose

---
[135] Reprinted with permission.
[136] It was called that in 2004, when the account was first published in this book.

predicted return would mark the end of Kali Yuga, a.k.a. the Iron Age or 'Age of Darkness' and initiate the beginning of the next cycle in the ancient Hindu calendar – the *Satya Yuga*, or, in common vernacular, the Golden Age.

While Vijay personally dismissed any such claims of being the Kalki Avatar [and still does, in 2019], there was little he could do to stop people from so addressing him. Due to these claims and rapidly growing popularity, a controversy was initiated by relatives of teenagers who sought to live and study at the monastery. Allegations of brainwashing circulated as fearful skeptics labeled the group a cult. Meanwhile, thousands of tearful pilgrims began to flock to *Satyaloka* to seek solace or divine help from the Avatar. Reports of miraculous healing and events ranging from fulfilled personal wishes to outright physical cures circulated like wildfire, and soon thousands continued to flood the small village to have the darshan of Vijay - Sri Bhagavan Mukteshwar, whom many simply referred to as *Kalki*. At one point, the monks concluded that an estimated 500,000 people had come to even have a momentary glimpse of the Master sitting in meditation. The movement began to grow so rapidly that some became alarmed and insisted that authorities investigate the school. Any and all allegations resulting from the investigation were ultimately dismissed and proved the organization to be harmless. Parents of students stepped forward to the press to assure the accusing public that their children had been given their permission and blessing to attend the school, and were quite pleased with the results. Having gained legitimacy by the authorities and the added positive public exposure, Satyaloka Monastery was acknowledged as a genuine safe haven for spiritual seekers. It was recognized as an institution that did indeed serve to aid the public, and in facilitating the resurrection of India's glorious Vedic culture which had prevailed thousands of years ago.

As a result of the initial controversy, however, Sri Mukteshwar retreated from public accessibility, closed the monastery to outside visitors, and only a select few were permitted brief tenures of stay. For a number of years following, Mukteshwar and his monks worked and studied quietly. When asked, he would remark that 'the world wasn't ready' for the profound experience he offered. Despite the restrictions, and though few ever heard of him outside of India, the movement continued to grow. By the early 1990s more than five million Hindus and a handful of westerners called themselves devotees or students.

The time frame of Sri Mukteshwar's early emergence corresponds with Benjamin Creme's initial press conference in Los Angeles in 1982. While Mukteshwar was in the midst of his retreat in the early to late 1980s, the anticipated London rendezvous with Maitreya and representatives of the press was cancelled due to an unspeakable interference. Meanwhile, at the same time in Medjugorje, the Blessed Mother appeared to explain to the visionaries her reasons for unexpected interference in 'the Plan.'

In 1997, Mukteshwar again opened the doors of his ashram and began to disseminate his teachings once more. He himself became publicly accessible, granting darshan to countless visitors. Curiously, Benjamin Creme held his second major press conference that same year to once more announce the imminent public appearance by Maitreya.

Is there a connection? An Eastern European follower and teacher of Sri Bhagavan's Dharma had written:

"...when people look at Kalki's living photo, not only a divine light is coming out of it. Many times a "living" Christ, Mary, various saints or great Masters like El Morya and Maitreya appear on Kalki's photo. They are all part of Kalki's "team" and have played an important role in preparing Mankind for Enlightenment. They are all helping Kalki who is now fulfilling what they begun, for Kalki is indeed fulfilling every promise and prophecy, given to all saints and in all Scriptures."

Several times, when I inquired directly with Dasaji or other monks about Mukteshwar's comments or perspective in the Maitreya connection, I got playfully evasive responses, and I frankly thought they just weren't familiar with it. A young man whom I later met that had spent time in Satyaloka had also been an active supporter of Benjamin Creme. He said that he, too had gotten primarily evasive responses when he tried to raise the Maitreya topic with the *Acharyas* (Sri Mukteshwar's direct disciples). He concluded, however, that he did recognize one of the Acharyas as being "a well-known Master," but explained that he could not disclose further details. I raised the topic once more with Dasaji, who finally said to me "You had better ask Sri Bhagavan yourself about that."

I agreed, and initially I had hoped to arrange to go to Satyaloka myself, but due to my inability to temporarily relinquish personal and professional responsibilities, I found need to resort to alternatives. Having secured permission to interview Sri Mukteshwar Bhagavan in advance, I instead drafted a letter. Included were a series of interview questions pertinent to the material in this book, along with a few personal inquiries. I faxed it to Dasaji, who personally took the letter to Sri Mukteshwar when she left for India a few days later. After waiting several weeks for a response, Dasaji returned from India and informed me that she had spoken with Sri Mukteshwar about my questions. She relayed his answer to me: "Tell him to come to India and take the *Mukti Yagna*, and all of his questions will be answered."

Though somewhat disappointed with the same prevailing evasiveness, I had arrived at a point where I trusted the wisdom of a great teacher such as this to know what was best. That was one irrefutable response I could live with. Based on my familiarity with the past attempts of others who sought explanations, I surrendered to the assumption that there must certainly be good reason for keeping a lid on any details relative to the whole ball of divine wax known as 'the Plan.'

My first experience of a Master's broad reach

In our initial telephone conversation, Dasaji had informed me that she would be on the East Coast in a matter of weeks, and would be willing to stop in Philadelphia if a significant enough number of people were interested. She gave me the name and contact of a chap named Dan, another local fellow who had invited her previously. I knew a number of other people who were fascinated and curious about all this Maitreya stuff and who definitely wanted to learn more. I told them I'd invited the student of an advanced yoga Master to Philadelphia to give a talk about her guru, his teachings, and the claims of associated miraculous phenomena.

After informing her that about two dozen friends agreed to attend, Dasaji arrived as planned with another teacher in training and addressed the audience. What began as the informal discussion I had promoted turned instead into *what I perceived* as an introductory meditation class. I kept trying to get someone's attention to inform him or her that most of my guests were experienced meditators and did not come to be given an introductory meditation lesson. My efforts failed, and I found myself fuming over the miscommunication. In my mind I was blaming certain people while simultaneously deducing how this could have happened. Outwardly, I politely followed suit by participating in the unfolding workshop.

Dasaji demonstrated breathing techniques accompanied by some very specific *mudras* - yogic positions of the fingers and hands. Afterward, we were instructed to lie down on our backs in the Hatha Yoga *Savasana* posture and conclude our meditation in that position for 15 minutes. While others lied in still repose, I was exasperated with the notion that my guest's time was being wasted. I had personally invited the majority of those in attendance, with many of them seasoned meditators from a variety of paths. These people didn't come to do this, I thought. They, like myself, had come to hear the miraculous and fantastic accounts associated with Sri Mukteshwar, I thought. Then came another thought, then another, and another. New thoughts kept arising at an increasingly rapid pace. As I tried to keep track of and "think" each of my thoughts, I began to notice myself getting increasingly stressed, agitated, and angry. I noticed that many of these thoughts and resulting frustration were related to an embarrassment I was generating based on the created notion that I was responsible for having been unintentionally deceptive to my guests. Then I started to blame, and I found my mind planning and rehearsing what I would say to this person, or to that one. No! Wait! I know, I'll say this. Wait! Better yet, I'll say....

The thoughts kept coming, and their speed accelerated. Soon, I noticed that I was witnessing my mind's activity as a sort of independent entity of its own. It seemed as if my mind was filling the empty space in the room with a never-ending parade of thoughts as if it was a 3-dimensional *IMAX-theatre* production. The thoughts began to take on a visually corresponding form and were flying about against and through and between and around like atoms and molecules, to the point where they seemed like they possessed their own physical forms which were flailing about aimlessly. I saw thoughts creating thoughts of their own, and those created thoughts that then spun off their own spawn -continuously multiplying at a calculated, increasing rate, like a pool of amoebas in rampant reproduction. Thoughts were layered upon layers upon layers into infinity, continually moving and transmuting, while the depth of the infinite space they occupied continually expanded to accommodate accordingly. They were multihued, while some were composed of words and others of amorphous shapes, with each one, large or small, possessing an indigenous yet equal measure of potency. They were alive - the thoughts themselves were conscious! The thoughts knew what they were thinking! I was witness to a veritable limitless sea - a universe - of thoughts.

Simultaneously, and perhaps more importantly, I noticed something else that was totally unexpected. I realized that I had unknowingly entered a transcendent state of witness-consciousness, and that 'I' was witnessing the activity of my own mind in a detached manner, as if they were simply a vast conglomerate of small television screens in constant channel-surfing mode. Understanding that such an experience of witness-consciousness to be one of the goals of meditation, I found myself abruptly and pleasantly surprised. I never had such a profound experience as this in all the years I'd practiced meditation. The speed, intensity, and depth to which the experience manifested led me to certainly acknowledge that something more than just an introductory workshop was happening here. Like a textbook, yogic dharana lifted right off the pages of Patanjali's *Yoga Sutras* or the mystical texts of Kashmir

Shaivism, I recognized that a deeper identification of 'I', that is, what I understood to be my inner Self, was the one inside me witnessing my own mental activity. I was experiencing myself as *That - the One,* the supreme, omniscient, all pervading consciousness. I was That! I *am* That! I was able to see that attachment to my thoughts and concepts were my own doing, and therein lied the very source of my own pain and agitation. I understood in a complex and timeless yet quite present and practical manner that I possessed complete control and freedom in allowing myself to be affected by thoughts and emotional reactions and stimulation. My thoughts weren't mine. I wasn't my thoughts. Thoughts were like the produce section of a supermarket - I was free to pick and choose the juiciest and best looking and in the quantity I wanted, if I wanted.

The potency of the experience lay in the fact that I had not voluntarily elected to contemplate this at the moment, but rather that I had been abruptly transported into a heightened state of awareness that was completely unanticipated, desired, or planned on. When the experience had peaked, I was at once humbled, and felt immediately liberated from my own anger, frustration, and irritation. At that instant, I was able to let go and begin to relax. Shortly afterwards, I heard Dasaji softly suggest that we slowly open our eyes to conclude the meditation.

As I sat up, I remained somewhat stunned and surprised. I hadn't anticipated such an experience and I actually enjoyed the fact that we had meditated after all. I rationalized, that, if Mukteshwar really was a Master, this would be quite consistent with what should be expected as a result of contact with one - even if remotely through one of his students. These beings aren't interested in impressive, academic semantics. They're only interested in helping humanity experience and witness the divinity in life found within ourselves.

As the evening concluded, a number of my guests approached me to remark about what a great experience they had, and to let them know if Dasaji were to ever visit again. I realized that my earlier anxiety about the evening's format was for naught. How could I have forgotten this after years of hanging out with gurus who had explained this over and over and over again and again? In any event, the clarity with which I saw both my mind and the experience of the futility of my own creation, as well as witnessing the Self, led me to conclude that Dasaji represented a very advanced presence, a presence which was palpably apparent that evening. Our innocent little gathering was, in actuality, nothing less than an introduction to the field of energy and grace of a Master. I just couldn't get over how quickly and powerfully my experience had manifested.

In the days that followed, I received a number of emails and phone calls about Dasaji's visit in which friends again reiterated their delight and interest in future workshops. Everyone, it turned out, had some positive experience relative to their own lives. I was somewhat taken aback, yet pleasantly surprised and pleased. I recognized that greater forces than I could define were afoot, and instinctively knew this had to have been the work of Sri Mukteshwar. And this I liked. If such a basic workshop could enable me to experience such a profound yet simple and harmless realization and state of awareness, then I imagined what the "advanced" workshops could offer. There was something grand going on here, and I wanted to learn more.

In the boot camp of a Master

In the months following I maintained contact with Dasaji, and eventually arranged for a return visit to conduct a one-day seminar the following Spring. Many of those who had joined us on that initial evening eagerly signed up, having invited additional friends and family members to join them. Twenty-five or thirty people registered to attend, and I was able to secure a local Buddhist meditation center that had graciously offered their entire two-story facility to us for the day at a reasonable rate.

The goal of this one-day workshop, as Dasaji described, was to give everyone an experience of their *Antaryamin* - their personal, inner connection with their respective spiritual deity, relative to their religious path or inclination. Entitled "Living with Joy: Awakening the Self Within - a retreat for Transformation," Dasaji began the day by teaching us all a key prayer called the *Moola Mantra*. Composed of Sanskrit terms and phrases, Dasaji explained that this mantra was of significant import at this particular time in human development due to the current, strategic position of the star known in Vedic astrology by the name Moola. The mantra itself, according to Sri Mukteshwar, she explained, is quite ancient, but has increased potency and healing properties due to the star's rare, current juxtaposition to the Earth, and enables the person chanting it to draw upon divine energies with virtual immediacy and ease, likening the mantra to a virtual backstage pass the divine.

The Moola Mantra, in the Sanskrit, is read as follows:

Om Satchitananda Parabrahma

Purushotama, Paramatma

Sri Bhagavati Samitha,

Sri Bhagavate Namaha

And translates as:

(Om Satchitananda Parabrahma) - We are calling on the highest energy, of all there is, the formless Consciousness of the Universe, [who is composed of] Pure Love, bliss, and joy, the supreme creator...

(Purushothama Paramatma) - Who has incarnated in human form to help guide mankind, Who comes to me in my heart, and becomes my inner voice whenever I ask...

(Sri Bhagavati Samitha)- The divine Mother, the power aspect of creation, Together within...

(Sri Bhagavate Namaha) - The Father of creation, which is unchangeable and permanent. I thank you and acknowledge this presence in my life. I ask for your guidance at all times.

In the ancient Hindu astrological tradition, the return of the Moola star in its current position signifies the advent of the cyclical return of Satya Yuga - the Golden Age - when the ability to directly experience a unity or oneness with God, Source, Universal Consciousness — whatever you prefer to call it - is now at its easiest in the entire 24,000-year cycle. It also signifies the time when the Lord himself returns to Earth via divinely ordained emissaries, primarily by manifesting as great advanced, enlightened sages known as *Avatara Purushas* – or, in western vernacular – Masters. Such beings, in turn, guide, uplift, heal, and enlighten each member of the human family by helping them to awaken their inner Self, or, Antaryamin, and know their direct connection to the creator.

In the book *The Dharma of Kalki,* one of Sri Mukteshwar's senior Acharyas had written:

"[Sri Mukteshwar] represents the continuum of all the earlier Avatara Purushas who have blessed this planet with their infinite grace. It is the preparation of the soil that they have ensured that has paved the way for the advent of the Supreme Being in flesh and blood on this blessed planet... [Sri Mukteshwar] thus represents the continuum of Krishna and Rama, of the lineage of the Buddha, of Moses, Abraham, Jesus and the Prophet Mohammed and of every seer and mystic who has walked through the glorious pathways of this planet.

[Sri Mukteshwar] explains to us the concept of Yugas (spiritual time zones) within a time cycle of 24,000 years, which is called a *Kalpa Chakra*. The 24,000-year time frame is divided as follows: 10,000 years of Satya Yuga, or the 'Golden Age'; 7200 years of *Treta Yuga* or the 'Silver Age'; 4400 years of *Dwapar Yuga* or the 'Bronze Age'; 2400 years of *Kali Yuga* or the 'Iron Age.'

Each of these Yugas are a period of distinct characteristics. They are indicative of a gradual and phased deterioration in the spiritual state of man. The Kali Yuga or the spiritual iron age is characterized by the upsurge of sentimentality and the death of genuine spiritual feeling. There is a hardening of the spiritual centre of being and almost an absence of sacredness within us. This is because the "Indweller" or the "Antaryamin" has been all but put to rest within us.

The "Indweller," in order to awaken our sleeping sensibilities, takes an external form and through an externally stimulated action, rejuvenates His [or Her] presence inside. This rejuvenation is within the realms of our being. The process is called the "Awakening of the Antaryamin."

His [or Her - God's] consciousness has descended into the realm of a distinct human consciousness much in the manner that milk would dissolve in water.[137] The earlier interventions within the period of the last 24,000 years have been [comparable to] the introduction of a piece of gold within a glass of water. There is definitely an influence, but to a limited extent. The awakening of the Antaryamin leads to the transformation of man. [Such a being capable of this] comes down only once in 24,000 years to fulfill this celestial mission. The Antaryamin itself can be awakened either by an internal or an external manifestation of the Supreme Reality in our lives, either in a formless fashion or in any form that is chosen either by the individual or over-ridden by the Creator.'

Sri Mukteshwar's teachers point out that the above referenced "Supreme Reality" with regard to the awakening of the Antaryamin is different for everyone. For some, it will manifest as Jesus or Mother Mary. For another it could be Padre Pio, Bhagavan Nityananda, Maitreya, the Prophet Mohammed or any personal deity relative to one's personal preference, upbringing, or cultural background.

"Christians *should* believe," Mukteshwar illustrates,

"that 'Jesus is the son of God', that 'They'll be saved by Jesus', that 'Jesus sacrificed himself for you.' Same is the case with Islam. Muslims *have* to believe that Mohammed is the last Prophet sent by God. Bhagavad Dharma [the study of Sri Bhagavan's teachings] is not built upon any person. This is the path of Truth. You can worship

---

[137] The allegorical description of the term "Paramahansa," a title ascribed to advanced, enlightened teachers of yoga. ie Paramahansa Yogananda, who was considered to have been an Avatara Purusha.

God in any form, be it Rama, Allah, Jesus, or Kalki. There are 600 Million ways for 600 Million people to attain liberation. I won't stress that this is the only way. This is also one of the ways, it is a way for the current generation. This way begins with freedom, ends with freedom, and is freedom in every step of the way."

What this man is proposing is the advent of a golden, glorious, advanced enlightened civilization the likes of which the world has not seen in thousands of years. In Satya Yuga, humanity has the potential to advance the global culture to the point of becoming nothing less than heaven-on-Earth - aka. – 'Satya Loka.'

The comparison to the assertions of Benjamin Creme, the Theosophists, of Alice Bailey and Blavatsky sent chills through my spine. The correlation of all of those writings and the words of Sri Mukteshwar and explanations offered by Dasaji were nothing less than startling. In fact, readers of this book thus far will note the remarkable similarities presented herein. The only difference, and perhaps the most vital one, is that here we are dealing with a tangible persona in Sri Mukteshwar, as opposed to the objectivity required when discussing the esoteric, intangible, and otherwise theoretical topics of Maitreya and ascended Masters.

But perhaps more significantly is that *millions* of Hindus to date have had countless mystical and spiritual experiences of Sri Mukteshwar as being the long awaited and returned *Kalki Avatar* - the Hindu equivalent of the returned Christ! Scores of testimonies offer that Sri Mukteshwar appeared to them while riding upon a white horse (the traditionally prophesied image of Kalki Avatar), or appeared to another dressed in white armor, healed this one of a chronic or fatal illness, helped their child with homework, helped another with household chores, or just appeared to have a friendly but instructional chat. Countless more in Russia, Europe, Asia, South America, Australia, and America continue to make similar claims. Others share, that, like the photo that had produced honey in India and California, the same photo was producing mounds of *Kumkuma* and sacred ash - items used in Hindu ritual.

I became convinced that Mukteshwar was an extremely advanced sage, and certainly one of those rare, legendary adepts. In this context, he's the new kid on the block. I wanted to know more. I eagerly prepared and participated in the seminar we had planned with Dasaji. It became the first of several I'd attend over the ensuing three years.

The Teachings of Sri Mukteshwar Bhagavan

In many ways, this book began as an effort to sort out all the data I'd collected over the years on the topics discussed herein. The reason I had been so passionate about getting to the bottom of things was because of my strange and mystical experiences recounted herein that I just needed to understand. As discussed, I knew others were having similar experiences, and the bookshelves are loaded with their tales. Interviewing some of those people was helpful in alleviating some of the anxiety and concern as to whether or not I was dealing with reality on the level. Many have dismissed my comments about miracles, about the stories of Maitreya and Masters, or the wonders of Hindu saints as a personal flight of fancy. Being surrounded by skeptics helped me develop my own measure of skepticism, enabling me to keep it all in check. In many ways, I'm grateful for those skeptics in my life. Had they not dismissed, scorned, or ridiculed me, I may not have arrived at the place I am now. I can say with full conviction that those mystics throughout history who were bold enough to share the story of their experience kept the human condition in balance in their own way, perhaps for the benefit of all of us.

What provided this conviction in the middle of my questioning was this contact with Sri Mukteshwar and his student teachers. Having spent numerous hours in discussions and group workshops and forums over the course of a year, it has been Sri Mukteshwar's explanations that have appropriately brought some measure of closure and summary to my long search for deepened understanding. The research and knowledge had been and remains wonderful, but in the end, it does, after all, boil down to one's own personal experience, perception and understanding.

One of the most significant purports of Sri Mukteshwar is his simple yet authoritative explanation of miraculous phenomena. When asked in an interview why some people have mystical experiences while many more do not, Sri Mukteshwar explained:

> "Yes, many people do not have mystical experiences. It is mainly due to biological reasons and psychological factors. The biological factors [which he further adds constitute 70% of the scenario] being your situation at the time of conception, health condition, food, weather, [the] body's response to the climate at the time of your experience. Your psychological factors [30%] depend on your karma…"

From there he explained that the karma interfering with one's ability to have a mystical experience, should they so desire one, can easily be removed through a yogic process termed *Samskara Shuddhi*. This process comprises a routine segment within the two, three, and seven-day workshops conducted regularly by his trained teachers who travel from city to city upon invitation. The process of Samskara Shuddhi is essentially a cleansing of the psychologically embedded conditioning - the emotionally bound mental blocks that basically mold and steer our lives on a subconscious and unconscious level. Samskaras can be things like fears or traumas we hold as a result of situations, persons, places, or things in our life that lead us down the road of compulsive behavior. Things like abuse, neglect, rejection, scars from being bullied, post-traumatic stress, etc., in all extremes. It may manifest in the way we relate to others, such as emotional reactions, anger, racism, or general indifference. To deal with the burden, we subscribe to food addictions, smoking, taking narcotics or alcohol. We may simply live our lives in a way we think is perfectly acceptable, but which is, in truth, nothing more than an arrogant, inner response and reflex of our conditioning.

Sri Mukteshwar explains in his lectures that our common experience in life in an unconscious state is nothing more than managed suffering. We shove emotional things under our self-created rugs, only to shuffle the same baggage from rug to new rug and so on. He says that there is no freedom in this, reiterating the words of all the great sages, prophets, saints and god men and women throughout history, who have had to learn this themselves as well. By living in such a way, we are nothing more than automatons. Liberation - Mukti - comes when one is free of the conditioning and hindrances. Processes like Samskara Shuddhi facilitate a relatively quick, safe and thorough method of remedying this consciously.

To aid in correcting the biological conditioning that prevents us from experiencing a freer existence, simple dietary approaches are suggested - never mandated. First and foremost is the adaptation of a vegetarian diet consisting of light foods. Without digressing too far on the topic, the summarization is that fruit and vegetables retain 'prana' - life force. They are essentially living foods. Prana implies that such foods still breathe, still grow and sustain their vital elements through sunlight and air. Over-processed foods, which comprise an enormous percentage of the western diet, are virtually devoid of prana. Animal flesh, on the other hand, loses its prana as soon as the creature is slaughtered, and begins an immediate process of decay once the life force leaves the deceased animal from which it came. While meat eating itself isn't rejected altogether, it is simply taught that those who choose to eat it should be educated about its effects on the physical body, mind, etc. In the practice of Yoga, it simply slows the process of achieving the desired goal of the practices.

Curiously, Sri Mukteshwar Bhagavan asserts, once that goal of enlightenment is attained, then anyone can choose to live anyway and eat anything they like.

During the preparatory phase in Bhagavad Dharma, dietary adjustments and psychological purging enable one's state of being to gradually become lighter and lighter, and the sense of feeling freer and freer begins to stabilize. But these comprise just two foundation points of the way prescribed by Sri Mukteshwar Bhagavan.

His workshops are broken down into a series of four subsequent stages, with each one addressing an essential, fundamental curriculum while simultaneously providing an environment for a heightened experience and insight of the topic discussed.

The first step in the process, Sri Bhagavan explains, is to get in touch with one's soul, one's own, respective inner Self - the *Antaryamin*, as described previously, as your personal image of or connection with the Divine. For example, for a Christian, the Antaryamin could be Christ, for a Catholic the Mother Mary or a preferred patron saint. For a Hindu it could be Ganesha, etc. For atheists or others who don't deify icons such as Muslims, it could simply be a brilliant light filled with fathomless love. As Sri Bhagavan explains:

"The Antaryamin is your inner guide and your supreme friend who can guide you and protect you. Today many a time you are in conflict. What is right and wrong? What is good and bad? You're unable to decide this. Even when you decide, many times you regret your decisions. But when the Antaryamin is awakened, you will exactly know how to respond to every situation of life. At every step you will have someone to guide you, on whom you can trust and who accepts you exactly as you are. And, also, when you have the Antaryamin, enlightenment is very easy.

Now I will tell you how the awakening of the Antaryamin actually happens. Basically, in our society, the kind of schooling, education and lifestyle one has, you are not allowed to experience and express your emotions. You are quite suppressed. That is why some have difficulty in getting in touch with their Antaryamin.

So, once you have got in touch with your suppressed emotions [through Samskara Shuddhi process] and if you invite the Antaryamin with your whole heart, it will awaken in you in the way it chooses or in the form you desire. To have the Antaryamin is the natural state of Man, it is your birthright; it is just like breathing or digesting.

In the Ancient days everybody was in touch with their Antaryamin... All that you must do is, from your heart, with emotion, with great feeling and with a bond, a liking, you must invite the Antaryamin and then it will awaken in you. It is not at all difficult."

Previously discussed on this topic were the astrological effects of the Moola star. Are there other factors that hinder our being in touch with the Antaryamin already? Sri Bhagavan continues:

"There is a lot of good and bad karma which effects your seeing or having an Antaryamin. For example, it depends on the thought pattern of your mother when you were in the womb, the situation at the time of your birth, again depending upon the doctors and nurses who received you, the feelings and emotions of relatives around you at that time of your birth and what happens to you for the first 6 hours after the birth. All these factors affect your having or receiving your Antaryamin."

One of Sri Bhagavan's monks further elaborated:

"Once the Antaryamin is activated in any form within you, the form of Sri Bhagavan, Jesus, Mary, Divine Light, Silence, or any form, then the Journey begins and the process of cleansing occurs, the cleansing of the negative energy [Samskaras] of your past lives, from conception, during your mother's womb, during your birth, and this process is not something that is only psychological, but also mystical, emotional and finally it is biological. Sri Bhagavan comes to them and does something to their physical body, though nothing happens to them outside, but then he performs something psychically that affects your DNA and suddenly you realize that you are in an altered state of Consciousness. The functioning of your Mind would be different. You do not know the meaning of suffering one fine morning. The whole thing could take place within 7 minutes, 7 days or 7 months but then you suddenly land into the state and you know it has not happened through your effort. It is a happening to you. It is a gift that is given to you."

The entire mission of Sri Mukteshwar Bhagavan's organization is nothing less than a passionate, consummate vision of uplifting human civilization. In the same way the founding fathers (and mothers) of the United States, for example, embraced the ideal of a Democratic society as engendered in ancient Greece, so Sri Bhagavan embraces the exemplary ideal that is the Vedic heritage of India's past. It should be made clear that it is not necessarily an exclusively Hindu, Indian, or Vedic agenda that is proposed as the right path for all, but rather an achievable foundation based on the core philosophical precepts of that culture, which can be universally embraced. In short, the mission statement reads like a poet's dream:

> "The mission of the foundation is to bring humanity into the golden era where each person would be enlightened. This institution strives for Enlightenment of Mankind. By Enlightenment we mean 'Freedom from all possible Suffering' in life and continue experiencing other states of consciousness. The ultimate transformation and salvation of the world will come through an individual here and there, each contributing his part to make up the whole and let the creation come forth."

Its rationale is explained:

> "To end the social, economic, political, family and personal problems, humanity's consciousness must undergo a change. The planet must be enlightened. The goal of the institution is to gather 60,000 people who wish to help humanity enter into this golden age. Once these 60,000 work on themselves and become enlightened then the rest of humanity can easily be enlightened."

While the ambition of Sri Mukteshwar seems like a lofty ideal that would certainly provide a nice alternative to the routine we know as modern living, his monks and he relay a more urgent message. Like the Madonna's pleas at Fatima in 1917, a similar, ominous message of warning is issued now.

One monk explained:

> "If mankind does not make it, it's going to be terrible. We are not here prophesying the doomsday but what is in store for man is evident. The way man's thoughts & emotions are structured today; we must know man and nature are one organism and not two separate entities. The ruthlessness, selfishness & brutality we have within us, the amount of violence that is there in our everyday life, all this is affected in the nature around us and very soon if man would go the way he is going, the tension he is building up because of the speed, competition and the struggle for survival, we seem to be moving towards inner death if we are not yet already. And if this is what is going to happen then we are going to have severe natural calamities.
>
> 'Mankind is going to have lot of diseases...because if the disease is inside that is going to manifest outside. Each one of us should only think, pause and look: "How am I living?" and we will know how we are going to be a few years from now, a few months from now. The speed at which the world is moving - what is going to

happen to man? And lots of people are going to go insane. We can already see it happening. Many are struggling to keep up their sanity. The world is moving towards disaster. If the pollution is going to increase because the kind of civilization we are in is the product of our mind and greed, then thousands are going to die out of lung diseases.

A large section of human population is going to be wiped out. That is what is in store for man. It is not that the earth is going to become a dead planet and the human race is going to be wiped out. No, but then lots and lots of people are going to die and those who are going to be left behind are going to be living in a huge graveyard and it is not a pleasant experience.

It's time that one becomes serious about life, serious about ourselves, serious about our fellow human beings, serious about suffering around us. We got the gift of thinking, feeling. We can't be dreaming and selfish any more. We have to buckle up.

I hope & pray that we can come across 60,000 serious people. I know that they are definitely there. If this is not going to happen... then we are in for a crisis. Mother earth is going to revolve [on her axis]. She is not going to take it on any more. The house is burning already. We can't wait any more. Today in India we can see, there is drought and to such places one of our enlightened dasas (monks) will go, sit down and go into a deep state of love & compassion. Then it rains. Earth is aching and seeking for enlightened people. That's what has to happen now."

However, to balance with a more upbeat alternative, the monk added;

"If all goes well and 60,000 people are enlightened then we make it. We also have got certain energy spots where we are going to build our *Golden City*.[138] This is the spot where the magnetic grid lines are working differently. The Vaastu of an ancient science of geo bio energy is tremendous in the spot. And it is here that Sri Bhagavan has impregnated his Consciousness into that land.

All that we need is 60,000 people becoming enlightened and

---

[138] Golden City here refers to a remarkable facility then (in 2002) under construction in the rainforests of Chennai District, Southern India, which is world renown for the ancient ruins of Vedic culture, designed under the direction, inspiration and design of Sri Bhagavan himself, for the benefit of mankind. Sri Bhagavan explained that certain buildings will, in fact, be 'enlightenment' rooms, in which one could enter, and due to a strategically aligned field of magnetic polarization, one will be enabled to experience stillness of mind, enabled to transcend their own suffering and karmic blocks, and experience their oneness with the divine. Once established, Sri Bhagavan intends to have 5000 enlightened people meditating there at all times, in rotation, who will serve as the stabilizing force which enable the entire globe to become enlightened. Golden City opened to the public in September, 2003, and is now known as O & O Academy.

5000 people in their enlightened state living in this place [Golden City] and meditating for mankind. It is not that these 5000 people have to be the same people. If at any given point of time out of 60,000 people for one month 5000 people decided to spend in meditation over there. Then over the next 1000 years of time things will be different. The [other] 55,000 who are outside are going to have so much power that is going to flow through them that as they touch, look and go into themselves others will be enlightened. That is what we are aiming for and our plan for the future.

If man *does* become enlightened...then, by...2024, there is going to be a different technology on this planet. We are going to have enlightened doctors, engineers, officers, peasants, housewives, mothers, children, all living, dreaming, and experiencing love. That is what is in store for man if he is going to be enlightened."

Curiously, this more positive assertion corresponds with the message Benjamin Creme had been relaying on behalf of Maitreya and his own Master for years as well. Like Mr. Creme's view that all of the calamity of the world is due to an influx of heightened energy being transmitted by the Masters, Sri Mukteshwar asserts the same. Another monk of his Dasa order, notes:

"We are now in the throes of a mighty spiritual awakening, unprecedented in the history of human kind. People from all walks of life are walking and talking with God in a tangible form. Their hearts have truly flowered, and for them, Heaven has met Earth. They have entered the Golden Age which is a state of consciousness as well as an astrological event."

This view explains the remarkable barrage of miracles, mystical visions and insights, the supernal encounters with angelic beings, Jesus, the Madonna, Maitreya and other saints as reported in journals like Share International Magazine, especially so in the past twenty plus years. Borrowing from the lessons of the Fatima warnings and the subsequent, global calamity from that point through World War II, is it any wonder that a Supreme, compassionate intelligence would send such signs and beings like Sri Mukteshwar Bhagavan into our world at this time? The aforementioned insanity referenced by the monk is already evident by simply reading, watching or listening to the news: Terrorism on every corner of the planet; bombings of buildings and suicide plane hijackings; threats of biological weapon attacks; the bellicose flaunting of the nuclear capabilities of various nations to neighboring countries and to the United Nations; Religious fanatics spreading mandates of hate, with accusations of heresy for those who seek peace and are unwilling to martyr themselves.

When asked of this a few years back, the Hindu spiritual teacher Satya Sai Baba commented "Things will get worse before they get better." How right he was. To what extent he was right is the question.

The late sage Paramahansa Yogananda wasn't as evasive. Prior to his death in 1952, Yogananda frequently shared his prophetic knowledge of future events. At various times, he told his students that the time toward the end of the Twentieth Century would pose unimaginable danger. "No corner of the world will be safe," he is quoted as saying. He made other predictions[139] that are chillingly manifesting at this writing.

Yet, Yogananda also made remarks that support the more positive vision of the ultimate future indicated herein.

"You are on the eve of a great spiritual awakening," he told his students, "a great change in the churches, where true souls will be drawn to seek the actual experience of God's presence." That, in a nutshell, describes Sri Bhagavan's explanation that we first and foremost get in touch with our Antaryamin.

As one of Sri Bhagavan's monks explained:

"That is how it has happened to all the previous sages and saints and mystics of the past, though some people were unaware of it. Now Sri Bhagavan is making it happen to anybody that is serious and seeking for it. Before this they are taken through a process [until] their consciousness gets connected. This is how all people land into this state."

Dr. Arthur J. Deikman, Clinical Professor of Psychiatry at the University of California, San Francisco, and a pioneering researcher in the scientific investigation of meditation, the mystical experience, and consciousness in its relation to psychotherapy, writes:

"The goal of psychotherapy is the relief of psychological suffering and the removal of obstacles to functioning in the world.[140] ...Western culture often overlooks the distinction between religion and mysticism, especially in the psychological and psychiatric literature. This is unfortunate because the mystical emphasis on self-development makes it consonant with modern psychotherapy. The

---

[139] Source: "The Road Ahead: World Prophecies of the famed Indian Mystic Paramahansa Yogananda, © 1973 by Swami Kriyananda. Ananda Publications.
[140] Source: Buddha Dharma Education Association; "Spirituality Expands a Therapist's Horizons, by Arthur J. Deikman, M.D. Available online @ http://www.buddhanet.net/psyspir3.htm. Reprinted courtesy of Dr. Arthur J. Deikman.

mystical tradition has been concerned with the very problems that modern psychotherapy has been unable to resolve. It makes sense, therefore, to investigate mysticism with a view to dealing more effectively with those problems and gaining wisdom as human beings."[141]

In his essay entitled "Deautomatization and the Mystic Experience," Deikman further substantiates (indirectly) Sri Mukteshwar's otherwise simplistic explanation of the Bhagavad Dharma process and goal. Deikman writes:

"To study the mystic experience one must turn initially to material that appears unscientific, is couched in religious terms, and seems completely subjective. Yet these religious writings are data and not to be dismissed as something divorced from the reality with which psychological science is concerned.

An intuitive experience is called mystical because it is considered beyond the scope of language to convey...a psychological model of the mystic experience [is] based on the assumption...that the process can be conceptualized as one of deautomatization. Deautomatization may be conceptualized as the undoing of automatization, presumably by *reinvesting actions and percepts with attention.*

In... the technique of contemplative meditation, one can see that it seems to constitute just such a manipulation of attention as is required to produce deautomatization. Since automatization normally accomplishes the transfer of attention from a percept or action to abstract thought activity, the meditation procedure exerts a force in the reverse direction [as an example of its traditional emphasis on stilling the modifications of the mind]. Automatization is a hierarchically organized developmental process [or, in Sri Bhagavan's terminology - 'conditioning'], so one would expect deautomatization to result in a shift toward a perceptual and cognitive organization characterized as "primitive," that is, an organization preceding the analytic, abstract, intellectual mode typical of present-day adult thinking."

A remarkable aspect about Deikman's summary is its indication that scientific, clinical research arrived at the same conclusion that a childlike, innocent and humble perspective provides the opening for mystical experience.

---

[141] Source: "The Observing Self," by Arthur J. Deikman, M.D., © 1983, Beacon Press. Chapter1, p4. Reprinted courtesy of Beacon Press.

The great teachers and prophets have long suggested this. For example, in the Gospel of Saint Matthew, Chapter 19, verses 13 -14, it's explained:

> "Then children were brought to [Jesus] that he might [bless] them and pray. The disciples rebuked the people, but Jesus said, "Let the children come to me, and do not hinder them, for to such belongs the kingdom of heaven."

Here, Jesus is referring to the "poor in spirit" - the humble, the innocent - mentioned in his Sermon on the Mount. By indicating that "to such belongs the kingdom of heaven," he's not just making a pleasant reference to children, but rather he is using the moment to suggest a teaching to the disciples, that they could perceive the kingdom of heaven had they a child-like manner of perception.

Deikman continues by explaining the universality of the mystic experience of an inner connection, of a oneness, and how, when that peak moment is achieved, it is almost always accompanied by fantastic visions and perception.

> "It is striking to note that classical accounts of mystic experience emphasize the phenomenon of Unity. Unity can be viewed as a dedifferentiation that merges all boundaries until the self is no longer experienced as a separate object and customary perceptual and cognitive distinctions are no longer available. Spiritual content dominates the description the mystic gives of the physical world...these accounts do suggest that a "new vision" takes place, colored by an inner exaltation. [Such] authors report perceiving a new brilliance to the world, of seeing everything as if for the first time.
>
> The sensations and ideation occurring during mystic deautomatization are often very unusual; they do not seem part of the continuum of everyday consciousness. "All at once without warning, he found himself wrapped around as it were by a flame colored cloud" (Bucke, 1961, p.8) Perceptions of encompassing light, infinite energy, ineffable visions, and incommunicable knowledge are remarkable in their seeming distinction from perceptions of the phenomena of the natural world. According to mystics, these experiences are different because they pertain to a higher transcendent reality. What is perceived is said to come from another world, or at least another dimension. Although such a possibility cannot be ruled out, many of the phenomena can be understood as representing *an unusual mode of perception*..."

One of the primary reasons this particular work of Deikman's caught my eye, in addition to its overall thesis, was the example used in the above paragraph. He quotes the statement of a clinical subject who experienced being wrapped or enveloped in "a flame colored cloud." I need not rehash the string of descriptions by Peterson, Krishnamurti, the Jeevashram School student and myself already mentioned herein. Did everyone experience this in the same manner? It's plausible. Deikman explains that the perception or reference to light in the mystical experience is not only universal in most accounts, it seems to be part and parcel in the package of such experience.

> "The concept of sensory translation offers an intriguing explanation for the ubiquitous use of light as a metaphor for mystic experience. *It may not be just a metaphor.* "Illumination" may be derived from an actual sensory experience occurring when in the cognitive act of unification, a liberation of energy takes place, or when a resolution of unconscious conflict occurs, permitting the experience of "peace," "presence," and the like. Liberated energy experienced as light may be the core sensory experience of mysticism."

Was this, perhaps, an explanation for the strange experience of mine mentioned in the previous chapter, when I experienced a flash of light emit from my crown chakra, a light that flooded the room in which I was sitting, which was accompanied by a sense of 'presence'? The crown chakra is the top of the pops in yogic study and practice. It is the seat of the experience of unity with the divine. Again, however, Deikman suggests that such an experience is actually consistent within all spiritual traditions, and can be viewed as a relatively *normal* experience.

> "Experiencing one's self as one with the universe or with God is the hallmark of the mystic experience, regardless of its cultural context. As [William] James (1929, p 410) puts it, "This overcoming of all the usual barriers between the individual and the Absolute is the great mystic achievement. In mystic states we both become one with the Absolute and we become aware of our oneness. This is the everlasting and triumphant mystical tradition, hardly altered by differences of clime or creed. In Hinduism, Neoplatonism, in Sufism, in Christian mysticism, in Whitmanism, we find the same recurring note, so that there is about mystical utterance an eternal unanimity which ought to make a critic stop and think..."

Finally, Dr. Deikman argues the point that all experience of the empirical world is scientifically proven to be illusory, and that the mystic experience constitutes what amounts to proverbial baby steps toward a more accurate perception of the universe as it really is. This is what the masters of yoga and Sufism and Buddhism and Kabala and all mystic traditions have been trying to tell us for ages! This is the grander explanation of Sri Bhagavan's teaching that we live our lives as slaves to our own conditioning. Deikman explains;

> "It is a commonplace fact that we do not experience the world directly. Instead, we have an experience of sensation and associated memories from which we infer the nature of the stimulating object. As far as anyone can tell, the actual *substance* of the perception is the electrochemical activity that constitutes perception and thinking.
>
> If awareness were turned back upon itself, as postulated for sensory translation, this fundamental [unity] of perceived reality - the electrochemical activity - might itself be experienced as truth about the outer world, rather than the inner one. Unity, the idea and the experience that we are one with the world and with God, would thus constitute a valid perception...
>
> Unity may in fact be a property of the real world that becomes perceptible via the techniques of meditation and renunciation, or under the special conditions...that create the spontaneous, brief mystic experience of untrained persons."

Here, Deikman just explained what is needed to manifest the 'Kingdom of God' in our world. His conclusions confirm, for example, the assertions of Jesus, when he said "The kingdom of God is at hand." It's right in front of our noses and we don't even see it. As the old Palmolive soap TV commercials would say, "You're soaking in it."

Deikman begins to summarize his dissertation by explaining the ideal environment and amount of personal effort required for mystical experience. What's fascinating in the context of this review of Sri Mukteshwar Bhagavan's work is that this offers a clinical description of Sri Bhagavan's prescribed methodology for facilitating global enlightenment.

> "A mystic...state is brought about by a deautomatization of hierarchically ordained structures that ordinarily conserve attentional energy for maximum efficiency in achieving the basic goals of the individual: biological survival as an organism and psychological survival as a personality.
>
> Under special goal conditions such as exist in religious mystics, the pragmatic systems of automatic selection are set aside or break down, in favor of alternate modes of consciousness whose

stimulus processing may be less efficient from a biological point of view but whose very inefficiency may permit the experience of aspects of the real world formerly excluded or ignored. The extent to which such a shift takes place is a function of the motivation of the individual, his particular neurophysiological state, and the environmental conditions encouraging or discouraging such a change."

Finally, Deikman concludes by reasserting that despite all previous suggestions, the mystic experience remains a highly individualized and personal one. This explains Sri Mukteshwar Bhagavan's remark when he says "There are 600 million ways for 600 million people" to attain enlightenment. While there may be similarities in the manifestation of the experience, i.e. 'balls of fire' or 'flashing light', etc, the resulting experience is highly personal - a direct one on one, heart to heart - with the creator. As Deikman cites, our experience of God can't be proven, but concludes that there really is no good reason why this experience or perception of life should be clinically questioned or denounced by any means.

"The mystic vision is one of unity, and modern physics lends some support to this perception when it asserts that the world and its living forms are variations of the same elements. However, there is no evidence that separateness and differences are illusions (as affirmed by Vedanta) or that God or a transcendent reality exists (as affirmed by Western religions). The available scientific evidence tends to support the view that the mystic experience is one of internal perception, and experience that can be ecstatic, profound, or therapeutic for purely internal reasons.

Regardless of ones's direction in the search to know what reality is, a feeling of awe, beauty, reverence, and humility seems to be the product of one's efforts. Since these emotions are characteristic of the mystic experience itself, *the question* of the epistemological validity of that experience may have less importance than was initially supposed."[142]

As a result of my participation in Sri Bhagavan's workshops over the span of a year, I began to enjoy an ever-growing clarity about my own experiences. In fact, it was sometime at or between the first and second level retreat when it occurred to me that I had seen this man in the photograph - Sri Mukteshwar - in a meditation vision nearly 23 years before. That image long

---

[142] All material from "Deautomatization and the mystic experience" (©1966) reprinted courtesy of Dr. Arthur J. Deikman.

ago had remained vividly etched in my mind, and I had always wondered who it had been. But the most fascinating part of that experience was that I never forgot that the vision came in the context of someone whom I would meet in the future. The photo bore the same stance, the same receding hairline, the same yellow clothes, the same salt and pepper greying beard, the same outstretched arms. It was all too amazing.

One personal issue in particular which came up was my ongoing, lifelong relationship to Jesus. I began to recognize that from an early age, Jesus had been the identity of my Antaryamin - my gateway to the experience of Self or Soul, my link to the Absolute. The many visions and alleged, perceived experiences were all manifestations of consciousness as filtered through my own spiritual apparatus. Jesus certainly did appear real to me because the conscious essence behind it was the Supreme Reality. This perception was notably heightened during my participation in a week-long Level 3 retreat held in the Trinity Retreat Center in West Cornwall, Connecticut in the summer of 2002. I enjoyed this retreat's location, and at least once daily I would make my way to a lovely little rustic chapel on the grounds where I would meditate and pray before a fantastic, hand-carved and painted wooden crucifix of Jesus that was suspended from the ceiling. When finished meditating, I would stay a little while longer, gazing at the life-like, hand-painted form of Christ and just contemplate while relishing a sweet depth of gratitude.

Dasaji led the retreat, which was attended by about 100 participants from across the United States. The retreat was extraordinarily powerful, and many people - myself included - had transforming, life resolving experiences. It was there that it became evident to me that Sri Bhagavan was quite present though physically thousands of miles away. It was only during this group's fourth and final level retreat held in India - the Mukti Yagna - the one for which I'd received a direct invitation from Sri Bhagavan himself – where one could spend real time with him.

Everyone attending the retreat shared incredible experiences of their release from personal traumas - some of which they experienced as being from previous incarnations. The *Samskara Shuddhi* segment, with its emphasis on a technique known as *Chakra Dhyana* was particularly powerful. It was if everyone had been given the keys to long locked and forgotten doors within that opened up to the buried crap that lie at the source of their personal suffering. One woman broke out into uncontrollable sobbing, then laughter, then sobbing, and so on. Everyone in the room evidently had some experience extraordinary and pertinent to themselves. The room was thick with Shakti, wild with energy, and yet remarkably stable, assuaging, and peaceful.

Later that evening, Dasaji opened the floor for anyone to share. One person claimed to have seen Sri Bhagavan step out of his photo and sit down for a while. A Hindu woman claimed to have a beatific vision of Ganesh. Some had past life recollections and understood that certain fears or behaviors they'd held since childhood were the result of a tragic death in a previous life, which they relived during the segment. From there, many shared general experiences they had since beginning to take the workshops. The shares flipped back and forth between practical results and mystical experiences. At one point, a woman shared that Sri Bhagavan had appeared to her, but was wearing 'humorous' clothing. Dasaji laughed, explained that he does that often, and then, turning to me, asked if I would share a story I had told her many months before.

With some reluctance, I recounted an incident I had shared with Dasaji in confidence, which, as with similar experiences with Benjamin Creme and his Master, she received confirmation from Sri Bhagavan's monks that I had been paid a visit from Sri Bhagavan himself in disguise.

In the year prior to the retreat, I had taken a temporary job in an upscale, fine furniture store, where each member of the staff served customers on a rotation system. At one point, a man walked in wearing baggy, blue denim overalls, some wild colored sports jersey beneath, a red baseball cap, and sneakers - a dress standard atypical of our normal, upscale clientele. As he approached the reception desk, I noted a few coworkers were laughing, and I wasn't sure if they were laughing at him or another topic of conversation. Either way, the coworkers seemed to judge the man based on his outfit, and though it was their turn, they elected not to serve him with the assumption that he wasn't a buyer. I felt immediate compassion for this poor fellow and had no tolerance for disrespect of anyone, regardless of the situation. So, though not my turn, I approached the man with my coworker's consent to offer him the service he deserved.

As I walked toward him, I noticed that he seemed to be approaching me, almost as if he had anticipated speaking with me anyway. He glanced over at my colleagues by the desk, seeming as though he actually preferred they wouldn't approach him. I greeted him, noticing a large, white letter 'B' on the front of his frayed baseball cap. The man had long, slicked back salt and pepper hair that curled at the shoulder, and a long, thick, straggly beard of the same color. Parts of it almost seemed to be in shades of olive green. His skin was tan in color, which stood out to me because it was the middle of winter. He wore classic, black-framed glasses with "Coke bottle" lenses so thick that his eyes seemed tiny behind them. He introduced himself simply as 'Phil.' As he spoke, I noticed he never looked directly at me, but rather his eyes were literally rolling around in their sockets the entire time. It was bizarre, and, frankly, somewhat humorous. But it was while I listened to him explain his reason for coming in, that, I had the thought, behind the glasses and all, the man looked remarkably like Sri Mukteshwar Bhagavan, whom I had only seen in a few photographs up until that point.

The man explained to me that he was "looking for a loveseat." I probed him for information on size, style, what decor, etc. He replied that it needed to be a 'firm' loveseat, and that he would not likely be buying today, but would need it when he moved into the area in a few months. The date he mentioned was the same day Dasaji was planning to come to Philadelphia to conduct the first one-day retreat we had planned. I thought it interesting that this man who looked like Sri Mukteshwar should mention that date. Meanwhile, I had escorted the man around the entire showroom, which had two floors and was as big as an airplane hangar. He spent a considerable amount of time sampling every single loveseat on display, which he would deem 'too soft' or 'not firm enough' or 'too firm' as we went on, his eyes still rolling all over and never looking directly at me. With each one, I explained the features and benefits, maintaining my personal credo of respect and courtesy. Yet, I also like to joke with customers to help them feel at ease. A few times the man laughed at some of my remarks, and we hit it off nicely.

When we wound up back near the entrance, he turned to me, with his rolling eyes becoming still and focused for the first time that day. He looked directly into my eyes, and said: "I like your style. You work the way I do. You could say that I'm in the retail business also. And when I come back I want to do business with you." He explained that he was moving from some sort of school or institution, and was settling into a smaller place that would need a loveseat. He made a few other remarks at the time that escape me now.

After he had left, I couldn't help but think about him. The whole encounter seemed oddly familiar, like the sort Benjamin Creme would confirm to be an encounter with Jesus, Maitreya, or another. There was just something about him, a sense about him. I kept thinking about how much he looked like the photos of Sri Bhagavan. Then I thought of the big letter 'B' on his red cap. Red - the color associated with Shakti, situated on his 'crown.' 'B' - for Bhagavan? Then, I started wondering if the whole 'love seat' thing was metaphoric reference to my own heart, and the testing of all the love seats a veiled metaphor for his mission of awakening 60,000 individuals, depending on their readiness. "Firm" could be interpreted as 'committed.' He said he was moving from a small school – just like the Jeevashram School in India. He said he was returning on the same date Dasaji was returning. 'Phil' - for Philadelphia? I started to chuckle to myself as I went about my other duties. My work partner came over and asked me about Phil. With a smile I said, "Girlfriend, that was God who just paid us a visit." My partner looked quizzically at me. "I'll explain it another time," I added.

When I next called Dasaji, I was curious about the incident, but I did have the hunch. Did Sri Bhagavan do that, I asked? Appear to people in disguises, etc? It was then that Dasaji shared that he did have that ability and, in fact, did it all the time. She shared a few examples, and said she would confirm it for me when she next called India. She later relayed to me that she had received confirmation from one of the monks who had relayed the inquiry to Sri Bhagavan, who confirmed that he had indeed paid me a visit guised as 'Phil.' It was explained that he did it as his way of responding to my interview questions which Dasaji had shared with him. Remarkable. Was I being too naïve or gullible to just accept Dasaji's word about this? I cautiously accepted what she had said, but, honestly, I was quite blown away and found the whole thing humorous. A Master with a fun sense of humor. I was growing to like this enlightened guy.

Our retreat session for the day ended thereafter. Everyone walked to the dining area in relative quiet, somewhat mesmerized by the depth and energy of personal experiences and internal purging that had occurred. After dinner and a brief, contemplative walk in an adjoining meadow at dusk, I retreated to bed.

On the morning of my fourth day of the Connecticut retreat, I was awakened in the early morning by an unprompted and completely 'deautomatized' experience. As I stirred from my slumber, there, sitting before me in full, 3-dimensional technicolor, was Jesus himself. So stunned by this apparition was I that I sat up immediately and opened my eyes, but when I did - he wasn't there! I quickly shut my eyes again, and there he was! It was some sort of internal vision unlike anything I'd experienced before. It was incredible! It was clear that the manifestation of this vision was beyond my control. Was I dreaming this? Or, had my routine attention to daily matters abated sufficiently enough to cause an opening, accompanied by the refreshed, mental stillness from the retreat, to create the ideal circumstance for a mystical experience just as Dr. Deikman's research had suggested?

Dream or authentic vision, this was so real I could almost reach out and touch the Lord's cloak. Jesus was smiling lovingly, appearing exactly as he does in the photo I had found years earlier, except in actual, deep flesh tones. At first glance, his face was about two feet away. When I looked the second time, he had leaned backward and sat at the end of by bed, with a backdrop of an extraordinarily beautiful blue sky, and I noted some lush, green foliage behind him. He was wearing a dark, reddish brown or burgundy colored garment, accented with a shawl or robe of deep crimson, remarkably like the "blood red" frock in the apparition described by Sister Anna Ali. The light emitting from all around him was glorious - heavenly - very hard to describe. It was as brilliant and golden and white as sunlight, but did not hurt my eyes. Around him was an intense dark corona, which only accentuated both the brilliant light behind him, and his three-dimensional form. The corona gave me the impression that the vision was almost like a projection, as if his form had pierced a subtle veil to allow himself to be seen.

He spoke to me, though his lips didn't move. I was too stunned to fully 'hear' what he may have been saying, but the essence of what was said was that he was letting me know that he was still with me (my Antaryamin!), was glad I was doing the inner work at this retreat, and was pleased with the good progress in my spiritual life. His presence and visit were simply a friendly acknowledgement. It was the most vivid, complete, real, direct such experience of Jesus in my life.

The vision faded and I lied in my bed thereafter absolutely enraptured and serene for about a half-hour, just allowing myself to relish the event. I wondered if I had somehow imagined or created the whole thing. Was it just an 'astral' image - a self-projected illusion borne of my innate spiritual desire, or was it generated by His will? Were the "words" I heard simply the voice of my own higher Self, my inner Antaryamin? Why was this particular vision so very real compared with other similar experiences? And while all these thoughts sought an empirical, rational explanation, I couldn't help but notice the deliciously serene state of bliss I was experiencing. It was simple and joyous, and I felt utterly connected - in union - with everything. All was as it should be. All was fine.

Then, having taken time to note the experience in my journal, I began my day. After the morning retreat session and culmination of lunchtime, I went back to the small, rustic and warm Christian chapel on the retreat site grounds. I sat quietly, gazing at the hand carved Crucifix hanging over the altar. I contemplated the remarkable lifetime of personal connection to this man called Jesus. I thanked my old friend for blessing me with such a wonderful visit and darshan, and for a lifetime of what amounted to an unquestioned depth of personal support. I then sat quietly a while longer, humbled and grateful.

That afternoon, I had shared my experience with Dasaji, and, later in the retreat session, she referenced my experience when answering the question of another.

"Consciousness manifested in the form of Christ for him" she said, motioning in my direction with her hand. That phraseology caught my attention. I had never heard it put that way before. Or, if I had, it was the first time I really 'got it', really understood it. In time I began to understand that my perception of the many apparitions of Jesus in the past, as well as those said to be of the Madonna or Maitreya, etc., were indeed due to my own, firmly established inner relationship with my own soul, my own Antaryamin, my own connection with God, with the Absolute. I'd had this ability all my life, but until now, never understood it, or never completely accepted it that way. This is exactly what I was taught in my formative Christian education. I had been taught to develop a personal relationship with Jesus from day one, and further taught that it was possible to develop a personal relationship with God as well. Who would have thought that it could manifest so literally for a working-class guy from South Philadelphia? For the first time in my life, I began to feel an increasing sense of fullness, of completeness in my life, that the long search for the elusive connection was over. There was nothing to look for. I had had it all along.

Part of this was also due to an ongoing dialog and contemplation of Sri Bhagavan's explanation about an organic propensity for mystical experience. I happen to enjoy both sides of the coin, both the empirical as well as the mystical. Sri Bhagavan simply explains, like Dr. Deikman, that mystical experience is a normal part of life. As quoted by Albert Einstein herein, *not having a mystical experience or connection is tantamount to death*. Sri Bhagavan's matter of fact explanation elucidated how a little girl in Fatima so long ago could see the object of her devotion - the blessed Mother. It explained how a woman who survived a coma would also see Jesus, how my own grandmother could claim to have met God on her childhood stoop in Ireland, how Maitreya could appear to hundreds of unassuming Africans and thousands of others around the globe. It also led to understanding why a being like Maitreya might remain evasive, and why a half-hearted search on behalf of an impartial, objectively minded press corps would produce no results, and how no search at all would produce even less. Of course Maitreya couldn't be found in the subjective world. "Seeing him" required the development of an inner connection first. Not necessarily an inner connection with him, but rather one's personal contact with their own Self, their own deity, their own Antaryamin. And even if the whole theory of Maitreya and a group of ascended Masters - initiated by Madame Blavatsky, sustained by Alice Bailey, and perpetuated by Benjamin Creme - was not true, even if the whole thing had been contrived by advanced, enlightened teachers of the Eastern spiritual traditions for the purpose of inspiring millions to seek something beyond the mundane, such a tale would have a positive, transforming effect on our culture.

By instilling the virtue of simply seeking, something would be found. Seek nothing and instead maintain an indifferent, skeptical attitude, and nothing is found. All that remains is what's in front of us. All that remains is our conditioned perception and our automatized behavior. But by electing to seek, seekers would move closer to that a-priori, innate connection with the divine that seems to have been lost. Was this the rationale of the Madonna visits at Fatima? At Lourdes? At Medjugorje? Was this the desired outcome of Mr. Creme's own Master - an individual he has asserted as being a living, flesh and blood person living thousands of miles from his London home? Is our very seeking the source of creating the perception of miraculous events throughout the world?

This Antaryamin teaching was as significant as any I'd come across in many years. I began to understand how I witnessed my own experience of a 'ball of grace' implode in the area of my heart at Mr. Creme's lecture during the overshadowing. It explained how a little boy named Gabriel Moyano could claim to heal on behalf of the Madonna, and visit the Christ in heaven on a moment's notice. All these experiences are like gifts that aid and cajole us on to embrace our a-priori, divine heritage, our connection with the absolute. All are as gifts from beyond, as gifts of the Masters among us.

The next morning, having completed the morning retreat session, I bid farewell as I had personal responsibilities to attend to. I packed my bags and set off on my long but ecstatic drive home on a pristine, perfect summer day. I contemplated the many remarkable insights gained at the retreat, and had more as I drove through the gorgeous, rural areas of Connecticut and New York State. I find driving a great form of meditation, providing moments of epiphany as sacrosanct as any had in a church or elsewhere. As the road turned onto a clearing, I realized I was at a fairly high altitude above the Hudson Valley. The vista before me was amazing, and I could see for miles in every direction. Just as the road ahead stretched before me as I descended back into the valley, I thought it analogous to my experience of life in recent years. And though I was driving back on roads previously traveled through towns I'd passed before, I was returning with an altogether refreshed and inspired perspective. The next chapter of this incredible, ongoing adventure had just begun.

Chapter Twelve

AWAKENING

"Awakening is not changing who you are but discarding who you are not."

Deepak Chopra

Twenty some years had passed since I wrote the majority of what you've just read, and fourteen since completing the 2004 revised edition with some added new material. On that drive described at the end of the previous chapter, I had stopped for lunch in a small rural café on the New York/Connecticut border and met one of my lifelong idols – the great American artist Jasper Johns. That was just one of many marvelous things that were left undocumented.

In the interim, life happened. I became a father and watched my child come of age all the way through to her college graduation. In 2003 I returned to college myself to pursue a degree at The University of Pennsylvania where I dedicated a fair amount of my time in Religious Studies. I was like a kid in a candy store, relishing courses on pre and early Christian Gnosticism with a professor who was among those world scholars engaged in translating the Dead Sea Scrolls; Hinduism with a tenured, Oxford educated scholar on the entirety of the culture and customs of India. I explored Existentialism, the Psychology of Religion, and Buddhist Psychology and belief with one of the most brilliant minds on those subjects I'd ever encountered. I exuberantly consumed works by Kant, Sartre, Buber, Phillip Reiff, Ken Wilbur, and an extended list of philosophers and spiritual luminaries from eastern and western traditions. My internal horizons on these subjects broadened considerably.

The biggest buzz in Penn's religious studies department at that time was the research then being conducted by Dr. Andrew Newberg which resulted in the book *Why God Won't Go Away: Brain Science and the Psychology of Belief*. Newberg and his associate Eugene D'Aquill had employed state of the art, high-tech imaging technology to scan and study the brains of Franciscan nuns during prayer, Buddhist monks in meditation, and more. What they found...

> "was that intensely focused spiritual contemplation triggers an alteration in the activity of the brain that leads one to perceive transcendent religious experiences as solid, tangible reality... the sensation that Buddhists call "oneness with the universe" and the Franciscans attribute to the palpable presence of God is not a delusion, or subjective psychology, or simple wishful thinking. The inescapable conclusion is that God seems to be hard-wired into the human brain...
>
> Is religion merely a product of biology—a neurological illusion—or does the very fact that our brains function in such a curious way argue that God is not only real, but reachable"[143]

I relished Dr. Newberg's work for evident, personally experiential reasons, and, frankly, felt somewhat vindicated. I tried several times to enroll in his classes, but each time, I was told, there was quite an extensive waiting list. I cited Dr. Newberg's work in at least one paper written while at Penn, and raised the topics of his research numerous times during healthy, in-class debates and discussions.

In short, my entire obsession in those years was about the simple need to understand the extraordinary experiences I'd had as well as those accounts I had been researching. It was Dr. Newberg's work that brought it all home, back to earth. My own take away was that such experiences were clinically authentic – and common!

After word about my book had circulated during those years, at some point I was invited to visit the home of a Hindu-American family in Northern New Jersey where I could witness first-hand the miraculous manifestation of honey and Kumkuma powder issuing from the same photo of Sri Mukteshwar Bhagavan I had written about. I accepted the invitation, and joining me for the adventure were my friends Sophia and Summer, my religious studies bestie from Penn.

We were greeted graciously by our host, Saadhvi, a charming, devout Hindu woman of sound, rational, and clinically leaning mind working as a practicing clinical psychologist. This I found reassuring. After introductions were exchanged and refreshments were enjoyed, Saadhvi asked if we would then like to see "the Murti photo" of Sri Bhagavan. We enthusiastically

[143] www.andrewnewberg.com. Accessed 12/17/2018

confirmed in unison. Saadhvi asked us to turn off our cell phones and led us to the door of a small room just off of her living room. She requested that we remain quiet and respectful while inside, explaining that this was her family's private Puja room — a home chapel where traditional Hindu prayer and oblations are performed daily - and welcomed us to sit a while and meditate.

The Puja room had no furniture aside from a low table adorned with a pristine white table cloth topped with traditional Hindu effigies of Ganesh, Laksmi, and some other deities. A garland of strung fresh marigolds and lemon leaves encircled the deities, and two lovely vases of flowers flanked either side. Resting before them was the framed portrait of Sri Mukteshwar, the same image I had seen in Share International magazine four years before. And there it was, right before my eyes. I was stunned to witness streams of honey caked with rich, red Kumkuma powder cascading down from Sri Bhagavan's hands in the photo, forming a small heap at the base of the frame. While my companions and I sat in awe of the phenomenon, now and then from the hands in the photo an additional small amount of Kumkuma would issue forth, trickle down and mildly disrupt the pile. This further entrenched my amazement and, of course, aroused suspicion. My discerning, doubting Thomas nature took hold as I stepped outside of the room and asked Saadhvi for permission to examine the back of the photo. She smiled with agreement, encouraging me to please do so. After reentering, I arched over the table and photo, carefully examining the reverse side. I was suspicious that there might be attached tubes or something that was causing this. I studied the fabric on the table, running my fingers along each side and along the back, trying to determine if some hidden apparatus was fueling this. On my knees, I crouched further and lifted the hem of the fabric to examine the underside of the table. There was nothing there either.

Resuming an upright posture on my knees, I gazed with widened eyes transfixed with wonder. I had never directly witnessed any miraculous phenomenon of this sort before. I was amazed, and humbled. It was as if the photo had become alive, much like a bleeding Madonna or Christ statue. My mind stopped. I became breathless. It was one of the most remarkable sites I'd ever beheld. Truly, I thought, the man in this photo was a living saint of the Hindu tradition. Being all too familiar with Hindu customs, I could do nothing else but close my eyes and pranam. I sat down to meditate for a short while, opening my eyes now and then to again gaze at the incredulous marvel before me.

After a short duration, the three of us emerged from the small room. We were all quite speechless, our minds collectively quietened. We thanked

Saadhvi as we prepared for our return home. All of us remained quiet for quite some time during our ride south along the New Jersey Turnpike. We couldn't find adequate words to describe our experience as none of us had encountered anything like that.

Fourteen years ago, this phenomenon was unique and extraordinary for us, and served as a stunning revelation in my research. Today, there is ample available evidence that photographs of Sri Bhagavan as well as his wife Sri Amma continue to produce sacred powders and fragrant oils throughout the world in the homes of devout Hindus. My friends and I were empirically aware that Sri Bhagavan was considered, in India, to be an Avatar – an incarnate divine teacher – and it wasn't long before we again became witness to his ability for miraculous healing.

In the months that followed, I met Carmela, a devout Catholic woman from Reading, Pennsylvania, who practiced the same yoga and meditation techniques as I. Carmela, I learned, had recently been diagnosed with Cervical cancer. This prognosis was quite traumatizing for her as only three years prior she had been diagnosed with breast cancer and had endured a rigorous treatment of radiation, chemotherapy and a lumpectomy. My heart went out to the woman. Having been so convinced of the plausibility of miraculous intervention from the many interviews and research I had done, I reached out to Carmela with a desire to help.

Carmela and I enjoyed spirited conversations about the Madonna apparitions, about our mutual fondness for the Easter Tridium – the three days of sacred celebration beginning with Holy Thursday and concluding with Easter Sunday – and of all things Catholic. I had shared with her some of the many stories of miraculous healing associated with a variety of resources, like the Holy Water from Lourdes and interventions from Padre Pio to the photograph of Maitreya's hand print that had been distributed by Benjamin Creme's Share International Magazine. With relation to her recent cancer prognosis, Carmela emotionally shared her fear of going through radiation treatment again, her fright that she was facing death, and tearfully explaining how she had been praying for a miracle to be cured.

By then, I was privy to a significant number of accounts of miraculous healings attributed to Sri Bhagavan and Sri Amma. I phoned Saadhvi, explained Carmela's plight and asked if she not only would pray for Carmela, but, if she was to be in touch with Sri Bhagavan again, to please relay her plea. Saadhvi graciously welcomed the opportunity to reach out to Sri Bhagavan on Carmela's behalf, and asked to have Carmela get in touch with her directly. Carmela recounted that Saadhvi did contact Sri Bhagavan, who replied by assuring Carmela that everything would turn out ok, and further informing her that she was being tested by God the way gold is tested in fire, that he was holding her in the palm of his hand, and that God's grace would take care of everything.

In the weeks that followed, Saadhvi encouraged Carmela to attend an upcoming class with Dasaji which I had organized. After explaining Carmela's situation and her interaction with Sri Bhagavan, Dasaji extended an invitation to other *Bhagavad Dharma* teachers living in my region who had also been trained in India as healers by Sri Bhagavan himself. A healing session for Carmela was arranged to be added after the final session of the class. Carmela voiced extreme delight, and that she would certainly arrange to be there.

The class I had organized featured two days of lecture, diksha transmission, yoga-centric contemplations, discussion, meditation, and samskara shuddhi processes. Due to the heightened level of shakti or sacred energy originating from Sri Bhagavan's exceptionally advanced level of Yoga mastery, many attendees were involuntarily experiencing past life regressions, reliving personal sources of trauma from which they were finally becoming healed, to extraordinary states of consciousness and well-being. By then, this had become expected. During the very first program I had hosted, when I had the experience of my own mind, a friend of mine who had lost a sister on the tragic Flight 93 that went down in Somerset, PA on 9/11/2001 was able to achieve a level of emotional resolve and closure about her sister's death previously unattainable for her. These processes were the core of the classes, designed to facilitate breakthroughs in each person's respective barrier that hindered the experience of personal awakening.

Carmela arrived after lunch on the second day to join us for the latter session. When that segment and the meditation concluded, Dasaji and the healers said they needed a few minutes to set up and prepare. All were asked to leave the room for a short duration, with the exception of Carmela and her husband Tom, myself, and some others who were assisting. Dasaji and the other women began to recite a series of prayers while offering an Arati light to the photo of Sri Bhagavan set on a puja. When they concluded, the others who elected to stay were invited to return to the room quietly, and Carmela was invited to sit in a chair that had been set near the puja. After Carmela took her place, the four women hovered their hands above Carmela's head while standing quietly with eyes closed. They maintained this posture for about three to seven minutes, after which Dasaji opened her eyes and announced "It's done."

While some friends began to assist with breaking down our event,

Carmela shared, that, during the healing she experienced a profound feeling of peacefulness, as if she was being flooded with God's grace. She and her husband thanked us all, expressed her hope for the best, and parted. Within a month, Carmela phoned me, her voice stammering with tears of gratitude. In one of the most sincere expressions of profound joy shared by another human being I'd ever experienced, Carmela explained that she had just returned from seeing her doctor. After examining her most recent biopsy results, Carmela was told that her cancer was gone. She was beyond grateful. It was simply extraordinary.

To this day - fourteen years after - Carmela has been cancer free, healthy, happy, and thriving, while working for the past thirteen years as an academic advisor at the Community College near her home. She is still appreciative of the care and kindness extended to her in her hour of need. She told me that she is grateful every minute of every day that the hand of God was over her during the a very low time in her life.

My experience with Carmela then had invigorated my enthusiasm for Sri Bhagavan's work, and in the year that followed I hosted one more, academically oriented public talk and meditation program with Sri Bhagavan's teachers geared towards my fellow students in the Religious Studies department at Penn. It was the last program I would organize before my personal and professional life interfered with my ability to schedule courses in subsequent years.

After graduating in 2007, thoughts of Masters, Maitreya and spiritual things were put on the back burner as I turned my focus on career and supporting a household and family, and with little time to tend to matters related to the book, I simply pulled it off the market. The original incarnation of *Masters Among Us* had received positive reviews in publications from Pakistan to London, had developed a reasonable following with relatively brisk sales in the U.S. and Australia, and had earned me the privilege of making quite a few new international friends.

In those years since, now and then I would get an email from the acquaintances I had made, from someone explaining how the book had facilitated a positive transformation in their life, or sometimes get word that one or another of the folks I had interviewed for the book had passed away. Among those were Benjamin Creme, who passed in 2016. I was saddened by this news as I had developed a fondness for Mr. Creme, along with great respect for his convictions. He was a wonderful, charming gentleman with quite an extraordinary story.

To this day, and to the best of my knowledge, no one fitting the description of Maitreya has stepped forward as Mr. Creme had passionately declared for decades. But having met Mr. Creme and witnessing the sincerity of his conviction first hand, I've always kept an open mind to the possibility on the back burner. I suppose it was around the time of Ben's death that I started to again think about this book, of the marvelous true accounts herein, and consider that maybe it was time to bring it out of retirement.

Another who had passed was the extraordinary Barbara Mark Hubbard. I was in the final stages of editing when I learned that she had passed in April of 2019. My heart sank as I sat back reflectively to let the news settle in. I recalled with great, heartfelt memory and gratitude the times Barbara and I had spoken on the phone during my interview sessions in 1999 - 2000. She had been so kind and gracious with her time, and loved to speak enthusiastically about her experiences shared earlier herein, as well as the expansive philosophical views associated therewith. I remain honored to have made her acquaintance in such a richly inspiring manner. Then again, Barbara Marx Hubbard was the living embodiment of inspiration. She will be missed, but her legacy lives on through the continuing educational work of her Foundation of Conscious Evolution.

As I continued to review the previous chapters, everything I've described in this book did happen and had only deepened my faith and fascination with these miraculous marvels of the creation we live in. This brought to light another point: I couldn't recall having recently seen many news segments with featured reports about miracles. Were miracles still occurring? Were people still claiming to have met Jesus or other saintly figures? Were people losing hope? Losing faith? Why no reports of spiritual magic?

I began to wonder if something had shifted. During the intervening years, there seemed to be a greater abundance of recurring news stories focused how the hominid inhabitants of our planet seemed to be becoming mentally unhinged. Compassion seemed to be a thing of the past, as if people had lost the capacity to love, let alone one another. The escalation of random mass shootings in schools, malls, and elsewhere was off the charts. Terrorism had reared its message of hate in a larger way than ever anticipated. It seemed as if no place in the world was safe anymore. Only a week after taking a trip to Nice, France in 2016 with my family, a 19-ton cargo truck was deliberately driven into crowds of people celebrating Bastille Day on a boulevard that we had just walked days before. 86 people were killed and over 450 injured. This was beginning to get a little too close for comfort.

Such scenarios of madness continued to pop up across the globe. In the sadness of my contemplation, I couldn't help but recall remarks made sixteen years earlier by Sri Mukteshwar Bhagavan indicating that this would happen, that "people would start losing their minds." In fact, Sri Bhagavan's whole mission, from day one, was the assertion that if he could help 64,000 people become enlightened by 2012, then things could begin to turn around, that humanity could benefit greatly, and that by the 2023, "everyone would be enlightened." That's just several years away at this point. Is such a phenomenon as mass enlightenment possible?

Curiously, this has become a topic of clinical research in the west. In one of Dr. Andrew Newberg's more recent works, entitled *How Enlightenment Changes your Brain*, he, with associate author Mark Robert Waldman, tackle what they describe as "the pinnacle of the human experience."

> "Through his brain-scan studies…[Dr. Newberg] has discovered the specific neurological mechanisms associated with the enlightenment experience—and how we might activate those circuits in our own brains."[144]

Not only is it possible, according to Dr. Newberg, but his current research continues to maintain his findings of 15 years ago, that our species is actually hard-wired for enlightenment. Suffering, as the Buddha discovered 2500 years ago, is only alleviated through attainment of enlightenment. According to scientific research that is consistent with the findings of ancient sages and, yes, masters of their respective traditions, we are actually designed to live in an enlightened state. This is exactly what Sri Bhagavan has been saying for more than 25 years. In fact, it's what all the great masters of Indian and Tibetan yoga have been saying for ages. What seems to distinguish Sri Bhagavan is that the service he offers is a precisely engineered, practical methodology designed to help interested aspirants attain a state of awakening, which is the gateway ultimately leading to a very natural attainment of enlightenment.

In those early years of my acquaintance with his mission, I learned that a number of readers of my book from various continents had been inspired to make the trip to India to meet Sri Bhagavan and take his courses which facilitated this awakening along with a conscious establishment of identification with one's Soul. Some of my own friends had participated in these courses as well. I saw them return home transformed, completely connected to their Soul-level Selves with enriched spiritual lives. My friend Dan reconnected with his Judaic roots, and has since enjoyed a deep, fulfilling practice of Judaism with his wife and children. My friend Cynthia, like myself, experienced a deeper connection to Jesus and became an active participant in

---

[144] www.andrewnewberg.com/books/how-enlightenment-changes-your-brain. Accessed 12/17/2018

her Catholic parish.

My friend Sophia had gone to India also. She had shared wonderful stories of then intimate, informal group darshans with the saintly man, describing Sri Bhagavan as "the coolest, most extraordinary person I've ever met!" Her stories were great. Nothing mystical or over the top, but, rather, that she had learned quite practical, accessible techniques and contemplations for facilitating awakening and practicing awareness - the forerunner to enlightenment.

"He made it sound so easy" Sophia shared. "Enlightenment isn't some lofty ideal that's hard to attain" she explained. "It starts with righting your relationships – with parents, your spouse, partner, whoever. To do that, we were taught to just practice awareness by taking a hard look at how we relate to others in our everyday lives." Sophia continued for some time, and it was a conversation we continued by phone for years following. I would employ some of the techniques she shared, and found them to be quite helpful. Sometime afterward, I was emailed a video clip of Sri Bhagavan giving a public talk about the unique nature of each individual's mystical experiences. As an offered example, Sri Bhagavan mentioned my name, this book, and his explanation that the experience of meeting Jesus I had during the Connecticut retreat had been completely authentic.

In the years since I had written about him, Sri Bhagavan's mission exploded into a worldwide phenomenon. When my friends went to India, they met him in Satyaloka, a humble village of thatched roof huts in the jungles of Chennai where his ashram was then located. At that time there may have been maybe twenty to fifty aspirants from multiple countries outside of India sitting and chatting with him at that time. Soon thereafter, when word spread globally, tens of thousands of spiritually hungry pilgrims flocked to meet this man who was declared by others to be a spiritual avatar. After 2006 the phenomenon of Sri Bhagavan's mission for world enlightenment went absolutely viral. His organization estimated that, as of 2018, more than 14 million people from across the globe have heard of Sri Bhagavan, taken his courses, or consider themselves followers.[145] I found it fascinating, that, in 2001, when I was originally researching for this book, there was very little information about him on the internet. At least not in English. At that time, my email correspondence with a monk was my main source of available information. Today, a quick Google search of Sri Bhagavan or Oneness unfolds an endless source of links, photos, videos, and information.

I was happy to see that this saintly man's mission had prospered, and that so many tens of thousands of people across the planet had benefited from his message, and quite likely from the same potent energy I had experienced in that first small gathering I had hosted in 2001. I would have liked to have made the trip to India to meet the man in person and witness the fabulous 'Golden City' then under construction in Andhra Pradesh, but personal responsibilities

---

[145] Source: Golden Age Movement archives.

made such a trip somewhat prohibitive.

From time to time over the next fourteen years, friends would share how Sri Bhagavan's organization had grown. Initially known as The Foundation for World Awakening, the ongoing expansion of content and curriculum brought about name changes, first to Oneness University, then to World Oneness University, and more recently O&O (Oneness & One World) Academy. Some of the original Dasa monks that had taken vows of renunciation in the traditional Indian manner had since returned to a secular lifestyle, with some continuing to teach while getting married and raising a family. Sri Bhagavan himself had also been addressed by different names: first as Sri Mukteshwar, then Sri Mukteshwar Bhagavan, Sri Kalki, Sri Kalki Bhagavan, and now, Sri Bhagavan or Sri AmmaBhagavan – so named by declaring his wife Amma and he to be two halves of the same being.

Though most westerners refer to him Sri Bhagavan, in India today he is yet revered by millions of devoted Hindus as the prophesized Kalki Avatar. Yet, as far as I could find, Sri Bhagavan has dismissed this designation himself, playfully pointing out that he has never ridden about on a white horse while brandishing a sword in the manner traditionally depicted in India's Puranic legend. One could, however, entertain the Puranic reference as a metaphor: seated on a horse would suggest leadership or authority, while the sword could simply refer to the tools needed to battle against falsehood and the limiting, egoic tendencies of our species. In the gospel of Matthew, verse 34-36, Jesus made a relative remark: "Think not that I have come to bring peace on the earth; I have not come to bring peace, but a sword."[146] Whichever perspective to which you subscribe, both refer to the internal battle one must wage to achieve that connection with the divine within ourselves. It's a blunt way of saying that there is some serious work to be done.

Sri Bhagavan has consistently maintained that his sole, simple mission was to help alleviate suffering, awaken humanity, and assist with ushering in the Golden Age, or, Satya Yuga - the next cyclical age of the ancient Hindu calendar. He has mathematically asserted that if a certain number of individuals based on population could become enlightened, then a shift in human consciousness would occur that would begin the process of lifting humanity from a culture of hatred and suffering to one of increasingly compassionate and interactive cooperation. He has always maintained that his primary goal was to help 64,000 people become enlightened. That's all that was needed.

But experiencing an enlightened state and maintaining it requires

---

[146] As translated in the Aramaic Bible in Plain English

consistent practice in the early stages. When many who flocked to his Indian retreat in the late 2000's found themselves unable to maintain the heightened state they had initially experienced, they moved on like spiritual window shoppers. The apathy of such browsers speaks volumes about the human condition. Our global culture has been defined by consumerist attitudes with demands for instant gratification. When not attained, the angels of our lesser natures lead us on to something else, some other new thing that might provide what we seek. We all do this. All the time.

Curiously, Sri Bhagavan asserts that what distinguishes this particular time in human history and evolution is that an assisted short cut to awakening and enlightenment is available, and that's his job. He recently remarked that the initial mission of his Oneness movement to affect a shift in human consciousness by 2012 had been completed. After then turning over the University directorship to his son, Krishna, in 2014, I learned that Sri Bhagavan and Sri Amma had elected to retire, moving from the massive complex that became the site of Oneness University to the serenity of a smaller country retreat. After learning that Sri Bhagavan would no longer be offering public programs, any remote hope I had retained to someday meet him in person was set aside. I always maintained a fondness for the guy. I liked his moxie, his sense of humor, and, quite frankly, I respected him for the dedication he maintained for his vision of an improved world, and concluded that he would just assume a quiet life of meditation in his jungle retreat, the way most sages and avatars of Indian lore had done for thousands of years. This wasn't necessarily the case.

While I was at work in late 2015, I engaged in a discussion about India, yoga, and meditation with a gentleman named Taber who shared how he had met Sri Bhagavan, had attended his 21-day retreat, and spent extended time in India with him a decade before. I smiled with delight, mentioning my book and my familiarity with Sri Bhagavan's work from 14 years prior. Taber found this to be serendipitous, and as we parted, he promised to keep in touch and continue the discussion another time.

Our conversation had reawakened my curiosity for this enlightened Master whom I had put out of my mind for some time. What was Sri Bhagavan up to these days, I began to wonder? Assuming the window of opportunity to meet him in person had passed, I thought fondly of this extraordinary yogi, and mentally wished him well. Taber had shared how his contact with Sri Bhagavan was so profound and life-transforming that initially it left him unsure if he wanted to leave India, claiming that during his time there, he had a profound healing experience.

In late Winter of 2018 I was invited to join Taber for dinner along with a group of exemplary friends, among whom was Dr. Clark, a clinical psychologist whose consulting firm works with organizations that address veteran's health related matters.

In the course of conversation, we began discussing the plight of veterans grappling with post-traumatic stress disorder and the types of organizations with whom Dr. Clark works. Taber shared his story about the healing of his own trauma with the aid of Sri Bhagavan, along with accounts of others who had claimed to have had similar healing experiences. Dr. Clark asked for my opinion. I replied by explaining how I'd written about him so many years ago specifically in the context of such miracles. Following some added prompting, I then rambled off a few example accounts of the miracles and such as found herein, while others shared some similar stories in response.

The topic of suicide came up, and I asked Dr. Clark about the nature of his work helping veterans that suffer with suicidal tendencies. The conversation spun in a few different directions on topics ranging from psychological trauma to the psychology of belief and religious experience. After a short while, Dr. Clark asked why I had inquired about that issue. I paused, unsure of how to reply. In true psychologist fashion, he then asked me directly if I had dealt with suicidal tendencies. I paused to think about that for a moment, then vaguely replied "Not consciously."

Dr. Clark sensed my hesitance, asking what I meant. I explained that it was a particularly sensitive topic for me as I had lost some friends to suicide, and once stayed on the phone through the night to talk a friend out of the act after they had phoned me to say goodbye. But that wasn't the whole answer.

I looked over at Taber, then continued by saying, "Well, I don't know if you believe in reincarnation or not, but many years ago the same spiritual teacher from India that Taber knows once told me that I had committed suicide in a previous life, and warned me that if I wasn't careful, I could potentially go down that path again."

Dr. Clark became transfixed, asking me to continue. The others became quiet to listen in. I had opened this can of worms, so now I had to serve it.

"I don't know about that for sure. I mean, who really knows their past lives, right? There's a reason God or nature keeps it veiled, I guess. I do believe that we come into this life to work out unfinished business from past lives, and if we keep our focus, it all works out by the time we leave. But I will say this: Though I didn't think of suicide realistically, meaning, that it was something I could actually do, in my view there were some very depressing, dark moments in my life when I felt like I was peering directly into that dark abyss. I felt it. I felt that I clearly understood what suicidal people experience in those moments. For me, I always held tight to a prayer, and in those darkest moments, when there seemed to be no hope or answer, I recalled the simple advice given to me by this teacher from India. I found it amazing that he had that rare ability to peer into one's past and future like many great saints and enlightened masters of legend. I don't know how else to say it, but, this man from India, Sri Bhagavan, well... I don't know another way to put this - he may have pretty much saved my life."

The jaws of all around me were agape, and for a moment not a word was uttered. All then expressed a keen interest to know more, so I obliged. The longer version of the story, which includes my first encounter with Saadhvi mentioned earlier, went something like this...

One evening I was sitting at home watching television when my cell phone rang. I didn't recognize the number. Telemarketing wasn't too much of a thing then and I figured it must have been work or client related, so I answered.

"Hello! Is this Tom?" asked an unfamiliar voice. I detected an Indian accent.

"It is."

"Hello, Tom. My name is Saadhvi. I have a message for you from Sri Bhagavan. He asked me to call you."

"Hello, Saadhvi! Sri Bhagavan? In India?" I was both surprised and suspicious. I never had met Sri Bhagavan, and though I did have those experiences shared in the previous chapter, I hadn't been in touch with him for some time at that point.

"Yes" Saadhvi replied.

"Are you phoning from India?"

"No. I'm in the United States, in New Jersey."

I was more confused. "Oh? How did you get my number?"

"Sri Bhagavan gave it to me."

I wasn't aware that Sri Bhagavan had my phone number, though I did suppose he could have gotten it from Dasaji, so I continued. "Well, this is an unexpected surprise. What is it that Sri Bhagavan wanted to relay?"

I thought perhaps it had something to do with the questions for my book which still remained unanswered.

"Sri Bhagavan wants to tell you to be aware, that it is very important for you to practice awareness at this time. He said to remember that your thoughts are not your thoughts, that what you sometimes feel emotionally aren't always your feelings."

As I listened to Saadhvi, I recognized maxims like those discussed by Dasaji in previous talks and courses I attended. Despite an otherwise pleasant demeanor, I detected some urgency in Saadhvi's tone.

"I am familiar with these teachings" I replied. "That's very thoughtful of Sri Bhagavan. But why is he stressing that it is important now?"

Saadhvi answered with a question: "Tell me: How are you doing?"

Her inquiry threw me.

"I'm fine... I guess."

She continued. "Have any issues been coming up for you lately that has caused difficulty?"

"Difficulty? In what way?"

"Like problems at work, at home, in your relationships?"

I felt the conversation was beginning to get a little personal, but familiar with the regressive therapy style of Sri Bhagavan's workshops, I went along.

"No more than usual. I mean, there is always something that disrupts the calm, but that's par for the course. My meditation practice keeps that in check."

Saadhvi continued. "What Sri Bhagavan means is that these are the things to be aware of, to practice awareness with. He's saying if things get difficult for you, that when these things come up, just remember that they are just thoughts, just emotions, and these are not you. They are not your thoughts. You are not your thoughts, your thoughts are not you. Will you remember this? Contemplate this?"

This wasn't far removed from how I learned to deal with most issues anyway, but somehow Saadhvi's directness made me instantly become more aware of it. I was grateful for the personal consideration this saintly man from India was extending.

"Yes, I will do that. Thank you, Saadhvi. I'm grateful that Sri Bhagavan was so thoughtful and asked you to phone me. Do you know what prompted him to do this so directly?"

It was unusual. Other than written replies by letter I'd received in years past from some of the Swamis with whom I'd studied, I never had received a phone call quite like this. Saadhvi was silent for a minute after I posed my question, and then she said this:

"Because of difficulties that you've referenced in your prayers. Sri Bhagavan said, that, in your previous life, in your last incarnation, you committed suicide. The Samskaras from that experience are still there. They are still working out in this incarnation. He said if you are not aware- if you don't practice awareness, and if you are not careful, that your mind and thoughts may compel you to do that again."

Now I was silent, stunned, and uncertain how to respond. I became suspicious, and questioned Saadhvi how I could know for sure that this message was from Sri Bhagavan, and why I shouldn't suspect her of being someone just trying to take advantage of me. Where was this coming from? I had never consciously harbored any inclinations for suicide in my life. Or had I?

I asked Saadhvi to tell me more about herself, and what authority she had to represent Sri Bhagavan. She explained that she was a clinical psychologist who helps Sri Bhagavan with students of his who may be having a difficult time processing their more deeply embedded Samskaras. That is, those residue impressions or forms of conditioning that keep us all bound, limited, and prevent us from experiencing our full soul potential. Saadhvi then asked me several questions and made some remarks about personal issues in my life of which there was no way she could have known. Some were issues so private that I'd never spoken of them to anyone, and some were related to events of my childhood. I was shocked.

"How do you know these things," I asked? "Who told you this?"

"Sri Bhagavan" was her simple reply.

What struck me was the absolute truth and clarity with which she made the remarks. It was certainly true that, privately, I had dealt with depression almost my entire life. It began when I was young, maybe 10 or so years old, when I practically sequestered myself in our house to avoid the emotional pain. On top of that, the neighborhood where I grew up was challenging at times for a young person trying to find their way. It had been one of the epicenters of violent racial conflict in the US, and I had been beaten, jumped, and almost killed before I was 16. Alcoholism and drug addiction had become rampant. Kids shooting heroin, crank or huffing bags of model glue in the corner of the playground was every day routine. Friends died, others were murdered. We had grown up in what otherwise might be considered a war zone. Depression prevailed as an undercurrent of life in our neighborhood. Everybody was just struggling to find the way to survive and get by. It took a few years for me to gradually emerge from my self-imposed depressed seclusion and start to find my way again. Frankly, these were the very reasons for which I began to practice meditation. For many years it was about battling depression.

There had been some dark, soul-searching moments in my youth, but, privately, the close kinship with God through prayer that I maintained was what always got me through. There were also those times when I felt like the God in which I had placed so much hope and reliance had abandoned me, but a quick recollection of Jesus' night in the garden would get me through.

After beginning to embrace a deeper spirituality when I was about 14 years old and going on religious retreats while investigating alternative philosophies and experimenting with the practice of meditation in high school, all of these things made a profoundly life-enhancing improvement in my life leaving me to believe I'd left those shadows of depression behind.

As life went on, other issues would trigger a return of depressive bouts: breaking up with a girlfriend, getting fired from a job, or just general uncertainty of direction. Throughout it all, prayer and meditation kept me balanced on this razor's edge that only I knew existed within me. In my mid-twenties I started to do drugs myself, mostly because it was always accessible – at work, with friends, at clubs. I saw myself going in a dark direction that I didn't like. Having witnessed the toll of drugs on people I knew from my neighborhood since I was a kid, I extricated myself post-haste and ran back to live in an ashram. After a year or so of living a relatively mendicant life while going through withdrawal, I still found myself profoundly unhappy. I consulted with the spiritual teacher Gurumayi, and asked what she suggested. To my surprise, she said that it would be better if I left the ashram, returned home, and pursued life head on. "The world will make you strong" she encouraged.

I took her advice. A year after returning home, my father passed away, and in short duration, I went back to my old, self-medicating ways and resumed a partying lifestyle. I had fantastic, memorable times, and made great, life-long friends. Yet, as John Lennon had sung, though I laughed and clowned, beneath that mask I was wearing a frown. Inwardly, I was still battling these demons of depression. This is the real reason I spent so many years exploring the different spiritual traditions and miraculous accounts described throughout this book. Despite a regular meditation practice and conversing with God in a very casual way, I was not able to comprehend why I couldn't grasp a full happiness even when my efforts were their best. I wanted answers! I enrolled in numerous self-help programs like Werner Erhard's est and its Forum and Landmark sequels, all things I thought could "cure" me and bring about permanent happiness. But nothing fulfilled me completely. They helped, and certainly provided the needed footing to grow into becoming a responsible adult. I eventually married, raised a beautiful child, and surrendered to the householder life, just as Muktananda had prescribed and his successor, Gurumayi, had reiterated.

When Saadhvi called me that night, I had been married for about eleven years at that point, and my daughter was then about 9 years old. It was during that time when I had been working three jobs at the same time just to keep things sustainable. Financial difficulty had put a strain on my marriage, and often I just didn't feel good about myself. I prayed regularly, always seeking permanent relief that never seemed to come. Yes! I say this despite the marvelous experiences shared throughout this book. How could I doubt that prayers were being answered? Yet, I questioned faith in anything and everything. I drank. I smoked. Despite it all, I kept my chin just above the water line. Though, outwardly, while extending the illusion that all was fine, inwardly, I was drowning.

So, for Saadhvi to call and relay this message from Sri Bhagavan while addressing some of these intimately personal issues that she couldn't have possibly known, you might understand how startled I was. At that time, there was no overtly dominant feeling of depression, though in the months following that phone call, some deeply dark moments came to the forefront. There were a few times when objective thoughts about why people commit suicide would cross my mind, and one or two times when I looked it directly in the eye. I can't say that I actually considered committing suicide, but I had seen how easily I could have. In those moments, as Sri Bhagavan had suggested, I maintained awareness that this was just a thought that would pass, and from having practiced yoga for so long, I easily identified it as a Samskara. Sometimes the emotional conflict was so intense that I perceived no end to it, that the anguish experienced in those moments was so challenging I wasn't sure if I would make to the other side, leaving me only with a feeling of profound hopelessness. And then, at some point in the midst of those darkest moments, in the back of my mind, I would hear that distant, still, silent voice say: "Your thoughts are not your thoughts. Be aware. This is not you."

By maintaining this practice of awareness, an inner balance began to steadily develop, and I was able to recognize a recurring pattern in each instance: a thought would come up, an emotional reaction would be triggered followed by anger, hatred, blame, or depression. At times the consummation was so great that I became the embodiment of these reactions. Yet, all the while, I was able to witness from a deeper place within, that this wasn't me. I knew myself not to be a hate-filled person, not an angry person, not one to blame indiscriminately - and, ultimately, not a depressed person. I saw depression as an illusory state unaffiliated with my innate nature. Once I became aware of this pattern, the unrelenting pressure would begin to gradually abate, and within a day or two, things would be normal. Later on, a similar incident would arise, yet they were never as pressuring as the time preceding, and each subsequent time lesser than that.

I started to understand that this was the ongoing process of release from latent Samskaras that is part and parcel to the practice of Raja yoga. And the more I understood that, then these psychologically challenging instances became more frequent, sometimes just as intense, sometimes less so. But each time they arose, dealing with it became a little easier. This, I recognized, was what is described as the trail of tears on the path of inner mastery. I understood that this is the lesson of the way of the cross, of Jesus' suffering while ascending Calvary. This had just been my cross, the way it manifested relative to my childhood impressions and traumas, of impressions transferred genetically from my parents and ancestors, and what seemed to be latent, leftover, unresolved impressions from previous lifetimes. The vision of Jesus and the crown of thorns years I had experienced years ago had come to me after praying during a particularly difficult time. I then thought I was being given a simple reminder from Jesus in response to my prayer, in which he was lovingly saying "You think you have it bad?" But now I understand the symbolism of the crown of thorns so intimately: it is this suffering in the mind borne of Samskaras, the impressions in our mind that we take on and to which we habitually continue to subscribe. We become so used to these impressions as part of our makeup that unconsciously we become addicted to indulging in pain.

Cultivating awareness of this is what I had signed on to when I accepted Shaktipat Diksha from Swami Muktananda to begin an advanced practice of yoga, and again when I opted to again receive Diksha from Sri Bhagavan through his emissary 32 years later. I suppose I didn't realize 'the path' would be so intense. Eventually I came to understand clearly that my depression was a result of my own managed suffering. I had adapted to it, dealt with it, assuming it would linger despite my efforts, so I just acknowledged and lived with it. I found temporal happiness in a variety of things, and became addicted to those actions and behaviors just to keep the demons at bay.

What had been fascinating about Saadhvi's relayed message from Sri Bhagavan was that it took on the same style of effect that I had when the Amish woman poked me in the chest to warn me about watching out for those buggies. In that instance, the same sharp jab woke me up just in time to avoid a potentially horrible accident. In this instance, Sri Bhagavan's simple words would come to mind whenever I succumbed to the darkest throes of depression. I came to see that it would take several more years for that Samskara to fully work itself out. Talk about untying a tough knot. I eventually was able to see that the karma one must endure for committing suicide is an unceasing hell of reliving it in the next life. When someone decides to take their own life with the thought of handing over the responsibility to a higher power, the truth is, as an individual soul - a jiva - the responsibility remains yours. You are given another chance to recognize that the life you are given is not yours to decide on your fate, that being born into a human form is a precious gift. The trials one endures in their respective life, no matter how perceptibly difficult, *are* the lessons to be learned. There is no other in that moment.

I also came to understand how suicide effects everyone around you, that it is the penultimate of selfish sins or transgressions. Once I allowed myself to peer directly into the very abyss that I feared, it no longer controlled me. After that, my depression symptoms just evaporated. And then, one day, after a lifetime of struggling with it, it was just gone. If something saddened me or proved to be emotionally or psychologically challenging, I found I had organically cultivated the new habit of just witnessing it, of being aware of it, and from that perspective I could deal with the situation objectively and detached. In other words, I had been healed. This enlightened man thousands of miles away whom I'd never met had helped save my life.

The conversation with Dr. Clark and the others continued, about the published work of Dr. Deikman, William James, and more accounts of miracles and healing. It evolved into an amazing, inspiring chat which left me with residual reflections that continued in the weeks and months that followed. I found myself with a renewed sense of gratitude for an intervention about which I had forgotten, and recalling all the amazing instances recounted in the earlier chapters of this book. It was during this time when I revisited this work and began editing for this revised edition. In that process, I recalled that Sri Bhagavan had never really answered my question about any truth to the school of thought on the return of Masters, and that he had once remarked that this book wasn't finished.

In late August of 2018, I was scrolling through my social media feed when I saw a notice for a three-day retreat offered for the first time ever in North America that would be highlighted with the attendance of Sri Bhagavan by Skype. I smiled, noting the serendipitous timing. Seventeen years had passed since I had first read about him, sixteen since I had reached out in an attempt to interview him, and more than a decade since his intervention for which I remain so grateful. I considered, that, not having been able to budget a trip to

India and given up all hope to meet him following his retirement, that this may be the one opportunity to spend some time in his company – albeit virtually - and maybe get my questions answered.

    I mulled the opportunity over for a few weeks, contemplating how I could budget the tuition. Despite its reasonable fee – which was ten times less than the cost of travelling to India fifteen years prior – I decided that I needed to find a way to make this happen. After a few weeks of putting it off, I considered an old adage I had learned decades before: Make the commitment and what you need will show up. So, heeding that advice, I followed suit, contacted the organizers and registered. In many self-help seminar programs I had attended through the years, it was often said that the process begins when you register. Sure enough, with minimal effort the funds needed came forth, and though the three-day retreat was yet a month away, within 48 hours, I would have one of the most profound personal spiritual experiences of my life.

Chapter Thirteen

CONCLUSION

"Be still, and know that I am God."

Psalm 46

Some nights, after getting home following a long work day, I wind down by writing or watching a little TV on a small sofa in our home office. One night just days after registering for the retreat, I had fallen asleep there and around five o'clock in the morning I was roused from my sleep and became conscious. I say conscious because I wasn't fully awakened from sleep in the normal sense of understanding. I awakened to full cognizance, but my body remained asleep. It wasn't like one of those paralyzed waking experiences either. I could move my body freely. It just remained at rest. What was most remarkable is that I was aware enough to witness what was going on. I experienced a profound serenity while then feeling a sensation as if the top of my skull had been opened, followed by my brain being gently lifted up and flipped upside down. I felt a burning sensation as if the fluid around my brain was boiling, but it wasn't painful. I recall feeling as if my brain were hovering independently in an aqueous, electrical solution. I experienced no fear. Something seemed completely right about it. Cognitively, I found myself simultaneously enveloped with a profound sense of union with…I wasn't sure how to describe it…God?

The extreme, rapturous level of joy that filled me was unearthly, like nothing I'd experienced before. I recognized it as the spiritual state I'd only known empirically from academic description as Sat-Chit-Ananda: Existence, Consciousness, and Bliss. I understood clearly that this was the state in which all the great saints and masters of yoga reveled and taught about, the goal of all spiritual and religious practice. This was the state of the Siddha Masters which Muktananda had earnestly implored we strive for. I understood it as the very experience Jesus had when he pronounced: "I and the Father are one." This was the "Kingdom of God" described by Jesus and passed on to his Apostles and Disciples before the true meaning became lost in time. I totally got it, experienced it, knew it, understood it, was living it in that moment.

And while all this was happening, I also witnessed a review of my entire spiritual life, from present going back. Images of landmark moments came forth as if I were reliving them again in that moment, and saw how they had all been connected, all part of what seemed to be a pre-ordained continuum that had order, purpose and planning, and executed with precision at the correct time in my life. I relived the encounter with Jesus I had while on the Connecticut retreat. I understood for the first time the meaning of a comment made to me by Gurumayi more than thirty years prior. I found myself once again in the company of Swami Muktananda in his ashram as if I had physically time-travelled and was there again. I reexperienced the moment and day on which I had received Shaktipat Diksha initiation from him. I saw memories of my times living and doing Seva in his ashrams and centers. I saw my first meeting with Swami Satchidananda, whose Integral Yoga techniques I'd begun when I was in high school, and his encouragement to study and spend time with Muktananda. I recalled meeting Sri Chinmoy, Swami Kriyananda, and Ammaji - the affectionate name for the incredible, extraordinarily saintly being Mata Amritanandamayiji, also known as "the hugging saint." My inner tour continued on as I witnessed moments in the Catholic vocational retreats I attended during my high school years, of Evangelical Christian church gatherings I'd attended with friends when we were teenagers, of my mother teaching me how to pray when I was very young, watching my dear grandmother saying the rosary in our parish church, and recalling some of my earliest epiphanies about the nature of God going back to as young as seven years old.

I had a profound recollection of my preference for the writings of Paramahansa Yogananda. I recalled how I had brought his book *Autobiography of a Yogi* with me when I went on the Catholic vocational retreats, and then, like a film camera zooming in for a closeup, my attention became focused on another book of his sitting on the coffee table of an apartment I had in summer of 1978 just after I had graduated from high school. The book, exactly as I remembered it, was *Man's Eternal Quest*. I had not thought of that book in at least twenty years. All the while, while the book was in my sphere of vision, a voice kept saying - not in audible words as we know it, but rather like an innate, intuitive knowing - "You know this. You know all of this. You know this already." Who was doing the speaking? Who was doing the watching? Who was the observer of this experience and who was experiencing it? Who was causing it to happen? I had simply fallen asleep on a sofa as I do from time to time. But all this – I hadn't experienced anything as profound as this since my episode of unfolding thoughts with Sri Bhagavan's representative teacher Dasaji eighteen years prior.

After about an hour had passed, I came to, drifting into the normal waking state as one does every morning. However, the profound experience of bliss, of complete contentment, mental stillness, rapturous joy – all remained. I felt so intimately connected and one with God, as if I had at long last attained the goal of yoga after practicing it for 45 years. This was it. This was the experience of Oneness, the unity-consciousness that Sri Bhagavan Mukteshwar had been teaching and referencing.

After fully awakening, I remember sitting up and pausing to digest it all. I couldn't help but note the uncanny timing for this to occur just two days after I had registered for the retreat. I was aware that the required applications had been reviewed in India. Had Sri Bhagavan been shown my application, prompting him to telepathically tune in to say hello? What a hello it was! I surfed easily through my routine tasks that day, floated into work without a care, maintaining an uplifted, blissful state while handling my professional duties with precision and care.

The state lingered for days. When I awoke each morning, I couldn't wait to sit and meditate and plunge again into that extraordinary state as if submerging myself into a warm, soothing, whirl-pooled bath. Throughout my workday, I'd intermittently check the time, wondering how much longer it would be before I could get home to meditate and enter that state again. When I did get home, I bypassed the beer or glass of wine I'd usually consume and immediately ascended to our second-floor office, sat on the same sofa, and went into some of the deepest meditations I'd had in years. In each of those sessions, I had profoundly clear understandings of circumstance. I would see, for example, how some reactionary perception of some person, place or thing was caused by some psychologically conditioned reflex I'd adapted from an incident earlier in life. I found myself incredibly appreciative of my wife of twenty-four years, recognizing how the good times along with our quarrelling and more difficult times had all been perfectly ordained, designed and played out with perfect balance in order to facilitate and strengthen personal spiritual growth. I experienced profound gratitude for all that she had contributed to my life. This prompted a keen perception of a deeper level of appreciation for the influence of everyone in my life. Every single incident of my life, I recognized, had played a key part in bringing me to this moment.

When I got up that first day, I searched through my vast collection of books to locate my copy of Man's Eternal Quest. I looked everywhere: in book cases on three floors of our home, in the night table beside our bed, in piles of books that needed to be filed, but could not find it. I concluded that I must have loaned it to a friend some years ago, so I dismissed it and gave up the search. I decided I'd just purchase a new copy at some point.

A day or so later, I was engaged with another project and was looking for a particular artwork of mine that I had wanted to work on. I searched in a portfolio that was leaning against one of my bookcases, but I couldn't find that, either. As I leaned the portfolio back against the bookcase and was simultaneously exiting the room, something caught my eye. I craned my neck backwards into the room from the doorway, leaned back, pulled the portfolio toward me, and there, on the third shelf down, in the very last position, was my old copy of Man's Eternal Quest. I swore I had looked there, and amused myself with the thought that a minor miracle had occurred.

From that point on, every night when I got home from work, I added the reading of a chapter from the book and then meditated. I reveled in Yogananda's words in depth for the first time since I was a teenager. I recalled some of the topics, and relived the original reading of those segments I had then highlighted. I was tuning into my seventeen-year-old self, feeling as if no time had transpired. Now and then, as I read a certain portion, I noted that a point discussed was something I had later learned first-hand from Swami Muktananda, how much I had then enjoyed Yogananda's frequent references to Jesus, the practical application of gospel excerpts that I had incorporated into my life since, and his perspectives on the synthesis of eastern and western philosophical schools and theisms.

My meditations continued to get stronger and deeper. One night I was a bit tired, and while meditating, the strain of trying to inwardly focus my eyeballs toward the 'third eye' pineal gland region was too much, so I rested my eyes and just allowed myself to relax even further. I noticed my meditation then got even deeper, and instantly thereafter I felt a jolt of Kundalini energy shoot up from the base of my spine to the inner center of my head. I experienced the spontaneous Kriya of my head forcibly being nodded to and fro. I laughed, asking myself silently: "Have I been doing this wrong all these years?" Inwardly I intuited "Yes! This is the proper way to meditate." Again, my head involuntarily nodded forward and back almost as a gesture of affirmation. This was the first time that I ever recognized Kundalini as a conscious, independent force of its own volition! I could see why the Hindu culture personified it as a Goddess. In Christian culture, this same energy is what is known as the Holy Spirit.

I felt areas of my brain I wasn't even aware of suddenly pulsing. I experienced a sensation within my brain like the unfolding of an umbrella, or the branches of a tree. The old metaphor of the opening of a lotus blossom came to mind, and again, I was fascinated and curious to find myself experiencing this familiar phenomenon so rooted in the ancient lore of yoga. The state I was experiencing was like relaxing in a garden, and suddenly I understood fully all the biblical legends: *This* was the garden of Eden. *This* was the burning bush to which Moses referred. *This* was the essence of the parable of the prodigal son. *This* was the Kingdom of God. Many aspects of Biblical parable became crystal clear in terms of mystical metaphor. I understood more deeply the tenants of Jesus and his union with the Father. I remained in this rapturous state for a considerable amount of time, and only became aware of my surroundings when I heard my wife getting ready for work. I looked at the clock. Seven hours had passed. I had never sat in meditation for seven hours in my life! Prior to that the longest session was maybe an hour or two, having only read about the great yogis of olden times sitting in meditation for longer durations. I never envisioned myself having the ability to do this. It was just ecstatic.

I sat for a short while, somewhat in a blissful daze, and suddenly found myself involuntarily reciting the *Our Father*, concurrently considering each word and sentence deeply and completely, reveling in its profound, inherent perfectness. I considered the fact that Jesus had composed it while fully comprehending Jesus' meaning. I again contemplated and marveled at what he meant by saying the Kingdom of God is at hand. I could see it so clearly. It's all around us, all the time, yet we don't see it. But that day, I did. I saw it lucidly, and I assure you, it's no fabrication. It can be experienced. It can be seen. It's not a place - it's a state of perception.

I began a regular practice of repeating the Our Father throughout my day, continuing to contemplate each word and phrase as if it were a living force of its own. Then I did the same with the Hail Mary, and this inspired a keen desire to recite the rosary. I appreciated that these were the prayers I had been taught in my youth, and fondly recalled my dear Irish grandmother who was never without a rosary in her hand or pocket. I went to the drawer where I thought I had kept my own rosary, but it wasn't there. As I looked about, I recalled a box in my office in which I had put some religious items when I painted the room some years back. The rosary wasn't there, but instead, I did find a Rudraksha bead mala my friend Sophia had brought back as a gift from Sri Bhagavan's retreat in India. This was cool, I thought. It wasn't a formal rosary, per se, but it had the same number of beads and I could alternate between traditional rosary recitation and mantra repetition. It didn't matter to me as both were the same and there was no conflict or existential crisis in combining the two. Both served the same purpose: to quiet the mind, open the heart, and kindle a closer union with God.

I continued these practices with profound gratitude that a lifetime of prayer, practice, and sadhana was at long last paying off. Everything that Muktananda had promised would result from the receipt of Shaktipat Diksha was becoming realized. Everything I had learned from just trying to live the teachings of Jesus the best I could was manifesting after a lifetime of devotion.

And then, after about a week or so, the deep inner connection and intense level of oneness began to dissipate. I couldn't understand why. It was like I had only been given a divine tease – a temporal taste of the fullness offered. I continued to pray and meditate, and contemplated reasons for this dissolution. Surely, I pondered, there was a lesson to be learned. I could comprehend that it was normal human conditioning that was limiting my access, and that this was an important lesson to learn. It was everyone's condition, and it was the very reason why great avatars like Jesus or Krishna descend into incarnation from time to time, to help us learn how to lift this veil that prevents us from living in the garden. Eventually I would come to learn that even such ecstatic states need to be transcended. Even this is just another distraction, another fodder for addiction. Although a preferable addiction, a truer experience was yet to be found, something more comprehensive and much deeper and broader than this profoundly exalted state.

After the passing of a few weeks, it was time for me to travel to Arlington, Virginia, for the scheduled retreat. Mindful that just registering had produced such amazing results, I had been looking forward to it as I hadn't been on a religious or spiritual retreat in many years. As I was packing, I noted the copy of *Man's Eternal Quest* sitting on my bureau. I smiled, recalling how it was one of the books I had frequently taken on my religious vocational retreats when I was in high school. Here I was at 58 feeling again like a 17-year-old as I packed the book to bring along as an old spiritual friend. After loading my car, I switched my mind onto pilgrimage mode, and made my way to Arlington.

The next morning, I headed to the retreat site at another hotel about a mile from where I was staying. About 120 or more people had converged for the occasion from all points east, and as far west as Iowa. Two other North American retreat sites in Colorado and Orange County, California were linked by satellite. The day began with forty minutes of gentle Hatha Yoga followed by meditation. After settling back into our seats, we were linked by satellite to

Satyaloka for class sessions taught by one of Sri Bhagavan's enlightened monks who'd been living there for almost twenty-five years. For the next three days, our class sessions included a deconstructed overview of habits and needs associated with the human condition which were presented as the common hindrances to attaining awakening, and, ultimately, enlightenment. Each session was punctuated with a guided meditation process, with liberal 90-minute breaks twice a day.

On the first day of the retreat, I made the following entry into my journal:

"I'm delighted to see photos of Jesus & Mary with Sacred Hearts exposed on the puja with the photo of Sri Bhagavan and Sri Amma. This makes it feel like home for me. The photos of Jesus/Mary complete my reconnection with saying the Our Father and Hail Mary…while I love Indian culture and traditions, the West needs re-awakening in Christian culture, in Christian terms, for Christians to understand…

Coming to this retreat is like a trip back in time for me, the 3 days like a brief respite in Baba's (Muktananda) ashram…

Just did the first extended Hatha Yoga session in many, many years. I was pleased to find that my body still retains enough relative limberness to do the postures… I took my first Hatha Yoga class when I was 17. I'm so grateful to have arrived at this point. I'm experiencing that the past 40 years was just a dance that I had to do in this world to complete some karma, or perhaps it was a schooling in the human conditioning and experience, on the commonality and bridge between Eastern and Western culture. I am the same being I was at 17 in an older body. It's as if nothing has transpired for 40 years, that I was just an actor in a play.

All such truths about the Self that have been relayed by sages and recorded in writing and oral tradition for thousands of years is true – it's all true. The Soul is a supreme principal residing in a human body vehicle. When the Bible says we are keepers of the creatures of the Earth, the notion occurred to me that it was referring to us as souls caring for these human forms we have been assigned, or selected. When you read the Bible from the perspective of the inner Self, it's much more understandable.

These are all lovely people here. Each one of them has recognized the spark offered by connection with this Avatar of our era, who has the ability to connect each of us to our True Selves, to our True Natures. I am in a room full of seasoned yogis. I overheard someone say they were a student of Yogi Amrit Desai. Another woman said she'd been a student of Transcendental Meditation at the Maharishi's University in Iowa. Another fellow I met had also studied with Gurumayi Chidvilasananda, and I, from my own path. I saw us all as respective representatives of yogic clans, like images of the assemblage of sages in ancient India, gathered to learn from a superior enlightened master. This is how we uplift our civilization in this time. The esteemed and enlightened must gather and be a living demonstration of wisdom, of sound decision making, of internal guidance."

Throughout the day, our Dasa instructor explained details on the significance of the Golden Age. She shared stories and showed video interviews with individuals who had experienced a healing or miraculous occurrence from their affiliation with Sri Bhagavan: A region in India that was destitute from drought experienced an onslaught of torrential rain following prayers offered during a traditional Homa; A young Asian girl born with Down Syndrome so severe and leaving her unable to talk was healed and is now an articulate spokesperson for an organization dedicated to helping others with the condition; an Indian man whose limbs were blown apart by a bomb experienced Sri Bhagavan appearing to him and putting him back together. Witnesses could not explain how the man survived. These stories just scratched the surface. In the weeks that followed, I would soon see that the accounts of miracles attributed to the intervention of Sri Bhagavan and Sri Amma were endless. Miracles are just the norm around these incredible beings.

On the next day, during one session, the Dasa explained the lineage of gurus from which Sri Bhagavan comes. In Indian custom, this is an important form of credential for any spiritual teacher. I was impressed that included on Sri Bhagavan's lineage were some of the great Siddha Masters that Swami Muktananda revered, wrote and spoke about, and whose photos were hung in all of his ashrams. Among those on the lineage were:

The legendary Sri Dattatreya Swami, who lived around 1149 AD, historically regarded as the first Guru of the Nath lineage of Shaivism, a master of Tantra, and composer of the Avadhuta Gita (Hymn of The Free), a devotional text still sung today;

Sri Pada Sri Vallaba - born in 1320 AD and revered to this day as an Avatar and reincarnation of Dattatrya during the dark age of Kali Yuga. Many miracles and healings have been attributed to his intervention;

Sri Narasimha Saraswati 1378 - 1459 AD, an enlightened monk in the same order and guru lineage as the great Shankaracharya and regarded as the second incarnation of Dattatreya. Narasimha is one of the great Yogis associated with Indian yoga lore because it is believed that in lieu of dying, he took mahasamadhi (final conscious departure) in a meditation posture under a tree. 300 years later, legend has it, a field worker's sickle was withdrawn with blood on it while clearing an ant hill. Upon digging a little deeper, Narasimha's body was found uncorrupted. To the field hand's astonishment, Narasimha then opened his eyes, thanked the worker for waking him, stood up, brushed himself off, and continued his mission for another 24 years under the name of Swami Samarth, more popularly known as Akalkot Swami.

Sri Akalkot Swami of Maharasthra, who lived until 1878, was regarded as an extraordinary Avadhoot - that is, a yoga Master of the highest caliber, possessing great spiritual power that is felt by believers to this day at his Samadhi shrine (burial place). Regarded as an incarnation of Sri Narasimha Saraswati, as a guru of the Dattatreya lineage he was also revered as the third incarnation of Dattatreya;

Akalkot Swami Samarth's disciple, Sai Baba of Shirdi, who lived from 1838 to 1918, is, perhaps, the most renowned of this lineage. He has been hailed as a peerless Siddha, a Master of yoga, regarded by some as an avatar and the 5th incarnation of Dattatreya. No one ever knew his specific religious affiliation as he taught in a manner that embodied both Hindu and Islamic canon, was strongly opposed to persecuting anyone for their caste or religion, regarding all as equal. While some legends claim he was born of a Brahmin family, he dressed in the attire of the Sufis and Muslims of his village. During the phenomenon of the Golden Orbs discussed earlier, many claimed to have seen the face of Sai Baba within it.

After the dinner break on the final day, we reconvened for the live skype session with Sri Bhagavan which, due to the time difference, was scheduled for 11:30 that night. We had been invited earlier to submit questions for him in advance. Though I did have plenty of questions, I was content enough and felt others needed the time for questioning him more than I. I just planned on enjoying Sri Bhagavan's virtual company and welcomed anything he wanted to discuss. Though I had never been able to make it to India, here, I thought, was India coming to me.

The Skype feed enabled our groups to be visible to Sri Bhagavan simultaneously, and when he came on, it brought a smile to my face while everyone else in the room cheered. There he was, the man himself. Sri Bhagavan smiled and waved, greeting everyone. After delivering a few opening remarks, the monk presented the questions to him from off camera.

As Sri Bhagavan spoke, I noted that he was just as described by those friends who had met him: eloquent, charming, intellectually engaging, and impressively knowledgeable of the human condition. He posed esoteric and lofty points with a casualness I had encountered with only a few individuals in my life, most notably Swamis Muktananda and Satchitananda. I considered the descriptions I had been offered in years past, that he was an Avatar and Master. It was a remarkable thought to consider as I watched him animatedly offer his answers.

Then, in his answer to one question, my ears perked when he began to speak of the phenomenon in which advanced, enlightened beings had the ability to manifest or bilocate themselves in a form that he termed "light beings." He spoke of it so pragmatically, suggesting matter-of-factly that it happens all the time, that it's just part and parcel to the vast intricacy of God's creation, that saintly beings possessed the capacity to do this whenever needed or desired, and that *we all had the capacity within us to do this as well.*

From his description, I understood that this is what Yogananda had described as our astral form - our spirit body that is just part of our packaging. Muktananda used to discuss this, too, during his talks about the four levels or bodies of the human being. This is also what Benjamin Creme had referred to as 'Masters,' and 'familiars' in the context of esoteric philosophy. For the first time, I understood fully what Creme had meant all through the years, and gained instant clarification on my experience of encountering Jesus on that retreat in Connecticut all those years ago. From Sri Bhagavan's explanation, it was made clear that Jesus is here, all the time, and can manifest at will wherever and whenever he liked. It made sense of the abilities of Padre Pio to be seen in two locations at the same time. It explained the long tradition of apparitions of the Madonna, and specifically brought to mind the illumined apparitions at Zeitoun, Egypt in 1970. And all those cinematic representations of an ethereal, transparent Christ transposed against a scene of blazing sun in a colorful, cloudy sky? By this assessment, all would be fairly accurate.

Sri Bhagavan continued to say that these 'light beings' - the light body of an enlightened being - could manifest in any form they wanted, which explained how Mr. Creme's Master's confirmations of encounters with Jesus, Maitreya, the Master who was the Madonna, or whomever appeared as normal people to those who sensed the occurrence of something supernatural. And then Sri Bhagavan made a somewhat humorous yet serious comment when he said to all of us that a light being could "even appear as you." I found this remark serendipitously amusing.

Only the night before, I had returned to my hotel following the evening retreat session, and not being quite ready for bed, I decided to step outside for some fresh air, a short walk, and a brief rest on the hotel's patio. Though it was early December, it wasn't too cold and I've always enjoyed exploring the local terrain when visiting temporal lodgings in places I'd never been nor may never visit again. As I stood outside gazing at the movement of clouds in the night sky, another hotel guest walked up and stood near me. I didn't pay it any mind until the fellow said to me: "So, we meet again."

I turned to look at the guy and said hello, but I didn't recognize him at all. I was confused because I hadn't really met anyone at the hotel. For the several days I was staying there, I had pretty much spent the majority of my time at the retreat site a mile down the road, only coming and going from my hotel by shuttle or taxi. The next thing the guy said immediately following, however, was even more curious.

"And look" he said, nodding downward and averting his eyes to my feet, "We're even wearing the same shoes." I looked down, and sure enough we both had on the same pair of Sketchers, which even appeared to be the same size as mine.

"Hey! How 'bout that!" I replied.

The guy just nodded and smiled, saying nothing else. Having grown up in the rough terrain of South Philadelphia, my first instinct is to not trust anyone. I wasn't sure what this guy wanted, and maybe nothing at all. Not wanting to be impolite, I inquired what brought him to the hotel. He explained that he was an I.T. specialist in town for some project involving an international teleconference. I knew nothing about I.T. and couldn't find words to continue the conversation. After a few short minutes of additional chit chat, I wished the guy a good night and excused myself. I thought it curious and couldn't fathom why the guy thought we'd met before. So, on that next night, when Bhagavan made the casual remark that light beings or Masters could even manifest to look like you, I laughed to myself with recognition. "Oh boy" I thought. "Here we go again."

Was there some meaning to glean from this experience? Did it bode auspiciously for things to come? I recalled James Twyman's encounter with the Madonna in Medjugorje, who had urged him to "Go beyond the form." That the answer wasn't to be found, as I had done, by following a trail of appearances by saints, angels, and Masters. While all of these miraculous events and supernal signs, wonders and experiences certainly add some truly exotic and inspiring spice to our lives, the underscoring lesson found in each occurrence is how they all goad us to look deeper within ourselves. They always have. That's the only place where the answers will be found, and that's where the real adventure truly begins

What I found most fascinating was that Sri Bhagavan's replies provided specific answers to some of the very interview questions I had sent to him in my letter fourteen years earlier. Many points about which I had then inquired were addressed. It was as if no time had transpired. I was stunned. *That* was absolutely magical.

Some of Bhagavan's remarks were expressed with an urgent tone, very much, I noted, like the messages from the Madonna during her apparitions in Medjugorje, compelling me to immediately recognize that Bhagavan and the Madonna were on the same team. Bhagavan voiced the importance of becoming spiritually awakened at this time in history as the future of humanity's evolution and survival depended on it. He explained his main mission of ushering in the Golden Age, and how the prevalence of living in an enlightened state actually had practical benefits in areas of human activity ranging from agriculture to technology sectors, from local community to government and political spheres. Enlightenment isn't an impractical dream – it's absolutely essential to our collective well-being. His offer – to help us attain that. Think about what I'm saying here. You've just read a book about apparitions of Masters. Here is one – a living avatar, an enlightened Master of Yoga and its related psychology – accessible and operating in the open, stating precisely the essential reasons for spiritual growth, and offering to help us kindle and nurture that.

After that, Sri Bhagavan and Sri Amma bid their farewells. The monk came back on and did the same, and then the retreat concluded. I said my goodbyes and took a Lyft ride back to my hotel. I ruminated on the Skype darshan and nuances of the retreat segments, recalling how the courses I'd taken with Sri Bhagavan's teachers in past years had only augmented and enhanced my existing personal practice quite nicely. I found it interesting that as long as I've been acquainted with his work he'd always said that he didn't want followers.

Sri Bhagavan in 2019

He just wanted to teach people techniques that could help reduce their suffering, which in turn could only serve to help alleviate the suffering of others. I had certainly recognized his extraordinary achievement as one of the most profound and accessible yoga masters I'd personally come across in my life. I saw him as an old friend – an old friend who cared deeply about humanity and simply sought to help.

At a time in our world when it seemed that so many were enduring a lot of pain and confusion, I welcomed his presence among us as sorely needed medicine. I concluded from his perspective that people were battling with life's difficulties in a much more stressed manner than was needed, thus triggering reactionary psychotic tendencies. Life doesn't have to be so hard and exasperating and can be eased by simply learning a few techniques that put one in their own driver's seat by just fine tuning a few inner dials of perception and understanding. Not only can we make our lives easier, but we can create a fulfilling sense of joy and personal contentment for ourselves.

As the old saying goes, God helps those who help themselves. While our tendency is to pray and conceptually cling to the hem of a saint's garment for help in times of crisis – which is always there and freely available when asked – there is a benefit to paying those blessings forward to others when we arrive on the other side of crisis. Maybe some things I've learned from this retreat and my lifetime of inner pursuit could be helpful to someone. This was the lesson of Jesus, of Saint Francis and so many saints and God-men and women of so many of the world's traditions. There are inspiring stories to learn from those spiritual masters, and the lesson to harvest is that we ourselves, each of us, have within us the potential to become the masters among us.

While unbuttoning my shirt as I prepared to go to bed, I wondered if a copy of Gideon's Bible might be in one of the drawers. In my travels over the years, I've appreciated their inclusion in hotel rooms, and enjoyed popping one open now and then for inspiration. After looking about, I found one in a night table. I took it out, set it on the chest height bureau, and opened it to a random page with anticipation of what lesson it might impart. I found myself on the page with the Gospel of Luke, chapter 9. As I read on, I chuckled with delight as there couldn't have been a more perfect passage relative to what I had just learned. It was the verses referring to the Transfiguration of Christ, which read:

> "[28]About eight days after Jesus said this, he took Peter, John and James with him and went up onto a mountain to pray. [29]As he was praying, the appearance of his face changed, and his clothes became as

bright as a flash of lightning. ³⁰Two men, Moses and Elijah, appeared in glorious splendor, talking with Jesus. ³¹ They spoke about his departure, which he was about to bring to fulfillment at Jerusalem. ³²Peter and his companions were very sleepy, but when they became fully awake, they saw his glory and the two men standing with him. ³³As the men were leaving Jesus, Peter said to him, "Master, it is good for us to be here. Let us put up three shelters—one for you, one for Moses and one for Elijah." (He did not know what he was saying.) ³⁴While he was speaking, a cloud appeared and covered them, and they were afraid as they entered the cloud. ³⁵A voice came from the cloud, saying, "This is my Son, whom I have chosen; listen to him."

I had known this gospel tale since childhood, and it is one of the passages that had formed the very root of my lifelong belief in the possibility of such divine phenomena. I understood that it clearly was an historically documented account of what Sri Bhagavan had described as the acts of 'light beings' which is what the Apostles were witnessing in their perception of Moses and Elijah, and Jesus adorned now in raiment "as bright as lightening," clearly demonstrating his 'light body.' I smiled. It's all been right there in the Bible the whole time. We've been told of these things for 2000 years. Why should we doubt now?

A few weeks later I was working on the first draft of this addendum, when I took a break to answer a phone call. After hanging up, I sat for a moment while reorienting myself into writing mode, and decided to scroll through the news on my cell phone. After weeding past the daily political stories, critiques of the *Saturday Night Live* year end Christmas show, and reviews of *Mary Poppins' Returns*, I stopped in my tracks when I saw this headline: "Texas Girl's Inoperable Brain Tumor Vanishes."

The story explained the plight of Roxli Doss, an eleven-year-old who was diagnosed in June of 2018 with Diffuse Intrinsic Pontine Glioma - a highly aggressive and difficult to treat type of inoperable brain tumor found at the base of the brain. Roxli had endured weeks of radiation treatment and had essentially been written off with limited time to live. In the meantime, her parents, Gena and Scott Doss, had been praying vigilantly for a miracle. When Dr. Virginia Harrod of Dell Children's Medical Center reviewed the most recent MRI scan, she remarked how stunned she was to find that the tumor was gone. Roxli's family considered it an answer to their prayers and a Christmas miracle. Thereafter Roxli resumed her normal life, enjoying her favorite activities again.[147] This was the first miracle story I had read in the news in a long time, and gave me great hope.

In the months following the retreat, those of us who had attended were offered the opportunity to continue our experience by participating in a free, guided series of monthly sadhana practices. Each month, a new contemplation and meditation technique was relayed from Sri Bhagavan by one of his monks, which we were to practice for just 7 minutes a day. I agreed to participate. The first five months brought about gradual awakening to subtle aspects of my personality that either hindered or supported spiritual growth. I witnessed with fascination as old stuff nestled in dark recessed crevices of my heart and mind seemed to be dredged and purged, leaving me feeling increasingly lighter, and more aware and appreciative of moment to moment living. It was a surprisingly easy series of techniques that produced extraordinarily expansive results. For example, in one instance, I noted how with regard to a personal issue that had bugged me for the past 12 or more years, I had desired change of one thing or another in an attempt to "fix" it. When I saw this and understood the secret of accepting situations as they were without wanting anything, any emotional pain that had lingered for years just evaporated. In another instance I became aware of an aspect of my personality that I had long considered playful and harmless was actually at the root of suffering for others around me. I saw my unwillingness to let go at first, but when I felt the pain of another who'd been hurt by what I thought were harmless words in jest, I had to embrace it, and it, too, transformed.

In early June, I received the transcript of a talk given by Sri Bhagavan on May 26, 2019. As I read on, I found some of the details extraordinary, in some instances providing explanations to many questions I had, and some of which this book has raised. I was gobsmacked.

He began his talk by explaining that, to date, 80,374 people had attended one of the Deeksha programs offered by his trained teachers throughout the world. This was in context with the previously asserted goal of his mission to enlighten 64000 people. Transference of Deeksha was the first step in the process.

From there, he briefly elucidated Sri Amma's then current teaching, which was about the effort required by aspirants to facilitate their spiritual awakening - which is step two in the process - which would then lead to step three - enlightenment. In a similar talk in April, he had relayed Sri Amma's lesson that "lazy people can't become enlightened." Sri Bhagavan clarified this point in this May discussion, by adding:

"This means that this Teaching requires you to put [forth some]

---

[147] Source: Fox News, December 17, 2018. Story by Frank Miles. https://foxnews.com/health/christmas-miracle-texas-girls-inoperable-brain-tumor-vanishes. Accessed 12/17/2018.

effort. Of course, you can take the help of Paramjyoti to put effort and do something about it."

In recent months, in all of his public discourse, Sri Bhagavan had been addressing the topic of Paramjyoti, which translates as "the Great Compassionate Light." I had been craning my cranium to fully grasp this concept for several months as it was raised numerous times. Since January of 2019, Sri Bhagavan has been asserting that students, devotees and disciples should veer away from worshiping photos of he and his wife, Sri Amma, which is a long-standing Indian custom and which had been popular as long as I could remember. Instead, he offered, was a photograph of an amorphous manifestation of pure light, taken during a moment of apparition experienced by a devotee. The account was supported by the testimonies of hundreds, thousands of students from around the world claiming to have encountered/experienced this precise phenomenon.

The "effort" referenced was, at minimum, the suggestion that the unawakened at least endeavor to practice a regular spiritual regimen. To reach out, as it were. How that effort manifests will be unique to each individual and relevant to their own experience of life.

"Suppose I ask a Question: 'who are you?'," Sri Bhagavan began…

"Each one of you will answer this question according to your level of consciousness. The level of consciousness depends on the stand you take in the many events that happened in your life. The stand you take depends on the meaning you give to an event. When an event occurs, you try to determine if it is useful, successful, great or useless. If someone scolds you saying 'you are useless' you are giving a meaning to yourself that you are useless. If you are praised, you give a different meaning. The meaning that you give is your belief system…

'Based on the inner meaning, you have an inner dialogue. You take a stand from these dialogues. If you are an unawakened person, you are nothing but the 'stand' you take. This stand is the story of your life. So the story of your life depends on the meaning you give to each event. This meaning again depends on the Karma or the childhood decision you took in the womb, or during delivery or the first 6 minutes, etc.

'You take different stands like, 'you are useless,' 'you are great,' 'you are successful,' etc. Based on this stand is your story. And these stories become your life. So you are the stand that you are.

So if you have to change your life, you have to change the stand, and change the meaning you have given to every event. If you put effort, you can change. But for that you should *see* that stand. The stand controls your emotion and feelings. And your life depends on these emotions and feelings. 'Yat Bhaavam, Tat Bhavati' [Quoting an ancient maxim, meaning "You are what you think", or, "you are what you believe"]. What you become - an engineer, Medical practitioner, great, useless - depends on what is your stand.

The most important thing is you should become conscious of the stand you have taken. Forget about awareness. You are that stand. You are merely the stand that you take.

Awakening is to make you enjoy your [worldly life]. You enjoy your coffee; you enjoy your food; you enjoy all things. Awakening is not for the other world. Awakening is for you to enjoy everything. You *should* enjoy everything. We do not see that as an obstacle for Awakening. But if you choose a life of denial, it is your choice. We do not say that you must leave all that. All we say is: if you are awakened, you will enjoy all these things. Our stand is: 'Have a good time and enjoy'. *That* is *our* stand."

In many regards, what Sri Bhagavan is saying here is not new. It speaks of the habitual tendency of our species that time and again, year after year, decade upon decade, from generation to generation, masters of yoga have advocated the same lesson repeatedly. In a 1943 talk, Paramahansa Yogananda said pretty much the same thing this way:

"One great stumbling block in the way...is our habits. In the morning we make up our minds to adhere to good, but during the day we forget our resolution...Many people don't understand the terrible nature of habit. Some persons form habits very quickly. This is all right when establishing good habits, but it is dangerous when performing actions that may create bad habits...Since you do not know what type of subconscious mind you have, or what hidden tendencies [i.e., "your stand] may be, it is best to avoid actions that may lead to harmful habits...If you make up your mind to do something good you must do it. Don't let anything stand in your way...All of us mean well, but habits sometimes make us do things against our will that are harmful to others and to ourselves.

'Your forefathers [speaking to an audience of Americans] came here to escape from rules that took freedom to act according to one's conscience. Freeborn Americans don't like to have anyone dictate to them. Why then should you let yourself be dictated by your habits?...You have allowed yourself to become a slave to bad habits.

'Just being born in America or in other democratic lands does not guarantee freedom of the mind and heart. To be free is to be able to perform right actions according to the dictates of one's own soul wisdom, not out of compulsion of habit, or blind obedience, or unreasoning fear. Wisdom confers true freedom, and that is the real spirit of America."[148]

And then, in his talk, Sri Bhagavan abruptly veered into a topic that floored me. In short, he clearly answered a question I had posed to him almost seventeen years prior. At that time, I now understand, he was unable to disclose too much, and pretty much then told me I would have to discover the answer for myself. That answer finally arrived.

"All the miracles in all religions" Sri Bhagavan began,

"Hinduism, Islam, Christianity, any religion - are done only by this Paramjyoti. Miracles of AmmaBhagavan, Satya Sai Baba, Shirdi Sai Baba - all are done by this Paramjyoti only. So when AmmaBhagavan are doing miracles, we are not doing it. The miracles of Sri Pada Sri Vallaba, miracles of Virgin Mary, oil and water coming out, the sun rotating, the rose petals falling down - everything is being done by this Paramjyoti only. In Mexico, the statue of Virgin Mary was seen bending to receive a garland. This was also done by Paramjyoti only. Hence, Paramjyoti is a being and it will be so."

The statue of Mary in Mexico at the moment it bowed to receive the wreath of flowers shown on the head. Photos courtesy of Foundation for World Awakening.

---

[148] Paramahansa Yogananda, "Creating and Destroying Habits at Will." Delivered Dec. 12, 1943, San Diego, CA. Man's Eternal Quest, Pp. 412-413. © 1975 Self Realization Fellowship. Reprinted with Permission.

Sri Bhagavan's mention of the Virgin Mary miracle struck a chord. I was reminded of Mary's words to the visionaries at Medjugorje, when she repeatedly referred to 'a plan', and a voiced connection to "The Plan" so-referenced by Benjamin Creme and the esotericists who claimed to have drawn their knowledge from a Tibetan Buddhist master, and 'The Masters' at large. In a previous chapter, I noted that Benjamin Creme's identification of Sri Bhagavan as a Master in the context of the esoteric tradition was the first time he had so identified a living, accessible person. Provided this was true, it was becoming evident that by and large the message was consistent with that of the Medjugorje Madonna as well as those claimed to have originated from ascended adepts.

Sri Bhagavan continued:

"So this is [what is meant by the name attributed to his course of study, aka] Bhagavad Dharma. The Mahavakyas, the Teachings of Lord Krishna, [the teachings of] Amma Bhagavan... the teachings of Surdas, Rama and that of all bhaktas - everything - came from this Paramjyoti... The Paramjyoti comes to people directly or through someone...All this [combined] is Bhagavad Dharma. It is time for Man to be awakened. Only Paramjyoti can do this. This Paramjyoti can only come to people as Rama, Krishna, Virgin Mary or in the forms of other Gods and great Beings...

'Bhagavad Dharma is phenomenon centric. Paramjyoti is the phenomenon... Paramjyoti was there from thousands of years. I am not a successor of Paramjyoti... There was a prophesy in China 2000 years back that India will connect Man and God. That is what [we see happening today]...it referred to awakening...Whatever it wants, only the phenomenon knows. I do not know... Sri Pada Sri Vallaba, Ramalinga, all became a part of the Paramjyoti. The Paramjyoti is the phenomenon... I think the work will be fast and dramatic, and crisis, accidents, depression will be taken care of. More people will be happy. Major problems will be solved..."

As I read the transcript about the phenomenon referenced by Sri Bhagavan as Paramjyoti (Para - Supreme, Jyoti - light) I wondered if this might be synonymous with what the Kabbalah called "The Ancient of Ancients." The import of Kabbalah implies that mystic experience of the transcendent divine is a natural, accessible function of humankind's existence, and the practice of awareness of which is considered integral to the study of the Torah to fully comprehend the esoteric, hidden meaning.

Paramjyoti also seemed to correlate with the descriptions relayed across a century offered herein, of Krishnamurti's experience, of the glowing forms of the Holy Family at Zeitun, of the 'ball of fire' described by Sri Bhagavan's monks, of the cloud that enveloped Jesus, Moses and Elijah during the Transfiguration, and of my own experience during Benjamin Creme's lecture at Saint Patrick's Cathedral in New York.

Sri Bhagavan clarified that, too, with his explanation:

"Now what do we mean by the word 'Paramjyoti', a phenomenon that is very important but cannot be understood or explained. What we do not understand, and cannot understand is called a phenomenon. We do not understand Paramjyoti. So it is called a phenomenon.

This phenomenon started in 1989 when the Golden Orb appeared in Satyaloka. It is not a ball, it is an orb. This Golden Orb when captured in camera appears small. But it not small. It is very huge. When it appeared, it was 2 stories tall. That is how it appeared in Satyaloka and the phenomenon named itself and [told] stories to children. It appeared to children first, not to adults. The children are very innocent. They have no religious or other bindings like adults. So the phenomenon appeared as the Golden Orb to children first. The Golden Orb became a golden being, took a human form. When we asked this being, it named itself as *Prajapati*."

The correlation to the Blessed Mother's preference for appearing to children at Lourdes and Fatima is noted. In a talk to a Hindu audience, Sri Bhagavan then furnished the answer to a question for which I had waited 16 years:

"All Gods and enlightened Masters merge with the Paramjyoti - Ramakrishna, Rama, Ramalinga, Ramana - all have merged with the Paramjyoti. They come and go. *Almost all are now coming to enlighten Mankind.*

All the great beings of all religions - be it Christians or Muslims or Hindus, anything - have merged with the Paramjyoti. This Supreme Light, when it is caught in the camera is small. Otherwise it is very huge, measuring many miles in the sky. It appears all over the world. Even yesterday many got experiences of this Paramjyoti. Not in India, but outside India.

The whole world is centered around this Paramjyoti... You will see this Jyoti when you die. You will feel Love - so much love. This Paramjyoti is a being. That is why we call it Sri Paramjyoti. It is enormous, loving, great and compassionate. You should experience it.

This is the Jyoti everyone will see after death. You can talk to people who were about to die. They will tell you stories about this Jyoti. If you pray, and have a bond with Paramjyoti, spontaneously you can see this Light."

I found Sri Bhagavan's description of Paramjyoti quite intriguing and revealing. Who hasn't pondered the descriptions of the light encountered by those who have shared and documented their near-death experiences? Case in point is the best-selling book *Proof of Heaven: A Neurosurgeon's Journey into the Afterlife* by Eben Alexander, M.D and similar works referenced earlier herein. But in books like Alexander's published primarily in the western world, descriptions of angelic beings and such prevail. Because of my own study of Hindu culture and belief, I had no qualms with comprehending Sri Bhagavan's description in a purely Hindu context. But what of those of us who don't share knowledge of this context? I found the answer by turning to the documented messages of the visionaries at Medjugorje.

While meditating one day, I began to contemplate the unseen hand of guidance I seemed to have experienced while working on this project. I reflected on the life review incident I had shortly after registering for the three-day retreat conducted by Sri Bhagavan's monks. The identity of the presence I had sensed during that incident had remained a mystery. I had wondered about it, but it occurred to me I had never directly asked internally who it was, if there was indeed an affiliated who to ask. So, I asked. Within short duration, a soft and serene image of the Blessed Mother, arms outstretched in loving welcome, silently emerged within my vision. I smiled. Of course, I thought. I had felt a deep kinship with the Madonna ever since I found the gifted Miraculous Medal, which I still wear on a chain around my neck today. It explained my inner-driven compulsion to pray the Our Father and Hail Mary with full focus and attention to their richly embedded meanings. I was being taught how to pray again! I then pranamed and thanked this Master who was the Madonna before concluding my meditation.

As I continued through my work day, I contemplated how perfect this connection to Mary was for me in many aspects. I had been born into a Catholic family, had been baptized and raised as Catholic, and when one really looks at the big picture while borrowing from the Hindu tradition, the Blessed Mother could be understood and viewed as the guru of Catholics. Though Jesus is the evident focus of Catholic Christian tradition, and to Jesus which She points, it has been Mary, through her repeated apparitions and communication of messages to the visionaries, that has served the role in western Christianity in a context identical to that of a true, saintly guru in the eastern tradition. A guru, in the accurate context of the term, is nothing more than a wise, experienced, and learned guide, and in some exceptionally rare cases, serves as a vehicle for bestowing grace. A true guru is one who does not enlist or exploit followers, but rather points the way for students to find access to the divinity that is already within each of them. Consider what I had written earlier in the transliterated response of Sufi Mystic Hamid to author Reshad Feild: "acceptance of Mary is the first requirement for the aspirant in order to awaken that inner spirit that is our personal connection to God. Hamid asserted to Field that what he was seeking, what all seekers, in fact, search for, is the spirit of God." This is precisely the central thrust in the messages from the Madonna of Medjugorje. When one reads the transcripts of those messages there is found simple, practical and inspiring advice pertinent to our present-day times.

I had inconsistently done just that for many years. My meditation vision of the Madonna prompted me to log online later that evening and catch up on the messages relayed by the visionaries at Medjugorje. I was pleasantly amused by the consistency of message I read that corresponded exactly to the maxims offered by Sri Bhagavan.

On June 25th, 2019, the Madonna's message was this:

"Dear children! I am thanking God for each of you. In a special way, little children, thank you for having responded to my call. *I am preparing you for the new times* that you may be firm in faith and persevering in prayer, so that the Holy Spirit may work through you and renew the face of the earth. I am praying with you for peace which is the most precious gift, even though satan wants war and hatred. You, little children, be my extended hands and proudly go with God. Thank you for having responded to my call."[149]

I found it fascinating how this pronouncement precisely paralleled Sri Bhagavan's twenty-plus year assertion that his own mission has been to facilitate the coming "new time" in phrasing known well to Hindus - The Golden Age. It would seem that the assertion presented for years by the late Benjamin Creme, that these two Masters work hand in hand in service of the same cause, was well founded.

In the archives of the Medjugorje messages, the Madonna made references to the new time on three additional occasions. On January 25, 1993, she said:

---

[149] https://www.medjugorje.com/medjugorje-messages/latest-25-message.html

"May every hatred and jealousy disappear from your life and your thoughts, and may there only dwell love for God and for your neighbor. Thus, only thus, shall you be able to discern the signs of this time. I am with you, and I guide you into a new time, a time which God gives you as grace, so that you may get to know Him more."[150]

On December 25, 1995, she said:

"Jesus is the King of Peace and only He can give you the peace that you seek. I am with you and I present you to Jesus in a special way, now in this new time in which one should decide for Him. This time is the time of grace."[151]

On October 25, 2000, she said:

"Dear children! Today I desire to open my Motherly Heart to you and to call you all to pray for my intentions. I desire to renew prayer with you and to call you to fast which I desire to offer to my Son Jesus for the coming of a new time - a time of spring."[152]

On July 5, 2019, in an apparition before a prayer group organized by the visionary Ivan Dragicevic, the Mother offered this urgent appeal:

"At this time, I especially desire to call you to decide for God. Put God in your lives and in your families in the first place. Leave the passing things of this world of materialism—all that distances you from my Son. Decide firmly. Live my messages."[153]

Remarkably, the tone was a match for the messages issuing from Sri Bhagavan. In the correspondence and transcripts for the first six months of 2019, he had voiced the need to get serious, and at one juncture - for the first time to my recollection - engaged in a discussion of hell. He voiced how terrible an experience it was, that it was not something we want to encounter, how he is trying to help us avoid the need to travel through that dark terrain, and how reorienting oneself to focus on cultivation of an inner connection with the Divine was imperative at this time if humanity is to come through unscathed. Concurrently he has replaced his own puja photo with an image of the apparition of Paramjyoti, explaining that all that he does is by the desire and will of Paramjyoti. I was beginning to sense that the Hindu Paramjyoti and the Judeo-Christian God the Father, or the Holy Spirit, were one in the same.

I did find it curious that Sri Bhagavan had been gradually withdrawing

---

[150] https://www.medjugorje.com/medjugorje-messages/search messages. html?q =new+time&lg= en&redirect=1
[151] Ibid
[152] Ibid
[153] https://www.medjugorje.com/medjugorje-today/medjugorje-headlines/make-a-list.html

himself from the forefront of his own mission. In July of 2019 I travelled to Princeton to attend a one-day course hosted by Sri Bhagavan's organization called "Journey into Awakening," an updated version of the very first course I had attended with Dasaji almost two decades ago. The course was conducted live from India by one of the monks with a link to 40 cities worldwide. On my arrival and throughout the day, I was mildly surprised to find no references to Sri Bhagavan or Sri Amma on display in photographs or in any context of the day long lectures. Instead, visible on screen throughout the duration of the program was the apparition photo of Paramjyoti.

I was mildly disappointed by this but that was just a personal preference. I have a fondness for Hindu-centric custom and the appeal of Sri Bhagavan first as an avatar of yogic wisdom and secondly as an enlightened Master in the broadest inclusive context of that term had been my attraction from the onset. The content of the course was presented in a more pragmatic fashion, in western scientific and psychological terminology, about the process needed for the brain to see through the mind's games and ultimately how changing the brain's functionality through effort and grace is how one is enabled to enjoy a deepened relation to the divine. It was fascinating to see what I have long understood as the standard maxims of yoga philosophy stripped almost completely of their traditional Indian flavor. The processes in which we participated included meditation and contemplation of seven key activities of the mind that hinder our growth. It was quite potent and my meditative experience was profound. At times I felt as if the inside of my cranium was getting scooped by a spoon, which I found to be curious because Sri Bhagavan himself had previously explained these processes as having a literal physical effect on the brain. He termed it surgery.

After waking the following day, I sat down on our back patio with a cup of Chai and contemplated these things. I thought about the Medjugorje apparitions and pondered that this discarnate entity - the Blessed Mother - had been appearing, guiding and delivering messages to humanity almost consistently since 1858 at Lourdes. Pause and think about that for a moment. Is this incredible phenomenon being taken for granted? What an extraordinary, miraculous thing occurs in our midst! How can anyone ignore this?

After a while, I took out my phone to check for messages and emails, and I was pleasantly surprised to find an email from Share International Magazine, Benjamin Creme's old publication, with a link to their most recent online edition. I smiled nostalgically as if hearing from an old friend after some time. I opened the link and first, as always, was the reprinting of a message from Ben's still unnamed Master. After recounting how communication technology today has transformed the world into an interdependent village that needs to find ways to work together to resolve our mutual problems, the Master concludes:

> "When men see the Christ the issues will be clearly placed before them: men now face the challenge to work together for the well-being of all, and to remake their ways of living with sufficiency the key, or to sound the death knell of a planet already sorely stressed, and so place their future in greatest jeopardy."[154]

Again, the parallel to the tone of the Messages from Medjugorje and Sri Bhagavan are noted. It is interesting to note how both Benjamin Creme's Master remained unnamed, unseen, and hence unapproachable, and "the Master who was the Madonna" appears to a select, trusted few in a non-physical form. Meanwhile, one known externalized Master in the person of Sri Bhagavan withdraws his outer accessibility. They all point to one thing in common: we shouldn't depend on them, to not cling to the hem of their cloak. They are simply furnishing the tools for us to do the work.

All the great teachers have said the same thing. In the ten months since I had the experience that guided me to read Yogananda's Man's Eternal Quest, by early July I had one remaining chapter to read. The one common strand running throughout every reprinted lecture is the same: establish your connection with God, with the Divine. Don't waste being born into this world without establishing that connection. Know your true purpose, destiny and divine kinship. The great Indian spiritual teacher, Anandamayi Ma - so named by Yogananda in 1920 and which means "Joy-Permeated Mother" - once said:

> "Do something to get near God. Some people like prayer, some like Japa [rosary bead praying] and some like to inquire: 'Who is he?' 'Who made the world?' Whatever you like best, do that. Fix a time every day and if you have no time then take it away from your sleep."

As I looked through the online edition of Share International, included was an article about J. D. Krishnamurti, which featured an excerpt from a talk he gave in Adyar in 1933. In all this swirl of consideration about the retreating Sri Bhagavan, the unidentified Master of Mr. Creme, the discarnate apparitions of the Blessed Mother, of Jesus, and tales of encounters with other extraordinary beings, Krishnamurti's words put a smile on my face:

Preceded by a quote from Maitreya, which read, "I have not come to create followers...Know that I am within you,"[155] Krishnamurti is then quoted

---

[154] Awakening to responsibility, Share International Magazine, May 2019. https://share-international.org. Accessed 7/10/2019.
[155] Krishamurti's Teaching, Maitreya's Teachings, 2005, Share International Magazine, May 2019. https://share-international.org. Accessed 7/10/2019.

thus:

> "Whether the Masters exist or do not exist... is not important, but what is important is to understand yourself... So to me whether or not Masters exist is quite irrelevant to action... Even though their existence be a fact is of no importance; for you to understand you must be independent, you must stand by yourself, completely stripped of all security... If you really search your hearts most of you will find that you are seeking security, comfort, places of safety, and in that search you provide yourselves with philosophies, gurus, systems of self-discipline; thus you are thwarting, continually narrowing down thought." [156]

Both excerpts appeased my wistful missing of Sri Bhagavan's presence in the course I had taken the day before. Both had delivered the same message. The ball was in my court. It's in all of our respective courts. The answers, the help, the guidance, the grace - it's all out there, all accessible, all ready to assist on our journey. It only requests our effort.

As the days went on, I found myself drawn to revisit websites associated with the Medjugorje apparitions and messages. Again and again, I listened to Our Lady's words with a keener ear. Between those daily messages and daily aphorisms issued by Sri Bhagavan's monks, I found them both saying the same things: prepare, pray, know that God exists.

Toward the end of July, 2019, I received a video from one of the Indian monks featuring the documented account of an apparition of the Paramjyoti phenomenon a day after it occurred. Pictured was a courtyard filled with astonished, prayerful monks and pilgrims, hands clasped and eyes transfixed on the slightly oblong and almost egg-shaped disc of brilliant, pulsating and undulating pure light in the sky above them. It immediately struck me as a modern-day recording of the similar event beheld by pilgrims in Fatima, Portugal, 102 years prior. This was the first such "live" recorded incident of this apparition that I had scene.

Two days later, I logged onto a website with news from Medjugorge where a local pilgrim had uploaded a virtually identical recording of pilgrims awaiting a scheduled apparition of the Madonna. A few minutes into the film, the light in the sky abruptly increases tenfold, and the woman filming breaks into an emotional, passionate outpouring of tears while voicing her love to Mary. In her account describing the situation afterward, she said that she

---

[156] Awakening to responsibility, Share International Magazine, May 2019. https://share-international.org. Accessed 7/10/2019.

witnessed the apparition, she had seen the Lady herself, and during which felt utterly compelled to surrender, merge and unite with the incomprehensible joy she experienced.

Another video posted on the Mystic Post website[157] captured an extraordinary "Miracle of the Sun" that occurred on July 2nd during one of the monthly apparitions to visionary Mirjana. At the onset, the sun is seen shining normally through hazy, overcast sky, when a few moments later it explodes and expands to ten times its normal previous size, filling the sky and landscape. The sun then continued to pulsate and radiate at this enormous size for several minutes before resuming its normal size.

On the same day I received this post, a July 30th report shared that an official Vatican delegation was en route to Medjugorje to give the sacred appearances "official recognition." I was kind of shocked to read this, as the article continued to explain that despite more than 40,000 accounted apparitions of the Blessed Mother in 38 years,[158] Pope Francis had only recently lifted an official ban on pilgrimage to the site in May of 2019.

The latter video struck me as current evidence of the described events of Fatima, Portugal in 1917, and my immediate thought upon seeing it was "Paramjyoti." Indeed, on June 23rd, 2019 Sri Bhagavan opened a monthly talk by saying:

> "What I would like to tell you is that The Paramjyoti phenomenon or the Great Compassionate Light has become very physical, sometimes very huge across the horizon, appearing in many places. It is appearing to all people very physical. Paramjyoti is appearing on skies, on people's heads…this [phenomenon] has been stepped up and you will see and hear more in the coming weeks. This is happening in various faiths, in all places, to both believers and non-believers - all are able to experience the Great Compassionate Light, Paramjyoti."[159]

In another talk on June 5th, Sri Bhagavan explained:
> "It is time for Man to become awakened. Only the Great Compassionate Light can do this. This, the Great Compassionate Light, can only come to people as Rama, Krishna, Virgin Mary or in the forms of other Gods and great beings."[160]

I found it interesting when one of the Madonna's Medjugorje messages suggested the need for human beings to examine their conscience as a gateway

---

[157] https://mysticpost.com
[158] https:"mysticpost.com/2019/07/july-30-2019-vatican-dignitaries-head-to-medjugorje-reports-of-imminent recognition/
[159] Transcript provided by a Dasa from Neemam, India, who is a direct student of Sri Bhagavan. Reprinted with permission.
[160] Ibid

for healing and conversion of heart. This is precisely what the methodology of Sri Bhagavan's courses entails. His whole system is based on diving deeply within the reflect on those embedded aspects of our conscience that hinder our spiritual growth. Where Mother Mary advocates a needed practice or "sadhana" as the Indian yoga masters would say, Sri Bhagavan provided the very means to do this. As I went back and forth reviewing transcripts of talks by Sri Bhagavan and the messages of Mary in Medjugorje, I found them completely compatible and complementary. It is quite evident, at least to this religious studies researcher, that both work for the same employer.

As the months went on, I continued with my daily practice which has always incorporated a fusion of eastern and western traditions. I updated it by adding 7 recitations of the Sri Paramjyoti mantra to Our Lady's recommended 7 recitations of The Glory Be prayer, 7 recitations of the Hail Mary, and 7 recitations of The Our Father, and concluding with 7 to 21 minutes of meditation. This combination seems to set the stage for the rest of the day of just living and functioning in a state of observation and awareness, while also mulling over a daily contemplation sent each morning from Sri Bhagavan's monks in India. Average, mundane routines increasingly became moments of blessed experience, where feeling gratitude for the simplest things became commonplace. On particularly busy days when my schedule didn't permit me to set aside the time at home to sit and do these practices, I just did it during my daily activity as a form of walking meditation.

In late July, an opportunity arose to test the full scope of the effectiveness of my daily practice when I was assigned to work in Las Vegas for an extended, three week stay. It's not nicknamed "Sin City" for no reason. Vegas provides a non-stop, 24-hour barrage on the senses - all the senses. It's loud, it's bright, it's fast-paced, with offers of all forms of entertainment options comin' atcha from all directions continuously.

Though I hadn't been to Vegas for at least a year, the appeal of The Strip and Vegas culture at large had lost most of its lustre for me, so it was relatively easy for me to just go there to do what I was assigned to do. I had a relatively demanding schedule, so often I did these practices as a silent, internal japa yoga practice while walking along the Strip, through casinos like the Bellagio, Caesar's Palace, and Planet Hollywood. This actually proved to be a remarkable experience, for, aside from inhaling the wafting smoke of legal marijuana that is prevalent everywhere in Vegas, my prayers and inward focus sustained me in a profoundly joyous and, yes, high state. I didn't need to do anything. Nothing attracted me and yet all was visually amusing and delightful. I just kind of walked and focused on this inner state and naturally occurring joy that bubbled up from within throughout my walk. I judged no one, no activity, or anything. I almost felt invisible, while organically experiencing the practice of the presence of God in the heart of Sin City. It was quite cool, and, I recall thinking, if this is what doing these practices will manifest for the long term, then sign me up. After so many years, the fruition of 40 years of sadhana was finally bearing fruit. All that I had sought had now arrived at my doorstep. My gratitude was - and is - unfathomable.

I specifically noticed - in Vegas - a notably increased cessation of thoughts and mental activity. My mind has generally become quiet. There are moments throughout my day when my experience is of simple thoughtlessness. No anxiety over trivial concerns, no fear of imagined scenarios, no animosity towards others or what they elect to believe or represent, no judgement of anything. Even more palpable is the absence of the persistent, underlying depression that had nagged me for years. Instead, I find myself permeated with an unplanned state of relatively consistent contentment. For the first time in my life, I witness my mind and thoughts serving me, not dependent on it or them for my well-being. Thoughts that come up are perceived like leaves floating on a stream, or a car that passes before you as you sit at a red light. It's almost as if my mind now presents a thought like a servant presenting a tray of tea and biscuits. I choose - without ego - how the thought will be addressed. If I perceive it doesn't serve the moment, it is dismissed. There is then a space, a brief gap of time, between that and the arrival or presentation of the next thought, when it, too, is reviewed for prescient merit or value. Most of the time. I'm only human.

By early September, the effects of my daily practice served me well during this tenure. This is what I wrote in my journal:

"I've been working in Vegas for 14 days now. Curiously, I find my experience not to be a draining one. Not so much for entertainment, et al, but rather by working with an attitude of service, I find myself experiencing the same state of mind performing my daily assigned duties in the Planet Hollywood Casino as when I lived and did seva (service) in a meditation ashram with Swami Muktananda.

Today, for example, I had to line up artworks for an artist to sign in a limited time due to his restricted availability, so it was important to stay on point and focused. As we proceeded to tackle the task together, it was kind of cool to witness myself go into that thoughtless state that is the goal of performing service as a yoga in a conscious manner. As the artist went along, I held his selection of pens in one hand while flipping through layers of unstretched canvases with the other as he signed each. There was a great flow to our conjoined activity, noting our mutual, thought-free focus on accomplishing the task. While we proceeded in relative silence, I perceived how my experience while serving and assisting the artist was identical to serving Muktananda in a similar manner. Back then, I would stand alongside Muktananda while he cooked, placing a rotating conveyor of empty pastry shells before him as he spooned his Samosa mix into each, which another assistant then took from the other side to fold and place on a baking sheet. The process then, like now, was a precisely orchestrated function of egoless teamwork. Assisting this artist in the same mode made it feel as if I was once again in the ashram 38 years ago, as if I had been transported in time and place. I was again that 20-year-old selfless servant sadhaka, just focused on executing the task at hand in the best possible manner. But then again, this made sense. The very purpose of spending time in a place like an ashram is to take the lessons learned back into the world of everyday living and utilize them where they're needed most."

After completing the art-signing task, I found the resulting quietened state of mind continuing to linger. As I walked into the casino which was the only thoroughfare to the elevators and my hotel room, I quietly reveled over the perception that I was able to organically experience what I enjoyed most about ashram life in the heart of the Vegas Strip. I stepped off of the tiled path to pause near a trash receptacle to review recent messages on my phone, barely noticing the din of endless, actively engaged slot machines, the thumping beat of dance music resounding through the ceiling speakers, and the continually moving parade of humanity in celebration mode all around me.

From amidst this, as if emerging from a dark, thicketed forest, a short woman of perhaps South American origin walked close to me with a small broom and long-handled dustpan. My attention was drawn from my phone as I watched how she carefully, consciously swept something off of the carpet near where I stood and emptied it into the trash can beside me. I perceived how she was fully focused on this task, just doing her Seva, her service.

She was no different than me, I thought, in this global ashram. We were both there to perform a service. I considered her internal experience in that moment as she appeared tired or perhaps just bored with her mundane routine. What was her experience of being alive? What was her life like when not cleaning a casino floor? Did she have a family? Did she long for the love of her parents left behind in another distant country?

Numerous questions like these arose in the brief moment I took to observe her, but one core question overshadowed them all: Was she happy? I leaned over to her, as she was about a foot shorter than myself, and took a moment to thank her for all the work she does to keep our casino playpen clean. As she looked up in in response, her eyes widened with appreciation, her face and totality of being beamed an immaculate smile filled with a conveyance of delight and an expression of joy. It was an amazing thing to witness her soul blossom right before me. Suddenly there was a common unity, a common humanity between us. In that instant, there was no separation, no difference between she and I. This was Oneness. Her expression alone displayed the recognition, sincerity, non-judgement, and equality in my thank you. In broken English, she then thanked me for thanking her. I was so happy to have shared this moment of happiness with her. Her joy was mine, and visa versa.

The experience served as clear evidence that even a place as loud and bustling and screaming as Las Vegas can provide the opportunity for a genuine spiritual experience with the right perspective when one maintains a focus within. The book of Romans, chapter 12 verse 2, reads: "Let God transform you into a new person by changing the way you think. Then you will learn to know God's will for you, which is good and pleasing and perfect." If there is any lesson to be gleaned from the entirety of this tome, it is this simple lesson engendered by the luminaries and masters of all human spiritual traditions, paths, and customs: change the way you think. Or, as my teacher, Muktananda, used to say, "Change the prescription of your glasses."

In all spiritual traditions, the advocation of 'surrender' is often presented. The implication belies the very heart and nexus of spiritual life - to let go, and let God. I've long found it fascinating that the very name of the religion of Islam is rooted in the Arabic word 'aslama' which interprets as 'Submission to God.' Recognition, acceptance and surrender or submission to the master is always voluntary. It cannot be enforced by external forces, whether it be the theocratic leaders of a religion or government, a guru, imam, priest, pastor, rabbi, or social peer pressure. Our species has been given the birth right of free will. Maxims such as 'no man can serve two masters' serve as a suggestion which leave us with a choice to acquire awareness of how we elect to live our lives, make the decisions we do, and pose the question of whether or not we have ears that hear and eyes that see. The latter is a direct invitation to the practice of awareness, and is truly left to each individual to make that choice. A true 'Master' of a spiritual tradition is just an individual who, at some point in their journey, allowed themselves to hear, see, recognize, accept, and yield to the profound revelation of the truth that sets one free.

The experience of absolute joy borne of this awakening is what they wish to share with those around them, whom they perceive as unnecessarily continuing to languish in perennial suffering. It's a simple lesson they wish to impart. Yet, to penetrate the quagmire that is the mind, which continues to distract and enslave those suffering individuals, volumes of teachings and practicums are offered as a means to gain a foothold on the path to personal - and collective - liberation. An external Master - seen or unseen, apparent or disguised, from any tradition - offers the one same fundamental service of utilizing any means possible to ring a sort of ancient, inaudible bell which is designed to awaken something deep within us that calls us back to very core truth of our essence and existence. Such is the duty and service of the awakened ones.

Through surrender to this subtle, familiar inner chime of the master, the mind instantly stills, and the still, small voice within gradually becomes luminous, loud and clear. As Psalm 46 offers, "Be still and know that I am God." It's the crux of the very secret of human existence. It is, at once, the very core, key and foundational secret learned and passed along by the masters among us - those spiritual luminaries of every path - who have ever offered their experienced assistance through the ages. They point the way to the junction where human suffering ends, and the path to our own innate mastery begins.

An apparition of Paramjyoti, the Great Compassionate Light,
captured by photo in India, 2019.

ACKNOWLEDGEMENTS

This work would not have been possible without the exemplary help and support of numerous individuals and organizations. With heartfelt gratitude I say

"Thank you." Your friendship is always cherished.

To: M.H. - for hanging in there unconditionally; To A.B.C., my guiding light and source of inspiration; to Pooki, my unfailing companion (during the first draft); N.L.K., my friend, sister, and unshakable cohort; To R.A, your faith is inspiring; To Sarah McKechnie and the folks at Lucis Trust; Mona, Tony ,and the folks at Tara/Share USA, for invaluable assistance, generosity, and insightfulness; A special thanks to Buddy Piper; A special thanks to Wayne Peterson for permission and the many hours of discussion; To Gill and all at Share International Magazine, for your gracious assistance; A special thanks to Share international Foundation and Share international Magazine and its editors for their gracious permission to use much material - the core of this book would not be possible without you; to the Philly Transmission Meditation group - for your support and interest from the get-go; Tim, Lon, and Betty from Colorado, for your invaluable contributions and testimony; A special thanks to Mickey Drake; To Uma H. for your excellent and insightful care, thoroughness, and professionalism, and to all the folks at SYDA Foundation who so graciously extended their "familial" support; To S.B.M., my kindred spirit and most ardent supporter; To mom, for your inexhaustible care, support, generosity, and love; Jack, Mike, and Jim, for your always evident and unconditional support; GM., your grace has kept me on my toes, your love has brought me to the doorstep of God; BM, for handing me a key for which I am forever indebted & eternally grateful; James, for your friendship, unselfish input, and exemplary assistance in editing; To Phyllis Creme for your review and support; To 'the Master', for you invaluable input and confirmations; To M., J., M. and friends; to E, for the inspiration to begin and the support to finish; to Zach, for your inspired and selfless support; A special thanks to Larry F., for your tireless support in so many gracious ways; to Ann S., for your wonderful and selfless measure of support and generosity; to SAB, TBD, others affiliated with the Foundation for World Awakening, for your support, and friendship, & to the monks of Satyaloka for your invaluable assistance; To Dr. Arthur J. Deikman, for the generous use of your material; To Adam Pallant and the Estate of Mary Lutyens; To Jen B., for your encouragement to resurrect this manuscript for the benefit of all.

A special thanks to the late Benjamin Creme, 1922 – 2016, for an incomparable measure of patience, graciousness and assistance; who once corrected me on the distinction between referring to someone from Scotland as Scotch or Scottish; who so generously opened his archives for my use; for offering his skills as an editor to support this young writer while working on my first book; and for your warmth, kindness, generosity and support: To you, my friend, I say: "Should old acquaintance be forgot, and ne'er brought to mind…We'll take a cup o' kindness yet, for old lang syne." Slainte', kind soul! God speed, my friend!

BIBLIOGRAPHY

Alcyone (Jiddu Krishnamurti), "At the Feet of the Master," © unknown, Quest Books, The Theosophical Publishing House, Wheaton, Ill., USA.

Bailey, Alice A., as follows: Extracts from the following have been reproduced with the permission of the Lucis Trust, which hold copyright: "Esoteric Astrology," pg. 477, © 1951, 12th printing 1979, Lucis Publishing Company. "A Treatise on White Magic," pg. 168, 533, © 1951/1979, 15th printing 1980, Lucis Publishing Company. "Discipleship in the New Age, Vol. 1" pg. 722, © 1952, 10th printing 1981, Lucis Publishing Company. "A Treatise on Cosmic Fire," © 1925/1964 Lucis Publishing Company. Material referenced, as follows: Section One - Division E - Motion on the Physical and Astral Planes, Part 5, 'The centers and initiation', pp.207 - 214. Section Two - Div. B - Manas as a Cosmic, Systemic and Human Factor, pp. 342 - 498; Div. D - Thought Elementals and Fire Elementals, Sec. II, Part 3, sub-sec. C - 'On Incarnation', d. 'The future coming of the Avatar', pg. 755. "The Reappearance of the Christ," pg.5, © 1948/1962, Lucis Publishing Company. "Esoteric Psychology: Vol. I" © 1984, Lucis Publishing Company. "Initiation-Human and Solar," pgs. 43 - 62, © 1922/1961, 15th printing 1984, Lucis Publishing Company. "Externalisation of the Hierarchy," pgs. vi, 474, 475, © 1957/1976, Lucis Publishing Company.

Blavatsky, H. P., "The Secret Doctrine: The Synthesis of Science, Religion, and Philosophy; Vol.'s I & II, © 1988 Centennial Edition, Theosophical University Press, Pasadena, CA, USA.

Brooks, Durgananda, Muller-Ortega, Mahony, Bailly, Sabharatham, "Meditation Revolution - a History and Theology of the Siddha Yoga Lineage" ©1997, the Muktabodha Indological Research Institute, Agama Press, South Fallsburg, New York, USA.

Chinmayananda, Swami, "Kindle Life," © unknown, Chinmaya Publications Trust, Madras, India.

Chodkiewicz, Michel, "Seal of the Saints: Prophethood and Sainthood in the Doctrine of Ibn 'Arabi," © 1993, The Islamic Texts Society, Cambridge, UK.

Church, W. H., "Edgar Cayce's Story of the Soul," ©1989 by W.H. Church, Assoc. for Research and Enlightenment, Inc., Virginia Beach, Virginia.

Creme, Benjamin, "The Reappearance of the Christ and the Masters of Wisdom," © 1980, The Tara Press, London; Tara Center, Hollywood, CA, USA. Permission courtesy Benjamin Creme.

Creme, Benjamin, "Maitreya's Mission: Volume I," © 1986, The Tara Press, London; Tara Center, Hollywood, CA, USA. Permission courtesy Benjamin Creme.

Creme, Benjamin, "Maitreya's Mission: Volume II," © 1993, The Tara Press, London; Tara Center, Hollywood, CA, USA. Permission courtesy Benjamin Creme.

Creme, Benjamin, "Maitreya's Mission: Volume III," © 1997, The Tara Press, London; Tara Center, Hollywood, CA, USA. Permission courtesy Benjamin Creme.

Creme, Benjamin, "Transmission: A Meditation for the New Age," © 1983, The Tara Press, London; Tara Center, Hollywood, CA, USA. Permission courtesy Benjamin Creme.

Corbin, Henry, "Temple and Contemplation," © 1986, Islamic Publications Limited, KPI Limited, London.

Culligan, Emmett J., "The Last World War," © 1952, Crestline Books, San Bernardino, CA, USA.

Dromgoole, W. A., "The Bridge Builder." Reprinted courtesy of The Master Teacher, Manhattan, KS, USA.

Eadie, Betty A., "Embraced by the Light," ©1992, Bantam Books, New York, USA.

Edwards, Paul/Pap, Arthur, "A Modern Introduction to Philosophy: 'A Priori Knowledge,' 53: pg. 612 - 623, "Immanuel Kant: Introduction to the Critique of Pure Reason," ©1965 by The Free Press, Collier-Macmillan Limited, London, UK.

Feild, Reshad, "The Last Barrier: A journey through the world of Sufi Teaching," ©1976 by Reshad T. Field. Harper & Row, New York, USA.

Gandhi, Mohandas K., "The Story of my Experiments with Truth," ©1948, Public Affairs Press, Washington, D.C., USA.

"Great Religions of the World," The Story of Man Library, National Geographic Book Service, ©1971, National Geographic Society

Guiley, Rosemary Ellen, "Harper's Encyclopedia of Mystical and Paranormal Experience," ©1991, Castle Books, Harper Collins Publishers, New York, USA.

Hancock, Graham, "Fingerprints of the Gods: The Evidence of Earth's Lost Civilization," ©1995, Crown Publishers, Inc., New York, USA.

Hatengdi, M. U., "Nityananda: The Divine Presence," ©1984, Rudra Press, Cambridge, MA, USA.

Hubbard, Barbara Marx, "The Hunger of Eve: One Woman's Odyssey Toward The Future" © 1989, Barbara Marx Hubbard. Published by Island Pacific NW, Eastsound, WA, USA. Permission courtesy of Barbara Marx Hubbard, President, The Foundation for Conscious Evolution.

Johnson, Julian, "The Path of the Masters: The Science of Surat Shabd Yoga," © 1939/1977, Radha Soami Satsang Beas, Punjab, India.

Kalki Spiritual Centre, Mumbai, "The Dharma of Kalki: An introduction," ©1998, Kalki Spiritual Centre, Mumbai, India

Kersten, Holger, "Jesus Lived In India," ©1986, Element Books Ltd., England, UK.

Levy, Edward, "'Look to Me and I Will Look to You': Sai Baba of Shirdi," from "Great Beings" series, Darshan Magazine, Vol. 21 - December 1988 © 1988, SYDA Foundation, USA.

Lutyens, Mary, "Krishnamurti - The Years of Awakening," © 1975, Farrar, Straus, and Giroux, New York. Permission courtesy Adam Pallant, the estate of Mary Lutyens

Meher Baba, "Discourses: Vol. II," © 1967, Adi K. IDasaji, Maharashtra, India.

Munshi, K.M./Diwakar, R.R., "Bhagavad Gita and Modern Life," © 1969, Bharatiya Vidya Bhavan, Bombay (Mumbai), India.

Muktananda, Swami, "Reflections of the Self," Copyright 1980, 1993 (2nd edition) SYDA Foundation, USA. Permission courtesy SYDA Foundation.

Muktananda, Swami, "Secret of the Siddhas," Copyright 1980, 1983, 1994 (3rd edition) SYDA Foundation, USA. Permission courtesy SYDA Foundation.

Muktananda, Swami, "I Am That: The Science of Hamsa from the Vijnana Bhairava," Copyright 1978; 1983, 1992 (3rd edition) SYDA Foundation, USA. Permission courtesy SYDA Foundation.

Muktananda, Swami, "The Perfect Relationship," Copyright 1980, 1999 (2nd edition) SYDA Foundation, USA. Permission courtesy SYDA Foundation.
Nicholson, Renold A., "Studies in Islamic Mysticism," © 1978, Cambridge University Press, Cambridge, UK.

Nikhilananda, Swami, "The Bhagavad Gita," translation and Introduction by author, ©1944, Ramakrishna-Vivekananda Center, New York, USA.

Ornstein, Robert E., "The Nature of human Consciousness," © 1973, Robert E. Ornstein; Publ: W.H. Freeman and Co., San Francisco, CA.; Ref: Section IV, pp 216 - 233, "Deautomatization and the Mystic Experience," by Arthur J. Deikman.

Pagels, Elaine, "The Gnostic Gospels," ©1979, Vintage Books, A division of Random House, Inc., New York.

Patanjali, Bhagawan Shree, "Aphorisms of Yoga," translated by Shree Purohit Swami, Introduction by W. B. Yeats, ©1975. Faber and Faber, London, UK.

Prabhavananda, Swami/Isherwood, Christopher, "How to Know God: The Yoga Aphorisms of Patanjali," © 1953/1969, Vedanta Society of Southern CA., USA. A Mentor Book, The New American Library, Inc., New York, USA.

Prabhavananda, Swami/Isherwood, Christopher, "Shankara's Crest Jewel of Discrimination (Viveka-Chudamani)," translated by authors, ©1978, Vedanta Press, Hollywood, CA, USA.

Prabhavananda, Swami, "The Sermon on the Mount according to Vedanta," ©1963/1972, Vedanta Society of California, a Mentor Book, The New American Library, Inc., New York, USA. Permission courtesy the Vedanta Society of California.

Saphier, Mahadev, "The Nirvana Sangha Committee: 'The Most Important Moment of Our Entire Life," Great Timers Newsletter, p.19, © 1999, SYDA Foundation, South Fallsburg, New York, USA. Permission courtesy SYDA Foundation.

Satyavan, "The Gayatri Mantra: Yoga for Beginners," © 1974 by S. K. Roy, Autumn Press, Inc., Brookline, MS, USA.

Schimmel, Annamarie, "Mystical Dimensions of Islam," © 1975, The University of North Carolina Press, USA.

SenSharma, Deba Brata, "The Philosophy of Sadhana: With special reference to the Trika Philosophy of Kashmir," © 1990, State University of New York Press, Albany, NY, USA.

Shah, Indries, "The Sufis; Introduction by Robert Graves," © 1964, 1971, Anchor Books/Random House, New York.

Share International Magazine, © 1982 - 2000. Referenced issues listed in footnotes. Permission courtesy Benjamin Creme, editor.

Singh, Dr. Jaideva, "Spanda Karikas," ©1980, Motilal Banarsidas, Delhi, India. Permission courtesy Mr. N. P. Jain, Motilal Banarsidas.

Singh, Dr. Jaideva, "Siva Sutras - The Yoga of Supreme Identity," ©1982, Motilal Banarsidas, Delhi, India. Permission courtesy Mr. N. P. Jain, Motilal Banarsidas.

Singh, Dr. Jaideva, "Pratyabhijnahrdayam - The Secret of Self-recognition," ©1980, Motilal Banarsidas, Delhi, India. Permission courtesy Mr. N. P. Jain, Motilal Banarsidas.

Singh, Dr. Jaideva, "Vijnanabhairava, or, Divine Consciousness," ©1979, Motilal Banarsidas, Delhi, India. Permission courtesy Mr. N. P. Jain, Motilal Banarsidas.

Smith, Huston, "The World's Religions," © 1991, Harper SanFrancisco™, Harper Collins Publishers, Inc., USA.

Stanford, Ray, "Fatima Prophecy," © 1987/88 Ballentine Books, New York.

Steiner, Rudolf, "Cosmic Memory," © 1987 Material used by permission of Garber Communications distributed by Anthroposophic Press, Hudson, NY 12534, USA.

Swahananda, Swami, "Service and Spirituality," © 1979, Sri Ramakrishna Math, Madras, India.

Szekely, Edmond Bordeaux, "The Essene Gospel of Peace," translated by author, © 1971, Academy of Creative Living, San Diego, CA, USA.

Tagore, Rabindranath, "Gitanjali," © 1913, Macmillan & Co., Ltd., London, UK.

Tagore, Rabindranath, "The Religion of Man," ©1961, Beacon Press, Boston, USA.

"The Dhammapada: The sayings of the Buddha," Rendered by Thomas Byrom/ Preface by Ram Dass, ©1976, Vintage Books/Random House, New York, USA.

"The Holy Bible - New American Catholic Edition," ©1961, Benzinger Brothers, Inc.

"The Holy Qur'an," Translation and Commentary by A. Yusef Ali, © 1934. Publisher unknown.

"The Koran," Translation by N. J. Dawood, ©1968, Penguin Books, Baltimore, MD. USA.

"The Lost Books of the Bible and the Forgotten Books of Eden," ©1926, LB Press, Cleveland, OH, USA.

"The Mother of Christ Crusade," ©1947, The Mother of Christ Crusade Inc.

"The Portable Plato," "The Republic: Book V" pgs. 491, 492© 1948/1970, The Viking Press, Inc. New York, USA;

"The Teaching of the Buddha," © 1966, Kenkyusha Printing, Tokyo, Japan.

"Thus Spake Shankara," © 1973, Sri Ramakrishna Math, Madras, India.

Universal Standard Encyclopedia, ©1954, Unicorn Publishers, Inc., New York, USA.

"Upanishads," translated by Patrick Olivelle, © 1996, Oxford University Press, Oxford, England, UK.

Venkateshananda, Swami, "The Concise Yoga Vasistha," © 1984, State University of New York Press, Abany, NY, USA.

Washington, Peter, "Madame Blavatsky's Baboon: A history of the mystics, mediums, and misfits who brought spiritualism to America" © 1993/1995, Schocken Books, New York, USA

"Webster's New World Dictionary of the American Language," ©1967 Websters, USA.

Wood, Ernest, "Seven Schools of Yoga: An Introduction," ©1976, A Quest Book, The Theosophical Publishing House, Wheaton, Ill., USA.

Yogananda, Paramahansa, "The Autobiography of a Yogi," pgs. 345, 349, ©1974, Self Realization Fellowship, Los Angeles, CA, USA. Permission courtesy Self Realization Fellowship, Los Angeles, CA, USA.

Yogananda, Paramahansa, "Man's Eternal Quest," ©1975, Self Realization Fellowship, Los Angeles, CA, USA.

Yogananda, Paramahansa, "Creating and Destroying Habits at Will." Delivered Dec. 12, 1943, San Diego, CA. Man's Eternal Quest, Pp. 412-413. © 1975 Self Realization Fellowship. Reprinted with Permission.

The following electronic publications were used as source material or reference from their online web sites and web pages:
http://www.uni-koeln.de/cgi-bin/SFgate - (Cologne Digital Sanskrit Lexicon)
http://www.ualberta.ca/~tlorentz/mast-av-disc.html (List of Masters)
http://www.netnews.org/bk/meditation/medi1147.html (Alice Bailey glossary)
http://www.netnews.org/bk/index.html (Alice Bailey books)
http://www.ishopper.com/manuscripts/research.html (Ancient manuscripts)
http://www.dayofdestiny.com/IndigenousUprising.html (Aztec information)
http://www.mcn.org/1/miracles/fricke.html (Personal miracle story)
http://www.sangha.net/messengers/ (Esoteric information)
http://www.simedia.org/Buddy/ (Buddy Piper's website)
http://www.mcn.org/1/miracles/Encounters2.html (tales of Christ encounters)
http://www.simedia.org/new/trdss.html (Dead Sea scrolls)
http://www.netnews.org/bk/discipleship1/toc.html (Discipleship in the New Age, by Alice Bailey)
http://www.iclnet.org/pub/resources/christian-history.html (Works by early church historians/theologians)
http://heavy.web.ipa.net/www.svpvril.com/svpweb5.html (Scientific reports on 'ether')
http://www.simedia.org/ (Share International media service)

http://home.webcom.se/religion/articles/Imam-Hussein.htm (Islamic history)
http://www.bible2000.org/index.htm (Apocryphal Biblical texts; the Koran)
http://www.medjugorje.org/medpage.htm (Official website of Medjugorje)
http://www.missionnet.com/miracles/index.html (miracle files; Madonna miracles)
http://www.shareintl.org/background/miracles/MI_nairobi_pictures.htm (the photos of Maitreya in Nairobi)
http://www.OPRAH.com (website of the Oprah Winfrey Show; 'see Spirit')
http://199.227.251.60/share-ind.html (articles on sharing as service)
http://www.shareintl.org/ (Share International website)
http://www.hooked.net/shareint/ (website of Share International Magazine)
http://www.siddhayoga.org (for information on Siddha Yoga Meditation, Bhagavan Nityananda, Swami Muktananda, Swami Chidvilasananda)
http://www.4tabloids.com/read.shtml (Source for Tabloids)
http://skepdic.com/theosoph.html (The Skeptics Dictionary)
http://dir.yahoo.com/Society_and_Culture/Religion_and_Spirituality/(Spirituality links at Yahoo.com)
https://www.medjugorje.org - Website of Medjugorje Web, featuring up to date messages from the Madonna, pilgrimage opportunities, and more.
http://www.sri-ammabhagavan.org - official website of Sri Bhagavan and Sri Amma.
https://sriammabhagavanfoundationindia.com - website of the India-based Sri AmmaBhagavan Foundation, the public charitable trust of Sri Bhagavan and his spouse, Sri Amma.
https://www.oo.academy - website of O & O Academy. the philosophy and meditation school for transforming human consciousness founded by Sri Bhagavan, his son and daughter-in-law Krishna and Preetha, and home of Ekam, the remarkable "Golden City" and Oneness Temple campus in Southern India.

FILM/VIDEO
"Miracles and Visions: Fact or Fiction," ©MCMXCVI, Kiviat Productions, Vidmark Entertainment.

www.ingramcontent.com/pod-product-compliance
Lightning Source LLC
Chambersburg PA
CBHW071233290426
44108CB00013B/1401